LPI LINUX CERTIFICATION

IN A NUTSHELL

LPI LINUX CERTIFICATION

IN A NUTSHELL

Third Edition

Adam Haeder, Stephen Addison Schneiter,
Bruno Gomes Pessanha, and James Stanger

O'REILLY®

Beijing · Cambridge · Farnham · Köln · Sebastopol · Taipei · Tokyo

LPI Linux Certification in a Nutshell, Third Edition

by Adam Haeder, Stephen Addison Schneiter, Bruno Gomes Pessanha, and James Stanger

Published by O'Reilly Media, Inc., 1005 Gravenstein Highway North, Sebastopol, CA 95472.

O'Reilly books may be purchased for educational, business, or sales promotional use. Online editions are also available for most titles (*http://my.safaribooksonline.com*). For more information, contact our corporate/institutional sales department: 800-998-9938 or *corporate@oreilly.com*.

Editor: Andy Oram
Production Editor: Adam Zaremba
Copyeditor: Genevieve d'Entremont
Proofreader: Jennifer Knight

Indexer: Jay Marchand
Cover Designer: Karen Montgomery
Interior Designer: David Futato
Illustrator: Robert Romano

Printing History:

May 2001:	First Edition.
July 2006:	Second Edition.
June 2010:	Third Edition.

RepKover.

This book uses RepKover™, a durable and flexible lay-flat binding.

ISBN: 978-0-596-80487-9

[M]

1276116172

Table of Contents

Preface

Certification of professionals is a time-honored tradition in many fields, including medicine and law. As small computer systems and networks proliferated over the last decade, Novell and Microsoft produced extremely popular technical certification products for their respective operating system and network technologies. These two programs are often cited as having popularized a certification market for products that had previously been highly specialized and relatively rare. These programs have become so popular that a huge training and preparation industry has formed to service a constant stream of new certification candidates.

Certification programs, offered by vendors such as Sun and Hewlett-Packard, have existed in the Unix world for some time. However, since Solaris and HP-UX aren't commodity products, those programs don't draw the crowds that the PC platform does. Linux, however, is different. Linux is both a commodity operating system and is PC-based, and its popularity continues to grow at a rapid pace. As Linux deployment increases, so too does the demand for qualified and certified Linux system administrators.

A number of programs such as the Linux Professional Institute (LPI), the Red Hat Certified Engineer (RHCE) program, and CompTIA's Linux+ have formed to service this new market. Each of these programs seeks to provide objective measurements of a Linux administrator's skills, but they approach the problem in different ways.

The RHCE program requires that candidates pass multiple exam modules, including two hands-on and one written, whose goals are to certify individuals to use their brand of products. The Linux+ program requires a single exam and is focused at entry-level candidates with six months' experience. LPI's program is a job-based certification and currently consists of three levels; this book focuses on the most basic level.

The Linux Professional Institute

The Linux Professional Institute (*http://www.lpi.org*) is a nonprofit organization formed with the single goal of providing a standard for vendor-neutral certification. This goal is being achieved by certifying Linux administrators through a modified open source development process. LPI seeks input from the public for its exam Objectives and questions, and anyone is welcome to participate. It has both paid and volunteer staff and receives funding from some major names in the computer industry. The result is a vendor-neutral, publicly developed program that is offered at a reasonable price.

LPI currently organizes its most popular Linux Professional Institute Certification (LPIC) series in three levels. This book covers the LPIC Level 1 Exams 101 and 102.

Level 1 is aimed at junior to midlevel Linux administrators with about two years of practical system administration experience. The Level 1 candidate should be comfortable with Linux at the command line as well as capable of performing simple tasks, including system installation and troubleshooting. Level 1 certification is required prior to obtaining Level 2 certification status.

All of LPI's exams are based on a published set of technical Objectives. These technical Objectives are posted on LPI's website and for your convenience printed at the beginning of each chapter within this book. Each Objective set forth by LPI is assigned a numeric weight, which acts as an indicator of the importance of the Objective. Weights run between 1 and 8, with higher numbers indicating more importance. An Objective carrying a weight of 1 can be considered relatively unimportant and isn't likely to be covered in much depth on the exam. Objectives with larger weights are sure to be covered on the exam, so you should study these closely. The weights of the Objectives are provided at the beginning of each chapter.

LPI offers its exams through Pearson VUE (*http://www.vue.com*), Thomson Prometric (*http://www.prometric.com*), and at on-site locations at special Linux events, such as trade shows. Before registering for any of these testing methods, you need to obtain an LPI ID number by registering directly with LPI. To obtain your LPI ID, visit *http://www.lpi.org/register.html*. Once you've received your LPI ID, you may continue your registration by registering with a testing center or special event. You can link to any of these registration options through LPI's website (*http://www.lpi .org/eng/certification/faq/procedure_for_taking_exams*).

In Vue and Prometric testing centers, the exams are delivered using a PC-based automated examination program. As of this writing, the exams are available in English, Japanese, Chinese (both Traditional and Simplified), German, Spanish, Portuguese, and French. Exam questions are presented in three different styles: multiple-choice single-answer, multiple-choice multiple-answer, and fill-in-the-blank. However, the majority of the questions on the exams are multiple-choice single-answer. Also, with the multiple-choice questions, the candidate is told exactly how many answers are correct.

For security purposes, multiple forms of each exam are available at testing centers to help minimize memorization and brain dumps of exams if candidates take them multiple times. Due to this, actual question numbers may vary slightly. LPI's psychometric team develops these forms and adjusts the scoring appropriately so all forms are equally difficult. The scores are between 200 and 800, and passing score is 500.

Audience for This Book

The primary audience for this book is, of course, candidates seeking the LPIC certification. These may range from administrators of other operating systems looking for a Linux certification to complement an MSCE certification to Unix administrators wary of a growing pool of Linux-certified job applicants. In any case, this book will help you with the specific information you require to be successful with the Level 1 Exams. Don't be fooled, however, as book study will not be enough to pass your exams. Remember, practice makes perfect!

Due to the breadth of knowledge required by the LPI Objectives and the book's one-to-one coverage, it also makes an excellent reference for skills and methods required for the day-to-day use of Linux. If you have a basic working understanding of Linux administration, the material in this book will help fill gaps in your knowledge while at the same time preparing you for the LPI Exams, should you choose to take them.

This book should also prove to be a valuable introduction for new Linux users and administrators looking for a broad, detailed introduction to Linux. Part of the LPI exam-creation process includes a survey of Linux professionals in the field. The survey results drive much of the content found on the exams. Therefore, unlike general-purpose introductory Linux books, all of the information in this book applies directly to running Linux in the real world.

Organization

This book is designed to exactly follow the Topics and Objectives established by LPI for Level 1. That means that the presentation doesn't look like any other Linux book you've read. Instead, you can directly track the LPI Objectives and easily measure your progress as you prepare.

The book is presented in two parts, one for Exam 101 and the other for Exam 102. Each part contains chapters dedicated to the LPI Topics, and each of those sections contains information on all of the Objectives set forth for the Topic. In addition, each part contains a practice exam (with answers), review questions and exercises, and a handy highlighter's index that can help you review important details.

Book Chapters

Each part of this book contains some combination of the following materials:

Exam overview
> Here you find an introduction to the exam along with details about the format of the questions.

Study guide

This chapter offers a few tips to prepare for the LPI Exams and introduces the Objectives contained in the Topic chapters that follow.

Topic chapters

A separate chapter covers each of the Topic areas on the exam. These chapters provide background information and in-depth coverage for each Objective, with "On the Exam" (see bottom of this page) tips dispersed throughout.

Review questions and exercises

This chapter reinforces important study areas with review questions. The purpose of this section is to provide you with a series of exercises that can be used on a running Linux system to give you valuable hands-on experience before you take the exams.

Practice test

The practice test is designed to be similar in format and content to the actual LPI Exams. You should be able to attain at least an 80 percent score on the sample test before attempting the live exam.

Highlighter's index

This unique chapter contains highlights and important facts culled from the Topic chapters. You can use this as review and reference material prior to taking the actual exams.

Conventions Used in This Book

This book follows certain typographical conventions:

Italic

Italic is used to indicate URLs, filenames, directories, commands, options, system components (such as usernames), and to highlight comments in examples.

`Constant Width`

Used to show the contents of files or the output from commands.

`Constant Width Bold`

Used in examples and tables to show commands or other text that should be typed literally by the user.

`Constant Width Italic`

Used to show arguments and variables that should be replaced with user-supplied values.

`#, $`

Used in some examples as the root shell prompt (#) and as the user prompt ($) under the Bourne or Bash shell.

On the Exam

Provides information about areas you should focus on when studying for the exam.

Indicates a tip, suggestion, or general note.

Indicates a warning or caution.

A final word about syntax: in many cases, the space between an option and its argument can be omitted. In other cases, the spacing (or lack of spacing) must be followed strictly. For example, -wn (no intervening space) might be interpreted differently from -w n. It's important to notice the spacing used in option syntax.

Using Code Examples

This book is here to help you get your job done. In general, you may use the code in this book in your programs and documentation. You do not need to contact us for permission unless you're reproducing a significant portion of the code. For example, writing a program that uses several chunks of code from this book does not require permission. Selling or distributing a CD-ROM of examples from O'Reilly books *does* require permission. Answering a question by citing this book and quoting example code does not require permission. Incorporating a significant amount of example code from this book into your product's documentation *does* require permission.

We appreciate, but do not require, attribution. An attribution usually includes the title, author, publisher, and ISBN. For example: "*LPI Linux Certification in a Nutshell*, Third Edition, by Adam Haeder et al. Copyright 2010 Adam Haeder, Stephen Addison Schneiter, Bruno Gomes Pessanha, and James Stanger. ISBN: 9780596804879."

If you feel your use of code examples falls outside fair use or the permission given here, feel free to contact us at *permissions@oreilly.com*.

How to Contact Us

We have tested and verified the information in this book to the best of our ability, but you may find that features have changed (or even that we have made mistakes!). As a reader of this book and as an LPI examinee, you can help us to improve future editions. Please let us know about any errors you find, as well as your suggestions for future editions, by writing to:

O'Reilly Media, Inc.
1005 Gravenstein Highway North
Sebastopol, CA 95472
800-998-9938 (in the United States or Canada)

707-829-0515 (international or local)
707-829-0104 (fax)

We have a web page for this book, where we list errata, examples, and any additional information. You can access this page at:

http://oreilly.com/catalog/9780596804879

To comment or ask technical questions about this book, send email to:

bookquestions@oreilly.com

For more information about our books, conferences, Resource Centers, and the O'Reilly Network, see our website at:

http://www.oreilly.com

If you have taken one or all of the LPIC Exams after preparing with this book and find that parts of this book could better address your exam experience, we'd like to hear about it. Of course, you are under obligation to LPI not to disclose specific exam details, but comments regarding the coverage of the LPI Objectives, level of detail, and relevance to the exam will be most helpful. We take your comments seriously and will do whatever we can to make this book as useful as it can be.

Safari® Books Online

 Safari Books Online is an on-demand digital library that lets you easily search over 7,500 technology and creative reference books and videos to find the answers you need quickly.

With a subscription, you can read any page and watch any video from our library online. Read books on your cell phone and mobile devices. Access new titles before they are available for print, and get exclusive access to manuscripts in development and post feedback for the authors. Copy and paste code samples, organize your favorites, download chapters, bookmark key sections, create notes, print out pages, and benefit from tons of other time-saving features.

O'Reilly Media has uploaded this book to the Safari Books Online service. To have full digital access to this book and others on similar topics from O'Reilly and other publishers, sign up for free at *http://my.safaribooksonline.com*.

Acknowledgments

For the third edition, we thank reviewers Don Corbet, Jon Larsen, Gregor Purdy, Rick Rezinas, G. Matt Rice, and Craig Wolf.

Adam Haeder dedicates his work to Tina, Erin, Ethan, Stanley, and Stefon: the reason I work so late into the night.

Bruno dedicates his work to his grandfather, Oswaldo Cabral Pessanha, in memoriam.

1

LPI Exams

LPI Exam 101 is one of two exams required for the LPIC Level 1 (officially referred to as LPIC 1) certification. In total, ten major Topic areas are specified for Level 1; this exam tests your knowledge on four of them.

Exam Topics are numbered using the *topic.objective* notation (e.g., 101.1, 101.2, 102.1). The 100 series topics represent LPI Level 1 certification topics, which are unique to all levels of LPI exams (e.g., 101, 102, 201, 202, etc.). The objective number represents the Objectives that are associated with the Topic area (e.g., 1, 2, 3, 4, and so on).

The Level 1 Topics are distributed between the two exams to create tests of similar length and difficulty without subject matter overlap. As a result, there's no requirement for or advantage to taking them in sequence, the only caveat being that you cannot be awarded an LPIC 2 or higher certifications until you pass the requirements for the lower-level certification.

Each Topic contains a series of Objectives covering specific areas of expertise. Each of these Objectives is assigned a numeric weight, which acts as an indicator of the importance of the Objective. Weights typically run between 1 and 8, with higher numbers indicating more importance. An Objective carrying a weight of 1 can be considered relatively unimportant and isn't likely to be covered in much depth on the exam. Objectives with larger weights are sure to be covered more heavily on the exam, so you should study these Topics closely. The weights of the Objectives are provided at the beginning of each Topic section. In the current version of LPI exams, all of the weighting totals for each exam add up to 60. With 60 questions per exam, this means that the weighting is exactly equivalent to how many questions the Objective will have in the exam.

The Topics for Exam 101 are listed in Table 1-1.

Table 1-1. LPI Topics for Exam 101

Name	Number of objectives	Description
System Architecture	3	These Objectives cover all the fundamentals of configuring common types of hardware on the system, managing the boot process, and modifying the run-levels of the system and the shut down or reboot process from the command line.
Linux Installation and Package Management	5	Objectives for this Topic include the basics of getting any LSB-compliant Linux distribution installed and installing applications. Some of the basics include partitioning hard drives, installing your choice of boot managers, managing shared libraries, and using Debian's *dpkg* and *apt* family of commands and RPM and Yellowdog Updater Modified (YUM) package management systems.
GNU and Unix Commands	8	This heavily weighted Topic addresses the most utilized command-line tools used on standard Linux systems as well as most commercial Unix systems. The Objectives detail working on a command line, processing text streams using command-line tools, managing files, manipulating text with pipes and redirects, monitoring system processes, managing task priorities, using regular expressions, and editing files with *vi*, *lilo*, syslog, and runlevels.
Devices, Linux Filesystems, and the Filesystem Hierarchy Standard	8	Objectives for this Topic include the creation of partitions and filesystems, filesystem integrity, mounting, quotas, permissions, ownership, links, and file location tasks.

As you can see from Table 1-1, the Topic numbers assigned by the LPI are not necessarily sequential. This is due to various modifications made by the LPI to its exam program as it developed. The Topic numbers serve only as reference and are not used on the exam.

Exam 101 lasts a maximum of 90 minutes and contains exactly 60 questions. The exam is administered using a custom application on a PC in a private room with no notes or other reference material. The majority of the exam is made up of multiple-choice single-answer questions. These questions have only one correct answer and are answered using radio buttons. Some of them present a scenario needing administrative action. Others seek appropriate commands for a particular task or proof of understanding of a particular concept. Some people may get an exam with an additional 20 items. These items are used to test new questions and don't count as part of the score. An additional 30 minutes is provided in this case, and there is no indication which items are unscored.

About 10 percent of the exam questions are multiple-choice multiple-answer questions, which are answered using checkboxes. These questions specify that they have multiple correct responses, each of which must be checked to get the item correct. There is no partial credit for partially answered items. This is probably the most difficult question style because the possibility of multiple answers increases the likelihood of forgetting to include an answer, even though the candidate is told in the question exactly how many answers to select. But they also are a good test of your knowledge of Unix commands, since an incorrect response on any one of the possible answers causes you to miss the entire question.

The exam also has fill-in-the-blank questions. These questions provide a one-line text area input box for you to fill in your answer. These questions check your knowledge of concepts such as important files and commands, plus common facts that you are expected to be aware of. Don't let this scare you, however, since most of these items accept a variety of answers. Unless specified otherwise, they are not case-sensitive and do not require full paths in your answers.

Exam 101 Study Guide

The first part of this book contains a section for each of the four Topics found on LPI Exam 101. Each section details certain Objectives, which are described here and on the LPI website (*http://www.lpi.org/eng/certification/the_lpic_program/lpic_1/ exam_101_detailed_objectives*).

Exam Preparation

LPI Exam 101 is thorough, but you should find it fairly straightforward if you have a solid foundation in Linux concepts. You won't come across questions intended to trick you, and you're unlikely to find ambiguous questions.

Exam 101 mainly tests your knowledge of facts, including commands and their common options, important file locations, configuration syntax, and common procedures. Your recollection of these details, regardless of your level of Linux administration experience, will directly influence your results.

For clarity, the material in the following sections is presented in the same order as the LPI Topics and Objectives. However, you may choose to study the Topics in any order you wish. To assist you with your preparation, Table 2-1 through Table 2-4 list the Topics and Objectives found on Exam 101. Objectives within each Topic occupy rows of the corresponding table, including the Objective's number, description, and weight. The LPI assigns a *weight* for each Objective to indicate the relative importance of that Objective on the exam on a scale of 1 to 8. We recommend that you use the weights to prioritize what you decide to study in preparation for the exams. After you complete your study of each Objective, simply check it off here to measure and organize your progress.

Table 2-1. System architecture (Topic 101)

Objective	Weight	Description
1	2	Determine and Configure Hardware settings
2	3	Boot the System
3	3	Change Runlevels and Shut Down or Reboot System

Table 2-2. Linux installation and package management (Topic 102)

Objective	Weight	Description
1	2	Design Hard Disk Layout
2	2	Install a Boot Manager
3	1	Manage Shared Libraries
4	3	Use Debian Package Management
5	3	Use RPM and YUM Package Management

Table 2-3. GNU and Unix commands (Topic 103)

Objective	Weight	Description
1	4	Work on the Command Line
2	3	Process Text Streams Using Filters
3	4	Perform Basic File Management
4	4	Use Streams, Pipes, and Redirects
5	4	Create, Monitor, and Kill Processes
6	2	Modify Process Execution Priorities
7	2	Search Text Files Using Regular Expressions
8	3	Perform Basic File Editing Operations Using vi or vim

Table 2-4. Devices, Linux filesystems, and the Filesystem Hierarchy Standard (Topic 104)

Objective	Weight	Description
1	2	Create Partitions and Filesystems
2	2	Maintain the Integrity of Filesystems
3	3	Control Filesystem Mounting and Unmounting
4	1	Set and View Disk Quotas
5	3	Manage File Permissions and Ownership
6	2	Create and Change Hard and Symbolic Links
7	2	Find System Files and Place Files in the Correct Location

3

System Architecture (Topic 101.1)

This Topic requires general knowledge of fundamental PC architecture facts that you must know before attempting any operating system installation. It includes this Objective:

Objective 1: Determine and Configure Hardware Settings
Candidates should be able to determine and configure fundamental system hardware. Weight: 2.

Objective 1: Determine and Configure Hardware Settings

Setting up a PC for Linux (or any other operating system) requires some familiarity with the devices installed in the system and their configuration. Items to be aware of include modems, serial and parallel ports, network adapters, SCSI adapters, hard drives, USB controllers, and sound cards. Many of these devices, particularly older ones, require manual configuration of some kind to avoid conflicting resources. The rest of the configuration for the system hardware is done in the PC's firmware, or Basic Input/Output System (BIOS).

BIOS

The firmware located in a PC, commonly called the BIOS, is responsible for bringing all of the system hardware to a state at which it is ready to boot an operating system. Systems vary, but this process usually includes system initialization, the testing of memory and other devices, and ultimately locating an operating system from among several storage devices. In addition, the BIOS provides a low-level system configuration interface, allowing the user to choose such things as boot devices and resource assignments. Quite a few BIOS firmware vendors provide customized versions of their products for various PC system architectures. Exams do require an understanding of the basics. For example, a laptop BIOS may differ significantly from a desktop system of similar capability from the same manufacturer. Due to these variations, it's impossible to test specifics, but the LPIC Level 1 exams do require an understanding of the basics.

At boot time, most PCs display a method of entering the BIOS configuration utility, usually by entering a specific keystroke during startup. Once the utility is started, a menu-based screen in which system settings can be configured appears. Depending on the BIOS vendor, these will include settings for disks, memory behavior, on-board ports (such as serial and parallel ports), and the clock, as well as many others.

Date and time

One of the basic functions of the BIOS is to manage the on-board hardware clock. This clock is initially set in the BIOS configuration by entering the date and time in the appropriate fields. Once set, the internal clock keeps track of time and makes the time available to the operating system. The operating system can also set the hardware clock, which is often useful if an accurate external time reference, such as an NTPD server (see Chapter 16), is available on the network while the system is running.

Disks and boot devices

Another fundamental configuration item required in BIOS settings is the selection of storage devices. Newer systems are able to detect and properly configure much of this hardware automatically. However, older BIOS versions require manual configuration. This may include the selection of floppy disk sizes and disk drive parameters.

Most PCs have at least three bootable media types: an internal hard disk (IDE or SCSI, or perhaps both), a CD-ROM drive (again IDE or SCSI), and a floppy disk. After initialization, the BIOS seeks an operating system (or an operating system loader, such as the Linux Loader [LILO]) on one or more of these media. By default, many BIOS configurations enable booting from the floppy or CD-ROM first, then the hard disk, but the order is configurable in the BIOS settings.

In addition to these default media types, many server motherboard BIOS (as well as high-end system motherboards) support booting from a network device such as a NIC with a bootable ROM. This is often used when booting diskless workstations such as Linux-based terminals.

On the Exam

You should be familiar with the general configuration requirements and layout of the BIOS configuration screens for a typical PC.

Using the /proc filesystem

When adding new hardware to an existing Linux system, you may wish to verify which resources the existing devices are using. The */proc* filesystem, the kernel's status repository, contains this information. The *proc* files, *interrupts*, *dma*, and *ioports*, show how system resources are currently utilized. (These files may not show devices unless their device files/drivers are open/active. This may make the problem harder to find if you're experiencing resource conflicts.) The following is an example

---

of *proc/interrupts* from a dual-CPU system with an Adaptec dual-AIC7895 SCSI controller:

```
# cat /proc/interrupts
           CPU0        CPU1
  0:    98663989          0           XT-PIC  timer
  1:       34698      34858      IO-APIC-edge  keyboard
  2:           0          0           XT-PIC  cascade
  5:        7141       7908      IO-APIC-edge  MS Sound System
  6:           6          7      IO-APIC-edge  floppy
  8:    18098274   18140354      IO-APIC-edge  rtc
 10:     3234867    3237313     IO-APIC-level  aic7xxx, eth0
 11:          36         35     IO-APIC-level  aic7xxx
 12:      233140     216205      IO-APIC-edge  PS/2 Mouse
 13:           1          0           XT-PIC  fpu
 15:       44118      43935      IO-APIC-edge  ide1
NMI:           0
ERR:           0
```

In this example, you can see that interrupt 5 is used for the sound system, so it isn't available for a second parallel port. The two SCSI controllers are using interrupts 10 and 11, respectively, while the Ethernet controller shares interrupt 10. You may also notice that only one of the two standard IDE interfaces is enabled in the system BIOS, freeing interrupt 14 use for another device.

Here are the *proc/dma* and *proc/ioports* files from the same system:

```
# cat /proc/dma
0: MS Sound System
1: MS Sound System
2: floppy
4: cascade
# cat /proc/ioports
0000-001f : dma1
0020-003f : pic1
0040-005f : timer
0060-006f : keyboard
0070-007f : rtc
0080-008f : dma page reg
00a0-00bf : pic2
00c0-00df : dma2
00f0-00ff : fpu
0170-0177 : ide1
02f8-02ff : serial(auto)
0370-0371 : OPL3-SAx
0376-0376 : ide1
0388-0389 : mpu401
03c0-03df : vga+
03f0-03f5 : floppy
03f7-03f7 : floppy DIR
03f8-03ff : serial(auto)
0530-0533 : WSS config
0534-0537 : MS Sound System
e800-e8be : aic7xxx
ec00-ecbe : aic7xxx
ef00-ef3f : eth0
```

```
ffa0-ffa7 : ide0
ffa8-ffaf : ide1
```

On the Exam

You should know how to examine a running Linux system's resource assignments using the */proc* filesystem.

Universal Serial Bus (USB) is a type of interface used to connect various types of peripherals, ranging from keyboards and mice to hard drives, scanners, digital cameras, and printers. The USB Objective covers the general architecture of USB, USB modules, and configuring USB devices.

USB Topology

USB devices are attached to a host in a tree through some number of hub devices. The *lsusb* command can be used to see how devices are physically attached to a Linux system.

```
# lsusb -t
Bus#  4
'-Dev#   1 Vendor 0x0000 Product 0x0000
Bus#  3
'-Dev#   1 Vendor 0x0000 Product 0x0000
  |-Dev#   2 Vendor 0x046d Product 0xc501
  '-Dev#   3 Vendor 0x0781 Product 0x0002
Bus#  2
'-Dev#   1 Vendor 0x0000 Product 0x0000
  |-Dev#   2 Vendor 0x0451 Product 0x2036
  | |-Dev#   5 Vendor 0x04b8 Product 0x0005
  | '-Dev#   6 Vendor 0x04b8 Product 0x0602
  '-Dev#   3 Vendor 0x0451 Product 0x2046
    '-Dev#   4 Vendor 0x056a Product 0x0011
Bus#  1
'-Dev#   1 Vendor 0x0000 Product 0x0000
```

USB Controllers

There are three types of USB host controllers:

- Open Host Controller Interface (OHCI)
- Universal Host Controller Interface (UHCI)
- Enhanced Host Controller Interface (EHCI)

OHCI and UHCI controllers are both USB 1.1 controllers, which are capable of a maximum of 12 Mbps. EHCI controllers are USB 2.0 controllers, which are capable of a theoretical maximum of 480 Mbps. To get greater than USB 1.1 speeds, you must have a USB 2.0 controller, as well as USB 2.0 devices, hubs, and cables. A USB 2.0 device attached to a USB 1.1 hub will only be able to run at USB 1.1 speeds.

USB Devices

There are several classes of USB devices, including the following:

Human Interface Device (HID)
  Input devices (mice, keyboards, etc.)

Communications device
  Modems

Mass storage device
  Disk devices, flash readers, etc.

Audio
  Sound devices

IrDA
  Infrared devices

Printer
  Printers and USB-to-parallel cables

USB Drivers

USB support was added to the Linux kernel in the 2.3.x development kernel series, then back-ported to 2.2.x, minus support for USB mass storage devices (due to SCSI changes in 2.3.x). The back-port was included in the 2.2.18 kernel release.

 There is *no* kernel USB support in 2.0.x and earlier.

The Linux kernel USB drivers fall into three categories:

Host controller drivers
  The USB host controller drivers include *usb-ohci.o* (OHCI driver), *usb-uhci.o* (UHCI driver), *uhci.o* (old "alternate" UHCI driver), and *ehci-hcd.o* (EHCI driver).

Class drivers
  The USB class drivers include *hid.o*, *usb-storage.o* (mass storage driver), *acm.o* (Automated Control Model [ACM] communications class driver, which deals with modems that emulate the standard serial modem AT command interface), *printer.o*, and *audio.o*.

Other device drivers
  There are many drivers for devices that either don't fit into one of the standard USB classes or don't work with one of the standard class drivers. Examples include *rio500.o* (the driver for the Diamond Rio 500 MP3 player) and *pwc.o* (the driver for various Philips webcams).

The Linux drivers implement USB support in layers. At the bottom is *usbcore.o*, which provides all of the generic USB support for the higher-level drivers as well as

USB hub support. The host controller drivers load in the middle of the stack. On top are the device and class drivers and any modules they require.

The following is an example of what you might see in */proc/modules* (or from the output of *lsmod*) on a system with several USB devices:

```
Module              Size    Used by
usb-storage         68628   0
scsi_mod            106168  2  [usb-storage]
evdev               5696    0  (unused)
printer             8832    0
wacom               7896    0  (unused)
keybdev             2912    0  (unused)
mousedev            5428    1
hid                 21700   0  (unused)
input               5824    0  [evdev wacom keybdev mousedev hid]
ehci-hcd            19432   0  (unused)
usb-uhci            25964   0  (unused)
usbcore             77760   1  [usb-storage printer wacom hid ehci-hcd \
                                   usb-uhci]
```

USB Hotplug

Modularized USB drivers are loaded by the generic */sbin/hotplug* support in the kernel, which is also used for other hotplug devices such as CardBus cards.

> Although not covered on the LPI exams, the Linux IEEE 1394 (also known as FireWire or i.Link) drivers have a similar design. If you understand how to set up USB devices, setting up IEEE 1394 devices should be easy.

Configuring specialized hardware has become easier and easier, even since the development of LPI's Level 2 Exams. Items such as LCD panels and serial UPS devices used to not be as common in our homes and offices, but today they are considered standard equipment.

When you prepared for Level 1, you became familiar with a number of the tools you must utilize when adding new hardware to your systems. For the Level 2 exams, you must be prepared to understand when to use them and the most efficient methods for installing your new devices.

Reporting Your Hardware

Before you tackle adding any new hardware devices to your system, it's useful to obtain information about the hardware you have installed. Some useful tools to report this information include *lsmod*, *lsdev*, and *lspci*.

lsmod

Syntax

```
lsmod [options]
```

Description

The *lsmod* command displays all the information available about currently loaded modules. Reviewing your loaded modules is often the first step in identifying possible problems, such as driver conflicts (quite frequently found with USB device drivers). This information can also be found in */proc/modules*. lsmod has only two options, neither of them affecting its operation.

Options

-h, --help
> Display help information.

-V, --version
> Display the version.

The output of *lsmod* is a series of columns identifying the module name, its size, its use number, and its status. A sample of *lsmod* output looks like this:

```
Module          Size  Used by    Not tainted
vfat           12844   0 (autoclean)
fat            38328   0 (autoclean) [vfat]
nfs            79960   0 (autoclean)
ide-scsi       11984   0 (autoclean)
ide-cd         35196   0 (autoclean)
cdrom          33440   0 (autoclean) [ide-cd]
tuner          11680   1 (autoclean)
tvaudio        14940   0 (autoclean) (unused)
bttv           73568   0 (autoclean)
videodev        8192   2 (autoclean) [bttv]
radeon        114244  28
agpgart        46752   3
parport_pc     18756   1 (autoclean)
lp              8868   0 (autoclean)
parport        36480   1 (autoclean) [parport_pc lp]
```

lsdev

Syntax

```
lsdev
```

Description

The *lsdev* command displays information about your system's hardware, such as interrupt addresses and I/O ports. The command is useful for obtaining information prior to installing devices that may have hardware addressing conflicts, such as ISA devices. This command uses DMA files in */proc* to also report I/O addresses and IRQ and DMA channel information. There are no options for *lsdev*.

lspci

The output of *lsdev* is very simple, similar to *lsmod*. It lists information in four columns: device name, DMA address, IRQ address, and I/O ports. The following is some sample output from *lsdev*:

```
Device          DMA   IRQ  I/O Ports
-------------------------------------------------
ATI                        c800-c8ff
bttv                  10
Creative                   e800-e81f ec00-ec07
dma                        0080-008f
dma1                       0000-001f
dma2                       00c0-00df
e100                       e000-e03f
EMU10K1               11   e800-e81f
fpu                        00f0-00ff
ide0                  14   01f0-01f7 03f6-03f6 fc00-fc07
ide1                  15   0170-0177 0376-0376 fc08-fc0f
Intel                      e000-e03f
keyboard               1   0060-006f
ohci1394              12
PCI                        0cf8-0cff c000-cfff
```

lspci

Syntax

    lspci [options]

Description

The *lspci* command displays information about your system's PCI buses and your installed PCI devices. This information is found primarily within */proc*.

Options

-t

Show a treelike diagram containing all buses, bridges, devices, and connections between them.

-vv

Very verbose mode.

Manipulating Modules

A module is dynamically linked into the running kernel when it is loaded. Much of Linux kernel module handling is done automatically. However, there may be times when it is necessary for you to manipulate the modules yourself, and you may come across the manipulation commands in scripts. For example, if you're having difficulty with a particular driver, you may need to get the source code for a newer version of the driver, compile it, and insert the new module in the running kernel. The commands listed in this section can be used to list, insert, remove, and query modules.

lsmod

Syntax

```
lsmod
```

Description

For each kernel module loaded, display its name, size, use count, and a list of other referring modules. This command yields the same information as is available in */proc/modules*.

Example

Here, *lsmod* shows that quite a few kernel modules are loaded, including filesystem (*vfat, fat*), networking (*3c59x*), and sound (*soundcore, mpu401*, etc.) modules, among others:

```
# lsmod
Module            Size  Used by
radeon          112996  24
agpgart          45824  3
parport_pc       18756  1 (autoclean)
lp                8868  0 (autoclean)
parport          36480  1 (autoclean) [parport_pc lp]
e100             59428  1
ohci1394         19976  0 (unused)
ieee1394         48300  0 [ohci1394]
scsi_mod        106168  0
evdev             5696  0 (unused)
printer           8832  0
wacom             7896  0 (unused)
emu10k1          68104  1
ac97_codec       13512  0 [emu10k1]
sound            73044  0 [emu10k1]
soundcore         6276  7 [emu10k1 sound]
keybdev           2912  0 (unused)
mousedev          5428  1
hid              21700  0 (unused)
input             5824  0 [evdev wacom keybdev mousedev hid]
ehci-hcd         19432  0 (unused)
usb-uhci         25964  0 (unused)
usbcore          77760  1 [printer wacom hid ehci-hcd usb-uhci]
ext3             87240  3
jbd              51156  3 [ext3]
```

insmod

Syntax

```
insmod [options] module
```

Description

Insert a module into the running kernel. The module is located automatically and inserted. You must be logged in as the superuser to insert modules.

Frequently used options

-s

Direct output to syslog instead of *stdout*.

-v

Set verbose mode.

Example

The *msdos* filesystem module is installed into the running kernel. In this example, the kernel was compiled with modular support for the *msdos* filesystem type, a typical configuration for a Linux distribution for i386 hardware. To verify that you have this module, check for the existence of */lib/modules/kernel-version/fs/msdos.o*:

```
# insmod msdos
/lib/modules/2.2.5-15smp/fs/msdos.o: unresolved symbol \
                        fat_add_cluster_Rsmp_eb84f594
/lib/modules/2.2.5-15smp/fs/msdos.o: unresolved symbol \
                        fat_cache_inval_inode_Rsmp_6da1654e
/lib/modules/2.2.5-15smp/fs/msdos.o: unresolved symbol \
                        fat_scan_Rsmp_d61c58c7
( ... additional errors omitted ... )
/lib/modules/2.2.5-15smp/fs/msdos.o: unresolved symbol \
                        fat_date_unix2dos_Rsmp_83fb36a1
# echo $?
```

This *insmod msdos* command yields a series of unresolved symbol messages and an exit status of 1, indicating an error. This is the same sort of message that might be seen when attempting to link a program that referenced variables or functions unavailable to the linker. In the context of a module insertion, such messages indicate that the functions are not available in the kernel. From the names of the missing symbols, you can see that the *fat* module is required to support the *msdos* module, so it is inserted first:

```
# insmod fat
```

Now the *msdos* module can be loaded:

```
# insmod msdos
```

Use the *modprobe* command to automatically determine these dependencies and install prerequisite modules first.

rmmod

Syntax

```
rmmod [options] modules
```

Description

The *rmmod* command is used to remove modules from the running kernel. You must be logged in as the superuser to remove modules, and the command will fail if the module is in use or being referred to by another module.

Frequently used options

-a

> Remove all unused modules.

-s

> Direct output to syslog instead of *stdout*.

Example

Starting with both the *fat* and *msdos* modules loaded, remove the *fat* module (which is used by the *msdos* module):

```
# lsmod
Module                  Size  Used by
msdos                   8348  0  (unused)
fat                    25856  0  [msdos]
# rmmod fat
rmmod: fat is in use
```

In this example, the *lsmod* command fails because the *msdos* module is dependent on the *fat* module. So, to unload the *fat* module, the *msdos* module must be unloaded first:

```
# rmmod msdos
# rmmod fat
```

The *modprobe -r* command can be used to automatically determine these dependencies and remove modules and their prerequisites.

modinfo

Syntax

```
modinfo [options] module_object_file
```

Description

Display information about a module from its *module_object_file*. Some modules contain no information at all, some have a short one-line description, and others have a fairly descriptive message.

Options

-a

> Display the module's author.

-d

> Display the module's description.

-p

> Display the typed parameters that a module supports.

Examples

In these examples, *modinfo* is run using modules compiled for a multiprocessing (SMP) kernel Version 2.2.5. Your kernel version, and thus the directory hierarchy containing modules, will be different.

```
# modinfo -d /lib/modules/2.2.5-15smp/misc/zftape.o
zftape for ftape v3.04d 25/11/97 - VFS interface for the
        Linux floppy tape driver. Support for QIC-113
        compatible volume table and builtin compression
        (lzrw3 algorithm)
# modinfo -a /lib/modules/2.2.5-15smp/misc/zftape.o
(c) 1996, 1997 Claus-Justus Heine
        (claus@momo.math.rwth-aachen.de)
# modinfo -p /lib/modules/2.2.5-15smp/misc/ftape.o
ft_fdc_base int, description "Base address of FDC
        controller."
Ft_fdc_irq int, description "IRQ (interrupt channel)
        to use."
ft_fdc_dma int, description "DMA channel to use."
ft_fdc_threshold int, description "Threshold of the FDC
        Fifo."
Ft_fdc_rate_limit int, description "Maximal data rate
        for FDC."
ft_probe_fc10 int, description "If non-zero, probe for a
        Colorado FC-10/FC-20 controller."
ft_mach2 int, description "If non-zero, probe for a
        Mountain MACH-2 controller."
ft_tracing int, description "Amount of debugging output,
        0 <= tracing <= 8, default 3."
```

modprobe

Syntax

modprobe [*options*] *module* [*symbol=value* ...]

Description

Like *insmod, modprobe* is used to insert modules. In fact, *modprobe* is a wrapper around *insmod* and provides additional functionality. In addition to loading single modules, *modprobe* has the ability to load modules along with their prerequisites or all modules stored in a specific directory. The *modprobe* command can also remove modules when combined with the *-r* option.

A module is inserted with optional *symbol=value* parameters. If the module is dependent upon other modules, they will be loaded first. The *modprobe* command determines prerequisite relationships between modules by reading *modules.dep* at the top of the module directory hierarchy (i.e., */lib/modules/2.2.5-15smp/modules.dep*).

You must be logged in as the superuser to insert modules.

Frequently used options

-*a*

Load all modules. When used with the *-t moduletype*, *all* is restricted to modules in the *moduletype* directory. This action probes hardware by successive module-insertion attempts for a single type of hardware, such as a network adapter (in which case the *moduletype* would be net, representing */lib/modules/kernel-version/kernel/net*). This may be necessary, for example, to probe for more than one kind of network interface.

-c

Display a complete module configuration, including defaults and directives found in */etc/ modules.conf* (or */etc/conf.modules* on older systems). The -c option is not used with any other options.

-l

List modules. When used with the *-t moduletype*, list only modules in directory *module type*. For example, if *moduletype* is net, then modules in */lib/modules/kernel-version/net* are displayed.

-r

Remove *module*, similar to *rmmod*. Multiple modules may be specified.

-s

Direct output to syslog instead of *stdout*.

-t moduletype

Attempt to load multiple modules found in the directory *moduletype* until a module succeeds or all modules in *moduletype* are exhausted. This action "probes" hardware by successive module-insertion attempts for a single type of hardware, such as a network adapter (in which case *moduletype* would be net, representing */lib/modules/kernel-version/kernel/ net*).

-v

Set verbose mode.

Example 1

Install the *msdos* filesystem module into the running kernel:

```
# modprobe msdos
```

Module *msdos* and its dependency, *fat*, will be loaded. *modprobe* determines that *fat* is needed by *msdos* when it looks through *modules.dep*. You can see the dependency listing using grep:

```
# grep /msdos.o: /lib/modules/2.2.5-15smp/modules.dep
/lib/modules/2.2.5-15smp/fs/msdos.o:
        /lib/modules/2.2.5-15smp/fs/fat.o
```

Example 2

Remove *fat* and *msdos* modules from the running kernel, assuming *msdos* is not in use:

```
# modprobe -r fat msdos
```

Example 3

Attempt to load available network modules until one succeeds:

```
# modprobe -t net
```

Example 4

Attempt to load all available network modules:

```
# modprobe -at net
```

Example 5

List all modules available for use:

```
# modprobe -l
/lib/modules/2.2.5-15smp/fs/vfat.o
/lib/modules/2.2.5-15smp/fs/umsdos.o
/lib/modules/2.2.5-15smp/fs/ufs.o
  . . .
```

Example 6

List all modules in the *net* directory for 3Com network interfaces:

```
# modprobe -lt net | grep 3c
/lib/modules/2.2.5-15smp/net/3c59x.o
/lib/modules/2.2.5-15smp/net/3c515.o
/lib/modules/2.2.5-15smp/net/3c509.o
/lib/modules/2.2.5-15smp/net/3c507.o
/lib/modules/2.2.5-15smp/net/3c505.o
/lib/modules/2.2.5-15smp/net/3c503.o
/lib/modules/2.2.5-15smp/net/3c501.o
```

Device Management Definitions

Hotplugging is often taken to mean the opposite of coldplugging—in other words, the ability of a computer system to add or remove hardware without powering the system down. Examples of devices that are coldpluggable include PCI (some PCI chipsets have hotplug support, but these are very expensive and almost exclusively used in server systems), ISA devices, and PATA devices.

In most computer systems, CPUs and memory are coldpluggable, but it is common for high-end servers and mainframes to feature hotplug capability of these components.

sysfs is a RAM-based filesystem initially based on ramfs. It provides a means to export kernel data structures, their attributes, and the linkages between them to the user space. *sysfs* contains several directory hierarchies showing the available hardware devices and attributes of the modules/drivers. It can be accessed by running:

```
# mount -t sysfs sysfs /sys
```

The udev process uses *sysfs* to get the information it needs about the hardware and creates dynamic device files as kernel modules are loaded. The directory */etc/udev.d* holds all the rules to be applied when adding or removing a device.

D-Bus is an application that uses *sysfs* to implement a message bus daemon. It is used for broadcasting system events such as "new hardware device added" or "printer queue changed" and is normally launched by an init script called *messagebus*.

The hald process is the daemon that maintains a database of the devices connected to the system in real time. The daemon connects to the D-Bus system message bus to provide an API that applications can use to discover, monitor, and invoke operations on devices.

4

Change Runlevels and Shut Down or Reboot System (Topics 101.2 and 101.3)

This Topic continues the subject of general knowledge of fundamental PC architecture. It includes these Objectives:

Objective 2: Boot the System
Candidates should be able to guide the system through the booting process. Weight: 3.

Objective 3: Change Runlevels and Shut Down or Reboot System
Candidates should be able to manage the runlevel of the system. This objective includes changing to single-user mode, shutdown, or rebooting the system. Candidates should be able to alert users before switching runlevel and properly terminate processes. This objective also includes setting the default runlevel. Weight: 3.

Objective 2: Boot the System

It is the job of a boot loader, such as LILO or GRUB, to launch the Linux kernel at boot time. In some cases, the boot loader has to deliver information to the Linux kernel that may be required to configure peripherals or control other behavior. This information is called a *kernel parameter*.

Boot-time Kernel Parameters

By default, your system's kernel parameters are set in your boot loader's configuration file (*/etc/lilo.conf* or */boot/grub/menu.lst*, and *boot/grub/grub.conf* on Red Hat and some other distributions). However, the Linux kernel also has the capability to accept information at boot time from a kernel command-line interface. You access the kernel command line through your installed boot loader. When your system boots, you can interrupt the "default" boot process when the boot loader displays and specify your desired kernel parameters. The kernel parameters on the command line look similar to giving arguments or options to a program during command-line execution.

For an example, let's say you wanted to boot with a root partition other than your default, */dev/hda1*. Using LILO, you could enter the following at the LILO prompt:

```
LILO: linux root=/dev/hda9
```

This command boots the kernel whose label is linux and overrides the default value of */dev/hda1* to */dev/hda9* for the root filesystem.

On the Exam

There are far too many kernel parameters to list in this book. Consequently, you must familiarize yourself with them in general terms so that you can answer questions on their form. Remember that they are specified to your boot loader as either a single item, such as ro, or *name=value* options such as root=/dev/hda2. Multiple parameters are always separated by a space.

Introduction to Kernel Module Configuration

Modern Linux kernels are *modular*, in that modules of code traditionally compiled into the kernel (say, a sound driver) are loaded as needed. The modules are separate from the kernel and can be inserted and removed by the superuser if necessary. Although parameters in the boot loader's configuration file and the kernel command line affect the kernel, they do not control kernel modules.

To send parameters to a kernel module, they are inserted into the file */etc/modules.conf* as text (in the past this configuration file was */etc/conf.modules*). Common module options you may find in your module configuration file are I/O address, interrupt, and DMA channel settings for your sound device. This file will also probably carry PCMCIA driver information when installed on laptops. Module configuration will probably be handled by your distribution's installation procedure but may require modifications if hardware is added or changed later. Example 4-1 shows a typical */etc/modules.conf* file.

Example 4-1. A typical /etc/modules.conf file

```
alias parport_lowlevel parport_pc
alias eth0 8139too
alias sound-slot-0 via82cxxx_audio
post-install sound-slot-0 /bin/aumix-minimal \
    -f /etc/.aumixrc -L >/dev/null 2>&1 || :
pre-remove sound-slot-0 /bin/aumix-minimal \
    -f /etc/.aumixrc -S >/dev/null 2>&1 || :
alias usb-controller usb-uhci
```

On the Exam

Read questions that ask about kernel or module parameters carefully. Kernel options can be passed on the kernel command line; module options are specified in *modules.conf*.

In this example, note that an alias named `sound-slot-0` is created for the audio driver `via82cxxx_audio`. Most devices won't need any additional configuration, but systems with older ISA cards may still need to pass options for I/O port, IRQ, and DMA channel settings. In addition, some drivers may need options to specify nonstandard settings. For example, an ISDN board used in North America will need to specify NI1 signaling to the driver:

```
options hisax protocol=4 type=40
```

Kernel boot-time messages

As the Linux kernel boots, it gives detailed status of its progress in the form of console messages. Modules that are loaded also yield status messages. These messages contain important information regarding the health and configuration of your hardware. Generally, the kinds of messages you will see are:

- Kernel identification
- Memory and CPU information
- Information on detected hardware, such as pointers (mice), serial ports, and disks
- Partition information and checks
- Network initialization
- Kernel module output for modules that load at boot time

These messages are displayed on the system console at boot time but often scroll off the screen too quickly to be read. The messages are also logged to disk and can easily be viewed using the *dmesg* command, which displays messages logged at the last system boot. For example, to view messages from the last boot sequence, simply pipe the output of *dmesg* to *less*:

```
# dmesg | less
```

It is also common to use *dmesg* to dump boot messages to a file for later inspection or archive, by simply redirecting the output:

```
# dmesg > bootmsg.txt
```

The kernel buffer used for log messages that *dmesg* displays is a fixed size, so it may lose some (or all) of the boot-time messages as the kernel writes runtime messages.

Reviewing system logs

In addition to kernel messages, many other boot-time messages will be logged using the syslog system. Such messages will be found in the system logfiles such as */var/log/messages*. For example, *dmesg* displays information on your network adapter when it was initialized. However, the configuration and status of that adapter is logged in */var/log/messages* as a result of the network startup. When examining and debugging boot activity on your system, you need to review both kinds of information. *syslogd*, its configuration, and logfile examination are covered in Chapter 16.

Objective 3: Change Runlevels and Shut Down or Reboot System

Linux has the same concept of *runlevels* that most Unix systems offer. This concept specifies different ways to use a system by controlling which services are running. For example, a system that operates as a web server is configured to boot and initiate processing in a runlevel designated for sharing data, at which point the web server is started. However, the same system could be booted into another runlevel used for emergency administration, when all but the most basic services are shut down, so the web server would not run.

One common use of runlevels is to distinguish between a system that offers only a text console and a system that offers a graphical user interface through the X Window System. Most end-user systems run the graphical user interface, but a server (such as the web server just discussed) is more secure and performs better without it.

Runlevels are specified by the integers 0 through 6. Runlevels 0 and 6 are unusual in that they specify the transitional states of shutdown and reboot, respectively. When an administrator tells Linux to enter runlevel 0, the operating system begins a clean shutdown procedure. Similarly, the use of runlevel 6 begins a reboot. The remaining runlevels differ in meaning slightly among Linux distributions and other Unix systems.

When a Linux system boots, the first process it begins is the *init* process, which starts all other processes. The *init* process is responsible for placing the system in the default runlevel, which is usually 2, 3, or 5 depending on the distribution and the use for the machine. Typical runlevel meanings are listed in Table 4-1.

Table 4-1. Typical runlevels

Runlevel	Description
0	Halt the system. Runlevel 0 is a special transitional state used by administrators to shut down the system quickly. This, of course, shouldn't be a default runlevel, because the system would never come up; it would shut down immediately when the kernel launches the init process. See also runlevel 6.
1, s, S	Single-user mode, sometimes called maintenance mode. In this mode, system services such as network interfaces, web servers, and file sharing are not started. This mode is usually used for interactive filesystem maintenance. The three choices 1, s, and S all mean the same thing.
2	Multiuser. On Debian-based systems, this is the default runlevel. On Red Hat–based systems, this is multiuser mode without NFS file sharing or the X Window System (the graphical user interface).

Runlevel	Description
3	On Red Hat–based systems, this is the default multiuser mode, which runs everything except the X Window System. This and levels 4 and 5 usually are not used on Debian-based systems.
4	Typically unused.
5	On Red Hat–based systems, full multiuser mode with GUI login. Runlevel 5 is like runlevel 3, but X11 is started and a GUI login is available. If your X11 cannot start for some reason, you should avoid this runlevel.
6	Reboot the system. Just like runlevel 0, this is a transitional device for administrators. It should not be the default runlevel, because the system would eternally reboot.

It is important to note that runlevels, like most things in Linux, are completely configurable by the end user. For the purposes of the LPIC test, it's important to know the standard meanings of each runlevel on Red Hat–based and Debian-based systems and how the runlevels work. However, in a production environment, runlevels can be modified to do whatever the system administrator desires.

Single-User Mode

Runlevel 1, the single-user runlevel, is a bare-bones operating environment intended for system maintenance. In single-user mode, remote logins are disabled, networking is disabled, and most daemons are not started. Single-user mode is used for system configuration tasks that must be performed with no user activity. One common reason you might be forced to use single-user mode is to correct problems with a corrupt filesystem that the system cannot handle automatically.

If you wish to boot directly into single-user mode, you may specify it at boot time with the kernel's command line through your boot loader. For instance, the GRUB boot loader allows you to pass arbitrary parameters to a kernel at boot time. In order to change the default runlevel, edit the line that boots your kernel in the GRUB interactive menu, adding a 1 or the word `single` to the end of the line to indicate single-user mode. These arguments are not interpreted as kernel arguments but are instead passed along to the init process. For example, if your default GRUB kernel boot line looks like this:

```
kernel /vmlinuz-2.6.27.21-170.2.56.fc10.i686 ro root=/dev/hda1 rhgb quiet
```

you can force the system to boot to runlevel 1 by changing this to:

```
kernel /vmlinuz-2.6.27.21-170.2.56.fc10.i686 ro root=/dev/hda5 rhgb quiet 1
```

or:

```
kernel /vmlinuz-2.6.27.21-170.2.56.fc10.i686 ro root=/dev/hda5 rhgb \
                                  quiet single
```

To switch into single-user mode from another runlevel, you can simply issue a runlevel change command with *init*:

```
# init 1
```

This is not the preferred way of taking a currently running system to runlevel 1, mostly because it gives no warning to the existing logged-in users. See the

---

explanation of the *shutdown* command later in this chapter to learn the preferred way of handling system shutdown.

Overview of the /etc Directory Tree and the init Process

By themselves, the runlevels listed in Table 4-1 don't mean much. It's what the *init* process does as a result of a runlevel specification or change that affects the system. The actions of *init* for each runlevel are derived from the style of initialization in Unix System V and are specified in a series of directories and script files under the */etc* directory.

When a Linux system starts, it runs a number of scripts in */etc* to initially configure the system and switch among runlevels. System initialization techniques differ among Linux distributions. The examples in this section are typical of a Red Hat–based system. Any distribution compliant with the Linux Standards Base (LSB) should look similar. The following describe these files:

/etc/rc.sysinit or /etc/init.d/rcS
> On Red Hat–based systems, *rc.sysinit* is a monolithic system initialization script. The Debian *rcS* script does the same job by running several small scripts placed in two different directories. In each case, the script is launched by *init* at boot time. It handles some essential chores to prepare the system for use, such as mounting filesystems. This script is designed to run before any system daemons are started.

/etc/rc.local
> Not used on Debian-based systems. On Red Hat–based systems, this file is a script that is called after all other *init* scripts (after all system daemons are started). It contains local customizations affecting system startup and provides an alternative to modifying the other *init* scripts. Many administrators prefer to avoid changing *rc.sysint* because those changes will be lost during a system upgrade. The contents of *rc.local* are not lost in an upgrade.

/etc/rc
> This file is a script that is used to change between runlevels. It is not provided on Debian.

The job of starting and stopping system services (also known as *daemons*, which are intended to always run in the background, such as web servers) is handled by the files and symbolic links in */etc/init.d* and by a series of runlevel-specific directories named */etc/rc0.d* through */etc/rc6.d*. These are used as follows:

/etc/init.d
> This directory contains individual startup/shutdown scripts for each service on the system. For example, the script */etc/init.d/httpd* is a Bourne shell script that performs some sanity checks before starting or stopping the Apache web server.
>
> These scripts have a standard basic form and take a single argument. Valid arguments include at least the words **start** and **stop**. Additional arguments are sometimes accepted by the script; examples are **restart**, **status**, and sometimes **reload** (to ask the service to reread its configuration file without exiting).

Administrators can use these scripts directly to start and stop services. For example, to restart Apache, an administrator could issue commands like these:

```
# /etc/init.d/httpd stop
# /etc/init.d/httpd start
```

or simply:

```
# /etc/init.d/httpd restart
```

Either form would completely shut down and start up the web server. To ask Apache to remain running but reread its configuration file, you might enter:

```
# /etc/init.d/httpd reload
```

This has the effect of sending the SIGHUP signal to the running *httpd* process, instructing it to initialize. Signals such as SIGHUP are covered in Chapter 6.

If you add a new service through a package management tool such as *rpm* or *dpkg*, one of these initialization files may be installed automatically for you. In other cases, you may need to create one yourself or, as a last resort, place startup commands in the *rc.local* file.

It's important to remember that these files are simply shell scripts that wrap the various options accepted by the different daemons on Linux. Not all Linux daemons recognize the command-line arguments **stop**, **start**, etc., but the scripts in */etc/init.d* make it easy to manage your running daemons by standardizing the commands that you use to control them.

The directories /etc/rc0.d through /etc/rc6.d

The initialization scripts in */etc/init.d* are not directly executed by the *init* process. Instead, each of the directories */etc/rc0.d* through */etc/rc6.d* contains symbolic (soft) links to the scripts in the */etc/init.d* directory. (These symbolic links could also be files, but using script files in each of the directories would be an administrative headache, because changes to any of the startup scripts would mean identical edits to multiple files.) When the *init* process enters runlevel *N*, it examines all of the links in the associated *rcN.d* directory. These links are given special names in the forms of *KNNname* and *SNNname*, described as follows:

K and S prefixes

These letters stand for *kill* and *start*, respectively. Each runlevel defines a state in which certain services are running and all others are not. The *S* prefix is used to mark files for all services that are to be running (started) for the runlevel. The *K* prefix is used for all other services, which should not be running.

NN

Sequence number. This part of the link name is a two-digit integer (with a leading zero, if necessary). It specifies the relative order for services to be started or stopped. The lowest number represents the first script executed by *init*, and the largest number is the last. There are no hard-and-fast rules for choosing these numbers, but it is important when adding a new service to be sure that it starts after any other required services are already running.

If two services have an identical start order number, the order is indeterminate but probably alphabetical.

name

By convention, the name of the script being linked to. *init* does not use this name, but including it makes maintenance easier for human readers.

As an example, when *init* enters the default runlevel (3 for the sake of this example) at boot time, all of the links with the *K* and *S* prefixes in */etc/rc3.d* will be executed in the order given by their sequence number (*S10network*, *S12syslog*, and so on). Links that start with *S* will be run with the single argument start to launch their respective services, and links that start with *K* will be run with the single argument stop to stop the respective service. Since K comes before S alphabetically, the *K* services are stopped before the *S* services are started. After the last of the scripts is executed, the requirements for runlevel 3 are satisfied.

Setting the Default Runlevel

To determine the default runlevel at boot time, *init* reads the configuration file */etc/inittab* looking for a line containing the word initdefault, which will look like this:

    id:N:initdefault:

In the preceding, *N* is a valid runlevel number, such as 3. This number is used as the default runlevel by init. The *S* scripts in the corresponding */etc/rcN.d* directory are executed to start their respective services. If you change the default runlevel for your system, it will most likely be in order to switch between the standard text login runlevel and the GUI login runlevel. In any case, never change the default runlevel to 0 or 6, or your system will not boot to a usable state.

Determining Your System's Runlevel

From time to time, you might be unsure just what runlevel your system is in. For example, you may have logged into a Linux system from a remote location and not know how it was booted or maintained. You may also need to know what runlevel your system was in prior to its current runlevel—perhaps wondering if the system was last in single-user mode for maintenance.

To determine this information, use the *runlevel* command. It displays the previous and current runlevel as integers, separated by a space, on standard output. If no runlevel change has occurred since the system was booted, the previous runlevel is displayed as the letter N. For a system that was in runlevel 3 and is now in runlevel 5, the output is:

    # runlevel
    3 5

For a system with a default runlevel of 5 that has just completed booting, the output would be:

    # runlevel
    N 5

---

runlevel does not alter the system runlevel. To do this, use the *init* command (or the historical alias *telinit*).

Changing runlevels with init and telinit

The *init* or *telinit* command sends signals to the executing *init* process, instructing it to change to a specified runlevel. You must be logged in as the superuser to use the *init* command.

Generally, you will use a runlevel change for the following reasons:

- To shut down the system using runlevel 0
- To go to single-user mode using runlevel 1
- To reboot the system using runlevel 6

init

Syntax

```
init n
```

Description

The command puts the system into the specified runlevel, *n*, which can be an integer from 1 through 6. *init* also supports S and s, which are equivalent to runlevel 1, and q, which tells *init* to reread its configuration file, */etc/inittab*.

Examples

Shut down immediately:

```
# init 0
```

Reboot immediately:

```
# init 6
```

Go to single-user mode immediately:

```
# init 1
```

or:

```
# init s
```

telinit

The *telinit* command may be used in place of *init*. *telinit* is simply a link to *init*, and the two may be used interchangeably.

System shutdown with shutdown

When shutdown is initiated, all users who are logged into terminal sessions are notified that the system is going down. In addition, further logins are blocked to prevent new users from entering the system as it is being shut down.

Syntax

```
shutdown [options] time [warning_message]
```

Description

The *shutdown* command brings the system down in a secure, planned manner. By default, it takes the system to single-user mode. Options can be used to halt or reboot the system instead. The command internally uses *init* with an appropriate runlevel argument to affect the system change.

The mandatory *time* argument tells the shutdown command when to initiate the shutdown procedure. It can be a time of day in the form *hh:m*, or it can take the form *+n*, where *n* is a number of minutes to wait. *time* can also be the word now, in which case the shutdown proceeds immediately.

warning_message is sent to the terminals of all users to alert them that the shutdown will take place. If the *time* specified is more than 15 minutes away, the command waits until 15 minutes remain before shutdown to make its first announcement. No quoting is necessary in *warning_message* unless the message includes special characters such as * or '.

Frequently used options

-f

Fast boot; this skips the filesystem checks on the next boot.

-h

Halt after shutdown.

-k

Don't really shut down, but send the warning messages anyway.

-r

Reboot after shutdown.

-F

Force filesystem checks on the next boot.

Examples

To reboot immediately (not recommended on a system with human users, because they will have no chance to save their work):

```
# shutdown -r now
```

To reboot in five minutes with a maintenance message:

```
# shutdown -r +5 System maintenance is required
```

To halt the system just before midnight tonight:

```
# shutdown -h 23:59
```

Following are the two most common uses of shutdown by people who are on single-user systems:

```
# shutdown -h now
```

and:

```
# shutdown -r now
```

These cause an immediate halt or reboots, respectively.

Although it's not really a bug, the *shutdown* manpage notes that omission of the required *time* argument yields unusual results. If you forget the *time* argument, the command will probably exit without an error message. This might lead you to believe that a shutdown is starting, so it's important to use the correct syntax.

On the Exam

You need to be familiar with the default runlevels and the steps that the init process goes through in switching between them.

Change Runlevels/
Shutdown/Reboot

5

Linux Installation and Package Management (Topic 102)

Many resources, such as the book *Running Linux (http://oreilly.com/catalog/ 9780596007607)* (O'Reilly), describe Linux installation. This section of the test does not cover the installation of any particular Linux distribution; rather, its Objectives focus on four installation Topics and packaging tools.

Objective 1: Design Hard Disk Layout
  This Objective covers the ability to design a disk partitioning scheme for a Linux system. The Objective includes allocating filesystems or swap space to separate partitions or disks and tailoring the design to the intended use of the system. It also includes placing */boot* on a partition that conforms with the BIOS's requirements for booting. Weight: 2.

Objective 2: Install a Boot Manager
  An LPIC 1 candidate should be able to select, install, and configure a boot manager. This Objective includes providing alternative boot locations and backup boot options using either LILO or GRUB. Weight: 2.

Objective 3: Manage Shared Libraries
  This Objective includes being able to determine the shared libraries that executable programs depend on and install them when necessary. The Objective also includes stating where system libraries are kept. Weight: 1.

Objective 4: Use Debian Package Management
  This Objective indicates that candidates should be able to perform package management on Debian-based systems. This indication includes using both command-line and interactive tools to install, upgrade, or uninstall packages, as well as find packages containing specific files or software. Also included is obtaining package information such as version, content, dependencies, package integrity, and installation status. Weight: 3.

Objective 5: Use Red Hat Package Manager (RPM)

An LPIC 1 candidate should be able to use package management systems based on RPM. This Objective includes being able to install, reinstall, upgrade, and remove packages as well as obtain status and version information on packages. Also included is obtaining package version, status, dependencies, integrity, and signatures. Candidates should be able to determine what files a package provides as well as find which package a specific file comes from. Weight: 3.

Objective 1: Design a Hard Disk Layout

Part of the installation process for Linux is designing the hard disk partitioning scheme. If you're used to systems that reside on a single partition, this step may seem to complicate the installation. However, there are advantages to splitting the filesystem into multiple partitions and even onto multiple disks.

You can find more details about disks, partitions, and Linux filesystem top-level directories in Chapter 7. This Topic covers considerations for implementing Linux disk layouts.

System Considerations

A variety of factors influence the choice of a disk layout plan for Linux, including:

- The amount of disk space
- The size of the system
- What the system will be used for
- How and where backups will be performed

Limited disk space

Filesystems and partitions holding user data should be maintained with a maximum amount of free space to accommodate user activity. When considering the physical amount of disk space available, the system administrator may be forced to make a trade-off between the number of partitions in use and the availability of free disk space. Finding the right configuration depends on system requirements and available filesystem resources.

When disk space is limited, you may opt to reduce the number of partitions, thereby combining free space into a single contiguous pool. For example, installing Linux on a PC with only 1 GB of available disk space might best be implemented using only a few partitions:

/boot

50 MB. A small */boot* filesystem in the first partition ensures that all kernels are below the 1024-cylinder limit for older kernels and BIOS.

/

850 MB. A large root partition holds everything on the system that's not in */boot*.

swap
> 100 MB.

Larger systems

On larger platforms, functional issues such as backup strategies and required filesystem sizes can dictate disk layout. For example, suppose a file server is to be constructed serving 100 GB of executable data files to end users via NFS. Such a system will need enough resources to compartmentalize various parts of the directory tree into separate filesystems and might look like this:

/boot
> 100 MB. Keep kernels under the 1024-cylinder limit.

swap
> 1 GB, depending on RAM.

/
> 500 MB (minimum).

/usr
> 4 GB. All of the executables in */usr* are shared to workstations via read-only NFS.

/var
> 2 GB. Since log files are in their own partition, they won't threaten system stability if the filesystem is full.

/tmp
> 500 MB. Since temporary files are in their own partition, they won't threaten system stability if the filesystem is full.

/home
> 90 GB. This big partition takes up the vast bulk of available space, offered to users for their home directories and data.

On production servers, much of the system is often placed on redundant media, such as mirrored disks. Large filesystems, such as */home*, may be stored on some form of disk array using a hardware controller.

Mount points

Before you may access the various filesystem partitions created on the storage devices, you first must list them in a filesystem table. This process is referred to as *mounting*, and the directory you are mounting is called a *mount point*. You must create the directories that you will use for mount points if they do not already exist. During system startup, these directories and mount points may be managed through the */etc/fstab* file, which contains the information about filesystems to mount when the system boots and the directories that are to be mounted.

Superblock

A superblock is a block on each filesystem that contains metadata information about the filesystem layout. The information contained in the block includes the type, size, and status of the mounted filesystem. The superblock is the Linux/Unix equivalent to Microsoft systems' file allocation table (FAT), which contains the information about the blocks holding the top-level directory. Since the information about the filesystems is important, Linux filesystems keep redundant copies of the superblock that may be used to restore the filesystem should it become corrupt.

MBR

The master boot record (MBR) is a very small program that contains information about your hard disk partitions and loads the operating system. This program is located in the first sector of the hard disk and is 512 bytes. If this file becomes damaged, the operating system cannot boot. Therefore, it is important to back up the MBR so that you can replace a damaged copy if needed. To make a backup of the MBR from the hard drive and store a copy to your */home* directory, use the *dd* command. An example of such a backup command is:

```
dd if=/dev/hda of=~/mbr.txt count=1 bs=512
```

The preceding example assumes that your hard drive is */dev/hda*. With this command you are taking one copy (`count=1`) consisting of 512 bytes (`bs=512`) from */dev/hda* (`if=/dev/hda`) and copying it to a file named *mbr.txt* in */home* (`of=~/mbr.txt`).

If you need to restore the MBR, you may use the following command:

```
dd if=~/mbr.txt of=/dev/hda count=1 bs=512
```

Booting from a USB device

Linux may be booted from a Live USB, similar to booting from a Live CD. One difference between booting to the USB opposed to the CD is that the data on the USB device may be modified and stored back onto the USB device. When using a Live USB distribution of Linux, you can take your operating system, favorite applications, and data files with you wherever you go. This is also useful if you have problems and are not able to boot your computer for some reason. You may be able to boot the system using the Live USB and access the hard drive and troubleshoot the boot issue.

In order to boot from the USB device, you will need to make the USB device bootable. This requires setting up at least one partition on the USB with the bootable flag set to the primary partition. An MBR must also write to the primary partition on the USB. There are many applications that can be used to create live USB distributions of Linux, including Fedora Live USB Creator and Ubuntu Live USB Creator. The computer may also need the BIOS to be configured to boot from USB.

Some older computers may not have support in the BIOS to boot from a USB device. In this case it is possible to redirect the computer to load the operating system from the USB device by using an initial bootable CD. The bootable CD boots the computer, loads the necessary USB drivers into memory, and then locates and loads the filesystem from the USB device.

System role

The role of the system should also dictate the optimal disk layout. In a traditional Unix-style network with NFS file servers, most of the workstations won't necessarily need all of their own executable files. In the days when disk space was at a premium, this represented a significant savings in disk space. Although space on workstation disks isn't the problem it once was, keeping executables on a server still eliminates the administrative headache of distributing updates to workstations.

Backup

Some backup schemes use disk partitions as the basic unit of system backup. In such a scenario, each of the filesystems listed in */etc/fstab* is backed up separately, and they are arranged so that each filesystem fits within the size of the backup media. For this reason, the available backup device capabilities can play a role in determining the ultimate size of partitions.

Using the *dd* command as discussed earlier, you can back up each of the individual partitions. The command may also be used to back up the entire hard drive. To back up a hard drive to another hard drive, you would issue the following command, where if=/dev/hdx represents the hard drive you want to back up and of=/dev/hyd represents the target or destination drive of the backup:

```
dd if=/dev/hdx of=/dev/hyd
```

If you are just interested in making a backup of the partition layout, you can also use the *sfdisk* command to create a copy of the partition table:

```
sfdisk -d /dev/hda > partition_backup.txt
```

Then, if you need to restore the partition table, you can use the *sfdisk* command again:

```
sfdisk /dev/hda < partition_backup.txt
```

Swap Space

When you install Linux, you're asked to configure a *swap*, or *virtual memory*, partition. This special disk space is used to temporarily store portions of main memory containing programs or program data that are not needed constantly, allowing more processes to execute concurrently. An old rule of thumb for Linux is to set the size of the system's swap space to be double the amount of physical RAM in the machine. For example, if your system has 512 MB of RAM, it would be reasonable to set your swap size to at least 1 GB. These are just guidelines, of course. A system's utilization of virtual memory depends on what the system does and the number and size of processes it runs. As hard disk and memory gets cheaper and Linux application footprints grow, the guidelines for determining swap sizes become more and more about personal preference. However, when in doubt, using twice the amount of main memory is a good starting point.

General Guidelines

Here are some guidelines for partitioning a Linux system:

- Keep the root filesystem (/) simple by distributing larger portions of the directory tree to other partitions. A simplified root filesystem is less likely to be corrupted.

- Separate a small /boot partition below cylinder 1024 for installed kernels used by the system boot loader. This does not apply to newer BIOS and kernels (e.g., 2.6.20).

- Separate /var. Make certain it is big enough to handle your logs, spools, and mail, taking their rotation and eventual deletion into account.

- Separate /tmp. Its size depends on the demands of the applications you run. It should be large enough to handle temporary files for all of your users simultaneously.

- Separate /usr and make it big enough to accommodate kernel building. Making it standalone allows you to share it read-only via NFS.

- Separate /home for machines with multiple users or any machine where you don't want to affect data during distribution software upgrades. For even better performance (for multiuser environments), put /home on a disk array and use Logical Volume manager (LVM).

- Set swap space to at least the same size (twice the size is recommended) as the main memory.

On the Exam

Since a disk layout is the product of both system requirements and available resources, no single example can represent the best configuration. Factors to remember include placing the old 2.2.x kernel below cylinder 1024, effectively utilizing multiple disks, sizing partitions to hold various directories such as /var and /usr, and the importance of the root filesystem and swap space size.

Objective 2: Install a Boot Manager

Although it is possible to boot Linux from a floppy disk, most Linux installations boot from the computer's hard disk. This is a two-step process that begins after the system BIOS is initialized and ready to run an operating system. Starting Linux consists of the following two basic phases:

Run the boot loader from the boot device
  It is the boot manager's job to find the selected kernel and get it loaded into memory, including any user-supplied options.

Launch the Linux kernel and start processes
  Your boot loader starts the specified kernel. The boot loader's job at this point is complete and the hardware is placed under the control of the running kernel, which sets up shop and begins running processes.

All Linux systems require some sort of boot loader, whether it's simply bootstrap code on a floppy disk or an application such as LILO or GRUB. Because the popularity of GRUB has grown, LPI has added it to the second release of the 101 exams.

LILO

The LILO is a small utility designed to load the Linux kernel (or the boot sector of another operating system) into memory and start it. A program that performs this function is commonly called a boot loader. LILO consists of two parts:

The boot loader

> This is a two-stage program intended to find and load a kernel. It's a two-stage operation because the boot sector of the disk is too small to hold the entire boot loader program. The code located in the boot sector is compact because its only function is to launch the second stage, which is the interactive portion. The first stage resides in the MBR or first boot partition of the hard disk. This is the code that is started at boot time by the system BIOS. It locates and launches a second, larger stage of the boot loader that resides elsewhere on disk. The second stage offers a user prompt to allow boot-time and kernel image selection options, finds the kernel, loads it into memory, and launches it.

The lilo command

> Also called the *map installer*, the *lilo* command is used to install and configure the LILO boot loader. The command reads a configuration file that describes where to find kernel images, video information, the default boot disk, and so on. It encodes this information along with physical disk information and writes it in files for use by the boot loader.

The boot loader

When the system BIOS launches, LILO presents you with the following prompt:

```
LILO:
```

The `LILO` prompt is designed to allow you to select from multiple kernels or operating systems installed on the computer and to pass parameters to the kernel when it is loaded. Pressing the Tab key at the LILO prompt yields a list of available kernel images. One of the listed images will be the default as designated by an asterisk next to the name:

```
LILO: <TAB>
linux*    linux_586_smp   experimental
```

Under many circumstances, you won't need to select a kernel at boot time because LILO will boot the kernel configured as the default during the install process. However, if you later create a new kernel, have special hardware issues, or are operating your system in a dual-boot configuration, you may need to use some of LILO's options to load the kernel or operating system you desire.

The LILO map installer and its configuration file

Before any boot sequence can complete from your hard disk, the boot loader and associated information must be installed by the LILO map installer utility. The *lilo* command writes the portion of LILO that resides to the MBR, customized for your particular system. Your installation program creates a correct MBR, but you'll have to repeat the command manually if you build a new kernel yourself.

lilo

Syntax

```
lilo [options]
```

The *lilo* map installer reads a configuration file and writes a map file, which contains information needed by the boot loader to locate and launch Linux kernels or other operating systems.

Frequently used options

-C config _ file
> Read the *config _ file* file instead of the default */etc/lilo.conf*.

-m map _ file
> Write *map _ file* in place of the default as specified in the configuration file.

-q
> Query the current configuration.

-v
> Increase verbosity.

LILO's configuration file contains options and kernel image information. An array of options is available. Some are global, affecting LILO overall, whereas others are specific to a particular listed kernel image. Most basic Linux installations use only a few of the configuration options. Example 5-1 shows a simple LILO configuration file.

Example 5-1. Sample /etc/lilo.conf file

```
boot = /dev/hda
timeout = 50
prompt
read-only
map = /boot/map
install = /boot/boot.b

image=/boot/bzImage-2.6.0
  label=test-2.6.0
  root=/dev/hda1
```

Each line in the example is described in the following list:

boot
> Sets the name of the hard disk partition device that contains the boot sector. For PCs with IDE disk drives, the devices will be */dev/hda*, */dev/hdb*, and so on.

timeout
> Sets the timeout in tenths of a second (deciseconds) for any user input from the keyboard. To enable an unattended reboot, this parameter is required if the **prompt** directive is used.

prompt
> Sets the boot loader to prompt the user. This behavior can be stimulated without the prompt directive if the user holds down the Shift, Ctrl, or Alt key when LILO starts.

read-only
> Sets the root filesystem to initially be mounted read-only. Typically, the system startup procedure will remount it later as read/write.

map
> Sets the location of the map file, which defaults to */boot/map*.

install
> Sets the file to install as the new boot sector, which defaults to */boot/boot.b*.

image
> Sets the kernel image to offer for boot. It points to a specific kernel file. Multiple image lines may be used to configure LILO to boot multiple kernels and operating systems.

label
> Sets the optional label parameter to be used after an image line and offers a label for that image. This label can be anything you choose and generally describes the kernel image. Examples include `linux` and `smp` for a multiprocessing kernel.

root
> Sets the devices to be mounted as root for the specified image (used after each image line).

There is more to configuring and setting up LILO, but a detailed knowledge of LILO is not required for this LPI Objective. It is important to review one or two sample LILO configurations to make sense of the boot process.

LILO locations

During installation, LILO can be placed either in the boot sector of the disk or in your root partition. If the system is intended as a Linux-only system, you won't need to worry about other boot loaders, and LILO can safely be placed into the boot sector. However, if you're running another operating system you should place its boot loader in the boot sector. Multiple-boot and multiple-OS configurations are beyond the scope of the LPIC Level 1 exams.

On the Exam

It is important to understand the distinction between *lilo*, the map installer utility run interactively by the system administrator, and the boot loader, which is launched by the system BIOS at boot time. Both are parts of the LILO package.

GRUB

GRUB is a multistage boot loader, much like LILO. It is much more flexible than LILO, as it includes support for booting arbitrary kernels on various filesystem types and for booting several different operating systems. Changes take effect at once, without the need for a command execution.

GRUB device naming

GRUB refers to disk devices as follows:

(*xdn*[,*m*])

The *xd* in this example will be either fd or hd—*floppy disk* or *hard disk*, respectively. The *n* refers to the number of the disk as seen by the BIOS, starting at 0. The optional ,*m* denotes the partition number, also starting at 0.

The following are examples of valid GRUB device names:

(fd0)
> The first floppy disk

(hd0)
> The first hard disk

(hd0,1)
> The second partition on the first hard disk

Note that GRUB does not distinguish between IDE and SCSI/SATA disks. It refers only to the order of the disks as seen by the BIOS, which means that the device number that GRUB uses for a given disk will change on a system with both IDE and SCSI/SATA if the boot order is changed in the BIOS.

Installing GRUB

The simplest way to install GRUB is to use the `grub-install` script.

For example, to install GRUB on the master boot record of the first hard drive in a system, invoke *grub-install* as follows:

```
# grub-install '(hd0)'
```

grub-install looks for a device map file (*/boot/grub/device.map* by default) to determine the mapping from BIOS drives to Linux devices. If this file does not exist, it will attempt to guess what devices exist on the system and how they should be mapped to BIOS drives. If *grub-install* guesses incorrectly, just edit */boot/grub/device.map* and rerun *grub-install*.

The device map file contains any number of lines in this format:

(*disk*) /dev/*device*

So, for example, on a system with a floppy and a single SCSI disk, the file would look like this:

```
(fd0)    /dev/fd0
(hd0)    /dev/sda
```

GRUB can also be installed using the *grub* command. The *grub-install* example shown earlier could also have been done as follows, assuming */boot* is on the first partition of the first hard disk:

```
# grub
grub> root (hd0,0)
grub> setup (hd0)
```

Booting GRUB

If there is no configuration file (or the configuration file does not specify a kernel to load), when GRUB loads it will display a prompt that looks like this:

```
grub>
```

GRUB expects a certain sequence of commands to boot a Linux kernel. They are as follows:

1. root *device*
2. kernel *filename* [*options*]
3. initrd *filename* – optional, only present if an initial ramdisk is required
4. boot

For example, the following sequence would boot a stock Red Hat 8.0 system with */boot* on */dev/hda1* and */* on */dev/hda2*:

```
grub> root (hd0,0)
grub> kernel /vmlinuz-2.4.18-14 ro root=/dev/hda2
grub> initrd /initrd-2.4.18-14.img
grub> boot
```

The GRUB configuration file

GRUB can be configured to boot into a graphical menu, allowing the user to bypass the GRUB shell entirely. To display this menu, GRUB needs a specific configuration file, */boot/grub/menu.lst*.

The location of this file may be different on your system. For example, on Red Hat systems the default configuration file is */boot/grub/grub.conf*.

The configuration file defines various menu options along with the commands required to boot each option. The earlier example of booting a stock Red Hat Fedora 8.0 system could have been accomplished with the following configuration file:

```
default=0
timeout=3
title Red Hat Linux (2.4.18-14)
        root (hd0,0)
        kernel /vmlinuz-2.4.18-14 ro root=/dev/hda2
        initrd /initrd-2.4.18-14.img
```

GRUB has many more features, including serial console support, support for booting other operating systems, and so on. For more information about GRUB, see the info documentation (*info grub* or *pinfo grub*) or the online documentation (*http:// www.gnu.org/software/grub*).

Objective 3: Manage Shared Libraries

When a program is compiled under Linux, many of the functions required by the program are linked from system *libraries* that handle disks, memory, and other functions. For example, when the standard C-language `printf()` function is used in a program, the programmer doesn't provide the `printf()` source code, but instead expects that the system already has a library containing such functions. When the compiler needs to link the code for `printf()`, it can be found in a system library and copied into the executable. A program that contains executable code from these libraries is said to be *statically linked* because it stands alone, requiring no additional code at runtime.

Statically linked programs can have a few liabilities. First, they tend to get large because they include executable files for all of the library functions linked into them. Also, memory is wasted when many different programs running concurrently contain the same library functions. To avoid these problems, many programs are *dynamically linked*. Such programs utilize the same routines but don't contain the library code. Instead, they are linked into the executable at runtime. This dynamic linking process allows multiple programs to use the same library code in memory and makes executable files smaller. Dynamically linked libraries are shared among many applications and are thus called *shared libraries*. A full discussion of libraries is beyond the scope of the LPIC Level 1 exams. However, a general understanding of some configuration techniques is required.

Shared Library Dependencies

Any program that is dynamically linked will require at least a few shared libraries. If the required libraries don't exist or can't be found, the program will fail to run. This could happen, for example, if you attempt to run an application written for the GNOME graphical environment but haven't installed the required GTK+ libraries. Simply installing the correct libraries should eliminate such problems. The *ldd* utility can be used to determine which libraries are necessary for a particular executable.

---

ldd

Syntax

    ldd *programs*

Description

Display shared libraries required by each of the *programs* listed on the command line. The results indicate the name of the library and where the library is expected to be in the filesystem.

Example

The *bash* shell requires three shared libraries:

    # ldd /bin/bash
    /bin/bash:

```
libtermcap.so.2 => /lib/libtermcap.so.2 (0x40018000)
libc.so.6 => /lib/libc.so.6 (0x4001c000)
/lib/ld-linux.so.2 => /lib/ld-linux.so.2 (0x40000000)
```

Linking Shared Libraries

Dynamically linked executables are examined at runtime by the shared object dynamic linker, *ld.so*. This program looks for dependencies in the executable being loaded and attempts to satisfy any unresolved links to system-shared libraries. If *ld.so* can't find a specified library, it fails, and the executable won't run.

To find a new library, *ld.so* must be instructed to look in */usr/local/lib*. There are a few ways to do this. One simple way is to add a colon-separated list of directories to the shell environment variable LD_LIBRARY_PATH, which will prompt *ld.so* to look in any directories it finds there. However, this method may not be appropriate for system libraries, because users might not set their LD_LIBRARY_PATH correctly.

To make the search of */usr/local/lib* part of the default behavior for *ld.so*, files in the new directory must be included in an index of library names and locations. This index is */etc/ld.so.cache*. It's a binary file, which means it can be read quickly by *ld.so*. To add the new library entry to the cache, first add its directory to the *ld.so.conf* file, which contains directories to be indexed by the *ldconfig* utility.

ldconfig

Syntax

```
ldconfig [options] lib_dirs
```

Description

Update the *ld.so* cache file with shared libraries specified on the command line in *lib_dirs*, in trusted directories */usr/lib* and */lib*, and in the directories found in */etc/ld.so.conf*.

Frequently used options

-p

Display the contents of the current cache instead of recreating it.

-v

Verbose mode. Display progress during execution.

Example 1

Examine the contents of the *ld.so* library cache:

```
# ldconfig -p
144 libs found in cache '/etc/ld.so.cache'
    libz.so.1 (libc6) => /usr/lib/libz.so.1
    libuuid.so.1 (libc6) => /lib/libuuid.so.1
    libutil.so.1 (libc6, OS ABI: Linux 2.2.5) => /lib/libutil.so.1
    libutil.so (libc6, OS ABI: Linux 2.2.5) => /usr/lib/libutil.so \
    libthread_db.so.1 (libc6, OS ABI: Linux 2.2.5) => /lib/libthread_db.so.1
    libthread_db.so (libc6, OS ABI: Linux 2.2.5) => /usr/lib/libthread_db.so
```

Example 2

Look for a specific library entry in the cache:

```
# ldconfig -p | grep ncurses
        libncurses.so.5 (libc6) => /usr/lib/libncurses.so.5
```

Example 3

Rebuild the cache:

```
# ldconfig
```

After */usr/local/lib* is added, *ld.so.conf* might look like this:

```
/usr/lib
/usr/i486-linux-libc5/lib
/usr/X11R6/lib
/usr/local/lib
```

Next, *ldconfig* is run to include libraries found in */usr/local/lib* in */etc/ld.so.cache*. It is important to run *ldconfig* after any changes in system libraries to be sure that the cache is up-to-date.

Objective 4: Use Debian Package Management

The Debian package management system is a versatile and automated suite of tools used to acquire and manage software packages for Debian Linux. The system automatically handles many of the management details associated with interdependent software running on your system.

Debian Package Management Overview

Each Debian package contains program and configuration files, documentation, and noted dependencies on other packages. The names of Debian packages have three common elements, including:

Package name
    A Debian package name is short and descriptive. When multiple words are used in the name, they are separated by hyphens. Typical names include *binutils*, *kernel-source*, and *telnet*.

Version number
    Each package has a version. Most package versions are the same as that of the software they contain. The format of package versions varies from package to package, but most are numeric (`major.minor.patchlevel`).

A file extension
    By default, all Debian packages end with the *.deb* file extension.

Figure 5-1 illustrates a Debian package name.

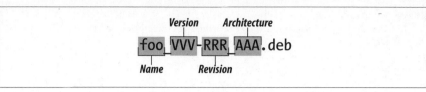

Figure 5-1. The structure of a Debian GNU/Linux package name

Managing Debian Packages

The original Debian package management tool is *dpkg*, which operates directly on *.deb* package files and can be used to automate the installation and maintenance of software packages. The alternative *apt-get* tool operates using package names, obtaining them from a predefined source (such as CD-ROMs, FTP sites, etc.). Both tools work from the command line.

The *dselect* command offers an interactive menu that allows the administrator to select from a list of available packages and mark them for subsequent installation. The *alien* command allows the use of non-Debian packages, such as the Red Hat RPM format.

For complete information on Debian package management commands, see details in their respective manpages.

dpkg

Syntax

    dpkg [options] action

Description

The Debian package manager command, *dpkg*, consists of an *action* that specifies a major mode of operation as well as zero or more *options*, which modify the action's behavior.

The *dpkg* command maintains package information in */var/lib/dpkg*. There are two files that are of particular interest:

available
    The list of all available packages.

status
    Contains package attributes, such as whether it is installed or marked for removal.

These files are modified by *dpkg, dselect*, and *apt-get*, and it is unlikely that they will ever need to be edited.

Frequently used options

-E
    Do not overwrite a previously installed package of the same version.

-G
    Do not overwrite a previously installed package with an older version of that same package.

-R (also --recursive)
> Recursively process package files in specified subdirectories. Works with *-i*, *--install*, *--unpack*, and so on.

Frequently used options

--configure package
> Configure an unpacked package. This involves setup of configuration files.

-i package_file (also --install package_file)
> Install the package contained in *package_file*. This involves backing up old files, unpacking and installation of new files, and configuration.

-l [pattern] (also --list [pattern])
> Display information for installed package names that match *pattern*.

-L package (also --listfiles package)
> List files installed from *package*.

--print-avail package
> Display details found in */var/lib/dpkg/available* about *package*.

--purge package
> Remove everything for *package*.

-r package (also --remove package)
> Remove everything except configuration files for *package*.

-s package (also --status package)
> Report the status of *package*.

-S search_pattern (also --search search_pattern)
> Search for a filename matching *search_pattern* from installed packages.

--unpack package_file
> Unpack *package_file*, but don't install the package it contains.

Example 1

Install a package using *dpkg -i* with the name of an available package file:

```
# dpkg -i ./hdparm_3.3-3.deb
(Reading database ... 54816 files and directories
  currently installed.)
Preparing to replace hdparm 3.3-3 (using hdparm_3.3-3.deb)
Unpacking replacement hdparm ...
Setting up hdparm (3.3-3) ...
```

Alternatively, use *apt-get install* with the name of the package. In this case, the package comes from the location or locations configured in */etc/apt/sources.list*. For this example, the location is *http://http.us.debian.org*:

```
# apt-get install elvis
Reading Package Lists... Done
Building Dependency Tree... Done
The following extra packages will be installed:
  libncurses4 xlib6g
The following NEW packages will be installed:
  elvis
```

```
2 packages upgraded, 1 newly installed, 0 to remove
  and 376 not upgraded.
Need to get 1678kB of archives. After unpacking 2544kB
  will be used.
Do you want to continue? [Y/n] y
Get:1 http://http.us.debian.org stable/main
  libncurses4 4.2-9 [180kB]
Get:2 http://http.us.debian.org stable/main
  xlib6g 3.3.6-11 [993kB]
Get:3 http://http.us.debian.org stable/main
  elvis 2.1.4-1 [505kB]
Fetched 1678kB in 4m11s (6663B/s)
(Reading database ... 54730 files and directories
 currently installed.)
Preparing to replace libncurses4 4.2-3 (using
  .../libncurses4_4.2-9_i386.deb) ...
Unpacking replacement libncurses4 ...
(installation continues...)
```

Example 2

Upgrading a package is no different from installing one. However, you should use the -G option when upgrading with *dpkg* to ensure that the installation won't proceed if a newer version of the same package is already installed.

Example 3

Use *dpkg -r* or *dpkg --purge* to remove a package:

```
# dpkg --purge elvis
(Reading database ... 54816 files and directories
  currently installed.)
Removing elvis ...
(purge continues...)
```

Example 4

Use the *dpkg -S* command to find a package containing specific files. In this example, *apt-get* is contained in the *apt* package:

```
# dpkg -S apt-get
apt: /usr/share/man/man8/apt-get.8.gz
apt: /usr/bin/apt-get
```

Example 5

Obtain package status information, such as version, content, dependencies, integrity, and installation status, using *dpkg -s*:

```
# dpkg -s apt
Package: apt
Status: install ok installed
Priority: optional
Section: admin
Installed-Size: 1388
(listing continues...)
```

Installation/Package Management

Example 6

List the files in a package using *dpkg -L* and process the output using *grep* or *less*:

```
# dpkg -L apt | grep '^/usr/bin'
/usr/bin
/usr/bin/apt-cache
/usr/bin/apt-cdrom
/usr/bin/apt-config
/usr/bin/apt-get
```

Example 7

List the installed packages using *dpkg -l*; if you don't specify a pattern, all packages will be listed:

```
# dpkg -l xdm
ii  xdm             3.3.2.3a-11    X display manager
```

Example 8

Use *dpkg -S* to determine the package from which a particular file was installed with the filename:

```
# dpkg -S /usr/bin/nl
textutils: /usr/bin/nl
```

---

apt-get

Syntax

```
apt-get [options] [command] [package_name ...]
```

Description

The *apt-get* command is part of the Advanced Package Tool (APT) management system. It does not work directly with *.deb* files like *dpkg*, but uses package names instead. *apt-get* maintains a database of package information that enables the tool to automatically upgrade packages and their dependencies as new package releases become available.

Frequently used options

-d

Download files, but do not install. This is useful when you wish to get a large number of package files but delay their installation to prevent installation errors from stopping the download process.

-s

Simulate the steps in a package change, but do not actually change the system.

-y

Automatically respond "yes" to all prompts, instead of prompting you for a response during package installation/removal.

Frequently used commands

dist-upgrade

Upgrade automatically to new versions of Debian Linux.

---

install
> Install or upgrade one or more packages by name.

remove
> Remove specified packages.

update
> Fetch a list of currently available packages. This is typically done before any changes are made to existing packages.

upgrade
> Upgrade a system's complete set of packages to current versions safely. This command is conservative and will not process upgrades that could cause a conflict or break an existing configuration; it also will not remove packages.

Additional commands and options are available. See the *apt-get* manpage for more information.

apt-get uses */etc/apt/sources.list* to determine where packages should be obtained. The file should contain one or more lines that look something like this:

```
deb http://http.us.debian.org/debian stable main contrib non-free
```

Example

Remove the *elvis* package using *apt-get*:

```
# apt-get remove elvis
Reading Package Lists... Done
Building Dependency Tree... Done
The following packages will be REMOVED:
  elvis
0 packages upgraded, 0 newly installed, 1 to remove
  and 376 not upgraded.
Need to get 0B of archives. After unpacking 1363kB
  will be freed.
Do you want to continue? [Y/n] y
(Reading database ... 54816 files and directories
  currently installed.)
Removing elvis ...
(removal continues...)
```

In this example, the user is required to respond with **y** when prompted to continue. Using the *-y* option to *apt-get* would eliminate this interaction.

dselect

Syntax

```
dselect
```

Description

dselect is an interactive, menu-driven, frontend tool for *dpkg* and is usually invoked without parameters. The *dselect* command lets you interactively manage packages by selecting them for installation, removal, configuration, and so forth. Selections are made from a locally stored list of available packages, which may be updated while running *dselect*. Package actions initiated by *dselect* are carried out using *dpkg*.

alien

Syntax

```
alien [--to-deb] [--patch=patchfile] [options] file
```

Description

Convert to or install a non-Debian (or "alien") package. Supported package types include Red Hat *.rpm*, Stampede *.slp*, Slackware *.tgz*, and generic *.tar.gz* files. rpm must also be installed on the system to convert an RPM package into a *.deb* package. The *alien* command produces an *output package* in Debian format by default after conversion.

Frequently used options

-i

Automatically install the output package and remove the converted package file.

-r

Convert package to RPM format.

-t

Convert package to a gzip tar archive.

Example

Install a non-Debian package on a Debian system using *alien* with the *-i* option:

```
# alien -i package.rpm
```

On the Exam

dselect, *apt-get*, and *alien* are important parts of Debian package management, but detailed knowledge of *dpkg* is of primary importance for Exam 101.

Objective 5: Use Red Hat Package Manager (RPM)

The Red Hat Package Manager is among the most popular methods for the distribution of software for Linux and is installed by default on most distributions. It automatically handles many of the management details associated with interdependent software running on your system.

RPM Overview

RPM automates the installation and maintenance of software packages. Built into each package are program files, configuration files, documentation, and dependencies on other packages. Package files are manipulated using the *rpm* command, which maintains a database of all installed packages and their files. Information from new packages is added to this database, and the database is consulted on a file-by-file basis for dependencies when packages are removed, queried, and installed. As with Debian packages, RPM packages have four common elements:

Name

An RPM package name is short and descriptive. If multiple words are used, they are separated by hyphens (not underscores, as you might expect). Typical names include *binutils*, *caching-nameserver*, *cvs*, *gmc*, *kernel-source*, and *telnet*.

Version

Each package has a version. Most package versions are the same as that of the software they contain. The format of package versions varies from package to package, but most are numeric (`major.minor.patchlevel`).

Revision

The revision tag is simply a release number for the package. It has no significance except to determine whether one package is newer than another when the version number does not change.

Architecture

Packages containing binary (compiled) files are by their nature specific to a particular type of system. For PCs, the RPM architecture designation is *i386*, meaning the Intel 80386 and subsequent line of microprocessors and compatibles.

Packages optimized for later x86 CPUs will have an architecture tag appropriate for the specific CPU the code is compiled for, such as *i586* for Intel Pentium (and compatible) processors, *i686* for Intel Pentium Pro and later processors (Pentium II, Celeron, Pentium III, and Pentium 4), or *athlon* for AMD Athlon.

Other possible architecture tags include *alpha, ia64, ppc*, and *sparc* (for the Alpha, Itanium, PowerPC, and SPARC architectures, respectively). Another arch tag, *noarch*, is used to indicate packages that can install on any architecture.

While the filename of an RPM package is not significant, Red Hat does have a standard naming scheme for its packages that most of the other RPM-based distributions also follow. It is constructed by tying these elements together in one long string.

Running rpm

The *rpm* command provides for the installation, removal, upgrade, verification, and other management of RPM packages. *rpm* has a bewildering array of options, including the traditional single-letter style (*-i*) and the double-dash full word style (*--install*). In most cases, both styles exist and are interchangeable.

Although configuring *rpm* may appear to be a bit daunting, its operation is simplified by being segmented into *modes*. *rpm* modes are enabled using one (and only one) of the *mode options*. Within a mode, additional mode-specific options become available to modify the behavior of *rpm*. The major modes of `rpm` and some of the most frequently used mode-specific options follow. For complete information on how to use and manage RPM packages, see the *rpm* manpage or the synopsis offered by *rpm --help*.

rpm

Syntax

```
rpm -i [options]
(also rpm --install)
rpm -U [options] (also rpm --upgrade)
rpm -e [options] (also rpm --uninstall)
rpm -q [options] (also rpm --query)
rpm -V [options] (also rpm --verify)
```

Install/upgrade mode

The *install mode* (*rpm -i*) is used to install new packages. A variant of install mode is the *upgrade mode* (*rpm -U*), where an installed package is upgraded to a more recent version. Another variant is the *freshen mode* (*rpm -F*), which upgrades only packages that have an older version already installed on the system. But *rpm*'s *-F* option has limited value, since it doesn't handle dependency changes at all. In other words, if a new version of a package requires that another package be installed, *-F* won't automatically install the new package, even if it is listed on the command line.

Frequently used install and upgrade options

--force
> Allows the replacement of existing packages and of files from previously installed packages; for upgrades, it allows the replacement of a newer package with an older one. (Literally, it is equivalent to setting all of the options *--replacepkgs*, *--replacefiles*, and *--oldpackage*.) *Use this option with caution.*

-h (also --hash)
> Prints a string of 50 hash marks (#) during installation as a progress indicator.

--nodeps
> Allows you to install a package without checking for dependencies. *This command should be avoided because it makes the dependency database inconsistent.*

--test
> Runs through all the motions except for actually writing files; it's useful to verify that a package will install correctly prior to making the attempt. Note that verbose and hash options cannot be used with *--test*, but *-vv* can.

-v
> Sets verbose mode. (Package names are displayed as the packages are being installed.)

-vv
> Sets really verbose mode. The manpage describes this as "print lots of ugly debugging information."

Example 1

To install a new package, simply use the *rpm -i* command with the name of a package file. If the new package depends upon another package, the install fails, like this:

```
# rpm -i gcc-2.96-113.i386.rpm
error: failed dependencies:
        binutils >= 2.11.93.0.2-6 is needed by gcc-2.96-113
```

```
        cpp = 2.96-113 is needed by gcc-2.96-113
        glibc-devel is needed by gcc-2.96-113
```

To correct the problem, the dependency must first be satisfied. In this example, *gcc* is dependent on *binutils, cpp,* and *glibc-devel,* which all must be installed first (or at the same time, as in this example):

```
# rpm -i binutils-2.11.93.0.2-11.i386.rpm cpp-2.96-113.i386.rpm \
  glibc-devel-2.2.5-44.i386.rpm gcc-2.96-113.i386.rpm
```

Example 2

Upgrading an existing package to a newer version can be done with the *-U* option. Upgrade mode is really a special case of the install mode, where existing packages can be superseded by newer versions. Using *-U*, a package can be installed even if it doesn't already exist, in which case it behaves just like *-i*:

```
# rpm -U gcc-2.96-113.i386.rpm
```

Uninstall mode

This mode is used to remove installed packages from the system. By default, *rpm* uninstalls a package only if no other packages depend on it.

Frequently used uninstall options

--nodeps
> *rpm* skips dependency checking with this option enabled. *This command should be avoided because it makes the dependency database inconsistent.*

--test
> This option runs through all the motions except for actually uninstalling things; it's useful to verify that a package can be uninstalled correctly without breaking other dependencies prior to making the attempt. Note that verbose and hash options cannot be used with *--test*, but *-vv* can.

Example

Package removal is the opposite of installation and has the same dependency constraints:

```
# rpm -e glibc-devel
error: removing these packages would break dependencies:
        glibc-devel is needed by gcc-2.96-113
```

Query mode

Installed packages and raw package files can be queried using the *rpm -q* command. Query mode options exist for package and information selection.

Frequently used query package selection options

-a (also --all)
> Display a list of all packages installed on the system. This is particularly useful when piped to *grep* if you're not sure of the name of a package or when you want to look for packages that share a common attribute.

-f filename (also --file)
> Display the package that contains a particular file.

Installation/Package Management

-p package_filename
> Query a package file (most useful with *-i*, described next).

Frequently used query information selection options

-c (also --configfiles)
> List only configuration files.

-d (also --docfiles)
> List only documentation files.

-i package
> Not to be confused with the *install mode*. Display information about an installed package, or when combined with *-p*, about a package file. In the latter case, *package* is a filename.

-l package (also --list)
> List all of the files contained in *package*. When used with *-p*, the *package* is a filename.

-R (also --requires)
> List packages on which this package depends.

Example 1

To determine the version of the software contained in an RPM file, use the query and package information options:

```
# rpm -qpi openssh-3.4p1-2.i386.rpm | grep Version
Version     : 3.4p1              Vendor: Red Hat, Inc.
```

For installed packages, omit the *-p* option and specify a package name instead of a package filename. Notice if you have multiple versions of the same package installed, you will get output for all of the packages:

```
# rpm -qi kernel-source | grep Version
Version     : 2.4.9              Vendor: Red Hat, Inc.
Version     : 2.4.18             Vendor: Red Hat, Inc.
Version     : 2.4.18             Vendor: Red Hat, Inc.
```

Example 2

List the files contained in a package:

```
# rpm -qlp gnucash-1.3.0-1.i386.rpm
/usr/bin/gnc-prices
/usr/bin/gnucash
/usr/bin/gnucash.gnome
/usr/doc/gnucash
/usr/doc/gnucash/CHANGES
  (...output continues ...)
```

For an installed package, enter query mode and use the *-l* option along with the package name:

```
# rpm -ql kernel-source
/usr/src/linux-2.4.18-14
/usr/src/linux-2.4.18-14/COPYING
/usr/src/linux-2.4.18-14/CREDITS
/usr/src/linux-2.4.18-14/Documentation
/usr/src/linux-2.4.18-14/Documentation/00-INDEX
/usr/src/linux-2.4.18-14/Documentation/BUG-HUNTING
```

```
/usr/src/linux-2.4.18-14/Documentation/Changes
(...output continues ...)
```

Example 3

List the documentation files in a package:

```
# rpm -qd at
/usr/doc/at-3.1.7/ChangeLog
/usr/doc/at-3.1.7/Copyright
/usr/doc/at-3.1.7/Problems
/usr/doc/at-3.1.7/README
/usr/doc/at-3.1.7/timespec
/usr/man/man1/at.1
/usr/man/man1/atq.1
/usr/man/man1/atrm.1
/usr/man/man1/batch.1
/usr/man/man8/atd.8
/usr/man/man8/atrun.8
```

Use -p for package filenames.

Example 4

List configuration files or scripts in a package:

```
# rpm -qc at
/etc/at.deny
/etc/rc.d/init.d/atd
```

Example 5

Determine what package a particular file was installed from. Of course, not all files originate from packages:

```
# rpm -qf /etc/fstab
file /etc/fstab is not owned by any package
```

Those that are package members look like this:

```
# rpm -qf /etc/aliases
sendmail-8.11.6-15
```

Example 6

List the packages that have been installed on the system:

```
# rpm -qa
(... hundreds of packages are listed ...)
```

To search for a subset with kernel in the name, pipe the previous command to grep:

```
# rpm -qa | grep kernel
kernel-source-2.4.18-24.7.x
kernel-pcmcia-cs-3.1.27-18
kernel-utils-2.4-7.4
kernel-doc-2.4.18-24.7.x
kernel-2.4.18-24.7.x
```

Verify mode

Files from installed packages can be compared against their expected configuration from the RPM database by using *rpm -V*.

Frequently used verify options

--nofiles
> Ignores missing files.

--nomd5
> Ignores MD5 checksum errors.

--nopgp
> Ignores PGP checking errors.

On the Exam

Make certain that you are aware of *rpm*'s major operational modes and their commonly used mode-specific options. Knowledge of specific options will be necessary. Read through the *rpm* manpage at least once.

YUM Overview

YUM (Yellowdog Updater Modified) is a package manager offering a fast way for installing, updating, and removing packages. The *yum* command has a very simple interface and functions similar to *rpm*, but *yum* additionally manages all of the dependencies for you. Yum will detect if dependencies are required for the installation of an application and, if need be, fetch the required dependency and install it. Yum has the ability to support multiple repositories for packages and has a simple configuration.

YUM is configured through the */etc/yum.conf* configuration file. A sample of the configuration file follows. Repositories may be added and modified through the */etc/yum.repos.d* directory:

```
# cat /etc/yum.conf
[main]
cachedir=/var/cache/yum
keepcache=0
debuglevel=2
logfile=/var/log/yum.log
exactarch=1
obsoletes=1
gpgcheck=1
plugins=1
installonly_limit=3

# This is the default. If you make this bigger yum won't see if the metadata
# is newer on the remote and so you'll "gain" the bandwidth of not having to
# download the new metadata and "pay" for it by yum not having correct
# information.
# It is especially important, to have correct metadata, for distributions
# like Fedora that don't keep old packages around. If you don't like this
```

```
# checking interrupting your command line usage, it's much better to have
# something manually check the metadata once an hour (yum-updatesd will do this).
# metadata_expire=90m

# PUT YOUR REPOS HERE OR IN separate files named file.repo
# in /etc/yum.repos.d
```

The most common commands used with *yum* are:

install
>Install a package or packages on your system.

erase
>Remove a package or packages from your system.

update
>Update a package or packages on your system.

list
>List a package or group of packages on your system.

search
>Search package details for the given string.

Checking installed packages

Check installed packages with *list*:

```
# yum list
```

This command will show all of the packages that are currently installed on your computer. It will also list available packages. In the following example the partial output is filtered through |*more* to display content one page at a time. Here you can see that some of the packages are installed (marked `installed`) and others are available through update (`@update`):

```
# yum list |more
Loaded plugins: refresh-packagekit
Installed Packages
Canna-libs.i586              3.7p3-27.fc11              installed
ConsoleKit.i586              0.3.0-8.fc11               installed
ConsoleKit-libs.i586         0.3.0-8.fc11               installed
ConsoleKit-x11.i586          0.3.0-8.fc11               installed
DeviceKit.i586               003-1                      installed
DeviceKit-disks.i586         004-4.fc11                 @updates
DeviceKit-power.i586         009-1.fc11                 @updates
GConf2.i586                  2.26.2-1.fc11              installed
GConf2-gtk.i586              2.26.2-1.fc11              installed
ImageMagick.i586             6.5.1.2-1.fc11             installed
MAKEDEV.i586                 3.24-3                     installed
NetworkManager.i586          1:0.7.1-8.git20090708.fc11 @updates
NetworkManager-glib.i586     1:0.7.1-8.git20090708.fc11 @updates
...
```

You can also check to see if a particular package is installed or available for install using the *list* command. The following example checks to see whether Samba is installed. From the output you see that the *samba* package is not installed but available for installation through the repository:

```
# yum list samba
Loaded plugins: refresh-packagekit
Available Packages
samba.i586                    3.3.2-0.33.fc11              fedora
```

If you need to collect information about a particular package, use the *info* command. In this situation we ask for information about the *httpd* service:

```
# yum info httpd
Loaded plugins: refresh-packagekit
Installed Packages
Name        : httpd
Arch        : i586
Version     : 2.2.11
Release     : 8
Size        : 2.6 M
Repo        : installed
Summary     : Apache HTTP Server
URL         : http://httpd.apache.org/
License     : ASL 2.0
Description: The Apache HTTP Server is a powerful, efficient, and extensible
            : web server.
```

Checking for updates

yum may be used to check for available updates for packages running on the computer. You can run the *check-updates* command to perform a check for any available package or specify a particular package you want to update. This example checks for any available updates:

```
# yum check-update
Loaded plugins: refresh-packagekit
gtk2.i586                         2.16.5-1.fc11              updates
mysql-libs.i586                   5.1.36-1.fc11             updates
selinux-policy.noarch             3.6.12-69.fc11            updates
selinux-policy-targeted.noarch    3.6.12-69.fc11            updates
```

Installing packages

Installing packages using *yum* is really quite straightforward. To install a package, you specify its name with the *install* command and the package name, along with any dependencies that will be downloaded and installed. This example installs the *samba* package:

```
# yum install samba
Loaded plugins: refresh-packagekit
Setting up Install Process
Resolving Dependencies
--> Running transaction check
---> Package samba.i586 0:3.3.2-0.33.fc11 set to be updated
--> Finished Dependency Resolution

Dependencies Resolved
```

```
===============================================================================
 Package          Arch          Version                 Repository       Size
===============================================================================
Installing:
 samba            i586          3.3.2-0.33.fc11         fedora          4.4 M

Transaction Summary
===============================================================================
Install      1 Package(s)
Update       0 Package(s)
Remove       0 Package(s)

Total download size: 4.4 M
Is this ok [y/N]:
Downloading Packages:
samba-3.3.2-0.33.fc11.i586.rpm                          | 4.4 MB       00:06
Running rpm_check_debug
Running Transaction Test
Finished Transaction Test
Transaction Test Succeeded
Running Transaction
  Installing      : samba-3.3.2-0.33.fc11.i586                           1/1

Installed:
  samba.i586 0:3.3.2-0.33.fc11

Complete!
```

Removing packages

Removing a package from your system is similar to the installation process. Two options remove packages: *remove* and *erase*. They perform the same function, but *remove* should be used with caution because it also can uninstall dependent packages:

```
# yum remove httpd
Loaded plugins: refresh-packagekit
Setting up Remove Process
Resolving Dependencies
--> Running transaction check
---> Package httpd.i586 0:2.2.11-8 set to be erased
--> Processing Dependency: httpd >= 2.2.0 for package: \
                gnome-user-share-2.26.0-2.fc11.i586
--> Running transaction check
---> Package gnome-user-share.i586 0:2.26.0-2.fc11 set to be erased
--> Finished Dependency Resolution

Dependencies Resolved
===============================================================================
 Package              Arch        Version           Repository       Size
===============================================================================
Removing:
 httpd                i586        2.2.11-8          installed        2.6 M

Removing for dependencies:
 gnome-user-share     i586        2.26.0-2.fc11     installed        809 k
```

```
Transaction Summary
========================================================================
Install      0 Package(s)
Update       0 Package(s)
Remove       2 Package(s)

Is this ok [y/N]: Y
```

6

GNU and Unix Commands
(Topic 103)

This Topic covers the essential skill of working interactively with Linux command-line utilities. Although it's true that GUI tools are available to manage just about everything on a Linux system, a firm understanding of command-line utilities is required to better prepare you to work on any LSB-compliant Linux distribution.

The family of commands that are part of Linux and Unix systems have a long history. Individuals or groups that needed specific tools contributed many of the commands in the early days of Unix development. Those that were popular became part of the system and were accepted as default tools under the Unix umbrella. Today, Linux systems carry new and often more powerful *GNU* versions of these historical commands, which are covered in LPI Topic 103.1.

This LPI Topic has eight Objectives:

Objective 1: Work on the Command Line
   This Objective states that a candidate should be able to interact with shells and commands using the command line. This includes using single shell commands and one-line command sequences to perform basic tasks on the command line, using and modifying the shell environment, including defining, referencing, and exporting environment variables, using and editing command history, and invoking commands inside and outside the defined path. Weight: 4.

Objective 2: Process Text Streams Using Filters
   This Objective states that a candidate should be able to apply filters to text streams. Tasks include sending text files and output streams through text utility filters to modify the output, and using standard Unix commands found in the GNU *coreutils* package. Weight: 3.

Objective 3: Perform Basic File Management
   This Objective states that candidates should be able to use the basic Linux commands to copy, move, and remove files and directories. Tasks include advanced file management operations such as copying multiple files recursively,

removing directories recursively, and moving files that meet a wildcard pattern. The latter task includes using simple and advanced wildcard specifications to refer to files, as well as using *find* to locate and act on files based on type, size, or time. This also includes usage of the commands *tar, cpio*, and *dd* for archival purposes. Weight: 4.

Objective 4: Use Streams, Pipes, and Redirects
This Objective states that a candidate should be able to redirect streams and connect them to efficiently process textual data. Tasks include redirecting standard input, standard output, and standard error, piping the output of one command to the input of another command, using the output of one command as arguments to another command, and sending output to both *stdout* and a file. Weight: 4.

Objective 5: Create, Monitor, and Kill Processes
This Objective states that a candidate should be able to manage processes. This includes knowing how to run jobs in the foreground and background, bring a job from the background to the foreground and vice versa, start a process that will run without being connected to a terminal, and signal a program to continue running after logout. Tasks also include monitoring active processes, selecting and sorting processes for display, sending signals to processes, and killing processes. Weight: 4.

Objective 6: Modify Process Execution Priorities
This Objective states that a candidate should be able to manage process execution priorities. The tasks include running a program with higher or lower priority, determining the priority of a process, and changing the priority of a running process. Weight: 2.

Objective 7: Search Text Files Using Regular Expressions
This Objective states that a candidate should be able to manipulate files and text data using regular expressions. This includes creating simple regular expressions containing several notational elements, as well as using regular expression tools to perform searches through a filesystem or file content. Weight: 2.

Objective 8: Perform Basic File Editing Operations Using vi
This Objective states a candidate should be able to edit files using *vi*. This includes *vi* navigation, basic *vi* modes, and inserting, editing, deleting, copying, and finding text. Weight: 3.

The tools and concepts discussed here represent important and fundamental aspects of working with Linux and are essential for your success on Exam 101.

Objective 1: Work on the Command Line

Every computer system requires a human interface component. For Linux system administration, a text interface is typically used. The system presents the administrator with a *prompt*, which at its simplest is a single character such as $ or #. The prompt signifies that the system is ready to accept typed commands, which usually occupy one or more lines of text. This interface is generically called the *command line*.

It is the job of a program called a *shell* to provide the command prompt and to interpret commands. The shell provides an interface layer between the Linux kernel and the end user, which is how it gets its name. The original shell for Unix systems was written by Stephen Bourne and was called simply *sh*. The default Linux shell is *bash*, the *Bourne-Again Shell*, which is a GNU variant of *sh*. This chapter will not cover all aspects of the *bash* shell. At this point, we are primarily concerned with our interaction with *bash* and the effective use of commands.

The Interactive Shell

The shell is a powerful programming environment, capable of automating nearly anything you can imagine on your Linux system. The shell is also your interactive interface to your system. When you first start a shell, it does some automated house-keeping to get ready for your use, and then presents a command prompt. The command prompt tells you that the shell is ready to accept commands from its *standard input* device, which is usually the keyboard. Shells can run standalone, as on a physical terminal, or within a window in a GUI environment. Whichever the case, their use is the same.

Shell variable basics

During execution, *bash* maintains a set of *shell variables* that contain information important to the execution of the shell. Most of these variables are set when *bash* starts, but they can be set manually at any time.

The first shell variable of interest in this topic is called PS1, which simply stands for *Prompt String 1*. This special variable holds the contents of the command prompt that are displayed when *bash* is ready to accept commands (there is also a PS2 variable, used when *bash* needs multiple-line input to complete a command). You can easily display the contents of PS1, or any other shell variable, by using the echo command with the variable name preceded by the $ symbol:

```
$ echo $PS1
\$
```

The \$ output tells us that PS1 contains the two characters \ and $. The backslash character tells the shell not to interpret the dollar symbol in any special way (that is, as a *metacharacter*, described later in this section). A simple dollar sign was the default prompt for *sh*, but *bash* offers options to make the prompt much more in-formative. On your system, the default prompt stored in PS1 is probably something like:

```
[\u@\h \W]\$
```

Each of the characters preceded by backslashes has a special meaning to *bash*, whereas those without backslashes are interpreted literally. In this example, \u is replaced by the username, \h is replaced by the system's hostname, \W is replaced by the unqualified path (or basename) of the current working directory, and \$ is replaced by a $ character (unless you are *root*, in which case \$ is replaced by #). This yields a prompt of the form:

```
[adam@linuxpc adam]$
```

How your prompt is formulated is really just a convenience and does not affect how the shell interprets your commands. However, adding information to the prompt, particularly regarding system, user, and directory location, can make life easier when hopping from system to system and logging in as multiple users (as yourself and *root*, for example). See the online documentation on *bash* (*http://www.gnu.org/soft ware/bash/manual/*) for more information on customizing prompts, including many more options you can use to display system information in your prompt.

Another shell variable that is extremely important during interactive use is PATH, which contains a list of all the directories that hold commands or other programs you are likely to execute. A default path is set up for you when *bash* starts. You may wish to modify the default to add other directories that hold programs you need to run.

Every file in the Linux filesystem can be specified in terms of its location. The *less* program, for example, is located in the directory */usr/bin*. Placing */usr/bin* in your PATH enables you to execute *less* by simply typing less rather than the explicit /usr/bin/less.

Also be aware that "." (the current directory) is not included in the PATH either implicitly (as it is in *DOS*) or explicitly for security reasons. To execute a program named *foo* in the current directory, simply run ./foo.

For *bash* to find and execute the command you enter at the prompt, the command must be one of the following:

- A bash *built-in* command that is part of *bash* itself
- An executable program located in a directory listed in the PATH variable
- An executable program whose filename you specify explicitly

The shell holds PATH and other variables for its own use. However, many of the shell's variables are needed during the execution of programs launched from the shell (including other shells). For these variables to be available, they must be *exported*, at which time they become *environment variables*. Environment variables are passed on to programs and other shells, and together they are said to form the *environment* in which the programs execute. PATH is always made into an environment variable. Exporting a shell variable to turn it into an environment variable is done using the *export* command:

```
$ export MYVAR
```

Do not include a preceding dollar sign when defining or exporting a variable (because in this command, you don't want the shell to expand the variable to its value). When a variable is exported to the environment, it is passed into the environment of all child processes. That is, it will be available to all programs run by your shell. Here is an example that displays the difference between a shell variable and an environment variable:

```
$ echo $MYVAR
```

No output is returned, because the variable has not been defined. We give it a value, and then echo its value:

```
$ MYVAR="hello"
$ echo $MYVAR
hello
```

We've verified that the variable MYVAR contains the value "hello". Now we spawn a subshell (or child process) and check the value of this variable:

```
$ bash
$ echo $MYVAR
```

Typing *bash* spawned another copy of the bash shell. This child process is now our current environment, and as you can see from the blank line that ends the example, the variable MYVAR is not defined here. If we return to our parent process and export the variable, it becomes an environment variable that can be accessed in all child processes:

```
$ exit
$ export MYVAR
$ bash
$ echo $MYVAR
hello
```

Typing the *export* command without any arguments will display all of the exported environment variables available to your shell. The *env* command will accomplish the same thing, just with slightly different output.

Along the same lines are the bash built-in commands *set* and *unset*. The command *set* with no arguments will display of list of currently set environment variables. The command *unset* will allow you to clear the value of an environment variable (assuming it is not read-only). The *set* command also gives you the ability to change the way *bash* behaves. The following are some examples of using *set* to modify your interactive shell.

To change to *vi*-style editing mode:

```
$ set -o vi
```

This example automatically marks variables that are modified or created for export to the environment of subsequent commands:

```
$ set -o allexport
```

To view the current settings for the variables that *set* can modify, run *set -o*.

Entering commands at the command prompt

Commands issued to the shell on a Linux system generally consist of four components:

- A valid command (a shell built-in, program, or script found among directories listed in the PATH, or an explicitly defined program)
- Command options, usually preceded by a dash
- Arguments
- Line acceptance (i.e., pressing the Enter key), which we assume in the examples

Each command has its own unique syntax, although most follow a fairly standard form. At minimum, a *command* is necessary:

```
$ ls
```

This simple command lists the contents of the current working directory. It requires neither options nor arguments. Generally, *options* are letters or words preceded by a single or double dash and are added after the command and separated from it by a space:

```
$ ls -l
```

The *-l* option modifies the behavior of *ls* by listing files in a longer, more detailed format. In most cases, single-dash options can be either combined or specified separately. To illustrate this, consider these two equivalent commands:

```
$ ls -l -a
$ ls -la
```

By adding the *-a* option, *ls* displays files beginning with a dot (which it hides by default). Adding that option by specifying *-la* yields the same result. Some commands offer alternative forms for the same option. In the preceding example, the *-a* option can be replaced with *--all*:

```
$ ls -l --all
```

These double-dash, full-word options are frequently found in programs from the GNU project. They cannot be combined like the single-dash options can. Both types of options can be freely intermixed. Although the longer GNU-style options require more typing, they are easier to remember and easier to read in scripts than the single-letter options.

Adding an *argument* further refines the command's behavior:

```
$ ls -l *.c
```

Now the command will give a detailed listing only of C program source files, if any exist in the current working directory.

 Using the asterisk in *.c allows any file to match as long as it ends with a .c extension. This is known as *file globbing*. More information on file globbing and using wildcards can be found later in this chapter.

Sometimes, options and arguments can be mixed in any order:

```
$ ls --all *.c -l
```

In this case, *ls* was able to determine that *-l* is an option and not another file descriptor.

Some commands, such as *tar* and *ps*, don't require the dash preceding an option because at least one option is expected or required. To be specific, *ps* doesn't require a dash when it is working like BSD's version of *ps*. Since the Linux version of *ps* is designed to be as compatible as possible with various other versions of *ps*, it sometimes does need a dash to distinguish between conflicting options. As an example, try *ps -e* and *ps e*. The first version invokes a Linux-specific option that shows everyone's processes, not just your own. The second version invokes the original BSD option that shows the environment variables available to each of your commands.

Also, an option often instructs the command that the subsequent item on the command line is a specific argument. For example:

```
$ sort name_list
```

```
$ sort -k 2 name_list
```

These commands invoke the *sort* command to sort the lines in the file *name_list*. The first command just sorts beginning with the first character of each line, whereas the second version adds the options -k 2. The -k option tells the command to break each line into fields (based on whitespace) and to sort the lines on a particular field. This option requires a following option to indicate which field to sort on. In this case, we have told *sort* to sort on the second field, which is useful if *name_list* contains people's names in a "Joe Smith" format.

Just as any natural language contains exceptions and variations, so does the syntax used for GNU and Unix commands. You should have no trouble learning the essential syntax for the commands you need to use often. The capabilities of the command set offered on Linux are extensive, making it highly unlikely that you'll memorize all of the command syntax you'll ever need. Most system administrators are constantly learning about features they've never used in commands they use regularly. It is standard practice to regularly refer to the documentation on commands you're using, so feel free to explore and learn as you go.

Entering commands not in the PATH

Occasionally, you will need to execute a command that is not in your path and not built into your shell. If this need arises often, it may be best to simply add the directory that contains the command to your path. However, there's nothing wrong with explicitly specifying a command's location and name completely. For example, the *ls* command is located in */bin*. This directory is most certainly in your PATH variable (if not, it should be!), which allows you to enter the *ls* command by itself on the command line:

```
$ ls
```

The shell looks for an executable file named *ls* in each successive directory listed in your PATH variable and will execute the first one it finds. Specifying the literal pathname for the command eliminates the directory search and yields identical results:

```
$ /bin/ls
```

Any executable file on your system may be started in this way. However, it is important to remember that some programs may have requirements during execution about what is listed in your PATH. A program can be launched normally but may fail if it is unable to find a required resource due to an incomplete PATH.

Entering multiple-line commands interactively

In addition to its interactive capabilities, the shell also has a complete programming language of its own. Many programming features can be very handy at the interactive command line as well. Looping constructs, including for, until, and while, are often used this way. (Shell syntax is covered in more detail in Chapter 13.) When you begin a command such as these, which normally spans multiple lines, *bash* prompts you for the subsequent lines until a valid command has been completed. The prompt you receive in this case is stored in shell variable PS2, which by default is >. For example, if you wanted to repetitively execute a series of commands each time with a different argument from a known series, you could enter the following:

```
$ var1=1
$ var2=2
$ var3=3
$ echo $var1
1
$ echo $var2
2
$ echo $var2
3
```

Rather than entering each command manually, you can interactively use *bash*'s for loop construct to do the work for you. Note that indented style, such as what you might use in traditional programming, isn't necessary when working interactively with the shell:

```
$ for var in $var1 $var2 $var3
> do
> echo $var
> done
1
2
3
```

You can also write this command on one line:

```
$ for var in $var1 $var2 $var3; do echo $var; done
1
2
3
```

The semicolons are necessary to separate the variables from the built-in bash functions.

Entering command sequences

There may be times when it is convenient to place multiple commands on a single line. Normally, *bash* assumes you have reached the end of a command (or the end of the first line of a multiple-line command) when you press Enter. To add more than one command to a single line, separate the commands and enter them sequentially with the *command separator*, a semicolon. Using this syntax, the following commands:

```
$ ls
$ ps
```

are, in essence, identical to and will yield the same result as the following single-line command that employs the command separator:

```
$ ls ; ps
```

On the Exam

Command syntax and the use of the command line are very important topics. Pay special attention to the use of options and arguments and how they are differentiated. Also be aware that some commands expect options to be preceded by a dash, whereas other commands do not. The LPI exams do not concentrate on command options, so don't feel like you need to memorize every obscure option for every command before taking the exams.

Command History and Editing

If you consider interaction with the shell as a kind of conversation, it's a natural extension to refer back to things "mentioned" previously. You may type a long and complex command that you want to repeat, or perhaps you need to execute a command multiple times with slight variation.

If you work interactively with the original Bourne shell, maintaining such a "conversation" can be a bit difficult. Each repetitive command must be entered explicitly, each mistake must be retyped, and if your commands scroll off the top of your screen, you have to recall them from memory. Modern shells such as *bash* include a significant feature set called *command history*, *expansion*, and *editing*. Using these capabilities, referring back to previous commands is painless, and your interactive shell session becomes much simpler and more effective.

The first part of this feature set is command history. When *bash* is run interactively, it provides access to a list of commands previously typed. The commands are stored in the history list *prior* to any interpretation by the shell. That is, they are stored before wildcards are expanded or command substitutions are made. The history list is controlled by the HISTSIZE shell variable. By default, HISTSIZE is set to 1,000 lines, but you can control that number by simply adjusting HISTSIZE's value. In addition to commands entered in your current *bash* session, commands from previous *bash* sessions are stored by default in a file called ~/.bash_history (or the file named in the shell variable HISTFILE).

If you use multiple shells in a windowed environment (as just about everyone does), the last shell to exit will write its history to ~/.bash_history. For this reason you may wish to use one shell invocation for most of your work.

To view your command history, use the *bash* built-in *history* command. A line number will precede each command. This line number may be used in subsequent *history expansion*. History expansion uses either a line number from the history or a portion of a previous command to re-execute that command. History expansion also allows a fair degree of command editing using syntax you'll find in the *bash* documentation. Table 6-1 lists the basic history expansion designators. In each case, using the designator as a command causes a command from the history to be executed again.

Table 6-1. Command history expansion designators

Designator	Description
!!	Spoken as *bang-bang*, this command refers to the most recent command. The exclamation point is often called *bang* on Linux and Unix systems.
!n	Refer to command *n* from the history. Use the *history* command to display these numbers.
!-n	Refer to the current command minus *n* from the history.
!string	Refer to the most recent command starting with string.
!?string	Refer to the most recent command containing string.
^string1^string2	Quick substitution. Repeat the last command, replacing the first occurrence of string1 with string2.

While using history substitution can be useful for executing repetitive commands, command history editing is much more interactive. To envision the concept of command history editing, think of your entire *bash* history (including that obtained from your ~/.bash_history file) as the contents of an editor's buffer. In this scenario, the current command prompt is the last line in an editing buffer, and all of the previous commands in your history lie above it. All of the typical editing features are available with command history editing, including movement within the "buffer," searching, cutting, pasting, and so on. Once you're used to using the command history in an editing style, everything you've done on the command line becomes available as retrievable, reusable text for subsequent commands. The more familiar you become with this concept, the more useful it can be.

By default, *bash* uses *key bindings* like those found in the Emacs editor for command history editing. (An editing style similar to the *vi* editor is also available.) If you're familiar with Emacs, moving around in the command history will be familiar and very similar to working in an Emacs buffer. For example, the key command Ctrl-p (depicted as C-p) will move up one line in your command history, displaying your previous command and placing the cursor at the end of it. This same function is also bound to the up-arrow key. The opposite function is bound to C-n (and the down arrow). Together, these two key bindings allow you to examine your history line by line. You may re-execute any of the commands shown simply by pressing Enter when it is displayed. For the purposes of Exam 101, you'll need to be familiar with this editing capability, but detailed knowledge is not required. Table 6-2 lists some of the common Emacs key bindings you may find useful in *bash*. Note that C- indicates the Ctrl key, and M- indicates the Meta key, which is usually Alt on PC keyboards (since PC keyboards do not actually have a Meta key).

> In circumstances where the Alt key is not available, such as on a terminal, using the Meta key means pressing the Escape (Esc) key, releasing it, and then pressing the defined key. The Esc key is not a modifier, but applications will accept the Esc key sequence as equivalent to the Meta key.

Table 6-2. Basic command history editing Emacs key bindings

Key	Description
C-p	Previous line (also up arrow)
C-n	Next line (also down arrow)
C-b	Back one character (also left arrow)
C-f	Forward one character (also right arrow)
C-a	Beginning of line
C-e	End of line
C-l	Clear the screen, leaving the current line at the top of the screen
M-<	Top of history
M->	Bottom of history
C-d	Delete character from right
C-k	Delete (kill) text from cursor to end of line
C-y	Paste (yank) text previously cut (killed)
M-d	Delete (kill) word
C-r*text*	Reverse search for *text*
C-s*text*	Forward search for *text*

Command substitution

bash offers a handy ability to do *command substitution*. This feature allows you to replace the result of a command with a script. For example, wherever $(*command*) is found, its output will be substituted. This output could be assigned to a variable, as in the system information returned by the command *uname –a*:

```
$ SYSTEMSTRING=$(uname -a)
$ echo $SYSTEMSTRING
Linux linuxpc.oreilly.com 2.6.24.7-92.fc8 #1 SMP Wed May 7 16:50:09 \
EDT 2008 i686 athlon i386 GNU/Linux
```

Another form of command substitution is `` `command` ``. The result is the same, except that the *back quote* (or *backtick*) syntax has some special rules regarding metacharacters that the $(command)$ syntax avoids. Refer to the *bash* manual at *http: //www.gnu.org/software/bash/manual/* for more information.

Applying commands recursively through a directory tree

There are many times when it is necessary to execute commands *recursively*. That is, you may need to repeat a command throughout all the branches of a directory tree. Recursive execution is very useful but also can be dangerous. It gives a single interactive command the power to operate over a much broader range of your system than your current directory, and the appropriate caution is necessary. Think twice before using these capabilities, particularly when operating as the superuser.

Some of the GNU commands on Linux systems have built-in recursive capabilities as an option. For example, *chmod* modifies permissions on files in the current directory:

```
$ chmod g+w *.c
```

In this example, all files with the *.c* extension in the current directory are given the group-write permission. However, there may be a number of directories and files in hierarchies that require this change. *chmod* contains the *-R* option (note the upper-case option letter; you may also use *--recursive*), which instructs the command to operate not only on files and directories specified on the command line, but also on all files and directories contained *beneath* the specified directories. For example, this command gives the group-write permission to all files in a source-code tree named */home/adam/src*:

```
$ chmod -R g+w /home/adam/src
```

Provided you have the correct privileges, this command will descend into each sub-directory in the *src* directory and add the requested permission to each file and directory it finds. Other example commands with this ability include *cp* (copy), *ls* (list files), and *rm* (remove files).

A more general approach to recursive execution through a directory is available by using the *find* command. *find* is inherently recursive and is intended to descend through directories executing commands or looking for files with certain attributes. At its simplest, *find* displays an entire directory hierarchy when you simply enter the command and provide a single argument of the target directory. If no options are given to *find*, it prints each file it finds, as if the option *-print* were specified:

```
$ find /home/adam/src
...files and directories are listed recursively...
```

As an example of a more specific use, add the *-name* option to search the same directories for C files (this can be done recursively with the *ls* command as well):

```
$ find /home/adam/src -name "*.c"
....c files are listed recursively...
```

find also can be used to execute commands against specific files by using the *-exec* option. The arguments following *-exec* are taken as a command to run on each *find* match. They must be terminated with a semicolon (;), which needs to be escaped (\;, for example) because it is a shell metacharacter. The string {} is replaced with the filename of the current match anywhere it is found in the command.

To take the previous example a little further, rather than execute *chmod* recursively against all files in the *src* directory, *find* can execute it against the C files only, like this:

```
$ find /home/adam/src -name "*.c" -exec chmod g+w {} \;
```

The *find* command is capable of much more than this simple example and can locate files with particular attributes such as dates, protections, file types, access times, and others. Although the syntax can be confusing, the results are worth some study of *find*.

Manpages

Traditional computer manuals covered everything from physical maintenance to programming libraries. Although the books were convenient, many users didn't always want to dig through printed documentation or carry it around. So, as space became available, the *man* (*manual*) command was created to put the books on the system, giving users immediate access to the information they needed in a searchable, quick-reference format.

There is a *manpage* for most commands on your system. There are also manpages for important files, library functions, shells, languages, devices, and other features. *man* is to your system what a dictionary is to your written language. That is, nearly everything is defined in detail, but you probably need to know in advance just what you're looking for.

man

Syntax

```
man [options] [section] name
```

Description

Format and display system manual pages from *section* on the topic of *name*. If *section* is omitted, the first manpage found is displayed.

Frequently used options

-a

Normally, *man* exits after displaying a single manpage. The *-a* option instructs *man* to display all manpages that match *name*, in a sequential fashion.

-d

Display debugging information.

-k

Search for manpages containing a given string.

-w

Print the locations of manpages instead of displaying them.

Example 1

View a manpage for *mkfifo*:

```
$ man mkfifo
...
```

Results for the first manpage found are scrolled on the screen.

Example 2

Determine what manpages are available for *mkfifo*:

```
$ man -wa mkfifo
/usr/share/man/man1/mkfifo.1
/usr/share/man/man3/mkfifo.3
```

This shows that two manpages are available, one in section 1 (*mkfifo.1*) of the manual and another in section 3 (*mkfifo.3*). See the next section for a description of manpage sections.

Example 3

Display the *mkfifo* manpage from manual section 3:

```
$ man 3 mkfifo
```

Manual sections

Manpages are grouped into *sections*, and there are times when you should know the appropriate section in which to search for an item. For example, if you were interested in the *mkfifo* C-language function rather than the command, you must tell the *man* program to search the section on library functions (in this case, section 3, *Linux Programmer's Manual*):

```
$ man 3 mkfifo
```

An alternative would be to have the *man* program search all manual sections:

```
$ man -a mkfifo
```

The first example returns the *mkfifo(3)* manpage regarding the library function. The second returns pages for both the command and the function. In this case, the pages are delivered separately; terminating the pager on the first manpage with Ctrl-C causes the second to be displayed.

Manual sections are detailed in Table 6-3.

Table 6-3. Man sections

Section	Description
1	User programs
2	System calls
3	Library calls
4	Special files (usually found in */dev*)
5	File formats
6	Games
7	Miscellaneous
8	System administration

Some systems might also have sections 9, *n*, and others, but only sections 1 through 8 are defined by the FHS.

The order in which *man* searches the sections for manpages is controlled by the `MANSECT` environment variable. `MANSECT` contains a colon-separated list of section numbers. If it is not set, *man* (as of version 1.5k) behaves as if it were set to `1:8:2:3:4:5:6:7:9:tcl:n:l:p:o`.

Manpage format

Most manpages are presented in a concise format with information grouped under well-known standard headings such as those shown in Table 6-4. Other manpage headings depend on the context of the individual manpage.

Table 6-4. Standard manpage headings

Heading	Description
Name	The name of the item, along with a description
Synopsis	A complete description of syntax or usage
Description	A brief description of the item
Options	Detailed information on each command-line option (for commands)
Return values	Information on function return values (for programming references)
See also	A list of related items that may be helpful
Bugs	Descriptions of unusual program behavior or known defects
Files	A list of important files related to the item, such as configuration files
Copying or copyright	A description of how the item is to be distributed or protected
Authors	A list of those who are responsible for the item

man mechanics

System manpages are stored mostly in */usr/share/man*, but may exist in other places as well. At any time, the manual pages available to the *man* command are contained within directories configured in your `man` configuration file, */etc/man.config*. This file contains directives to the *man*, telling it where to search for pages (the `MANPATH` directive), the paging program to use (`PAGER`), and many others. This file essentially controls how *man* works on your system. To observe this, use the debug (*-d*) option to *man* to watch as it constructs a *manpath* (a directory search list) and prepares to display your selection:

```
$ man -d mkfifo
```

Objective 2: Process Text Streams Using Filters

Many of the commands on Linux systems are intended to be used as *filters*, meaning that multiple commands can be piped together to perform complex operations on text. Text fed into the command's standard input or read from files is modified in some useful way and sent to standard output or to a new file, leaving the original source file unmodified. Multiple commands can be combined to produce *text streams*, which modify text at each step. This section describes basic use and syntax for the filtering commands important for Exam 101. Refer to a Linux command reference for full details on each command and the many other available commands.

cat

Syntax

```
cut options [files]
```

Description

Concatenate files and print on the standard output. Cat is often used as the first command in a text stream, as it simply sends the contents of a file (or multiple files) to the standard output.

Frequently used options

-s
> Never output more than one single blank line.

-v
> Display nonprinting characters (these usually are not displayed).

-A
> Display nonprinting characters, display $ at the end of each line, and display Tab characters as ^I.

Example

Send the contents of the file */etc/passwd* to the file */tmp/passwd*:

```
$ cat /etc/passwd > /tmp/passwd
```

cut

Syntax

```
cut options [files]
```

Description

Cut out (that is, print) selected columns or fields from one or more *files*. The source file is not changed. This is useful if you need quick access to a vertical slice of a file. By default, the slices are delimited by a Tab character.

Frequently used options

-blist
> Print bytes in *list* positions.

-clist
> Print characters in *list* columns.

-ddelim
> Set field delimiter (default is ;).

-flist
> Print *list* fields.

Example

Show usernames (in the first colon-delimited field) from */etc/passwd*:

```
$ cut -d: -f1 /etc/passwd
```

expand

Syntax

> expand [*options*] [*files*]

Description

Convert Tabs to spaces. Sometimes the use of Tab characters can make output that is attractive on one output device look bad on another. This command eliminates Tabs and replaces them with the equivalent number of spaces. By default, Tabs are assumed to be eight spaces apart.

Frequently used options

-tnumber
> Specify Tab stops in place of the default 8.

-i

> Initial; convert only at start of lines.

fmt

Syntax

> fmt [*options*] [*files*]

Description

Format text to a specified width by filling lines and removing newline characters. Multiple *files* from the command line are concatenated.

Frequently used options

-u
> Use uniform spacing: one space between words and two spaces between sentences.

-w width
> Set line width to *width*. The default is 75 characters.

head

Syntax

> head [*options*] [*files*]

GNU/Unix
Commands

Description

Print the first few lines of one or more files (the "head" of the file or files). When more than one file is specified, a header is printed at the beginning of each file, and each is listed in succession.

Frequently used options

-c n

Print the first *n* bytes, or if *n* is followed by k or m, print the first *n* kilobytes or megabytes, respectively.

-nn

Print the first *n* lines. The default is 10.

---

join

Syntax

```
join [options] file1 file2
```

Description

Print a line for each pair of input lines, one each from *file1* and *file2*, that have identical *join fields*. This function could be thought of as a very simple database table join, where the two files share a common index just as two tables in a database would.

Frequently used options

-j1field
Join on *field* of *file1*.

-j2field
Join on *field* of *file2*.

-jfield
Join on *field* of both *file1* and *file2*.

Example

Suppose *file1* contains the following:

```
1 one
2 two
3 three
```

and *file2* contains:

```
1 11
2 22
3 33
```

Issuing the command:

```
$ join -j 1 file1 file2
```

yields the following output:

```
1 one 11
2 two 22
3 three 33
```

---

nl

Syntax

```
nl [options] [files]
```

Description

Number the lines of *files*, which are concatenated in the output. This command is used for numbering lines in the body of text, including special header and footer options normally excluded from the line numbering. The numbering is done for each *logical page*, which is defined as having a header, a body, and a footer. These are delimited by the special strings \:\:\:, \: \:, and \:, respectively.

Frequently used options

-b style
> Set body numbering style to *style*, which is t by default (styles are described next).

-f style
> Set footer number style to *style* (n by default).

-h style
> Set header numbering style to *style*, (n by default).

Styles can be in these forms:

A
> Number all lines.

t
> Number only nonempty lines.

n
> Do not number lines.

pREGEXP
> Number only lines that contain a match for regular expression *REGEXP*.

Example

Suppose file *file1* contains the following text:

```
\:\:\:
header
\:\:
line1
line2
line3
\:
footer
\:\:\:
header
```

GNU/Unix Commands

```
\:\:
line1
line2
line3
\:
footer
```

If the following command is given:

```
$ nl -h a file1
```

the output would yield numbered headers and body lines but no numbering on footer lines. Each new header represents the beginning of a new logical page and thus a restart of the numbering sequence:

```
       1  header
       2  line1
       3  line2
       4  line3
footer
       1  header
       2  line1
       3  line2
       4  line3
footer
```

od

Syntax

```
od [options] [files]
```

Description

Dump files in octal and other formats. This program prints a listing of a file's contents in a variety of formats. It is often used to examine the byte codes of binary files but can be used on any file or input stream. Each line of output consists of an octal byte offset from the start of the file followed by a series of tokens indicating the contents of the file. Depending on the options specified, these tokens can be ASCII, decimal, hexadecimal, or octal representations of the contents.

Frequently used options

-t type
> Specify the *type* of output.

Typical types include:

A
> Named character

c
> ASCII character or backslash escape

O
> Octal (the default)

x
Hexadecimal

Example

If *file1* contains:

```
a1\n
A1\n
```

where \n stands for the newline character, the *od* command specifying named characters yields the following output:

```
$ od -t a file1
00000000   a   1   nl   A   1   nl
00000006
```

A slight nuance is the ASCII character mode. This *od* command specifying named characters yields the following output with backslash-escaped characters rather than named characters:

```
$ od -t c file1
00000000   a   1   \n   A   1   \n
00000006
```

With numeric output formats, you can instruct *od* on how many bytes to use in interpreting each number in the data. To do this, follow the type specification by a decimal integer. This *od* command specifying single-byte hex results yields the following output:

```
$ od -t x1 file1
00000000   61 31 0a 41 31 0a
00000006
```

Doing the same thing in octal notation yields:

```
$ od -t o1 file1
00000000   141 061 012 101 061 012
00000006
```

If you examine an ASCII chart with hex and octal representations, you'll see that these results match those tables.

paste

Syntax

```
paste [options] [files]
```

Description

Paste together corresponding lines of one or more *files* into vertical columns. Similar in function to the *join* command, but simpler in scope.

Frequently used options

-dn
Separate columns with character *n* in place of the default Tab.

-s

    Merge lines from one file into a single line. When multiple files are specified, their contents are placed on individual lines of output, one per file.

For the following three examples, *file1* contains:

```
1
2
3
```

and *file2* contains:

```
A
B
C
```

Example 1

A simple *paste* creates columns from each file in standard output:

```
$ paste file1 file2
1    A
2    B
3    C
```

Example 2

The column separator option yields columns separated by the specified character:

```
$ paste -d'@' file1 file2
1@A
2@B
3@C
```

Example 3

The single-line option (*-s*) yields a line for each file:

```
$ paste -s file1 file2
1    2    3
A    B    C
```

pr

Syntax

```
pr [options] [file]
```

Description

Convert a text file into a paginated, columnar version, with headers and page fills. This command is convenient for yielding nice output, such as for a line printer from raw, uninteresting text files. The header will consist of the date and time, the filename, and a page number.

Frequently used options

-d

    Double space.

-hheader
> Use *header* in place of the filename in the header.

-llines
> Set page length to *lines*. The default is 66.

-o width
> Set the left margin to *width*.

sort

Syntax

```
sort [options] [files]
```

Description

Write input to *stdout* (standard out), sorted alphabetically.

Frequently used options

-f
> Case-insensitive sort.

-kPOS1[,POS2]
> Sort on the key starting at *POS1* and (optionally) ending at *POS2*.

-n
> Sort numerically.

-r
> Sort in reverse order.

-tSEP
> Use *SEP* as the key separator. The default is to use whitespace as the key separator.

Example

Sort all processes on the system by resident size (RSS in ps):

```
$ ps aux | sort -k 6 -n
USER     PID   %CPU %MEM VSZ    RSS  TTY   STAT START TIME  COMMAND
root     2     0.0  0.0  0      0    ?     SW   Feb08 0:00  [keventd]
root     3     0.0  0.0  0      0    ?     SWN  Feb08 0:00  [ksoftirqd_CPU0]
root     4     0.0  0.0  0      0    ?     SW   Feb08 0:01  [kswapd]
root     5     0.0  0.0  0      0    ?     SW   Feb08 0:00  [bdflush]
root     6     0.0  0.0  0      0    ?     SW   Feb08 0:00  [kupdated]
root     7     0.0  0.0  0      0    ?     SW   Feb08 0:00  [kjournald]
root     520   0.0  0.3  1340   392  tty0  S    Feb08 0:00  /sbin/mingetty tt
root     335   0.0  0.3  1360   436  ?     S    Feb08 0:00  klogd -x
root     1     0.0  0.3  1372   480  ?     S    Feb08 0:18  init
daemon   468   0.0  0.3  1404   492  ?     S    Feb08 0:00  /usr/sbin/atd
root     330   0.0  0.4  1424   560  ?     S    Feb08 0:01  syslogd -m 0
root     454   0.0  0.4  1540   600  ?     S    Feb08 0:01  crond
root     3130  0.0  0.5  2584   664  pts/0 R    13:24 0:00  ps aux
root     402   0.0  0.6  2096   856  ?     S    Feb08 0:00  xinetd -stayalive
root     385   0.0  0.9  2624   1244 ?     S    Feb08 0:00  /usr/sbin/sshd
```

```
root    530  0.0  0.9  2248  1244 pts/0 S    Feb08  0:01  -bash
root   3131  0.0  0.9  2248  1244 pts/0 R    13:24  0:00  -bash
root    420  0.0  1.3  4620  1648 ?     S    Feb08  0:51  sendmail: accepti
root    529  0.0  1.5  3624  1976 ?     S    Feb08  0:06  /usr/sbin/sshd
```

split

Syntax

```
split [option] [infile] [outfile]
```

Description

Split *infile* into a specified number of line groups, with output going into a succession of files, *outfile*aa, *outfile*ab, and so on (the default is *xaa*, *xab*, etc.). The *infile* remains unchanged. This command is handy if you have a very long text file that needs to be reduced to a succession of smaller files. This was often done to email large files in smaller chunks, because at one time it was considered bad practice to a send a single large email message.

Frequently used option

-n

Split the *infile* into *n*-line segments. The default is 1,000.

Example

Suppose *file1* contains:

```
1  one
2  two
3  three
4  four
5  five
6  six
```

Then the command:

$ split -2 file1 splitout_

yields as output three new files, *splitout_aa*, *splitout_ab*, and *splitout_ac*.

The file *splitout_aa* contains:

```
1  one
2  two
```

splitout_ab contains:

```
3  three
4  four
```

and *splitout_ac* contains:

```
5  five
6  six
```

tac

Syntax

```
tac [file]
```

Description

This command is named as an opposite for the *cat* command, which simply prints text files to standard output. In this case, *tac* prints the text files to standard output with lines in reverse order.

Example

Suppose *file1* contains:

```
1   one
2   two
3   three
```

Then the command:

$ tac file1

yields as output:

```
3   three
2   two
1   one
```

tail

Syntax

```
tail [options] [files]
```

Description

Print the last few lines of one or more *files* (the "tail" of the file or files). When more than one file is specified, a header is printed at the beginning of each file, and each is listed in succession.

Frequently used options

-cn

> This option prints the last *n* bytes, or if *n* is followed by k or m, the last *n* kilobytes or megabytes, respectively.

-nm

> Prints the last *m* lines. The default is 10.

-f

> Continuously display a file as it is actively written by another process ("follow" the file). This is useful for watching logfiles as the system runs.

GNU/Unix
Commands

tr

Syntax

```
tr [options] [string1 [string2]]
```

Description

Translate characters from *string1* to the corresponding characters in *string2*. *tr* does *not* have file arguments and therefore must use standard input and output.

Note that *string1* and *string2* should contain the same number of characters since the first character in *string1* will be replaced with the first character in *string2* and so on.

Either *string1* or *string2* can contain several types of special characters. Some examples follow, although a full list can be found in the **tr** manpage.

a-z

All characters from *a* to *z*.

**

A backslash (\) character.

\nnn

The ASCII character with the octal value *nnn*.

\x

Various control characters:

```
\a      bell
\b      backspace
\f      form feed
\n      newline
\r      carriage return
\t      horizontal tab
\v      vertical tab
```

Frequently used options

-c

Use the complement of (or all characters *not* in) *string1*.

-d

Delete characters in *string1* from the output.

-s

Squeeze out repeated output characters in *string1*.

Example 1

To change all lowercase characters in *file1* to uppercase, use:

```
$ cat file1 | tr a-z A-Z
```

or:

```
$ cat file1 | tr '[:lower:]' '[:upper:]'
```

Example 2

To suppress repeated whitespace characters from *file1*:

```
$ cat file1 | tr -s '[:blank:]'
```

Example 3

To remove all non-printable characters from *file1* (except the newline character):

```
$ cat file1 | tr -dc '[:print:]\n'
```

---

unexpand

Syntax

```
unexpand [options] [files
```

Description

Convert spaces to Tabs. This command performs the opposite action of *expand*. By default, Tab stops are assumed to be every eight spaces.

Frequently used options

-a

Convert all spaces, not just leading spaces. Normally *unexpand* will work only on spaces at the beginning of each line of input. Using the *-a* option causes it to replace spaces anywhere in the input.

 This behavior of *unexpand* differs from *expand*. By default, *expand* converts all Tabs to spaces. It requires the *-i* option to convert only leading spaces.

-t number

Specify Tab stops in place of the default 8.

---

uniq

Syntax

```
uniq [options] [input [output]]
```

Description

Writes *input* (or *stdin*) to *output* (or *stdout*), eliminating adjacent duplicate lines.

Since *uniq* works only on adjacent lines of its input, it is most often used in conjunction with *sort*.

Frequently used options

-d

Print only nonunique (repeating) lines.

-u
>   Print only unique (nonrepeating) lines.

Examples

Suppose *file* contains the following:

>   b
>   b
>   a
>   a
>   c
>   d
>   c

Issuing the command `uniq` with no options:

```
$ uniq file
```

yields the following output:

>   b
>   a
>   c
>   d
>   c

Notice that the line with c is repeated, since the duplicate lines were not adjacent in the input file. To eliminate duplicate lines regardless of where they appear in the input, use **sort** on the input first:

```
$ sort file | uniq
a
b
c
d
```

To print only lines that never repeat in the input, use the *-u* option:

```
$ sort file | uniq -u
d
```

To print only lines that *do* repeat in the input, use the *-d* option:

```
$ sort file | uniq -d
a
b
c
```

WC

Syntax

```
wc [options] [files]
```

Description

Print counts of characters, words, and lines for *files*. When multiple files are listed, statistics for each file output on a separate line with a cumulative total output last.

Frequently used options

-c

    Print the character count only.

-l

    Print the line count only.

-w

    Print the word count only.

Example 1

Show all counts and totals for *file1*, *file2*, and *file3*:

```
$ wc file[123]
```

Example 2

Count the number of lines in *file1*:

```
$ wc -l file1
```

Objective 3: Perform Basic File Management

This section covers basic file and directory management, including filesystems, files and directories, standard file management commands, their recursive capabilities (where applicable), and wildcard patterns (also known as file globbing).

Filesystem Objects

Nearly every operating system in history structures its collection of stored objects in a *hierarchy*, which is a tree of objects containing other objects. This hierarchy allows a sane organization of objects and allows identically named objects to appear in multiple locations, an essential feature for multiuser systems such as Linux. Information about each object in the filesystem is stored in a table (which itself is part of the filesystem), and each object is numbered uniquely within that table. Although there are a few special object types on Linux systems, the two most common are *directories* and *files*.

Directories and files

A directory is a container intended to hold objects such as files and other directories. A directory's purpose is primarily for organization. A file, on the other hand, exists within the directory, and its purpose is to store raw data. At the top of all Linux filesystem hierarchies is a directory depicted simply by /; this is known as the *root* directory. Beneath / are named directories and files in an organized and well-defined tree. To describe these objects, you simply refer to them by name separated by the / character. For example, the object *ls* is an executable program stored in a directory called */bin* under the root directory; it is depicted simply as */bin/ls*.

Don't confuse *root* directory with the username *root*, which is separate and distinct. There's also often a directory named */root* for the root user. Keeping */*, */root*, and the *root* user straight in a conversation can be a challenge.

Inodes

The identification information for a filesystem object is known as its *inode*. Inodes carry information about objects, such as where they are located on disk, their modification time, security settings, and so forth. Each Linux *ext3* filesystem is created with a finite number of inodes that is calculated based on the size of the filesystem and other options that are given to *mke2fs* (the command used to create an ext2 or ext3 filesystem on a partition). Multiple objects in the filesystem can share the same inode; this concept is called *linking*.

File and directory management commands

Once a hierarchy is defined, there is a never-ending need to manage the objects in the filesystem. Objects are constantly created, read, modified, copied, moved, and deleted, so wisely managing the filesystem is one of the most important tasks of a system administrator. In this section, we discuss the basic command-line utilities used for file and directory management. There are GUI tools for this task, but the LPI Level 1 exams only test on command-line tools, and although GUI tools are sometimes more intuitive, a good system administrator should always be always be able to administer his or her system from the command line.

---

bzip2

Syntax

```
bzip2 [options] [filenames ...]
bunzip2 [options] [filenames ...]
```

Description

Compress or uncompress files using the Burrows-Wheeler block sorting text compression algorithm and Huffman coding. *bzip2* is generally considered one of the most efficient compression programs available for Linux systems. Files compressed with *bzip2* usually have the extension *.bz2*.

Frequently used options

-d

Decompress a file. *bzip2 –d* is the same as *bunzip2*.

-1 to -9

Set the block size to 100k, 200k, 300k...900k when compressing. This essentially means that -1 compresses faster but leaves larger compressed files, whereas -9 compresses more slowly but results in smaller files.

Example 1

Compress the file /etc/largefile using the highest level of compression. It will be compressed and renamed /etc/largefile.bz2:

```
$ bzip2 -9 /etc/largefile
```

Example 2

Uncompress /etc/largefile.bz2. It will be uncompressed and renamed /etc/largefile:

```
$ bunzip2 /etc/largefile.bz2
```

or:

```
$ bzip2 -d /etc/largefile.bz2
```

---

cp

Syntax

```
cp [options] file1 file2
cp [options] files directory
```

Description

In the first command form, copy *file1* to *file2*. If *file2* exists and you have appropriate privileges, it will be overwritten without warning (unless you use the -i option). Both *file1* and
file2 can be any valid filename, either fully qualified or in the local directory. In the second
command form, copy *files* to *directory*. Note that the presence of multiple files implies that
you wish to copy the files to a directory. If *directory* doesn't exist, an error message will be
printed. This command form can get you in trouble if you attempt to copy a single file into a
directory that doesn't exist, as the command will be interpreted as the first form and you'll end
up with *file2* instead of *directory*.

Frequently used options

-f

Force an overwrite of existing files in the destination.

-i

Prompt *interactively* before overwriting destination files. It is common practice (and advised) to alias the *cp* command to *cp -i* to prevent accidental overwrites. You may find that
this is already done for you for the *root* user on your Linux system.

-p

Preserve all information, including owner, group, permissions, and timestamps. Without
this option, the copied file or files will have the present date and time, default permissions,
owner, and group.

-r, -R

Recursively copy directories. You may use either upper- or lowercase for this option. If
file1 is actually a directory instead of a file and the recursive option is specified, *file2* will
be a copy of the entire hierarchy under directory *file1*.

-v

Display the name of each file verbosely before copying.

Example 1

Copy the messages file to the local directory (specified by **.**):

```
$ cp /var/log/messages .
```

Example 2

Make an identical copy, including preservation of file attributes, of directory *src* in new directory *src2*:

```
$ cp -Rp src src2
```

Copy *file1, file2, file5, file6*, and *file7* from the local directory into your home directory (in bash):

```
$ cp file1 file2 file[567] ~
```

On the Exam

Be sure to know the difference between a file destination and a directory destination and how to force an overwrite of existing objects.

---

cpio

Syntax

```
cpio -o [options] < [filenames ...] > [archive]
cpio -i < [archive]
cpio -p [destination-directory] < [filenames...]
```

Description

cpio is used to create and extract archives, or copy files from one place to another. No compression is done natively on these archives; you must employ *gzip* or *bzip2* if you desire compression.

Frequently used options

-o

Copy-out mode. This mode is used to create an archive.

-i

Copy-in mode. This mode is used to copy files out of an archive.

-p

Copy-pass mode. Don't create an archive; just copy files from one directory tree to another.

Example 1

Create an archive that contains all the files in the current working directory:

```
$ ls | cpio -ov > /tmp/archive.cpio
```

Notice that instead of passing files to archive to *cpio* on the command line, we had the *ls* command create a list of files for us, which we then send to the *cpio* command via standard input using the | (vertical bar) character.

Example 2

Extract all the files from the archive we just created:

```
$ cpio -iv < /tmp/archive.cpio
```

dd

Syntax

```
dd [options]
```

Description

dd converts and copies files. It is one of the few commands in the Linux world that can operate directly on block devices, rather than requiring access through the filesystem layer. This is especially useful when performing backups of block devices, such as hard drive partitions, CD-ROMs, or floppy disks.

Frequently used options

-if=file
> Read from *file* instead of standard input.

-of=file
> Output to *file* instead of standard output.

-ibs=n
> Read *n* bytes at a time.

-obs=n
> Write *n* bytes at a time.

-conv=list
> Perform the conversions defined in *list*.

Example 1

Create an image of the compact disc currently in the default CD drive (*/dev/cdrom*):

```
$ dd if=/dev/cdrom of=/tmp/cd.img
```

Example 2

Copy */tmp/file* to */tmp/file2*, converting all characters to lowercase:

```
$ dd if=/tmp/file of=/tmp/file2 conv=lcase
```

file

Syntax

```
file [options] [file]
```

Description

file is designed to determine the kind of file being queried. Because Linux (and other Unix-like systems) don't require filename extensions to determine the type of a file, the *file* command is useful when you're unsure what kind of file you're dealing with. *file* accomplishes this by performing three sets of tests on the file in question: filesystem tests, magic tests, and language tests. Filesystem tests involved examining the output of the "stat" system call. Magic tests are used to check for files with data in particular fixed formats. If neither of these tests results in a conclusive answer, a language test is performed to determine whether the file is some sort of text file.

Frequently used options

-f namefile
> Read the names of the files to be examined from *namefile* (one per line) before the argument list.

-z

> Try to look inside compressed files.

Example 1

Determine the file type of the currently running kernel:

```
$ file /boot/vmlinuz-2.6.27.29-170.2.78.fc10.i686
/boot/vmlinuz-2.6.27.29-170.2.78.fc10.i686: Linux kernel x86 boot executable \
 RO-rootFS, root_
0x902, swap_dev 0x2, Normal VGA
```

Example 2

Determine the file type of */etc/passwd*:

```
$ file /etc/passwd
/etc/passwd: ASCII text
```

---

find

Syntax

```
find [options] [path...] [expression]
```

Description

find searches recursively through directory trees for files or directories that match certain characteristics. *find* can then either print the file or directory that matches or perform other operations on the matches.

Frequently used options

-mount
> Do not recursively descend through directories on mounted filesystems. This prevents *find* from doing a potentially very long search over an NFS-mounted share, for example.

-maxdepth X

 Descend at most *X* levels of directories below the command-line arguments. `-maxdepth 0` eliminates all recursion into subdirectories.

Example 1

Find all files in */tmp* that end in *.c* and print them to standard out:

```
$ find /tmp -name "*.c"
```

The expression `"*.c"` means "all files that end in .c". This is an example of *file globbing* and is explained in detail later in this Objective.

Example 2

Find files (and only files) in */tmp* older than seven days. Do not recurse into subdirectories of */tmp*:

```
$ find /tmp -maxdepth 1 -type f -daystart -ctime +7
```

Example 3

Find files in */usr* that have the `setuid` permission bit set (mode 4000):

```
$ find /usr -perm -4000
```

gzip and gunzip

Syntax

```
gzip [options] [filenames ...]
gunzip [options] [filenames ...]
```

Description

Compress or uncompress files using Lempel-Ziv coding. *gzip* is one of the most common compression formats found on Linux systems, although it is starting to be replaced by the more efficient *bzip2*. Files compressed with *gzip* usually have the extension *.gz*. Command-line options for *gzip* are very similar to those for *bzip2*.

Frequently used options

-d

 Decompress a file. *gzip -d* is the same as *gunzip*.

-r

 Travel the directory structure recursively. If any of the filenames specified on the command line are directories, *gzip* will descend into the directory and compress all the files it finds there (or decompress them in the case of *gunzip*).

Example 1

Compress the file */etc/largefile*. It will be compressed and renamed */etc/largefile.gz*:

```
$ gzip /etc/largefile
```

Example 2

Uncompress */etc/largefile.gz*. It will be uncompressed and renamed */etc/largefile*:

```
$ gunzip /etc/largefile.gz
```

or:

```
$ gzip -d /etc/largefile.gz
```

mkdir

Syntax

```
mkdir [options] directories
```

Description

Create one or more *directories*. You must have write permission in the directory where *directories* are to be created.

Frequently used options

-mmode
> Set the access rights in the octal format *mode* for *directories*.

-p
> Create intervening parent directories if they don't exist.

Examples

Create a read-only directory named *personal*:

```
$ mkdir -m 444 personal
```

Create a directory tree in your home directory, as indicated with a leading tilde (~), using a single command:

```
$ mkdir -p ~/dir1/dir2/dir3
```

In this case, all three directories are created. This is faster than creating each directory individually.

On the Exam

Verify your understanding of the tilde (~) shortcut for the home directory, and the shortcuts . (for the current directory) and .. (for the parent directory).

---

mv

Syntax

```
mv [options] source target
```

Description

Move or rename files and directories. For *targets* on the same filesystem (partition), moving a file doesn't relocate the contents of the file itself. Rather, the directory entry for the target is updated with the new location. For *targets* on different filesystems, such a change can't be made, so files are copied to the target location and the original sources are deleted.

If a target file or directory does not exist, *source* is renamed to *target*. If a *target* file already exists, it is overwritten with *source*. If *target* is an existing directory, *source* is moved into that directory. If *source* is one or more files and *target* is a directory, the files are moved into the directory.

Frequently used options

-*f*

Force the move even if *target* exists, suppressing warning messages.

-*i*

Query interactively before moving files.

rm

Syntax

```
rm [options] files
```

Description

Delete one or more files from the filesystem. To remove a file, you must have write permission in the directory that contains the file, but you do not need write permission on the file itself. The *rm* command also removes directories when the *-d, -r,* or *-R* option is used.

Frequently used options

-*d*

Remove directories even if they are not empty. This option is reserved for privileged users.

-*f*

Force removal of write-protected files without prompting.

-*i*

Query interactively before removing files.

-*r,-R*

If the file is a directory, recursively remove the entire directory and all of its contents, including subdirectories.

rmdir

Syntax

```
rmdir [option] directories
```

Description

Delete *directories*, which must be empty.

Frequently used option

-p

> Remove *directories* and any intervening parent directories that become empty as a result. This is useful for removing subdirectory trees.

On the Exam

Remember that recursive remove using *rm –R* removes directories too, even if they're not empty. Beware the dreaded *rm –Rf /*, which will remove your entire filesystem!

---

touch

Syntax

```
touch [options] files
```

Description

Change the access and/or modification times of *files*. This command is used to refresh time-stamps on files. Doing so may be necessary, for example, to cause a program to be recompiled using the date-dependent *make* utility.

Frequently used options

-a

> Change only the access time.

-m

> Change only the modification time.

-t timestamp

> Instead of the current time, use *timestamp* in the form of [[CC]YY]MMDDhhmm[.ss]. For example, the timestamp for January 12, 2001, at 6:45 p.m. is 200101121845.

File-Naming Wildcards (File Globbing)

When working with files on the command line, you'll often run into situations in which you need to perform operations on many files at once. For example, if you are developing a C program, you may want to *touch* all of your .c files in order to be sure to recompile them the next time you issue the *make* utility to build your program. There will also be times when you need to move or delete all the files in a directory or at least a selected group of files. At other times, filenames may be long or difficult to type, and you'll want to find an abbreviated alternative to typing the filenames for each command you issue (see Table 6-5).

To make these operations simpler, all shells on Linux offer *file-naming wildcards*.

Wildcards are expanded by the shell, not by commands. When a command is entered with wildcards included, the shell first expands all the wildcards (and other types of expansion) and passes the full result on to the command. This process is invisible to you.

Rather than explicitly specifying every file or typing long filenames, you can use *wildcard characters* in place of portions of the filenames, and the shell can usually do the work for you. For example, the shell expands *.txt* to a list of all the files that end in *.txt*. File wildcard constructs like this are called *file globs*, and their use is awkwardly called *globbing*. Using file globs to specify multiple files is certainly a convenience, and in many cases is required to get anything useful accomplished. Wildcards for shell globbing are listed in Table 6-5.

Table 6-5. Common file-naming wildcards

Wildcard	Description
*	Commonly thought to "match anything," it actually will match zero or more characters (which includes "nothing"!). For example, x* matches files or directories *x*, *xy*, *xyz*, *x.txt*, *xy.txt*, *xyz.c*, and so on.
?	Match exactly one character. For example, x? matches files or directories *xx*, *xy*, *xz*, but not *x* and not *xyz*. The specification x?? matches *xyz*, but not *x* and *xy*.
[*characters*]	Match any single character from among *characters* listed between the brackets. For example, x[yz] matches *xy* and *xz*.
[!*characters*]	Match any single character other than *characters* listed between the brackets. For example, x[!yz] matches *xa* and *x1* but does not match *xy* or *xz*.
[*a-z*]	Match any single character from among the range of characters listed between the brackets and indicated by the dash (the dash character is not matched). For example, x[0-9] matches *x0* and *x1*, but does not match *xx*. Note that to match both upper- and lowercase letters (Linux filenames are case-sensitive), you specify [a-zA-Z]. Using x[a-zA-Z] matches *xa* and *xA*.
[!*a-z*]	Match any single character from among the characters not in the range listed between the brackets.
{*frag1,frag2,frag3,...*}	Create strings *frag1*, *frag2*, *frag3*, etc. For example, file_{one,two,three} yields the strings *file_one*, *file_two*, and *file_three*. This is a special operator named *brace expansion* that can be used to match filenames but isn't specifically a file wildcard operator and does not examine directories for existing files to match. Instead, it will expand *any string*.
	For example, it can be used with echo to yield strings totally unrelated to existing filenames:
	`$ echo    string_{a,b,c}` `string_a string_b    string_c`

A few examples of the useful things you can do with wildcards follow:

- If you remember part of a filename but not the whole thing, use wildcards with the portion you remember to help find the file. For example, if you're working in a directory with a large number of files and you know you're looking for a file named for Linux, you may enter a command like this:

```
$ ls -l *inux*
```

- When working with groups of related files, wildcards can be used to help separate the groups. For example, suppose you have a directory full of scripts you've written. Some are Perl scripts, for which you've used an extension of *.pl*, and some are Python, which have a *.py* extension. You may wish to separate them into new, separate directories for the two languages like this:

```
$ mkdir perl python
$ mv *.pl perl
$ mv *.py python
```

- Wildcards match directory names as well. Suppose you have a tree of directories starting with *contracting*, where you've created a directory for each month (that is, *contracting/january*, *contracting/february*, through *contracting/december*). In each of these directories are stored invoices, named simply *invoice_custa_01.txt*, *invoice_custa_02.txt*, *invoice_custb_01.txt*, and so on, where *custa* and *custb* are customer names of some form. To display all of the invoices, wildcards can be used:

```
$ ls con*/*/inv*.txt
```

The con* matches *contracting*. The second * matches all directories under the *contracting* directory (*january* through *december*). The last * matches all the customers and each invoice number for each customer.

See the *bash* manpages or info page for additional information on how *bash* handles expansions and on other expansion forms.

Objective 4: Use Streams, Pipes, and Redirects

Among the many beauties of Linux and Unix systems is the notion that *everything is a file*. Things such as disk drives and their partitions, tape drives, terminals, serial ports, the mouse, and even audio are mapped into the filesystem. This mapping allows programs to interact with many different devices and files in the same way, simplifying their interfaces. Each device that uses the file metaphor is given a *device file*, which is a special object in the filesystem that provides an interface to the device. The kernel associates device drivers with various device files, which is how the system manages the illusion that devices can be accessed as if they were files. Using a terminal as an example, a program reading from the terminal's device file will receive characters typed at the keyboard. Writing to the terminal causes characters to appear on the screen. Although it may seem odd to think of your terminal as a file, the concept provides a unifying simplicity to Linux and Linux programming.

Standard I/O and Default File Descriptors

Standard I/O is a capability of the shell, used with all text-based Linux utilities to control and direct program input, output, and error information. When a program is launched, it is automatically provided with three *file descriptors*. File descriptors are regularly used in programming and serve as a "handle" of sorts to another file. We have mentioned these already in our discussion of text streams and "piping" together programs on the command line. Standard I/O creates the following file descriptors:

Standard input (abbreviated stdin)
> This file descriptor is a text input stream. By default it is attached to your keyboard. When you type characters into an interactive text program, you are feeding them to standard input. As you've seen, some programs take one or more filenames as command-line arguments and ignore standard input. Standard input is also known as *file descriptor 0*.

Standard output (abbreviated stdout)
> This file descriptor is a text output stream for normal program output. By default it is attached to your terminal (or terminal window). Output generated by commands is written to standard output for display. Standard output is also known as *file descriptor 1*.

Standard error (abbreviated stderr)
> This file descriptor is also a text output stream, but it is used exclusively for errors or other information unrelated to the successful results of your command. By default, standard error is attached to your terminal just like standard output. This means that standard output and standard error are commingled in your display, which can be confusing. You'll see ways to handle this later in this section. Standard error is also known as *file descriptor 2*.

Standard output and standard error are separated because it is often useful to process normal program output differently from errors.

The standard I/O file descriptors are used in the same way as those created during program execution to read and write disk files. They enable you to tie commands together with files and devices, managing command input and output in exactly the way you desire. The difference is that they are provided to the program by the shell by default and do not need to be explicitly created.

Pipes

From a program's point of view there is no difference between reading text data from a file and reading it from your keyboard. Similarly, writing text to a file and writing text to a display are equivalent operations. As an extension of this idea, it is also possible to tie the output of one program to the input of another. This is accomplished using a *pipe* symbol (|) to join two or more commands together, which we have seen some examples of already in this chapter. For example:

```
$ grep "01523" order* | less
```

This command searches through all files whose names begin with order to find lines containing the word 01523. By creating this pipe, the standard output of *grep* is sent to the standard input of *less*. The mechanics of this operation are handled by the shell and are invisible to the user. Pipes can be used in a series of many commands.

When more than two commands are put together, the resulting operation is known as a *pipeline* or *text stream*, implying the flow of text from one command to the next.

As you get used to the idea, you'll find yourself building pipelines naturally to extract specific information from text data sources. For example, suppose you wish to view a sorted list of inode numbers from among the files in your current directory. There are many ways you could achieve this. One way would be to use *awk* in a pipeline to extract the inode number from the output of *ls*, then send it on to the *sort* command and finally to a pager for viewing (don't worry about the syntax or function of these commands at this point):

```
$ ls -i * | awk '{print $1}' | sort -nu | less
```

The pipeline concept in particular is a feature of Linux and Unix that draws on the fact that your system contains a diverse set of tools for operating on text. Combining their capabilities can yield quick and easy ways to extract otherwise hard-to-handle information. This is embodied in the historical "Unix Philosophy":

- Write programs that do one thing and do it well.
- Write programs to work together.
- Write programs to handle text streams, because that is a universal interface.

Redirection

Each pipe symbol in the previous pipeline example instructs the shell to feed output from one command into the input of another. This action is a special form of *redirection*, which allows you to manage the origin of input streams and the destination of output streams. In the previous example, individual programs are unaware that their output is being handed off to or from another program because the shell takes care of the redirection on their behalf.

Redirection can also occur to and from files. For example, rather than sending the output of an inode list to the pager *less*, it could easily be sent directly to a file with the > redirection operator:

```
$ ls -i * | awk '{print $1}' | sort -nu > in.txt
```

When you change the last redirection operator, the shell creates an empty file (*in.txt*) and opens it for writing, and the standard output of *sort* places the results in the file instead of on the screen. Note that, in this example, anything sent to standard error is still displayed on the screen. In addition, if your specified file, *in.txt*, already existed in your current directory, it would be overwritten.

Since the > redirection operator *creates* files, the >> redirection operator can be used to append to existing files. For example, you could use the following command to append a one-line footnote to *in.txt*:

```
$ echo "end of list" >> in.txt
```

Since *in.txt* already exists, the quote will be appended to the bottom of the existing file. If the file didn't exist, the >> operator would create the file and insert the text "end of list" as its contents.

It is important to note that when creating files, the output redirection operators are interpreted by the shell *before* the commands are executed. This means that any output files created through redirection are opened first. For this reason you cannot modify a file in place, like this:

```
$ grep "stuff" file1 > file1
```

If *file1* contains something of importance, this command would be a disaster because an empty *file1* would overwrite the original. The *grep* command would be last to execute, resulting in a complete data loss from the original *file1* file because the file that replaced it was empty. To avoid this problem, simply use an intermediate file and *then* rename it:

```
$ grep "stuff" file1 > file2
$ mv file2 file1
```

Standard input can also be redirected, using the redirection operator <. Using a source other than the keyboard for a program's input may seem odd at first, but since text programs don't care about where their standard input streams originate, you can easily redirect input. For example, the following command will send a mail message with the contents of the file *in.txt* to user *jdean*:

```
$ mail -s "inode list" jdean < in.txt
```

Normally, the *mail* program prompts the user for input at the terminal. However, with standard input redirected *from* the file *in.txt*, no user input is needed and the command executes silently. Table 6-6 lists the common standard I/O redirections for the *bash* shell, specified in the LPI Objectives.

Table 6-6. Standard I/O redirections for the bash shell

Redirection function	Syntax for bash
Send *stdout* to *file*.	`$ cmd > file` `$ cmd 1> file`
Send *stderr* to *file*.	`$ cmd 2> file`
Send both *stdout* and *stderr* to *file*.	`$ cmd > file 2>&1`
Send *stdout* to *file1* and *stderr* to *file2*.	`$ cmd > file1 2> file2`
Receive *stdin* from *file*.	`$ cmd < file`
Append *stdout* to *file*.	`$ cmd >> file` `$ cmd 1>> file`
Append *stderr* to *file*.	`$ cmd 2>> file`
Append both *stdout* and *stderr* to *file*.	`$ cmd >> file 2>&1`
Pipe *stdout* from *cmd1* to *cmd2*.	`$ cmd1	cmd2`
Pipe *stdout* and *stderr* from *cmd1* to *cmd2*.	`$ cmd1 2>&1	cmd2`

Using the tee Command

Sometimes you'll want to run a program and send its output to a file while at the same time viewing the output on the screen. The *tee* utility is helpful in this situation.

tee

Syntax

    tee [options] files

Description

Read from standard input and write both to one or more *files* and to standard output (analogous to a tee junction in a pipe).

Option

-*a*

  Append to *files* rather than overwriting them.

Example

Suppose you're running a pipeline of commands *cmd1*, *cmd2*, and *cmd3*:

    $ cmd1 | cmd2 | cmd3 > file1

This sequence puts the ultimate output of the pipeline into *file1*. However, you may also be interested in the intermediate result of *cmd1*. To create a new *file_cmd1* containing those results, use *tee*:

    $ cmd1 | tee file_cmd1 | cmd2 | cmd3 > file1

The results in *file1* will be the same as in the original example, and the intermediate results of *cmd1* will be placed in *file_cmd1*.

The xargs Command

Sometimes you need to pass a list of items to a command that is longer than your shell can handle. In these situations, the *xargs* command can be used to break down the list into smaller sublists.

xargs

Syntax

```
xargs [options] [command] [initial-arguments]
```

Description

Execute *command* followed by its optional *initial-arguments* and append additional arguments found on standard input. Typically, the additional arguments are filenames in quantities too large for a single command line. *xargs* runs *command* multiple times to exhaust all arguments on standard input.

Frequently used options

-n maxargs
> Limit the number of additional arguments to *maxargs* for each invocation of *command*.

-p
> Interactive mode. Prompt the user for each execution of *command*.

Example

Use *grep* to search a long list of files, one by one, for the word "linux":

```
$ find / -type f | xargs -n 1 grep -H linux
```

find searches for normal files (*-type f*) starting at the root directory. *xargs* executes *grep* once for each of them due to the *-n 1* option. *grep* will print the matching line preceded by the filename where the match occurred (due to the *-H* option).

Objective 5: Create, Monitor, and Kill Processes

This Objective looks at the management of *processes*. Just as file management is a fundamental system administrator's function, the management and control of processes is also essential for smooth system operation. In most cases, processes will live, execute, and die without intervention from the user because they are automatically managed by the kernel. However, there are times when a process will die for some unknown reason and need to be restarted. Or a process may "run wild" and consume system resources, requiring that it be terminated. You will also need to instruct running processes to perform operations, such as rereading a configuration file.

Processes

Every program, whether it's a command, application, or script, that runs on your system is a *process*. Your shell is a process, and every command you execute from the shell starts one or more processes of its own (referred to as *child processes*). Attributes and concepts associated with these processes include:

Lifetime
> A process lifetime is defined by the length of time it takes to execute (while it "lives"). Commands with a short lifetime such as *ls* will execute for a very short

time, generate results, and terminate when complete. User programs such as web browsers have a longer lifetime, running for unlimited periods of time until terminated manually. Long-lifetime processes include server daemons that run continuously from system boot to shutdown. When a process terminates, it is said to *die* (which is why the program used to manually signal a process to stop execution is called *kill*; succinct, though admittedly morbid).

Process ID (PID)
> Every process has a number assigned to it when it starts. PIDs are integer numbers unique among all running processes.

User ID (UID) and Group ID (GID)
> Processes must have associated privileges, and a process's UID and GID are associated with the user who started the process. This limits the process's access to objects in the filesystem.

Parent process
> The first process started by the kernel at system start time is a program called *init*. This process has PID 1 and is the ultimate parent of all other processes on the system. Your shell is a descendant of *init* and the parent process to commands started by the shell, which are its *child* processes, or *subprocesses*.

Parent process ID (PPID)
> This is the PID of the process that created the process in question.

Environment
> Each process holds a list of variables and their associated values. Collectively, this list is known as the *environment* of the process, and the variables are called *environment variables*. Child processes inherit their environment settings from the parent process unless an alternative environment is specified when the program is executed.

Current working directory
> The default directory associated with each process. The process will read and write files in this directory unless they are explicitly specified to be elsewhere in the filesystem.

On the Exam

The parent/child relationship of the processes on a Linux system is important. Be sure to understand how these relationships work and how to view them. Note that the *init* process always has PID 1 and is the ultimate ancestor of all system processes (hence the nickname "mother of all processes"). Also remember the fact that if a parent process is killed, all its children (subprocesses) die as well.

Process Monitoring

At any time, there could be tens or even hundreds of processes running together on your Linux system. Monitoring these processes is done using three convenient utilities: *ps*, *pstree*, and *top*.

---

ps

Syntax

```
ps [options]
```

Description

This command generates a one-time snapshot of the current processes on standard output.

Frequently used options

-a

> Show processes that are owned by other users and attached to a terminal. Normally, only the current user's processes are shown.

-f

> "Full-format" listing. This option prints command arguments in addition to the command itself.

-l

> Long format, which includes priority, parent PID, and other information.

-u

> User format, which includes usernames and the start time of processes.

-w

> Wide output format, used to eliminate the default output line truncation. Specify it twice (*-ww*) for unlimited width.

-x

> Include processes without controlling terminals. Often needed to see daemon processes and others not started from a terminal session.

-C cmd
> Display instances of command name *cmd*.

-U user
> Display processes owned by username *user*.

Examples

Simply entering the *ps* command with no options will yield a brief list of processes owned by you and attached to your terminal:

```
$ ps
```

Use the *-a*, *-u*, and *-x* options to include processes owned by others and not attached to terminals as well as to display them in the "user" mode. The command is valid with or without the dash:

```
$ ps -aux
$ ps aux
```

In this case, the dash is optional. However, certain *ps* options require the dash. (See the manpage for details.)

If you are interested in finding process information on a particular command, use the *-C* option. This command displays all web server processes:

```
$ ps u -C httpd
```

You'll note that the -C option *requires* the dash, but the *u* option won't work with it if a dash is included. This confusion exists because the *ps* command as implemented on Linux understands options in three differing forms:

Unix98 *options*
  These may be grouped and must be preceded by a dash.

BSD *options*
  These may be grouped and must *not* be used with a dash.

GNU long *options*
  These options are preceded by two dashes.

 The Linux *ps* tries to be compatible with *ps* from various other systems. How it interprets various command-line options, which determines how compatible it is with other versions of *ps*, can be controlled by setting I_WANT_A_BROKEN_PS, PS_PERSON ALITY, and various other environment variables. See the *ps* man-page for details.

All of these option types may be freely intermixed. Instead of the -C option, you may wish to use *ps* with other options that you usually use and pipe the output to *grep*, searching for process names, PIDs, or anything else you know about the process:

```
$ ps aux | grep httpd
```

In this case, the result would be the same list of *httpd* servers, as well as the *grep* command itself.

pstree

Syntax

```
pstree [options] [pid|user]
```

Description

This command displays a hierarchical list of processes in a tree format. *pstree* is very handy for understanding how parent/child process relationships are set up.

If the PID is specified, the displayed tree is rooted at that process. Otherwise, it is rooted at the *init* process, which has PID 1. If *user* (a valid username) is specified, trees for all processes owned by *user* are shown. The tree is represented using characters that appear as lines, such as | for vertical lines and + for intersections (VT100 line-drawing characters, displayed as solid lines by most terminals, are optional). The output looks similar to this:

```
httpd-+-httpd
      |-httpd
      |-httpd
      |-httpd
      '-httpd
```

By default, visually identical branches of the tree are merged to reduce output. Merged lines are preceded by a count indicating the actual number of similar processes. The preceding example is normally displayed on a single line:

```
httpd---5*[httpd]
```

This behavior can be turned off with the -c option.

Frequently used options

-a

Display command-line arguments used to launch processes.

-c

Disable the compaction of identical subtrees.

-G

Use the VT100 line-drawing characters instead of plain characters to display the tree. This yields a much more pleasing display but may not be appropriate for printing or paging programs.

-h

Highlight the ancestry of the current process (usually the shell). The terminal must support highlighting for this option to be meaningful.

-n

The default sort order for processes with the same parent is alphanumerically by name. This option changes this behavior to a numeric sort by PID.

-p

Include PIDs in the output.

Example

Display a process tree including PIDs:

```
# pstree -p
init(1)-+-atd(468)
        |-bdflush(5)
        |-crond(454)
        |-httpd(440)-+-httpd(450)
        |            |-httpd(451)
        |            |-httpd(452)
        |            |-httpd(453)
        |            |-httpd(455)
        |            |-httpd(456)
        |            |-httpd(457)
        |            '-httpd(458)
        |-keventd(2)
        |-kjournald(7)
        |-klogd(335)
        |-ksoftirqd_CPU0(3)
        |-kswapd(4)
        |-kupdated(6)
        |-login(475)---bash(478)---pstree(518)
        |-sendmail(420)
        |-sshd(385)
        |-syslogd(330)
        '-xinetd(402)
```

top

Syntax

```
top [options]
```

Description

The *top* command offers output similar to *ps*, but in a continuously updated display. This is useful for situations in which you need to watch the status of one or more processes or to see how they are using your system.

In addition, a header of useful uptime, load, CPU status, and memory information is displayed. By default, the process status output is generated with the most CPU-intensive processes at the top of the listing (and is named for the "top" processes). To format the screen, *top* must understand how to control the terminal display. The type of terminal (or terminal window) in use is stored in the environment variable TERM. If this variable is not set or contains an unknown terminal type, *top* may not execute.

Popular command-line options

Dashes are optional in *top* options:

-b

> Run in batch mode. This is useful for sending output from *top* to other programs or to a file. It executes the number of iterations specified with the -*n* option and terminates. This option is also useful if *top* cannot display on the terminal type you are using.

-d *delay*

> Specify the *delay* in seconds between screen updates. The default is five seconds.

-i

> Ignore idle processes, listing only the "interesting" ones taking system resources.

-*n num*

> Display *num* iterations and then exit, instead of running indefinitely.

-q

> Run with no delay. If the user is the superuser, run with highest possible priority. This option causes *top* to update continuously and will probably consume any idle time your CPU had. Running *top -q* as superuser will seriously affect system performance and is not recommended.

-s

> Run in secure mode. Some of *top*'s interactive commands can be dangerous if running as the superuser. This option disables them.

Frequently used interactive options

Once *top* is running interactively, it can be given a number of commands via the keyboard to change its behavior. These commands are single-key commands, some of which cause *top* to prompt for input:

spacebar

> Refresh the screen.

h

> Generate a help screen.

k

Kill a process. You will be prompted for the PID of the process and the signal to send it. (The default signal is 15, *SIGTERM*.) See "Terminating Processes" on page 117.

n

Change the number of processes to show. You will be prompted to enter an integer number. The default is 0, which indicates that the screen should be filled.

q

Quit the program.

r

Change the priority of a process (*renice*). You will be prompted for the PID of the process and the value to nice it to (see *nice* and *renice* in "Objective 6: Modify Process Execution Priorities" on page 120). Entering a positive value causes a process to lose priority. If the superuser is running *top*, a negative value may be entered, causing a process to get a higher than normal priority. This command is not available in secure mode.

s

Change the delay in seconds between updates. You will be prompted for the delay value, which may include fractions of seconds (e.g., 0.5).

Example 1

Simply executing *top* without options gives a full status display updated every five seconds:

```
$ top
```

Use the *q* command to quit.

Example 2

To run *top* with a faster refresh rate, use the interval option, specified here with a one-second refresh:

```
$ top -d 1
```

Example 3

You may wish to use *top* to log its output to a file. Use the *-b* (batch) option for this purpose. In this batch example, the *-i* option eliminates idle processes, the *-n* option, with its argument, indicates five iterations, and the *-d* option indicates a one-second interval. Results will be redirected to *file1*. This command will take five seconds to execute and does not use the optional dashes:

```
$ top -bi -n 5 -d 1 > file1
```

The single-key interactive commands can be used when *top* is running interactively. For example, if you type the *h* command, *top* displays a help screen. If you enter the *n* command, *top* prompts you for the number of lines you wish to display.

Using *top* to change the *nice* (priority modifier) value for a process is discussed in "Objective 6: Modify Process Execution Priorities" on page 120.

free

Syntax

```
free [options]
```

Description

Display amount of free and used memory in the system.

Frequently used options

-b

Show memory usage in bytes.

-k

Show memory usage in kilobytes.

-m

Show memory usage in megabytes.

-t

Display a line showing totals.

-s X

Continuous operation at *X* second intervals.

Example

Display current memory usage in megabytes and display a total line:

```
$ free -tm
                 total      used      free    shared   buffers    cached
Mem:              2023      1874       149         0        77      1089
-/+ buffers/cache:           707      1316
Swap:             4031       351      3680
Total:            6055      2225      3830
```

This tells me that I have 2,023 megabytes of system memory (2 gigabytes) and 4,031 megabytes (about 4 gigabytes) of swap space. I'm currently using 1,874 megabytes of memory, leaving 149 free.

uptime

Syntax

```
uptime
```

Description

uptime gives a one-line display of the following information: the current time, how long the system has been running, how many users are currently logged on, and the system load averages for the past 1, 5, and 15 minutes.

Examples

```
$ uptime
13:17:57 up 214 days,  2:52,  4 users,  load average: 0.09, 0.03, 0.01
```

Load average on a Linux system is defined as the number of blocking processes in the run queue averaged over a certain time period. A blocking process is a process that is waiting on a resource to continue, usually the CPU, disk I/O, or network. Many processes waiting in the run queue will drive up the load average of your system. It's not uncommon to see a load average over 1; that just means for the designated time interval (1, 5 or 15 minutes) there was an average of at least one process waiting on resources in the run queue. This is usually indicative of a busy system and might not necessarily mean anything is amiss. However, high load averages will negatively affect system performance, so it's always a good idea to be aware of what is causing them. Here is the uptime output of a relatively busy web server:

```
$ uptime
1:20pm  up 3 days 15:49,  1 user,  load average: 1.47, 1.10, 0.83
```

Signaling Active Processes

Each process running on your system listens for *signals*, simple messages sent to the process either by the kernel or by a user. The messages are sent through inter-process communication. They are single-valued, in that they don't contain strings or command-like constructs. Instead, signals are numeric integer messages, predefined and known by processes. Most have an implied action for the process to take. When a process receives a signal, it can (or may be forced to) take action.

For example, if you are executing a program from the command line that appears to hang, you may elect to type Ctrl-C to abort the program. This action actually sends an *SIGINT* (interrupt signal) to the process, telling it to stop running.

There are more than 32 signals defined for normal process use in Linux. Each signal has a name and a number (the number is sent to the process; the name is only for our convenience). Many signals are used by the kernel, and some are useful for users. Table 6-7 lists popular signals for interactive use.

Table 6-7. Frequently used interactive signals

Signal name[a]	Number	Meaning and use
HUP	1	Hang up. This signal is sent automatically when you log out or disconnect a modem. It is also used by many daemons to cause the configuration file to be reread without stopping the daemon process. Useful for things like an *httpd* server that normally reads its configuration file only when the process is started. A *SIGHUP* signal will force it to reread the configuration file without the downtime of restarting the process.
INT	2	Interrupt; stop running. This signal is sent when you type Ctrl-C.
KILL	9	Kill; stop unconditionally and immediately. Sending this signal is a drastic measure, as it cannot be ignored by the process. This is the "emergency kill" signal.
TERM	15	Terminate, nicely if possible. This signal is used to ask a process to exit gracefully, after its file handles are closed and its current processing is complete.
TSTP	20	Stop executing, ready to continue. This signal is sent when you type Ctrl-Z. (See the later section "Shell Job Control" for more information.)

Signal name[a]	Number	Meaning and use
CONT	18	Continue execution. This signal is sent to start a process stopped by *SIGTSTP* or *SIGSTOP*. (The shell sends this signal when you use the *fg* or *bg* commands after stopping a process with Ctrl-Z.)

[a] Signal names often will be specified with a SIG prefix. That is, signal HUP is the same as signal SIGHUP.

As you can see from Table 6-7, some signals are invoked by pressing well-known key combinations such as Ctrl-C and Ctrl-Z. You can also use the *kill* command to send any message to a running process. The *kill* command is implemented both as a shell built-in command and as a standalone binary command. For a complete list of signals that processes can be sent, refer to the file */usr/include/bits/signum.h* on your Linux install, which normally is installed with the *glibc-headers* package.

kill

Syntax

```
kill [-s sigspec | -sigspec] [pids]
kill -l [signum]
```

Description

In the first form, *kill* is used with an optional *sigspec*. This is a signal value, specified as either an integer or the signal name (such as *SIGHUP*, or simply *HUP*). The *sigspec* is case-insensitive but is usually specified with uppercase letters. The *bash* built-in *kill* is case-insensitive, both when using the -s*sigspec* and the -*sigspec* forms, but the standalone *kill* is only case-insensitive in the -s*sigspec* form. For this reason, it is best to use uppercase signal names. You may use -s*sigspec* or simply -*sigspec* to make up the signal value or name. If a *sigspec* is not given, then *SIGTERM* (signal 15, "exit gracefully") is assumed. The *sigspec* is followed by one or more PIDS to which the signal is to be sent. In the second form with the -l option, *kill* lists the valid signal names. If *signum* (an integer) is present, only the signal name for that number will be displayed.

Examples

This command displays the signal name *SIGTERM*, the name of signal 15, and the default when *kill* is used to signal processes:

```
$ kill -l 15
TERM
```

All of the following commands will send *SIGTERM* to the processes with PIDs 1000 and 1001:

```
$ kill 1000 1001
$ kill -15 1000 1001
$ kill -SIGTERM 1000 1001
$ kill -sigterm 1000 1001
$ kill -TERM 1000 1001
$ kill -s 15 1000 1001
$ kill -s SIGTERM 1000 1001
```

If those two processes are playing nicely on your system, they'll comply with the *SIGTERM* signal and terminate when they're ready (after they clean up whatever they're doing). Not all processes will comply, however. A process may be hung in such a way that it cannot respond, or it may have *signal handling* code written to trap the signal you're trying to send. To force a process to die, use the strongest *kill*:

```
$ kill -9 1000 1001s
$ kill -KILL 1000 1001
```

These equivalent commands send the *KILL* signal to the process, which the process cannot ignore. The process will terminate immediately without closing files or performing any other cleanup. Because this may leave the program's data in an inconsistent state, using the *KILL* signal should be a last resort. When a process is blocked waiting for I/O, such as trying to write to an unavailable NFS server or waiting for a tape device to complete rewinding, the *KILL* signal may not work. See "Terminating Processes" below.

The *httpd* daemon will respond to the *HUP* signal by rereading its configuration files. If you've made changes and want *httpd* to reconfigure itself, send it the *HUP* signal:

```
$ kill -HUP 'cat /var/run/httpd.pid'
```

Many other daemons respond to *SIGHUP* this way.

The back quotes are replaced by the shell with the contents of the file *httpd.pid*, which *httpd* creates when it starts.

Other programs allow you to send signals to processes without indicating their PID. *killall* will send a signal to all processes that match a given name, and *killproc* will send a signal to all process that match a full pathname.

On the Exam

Note that *kill* is used for sending all kinds of signals, not just termination signals. Also, be aware of the difference between the PID you intend to kill and the signal you wish to send it. Since they're both integers, they can sometimes be confused.

Terminating Processes

Occasionally, you'll find a system showing symptoms of high CPU load or one that runs out of memory for no obvious reason. This often means an application has gone out of control on your system. You can use *ps* or *top* to identify processes that may be having a problem. Once you know the PID for the process, you can use the *kill* command to stop the process nicely with *SIGTERM* (`kill -15 PID`), escalating the signal to higher strengths if necessary until the process terminates.

Occasionally you may see a process displayed by *ps* or *top* that is listed as a *zombie*. These are processes that are stuck while trying to terminate and are appropriately said to be in the *zombie state*. Just as in the cult classic film *Night of the Living Dead*, you can't kill zombies, because they're already dead!

If you have a recurring problem with zombies, there may be a bug in your system software or in an application.

Killing a process will also kill all of its child processes. For example, killing a shell will kill all the processes initiated from that shell, including other shells.

Shell Job Control

Linux and most modern Unix systems offer *job control*, which is the ability of your shell (with support of the kernel) to stop and restart executing commands, as well as place them in the *background* where they can be executed. A program is said to be in the *foreground* when it is attached to your terminal. When executing in the background, you have no input to the process other than sending it signals. When a process is put in the background, you create a *job*. Each job is assigned a job number, starting at 1 and numbering sequentially.

The basic reason to create a background process is to keep your shell session free. There are many instances when a long-running program will never produce a result from standard output or standard error, and your shell will simply sit idle waiting for the program to finish. Noninteractive programs can be placed in the *background* by adding a & character to the command. For example, if you start firefox from the command line, you don't want the shell to sit and wait for it to terminate. The shell will respond by starting the web browser in the background and will give you a new command prompt. It will also issue the job number, denoted in square brackets, along with the PID. For example:

```
$ /usr/bin/firefox &
[1]  1748
```

Here, firefox is started as a background process. Firefox is assigned to job 1 (as denoted by [1]), and is assigned PID 1748. If you start a program and forget the & character, you can still put it in the background by first typing Ctrl-Z to stop it:

```
^Z
[1]+  Stopped        firefox
```

Then, issue the *bg* command to restart the job in the background:

```
$ bg
[1]+ /usr/bin/firefox &
```

When you exit from a shell with jobs in the background, those processes may die. The utility *nohup* can be used to protect the background processes from the hangup signal (*SIGHUP*) that it might otherwise receive when the shell dies. This can be used to simulate the detached behavior of a system daemon.

Putting interactive programs in the background can be quite useful. Suppose you're logged into a remote Linux system, running Emacs in text mode. Rather than exit from the editor when you need to drop back to the shell, you can simply press Ctrl-Z. This stops Emacs, puts it in the background, and returns you to a command prompt. When you are finished, you resume your Emacs session with the *fg* command, which puts your stopped job back into the foreground.

Background jobs and their status can be listed by issuing the *jobs* command. Stopped jobs can be brought to the foreground with the *fg* command and optionally placed into the background with the Ctrl-Z and bg sequence.

bg

Syntax

```
bg [jobspec]
```

Description

Place *jobspec* in the background, as if it had been started with **&**. If *jobspec* is not present, then the shell's notion of the *current job* is used, as indicated by the plus sign (+) in output from the *jobs* command. Using this command on a job that is stopped will allow it to run in the background.

fg

Syntax

```
fg [jobspec]
```

Description

This command places the specified job in the foreground, making it the current job. If *job spec* is not present, the shell's notion of the current job is used.

jobs

Syntax

```
jobs [options] [jobspecs]
```

Description

List the active jobs. The optional *jobspecs* argument restricts output to information about those jobs.

Frequently used option

-l

    Also list PIDs.

nohup

Syntax

```
nohup [options] [command] [args...]
```

Description

Run a command immune to hangups, with output to a non-TTY terminal.

Example 1

Run the command */opt/bin/myscript.sh* in the background, with standard output and standard error redirected to *nohup.out*:

```
$ nohup /opt/bin/myscript.sh &
[1] 12611
```

On the Exam

Be sure to know how to display background jobs and how to switch among them.

Objective 6: Modify Process Execution Priorities

Part of Linux's flexibility is to let users and administrators prioritize process execution. This feature is handy when you have a high-load machine and want to make sure special processes (like yours!) get more rights to use system resources than others. It also is useful if you have a process that's gone haywire and you want to debug the problem prior to killing it. On the flip side, you can bury nonessential processes, giving them the lowest priority so they don't ever conflict with other processes.

Generally, on a day-to-day basis, you don't need to worry about execution priority, because the kernel handles it automatically. Each process's priority level is constantly and dynamically raised and lowered by the kernel according to a number of parameters, such as how much system time it has already consumed and its status (perhaps waiting for I/O; such processes are favored by the kernel). Linux gives you the ability to bias the kernel's priority algorithm, favoring certain processes over others.

The priority of a process can be determined by examining the PRI column in the results produced from issuing either the *top* or *ps -l* commands. The values displayed are relative; the higher the priority number, the more CPU time the kernel offers to the process. The kernel does this by managing a queue of processes. Those with high priority are given more time, and those with low priority are given less time. On a heavily loaded system, a process with a very low priority may appear stalled.

nice

One of the parameters used by the kernel to assign process priority is supplied by the user and is called a *nice number*. The *nice* command[*] is used to assign a priority number to the process. It is so named because it normally causes programs to execute with lower priority levels than their default. Thus, the process is being "nice" to other processes on the system by yielding CPU time. With this scheme, more "niceness" implies a lower priority, and less niceness implies a higher priority.

By default, user processes are created with a *nice number* of zero. Positive numbers lower the priority relative to other processes, and negative numbers raise it. For

---

[*] Some shells, not including *bash*, have a built-in *nice* command.

example, if you have a long-running utility and don't want to impact interactive performance, a positive nice number will lower the job's priority and improve interactive performance.

Nice numbers range from –20 to +19. Any user can start a process with a positive nice number, but only the superuser (**root**) can lower a process's nice number and thus raise its priority. Remember, the lower the nice number, the higher the priority to the CPU.

nice

Syntax

```
nice [-n adjustment] [command ]
nice [-adjustment] [command ]
```

Description

The *nice* command alters another process's nice number at start time. For normal users, *adjustment* is an integer from 1 to 19. If you're the superuser, the *adjustment* range is from –20 to 19. If an *adjustment* number is not specified, the process's nice number defaults to 10. The *command* consists of any command that you might enter on the command line, including all options, arguments, redirections, and the background character **&**.

If both *adjustment* and *command* are omitted, *nice* displays the current scheduling priority, which is inherited.

Example 1

The following command starts a program in the background with reduced priority, using the default nice number of 10:

```
$ nice somecmd -opt1 -opt2 arg1 arg2 &
```

Example 2

As superuser, you can start programs with elevated priority. These equivalent commands start the *vi* editor with a higher priority, which may be necessary for administrative purposes if the system is exceptionally slow:

```
# nice --10 vi /etc/hosts.deny
# nice -n -10 vi /etc/hosts.deny
```

Note the double dash (`--10`) in the first form. The first dash indicates that an option follows, whereas the second dash indicates a negative number.

Be careful when using *nice* on interactive programs such as editors, word processors, or browsers. Assigning a program a positive nice number will most likely result in sluggish performance. Remember, the higher the positive number, the lower the resulting priority level.

For that reason, you should try not to assign positive nice numbers to foreground jobs on your terminal. If the system gets busy, your terminal could hang awaiting CPU time, which has been sacrificed by *nice*.

GNU/Unix Commands

Changing nice numbers on running processes

The *nice* command works to change the nice number for new processes only at the time that they're started. To modify a running program, use the *renice* command.

renice

Syntax

```
renice [+|-]nicenumber [option] targets
```

Description

Alter the *nicenumber* to set the scheduling priority of one or more running **target** processes. By default, *renice* assumes that the **targets** are numeric PIDs. One or more **option**s may also be used to interpret **targets** as processes owned by specific users.

Frequently used options

-u

Interpret **targets** as usernames, affecting all processes owned by those users.

-p

Interpret **targets** as PIDs (the default).

Examples

This command will lower the priority of the process with PID 501 by increasing its nice number to the maximum:

```
$ renice 20 501
```

The following command can be used to increase the priority of all of user *adamh*'s processes as well as the process with PID 501:

```
# renice -10 -u adamh -p 501
```

In this command, -10 indicates a nice value of negative 10, thus giving PID 501 a higher priority on the system. A dash isn't used for the nice value, because the dash could be confused for an option, such as *-u*.

On the Exam

Be sure to know the range and meaning of nice numbers and how to change them for new and existing processes. Also note that *nice* and *renice* specify their numbers differently. With *nice*, a leading dash can indicate a nice number (e.g., -10), including a negative one with a second dash (e.g., --10). On the other hand, *renice* does not need the dash.

You can renice processes interactively using *top*'s text interface by using the single-keystroke *r* command. You will be prompted for the PID of the process whose nice number you wish to change and for the new nice number. If you are the superuser, you can enter negative values. The new nice number will be displayed by *top* in the column labeled NI for the process you specify.

Objective 7: Search Text Files Using Regular Expressions

Linux offers many tools for system administrators to use for processing text. Many, such as *sed, awk*, and *perl*, are capable of automatically editing multiple files, providing you with a wide range of text-processing capability. To harness that capability, you need to be able to define and delineate specific text segments from within files, text streams, and string variables. Once the text you're after is identified, you can use one of these tools or languages to do useful things to it.

These tools and others understand a loosely defined pattern language. The language and the patterns themselves are collectively called regular expressions (often abbreviated just *regexp* or *regex*). Regular expressions are similar in concept to file globs, but many more special characters exist for regular expressions, extending the utility and capability of tools that understand them.

Two tools that are important for the LPIC Level 1 exams and that make use of regular expressions are *grep* and *sed*. These tools are useful for text searches. There are many other tools that make use of regular expressions, including the *awk*, Perl, and Python languages and other utilities, but you don't need to be concerned with them for the purpose of the LPIC Level 1 exams.

Regular expressions are the topic of entire books, such as *Mastering Regular Expressions (http://oreilly.com/catalog/9780596528126/)* (O'Reilly). Exam 101 requires the use of simple regular expressions and related tools, specifically to perform searches from text sources. This section covers only the basics of regular expressions, but it goes without saying that their power warrants a full understanding. Digging deeper into the regular expression world is highly recommended in your quest to become an accomplished Linux system administrator.

Regular Expression Syntax

It would not be unreasonable to assume that some specification defines how regular expressions are constructed. Unfortunately, there isn't one. Regular expressions have been incorporated as a feature in a number of tools over the years, with varying degrees of consistency and completeness. The result is a cart-before-the-horse scenario, in which utilities and languages have defined their own flavor of regular expression syntax, each with its own extensions and idiosyncrasies. Formally defining the regular expression syntax came later, as did efforts to make it more consistent. Regular expressions are defined by arranging strings of text, or *patterns*. Those patterns are composed of two types of characters, *literals* (plain text or literal text) and *metacharacters*.

Like the special file *globbing* characters, regular expression metacharacters take on a special meaning in the context of the tool in which they're used. There are a few metacharacters that are generally thought of to be among the "extended set" of metacharacters, specifically those introduced into *egrep* after *grep* was created.

The *egrep* command on Linux systems is simply a wrapper that runs *grep -E*, informing *grep* to use its extended regular expression capabilities instead of the basic ones. Examples of metacharacters include the ^ symbol, which means "the beginning of a line," and the $ symbol, which means "the end of a line." A complete listing of metacharacters follows in Tables 6-8 through 6-11.

 The backslash character (\) turns off (escapes) the special meaning of the character that follows, turning metacharacters into literals. For nonmetacharacters, it often turns on some special meaning.

Table 6-8. Regular expression position anchors

Regular expression	Description
^	Match at the beginning of a line. This interpretation makes sense only when the ^ character is at the lefthand side of the *regex*.
$	Match at the end of a line. This interpretation makes sense only when the $ character is at the righthand side of the *regex*.
\<\>	Match word boundaries. Word boundaries are defined as whitespace, the start of line, the end of line, or punctuation marks. The backslashes are required and enable this interpretation of < and >.

Table 6-9. Regular expression POSIX character classes

Character class	Description
[:alnum:]	Alphanumeric [a-zA-Z0-9]
[:alpha:]	Alphabetic [a-zA-Z]
[:blank:]	Spaces or Tabs
[:cntrl:]	Control characters
[:digit:]	Numeric digits [0-9]
[:graph:]	Any visible characters
[:lower:]	Lowercase [a-z]
[:print:]	Noncontrol characters
[:punct:]	Punctuation characters
[:space:]	Whitespace
[:upper:]	Uppercase [A-Z]
[:xdigit:]	Hex digits [0-9a-fA-F]

Table 6-10. Regular expression character sets

Regular expression	Description
[abc][a-z]	Single-character groups and ranges. In the first form, match any single character from among the enclosed characters a, b, or c. In the second form, match any single character from among the range of characters bounded by a and z (POSIX character classes can also be used, so [a-z] can be replaced with [[:lower:]]). The brackets are for grouping only and are not matched themselves.

Regular expression	Description
[^abc][^a-z]	Inverse match. Match any single character not among the enclosed characters a, b, and c or in the range a-z. Be careful not to confuse this inversion with the anchor character ^, described earlier.
.	Match any single character except a newline.

Table 6-11. Regular expression modifiers

Basic regular expression	Extended regular expression (egrep)	Description
*	*	Match an unknown number (zero or more) of the single character (or single-character *regex*) that precedes it.
\?	?	Match zero or one instance of the preceding *regex*.
\+	+	Match one or more instances of the preceding *regex*.
\{*n*,*m*\}	{*n*,*m*}	Match a range of occurrences of the single character or *regex* that precedes this construct. \{*n*\} matches *n* occurrences, \{*n*,\} matches at least *n* occurrences, and \{*n*,*m*\} matches any number of occurrences from *n* to *m*, inclusively.
|	|	Alternation. Match either the *regex* specified before or after the vertical bar.
\(*regex*\)	(*regex*)	Grouping. Matches *regex*, but it can be modified as a whole and used in back-references. (\1 expands to the contents of the first \(\), and so on, up to \9.)

It is often helpful to consider regular expressions as their own language, where literal text acts as words and phrases. The "grammar" of the language is defined by the use of metacharacters. The two are combined according to specific rules (which, as mentioned earlier, may differ slightly among various tools) to communicate ideas and get real work done. When you construct regular expressions, you use metacharacters and literals to specify three basic ideas about your input text:

Position anchors
> A position anchor is used to specify the position of one or more character sets in relation to the entire line of text (such as the beginning of a line).

Character sets
> A character set matches text. It could be a series of literals, metacharacters that match individual or multiple characters, or combinations of these.

Quantity modifiers
> Quantity modifiers follow a character set and indicate the number of times the set should be repeated.

Using grep

A long time ago, as the idea of regular expressions was catching on, the line editor ed contained a command to display lines of a file being edited that matched a given regular expression. The command is:

```
g/regular expression/p
```

That is, "on a global basis, print the current line when a match for *regular expres sion* is found," or more simply, "global *regular expression* print." This function was so useful that it was made into a standalone utility named, appropriately, *grep*. Later, the regular expression grammar of *grep* was expanded in a new command called *egrep* (for "extended *grep*"). You'll find both commands on your Linux system today, and they differ slightly in the way they handle regular expressions. For the purposes of Exam 101, we'll stick with *grep*, which can also make use of the "extended" regular expressions when used with the -*E* option. You will find some form of *grep* on just about every Unix or Unix-like system available.

grep

Syntax

```
grep [options] regex [files]
```

Description

Search *files* or standard input for lines containing a match to regular expression *regex*. By default, matching lines will be displayed and nonmatching lines will not be displayed. When multiple files are specified, *grep* displays the filename as a prefix to the output lines (use the -*h* option to suppress filename prefixes).

Frequently used options

-*c*

Display only a count of matched lines, but not the lines themselves.

-*h*

Display matched lines, but do not include filenames for multiple file input.

-*i*

Ignore uppercase and lowercase distinctions, allowing abc to match both abc and ABC.

-*n*

Display matched lines prefixed with their line numbers. When used with multiple files, *both* the filename and line number are prefixed.

-*v*

Print all lines that *do not* match *regex*. This is an important and useful option. You'll want to use regular expressions not only to *select* information but also to *eliminate* information. Using -*v* inverts the output this way.

-*E*

Interpret *regex* as an extended regular expression. This makes *grep* behave as if it were *egrep*.

Examples

Since regular expressions can contain both metacharacters and literals, *grep* can be used with an entirely literal *regex*. For example, to find all lines in *file1* that contain either *Linux* or *linux*, you could use *grep* like this:

```
$ grep -i linux file1
```

In this example, the *regex* is simply `linux`. The uppercase `L` in `Linux` will match since the command-line option *-i* was specified. This is fine for literal expressions that are common. However, in situations in which *regex* includes regular expression metacharacters that are also shell special characters (such as `$` or `*`), the *regex* must be quoted to prevent shell expansion and pass the metacharacters on to *grep*.

As a simplistic example of this, suppose you have files in your local directory named *abc*, *abc1*, and *abc2*. When combined with *bash*'s *echo* built-in command, the `abc*` wildcard expression lists all files that begin with `abc`, as follows:

```
$ echo abc*
abc abc1 abc2
```

Now, suppose that these files contain lines with the strings `abc`, `abcc`, `abccc`, and so on, and you wish to use *grep* to find them. You can use the shell wildcard expression `abc*` to expand to all the files that start with `abc` as displayed with *echo* in the previous example, and you'd use an identical regular expression `abc*` to find all occurrences of lines containing `abc`, `abcc`, `abccc`, etc. Without using quotes to prevent shell expansion, the command would be:

```
$ grep abc* abc*
```

After shell expansion, this yields:

```
grep abc abc1 abc2 abc abc1 abc2   no!
```

This is *not* what you intended! *grep* would search for the literal expression `abc`, because it appears as the first command argument. Instead, quote the regular expression with single or double quotes to protect it (the difference between single quotes and double quotes on the command line is subtle and is explained later in this section):

```
$ grep 'abc*' abc*
```

or:

```
$ grep "abc*" abc*
```

After expansion, both examples yield the same results:

```
grep abc* abc abc1 abc2
```

Now this is what you're after. The three files *abc*, *abc1*, and *abc2* will be searched for the regular expression `abc*`. It is good to stay in the habit of quoting regular expressions on the command line to avoid these problems; they won't be at all obvious, because the shell expansion is invisible to you unless you use the *echo* command.

GNU/Unix Commands

On the Exam

The use of *grep* and its options is common. You should be familiar with what each option does, as well as the concept of piping the results of other commands into *grep* for matching.

Using sed

sed, the *stream editor*, is a powerful filtering program found on nearly every Unix system. The *sed* utility is usually used either to automate repetitive editing tasks or to process text in pipes of Unix commands (see "Objective 4: Use Streams, Pipes, and Redirects," earlier in this chapter). The scripts that *sed* executes can be single commands or more complex lists of editing instructions.

sed

Syntax

```
sed [options] 'command1' [files]
sed [options] -e 'command1' [-e 'command2'...] [files]
sed [options] -f script [files]
```

Description

The first form invokes *sed* with a one-line *command1*. The second form invokes *sed* with two (or more) commands. Note that in this case the *-e* parameter is required for each command specified. The commands are specified in quotes to prevent the shell from interpreting and expanding them. The last form instructs *sed* to take editing commands from file *script* (which does not need to be executable). In all cases, if *files* are not specified, input is taken from standard input. If multiple *files* are specified, the edited output of each successive file is concatenated.

Frequently used options

-e cmd

> The *-e* option specifies that the next argument (*cmd*) is a *sed* command (or a series of commands). When specifying only one string of commands, the *-e* is optional.

-f file

> *file* is a *sed* script.

-g

> Treat all substitutions as global.

The *sed* utility operates on text through the use of *addresses* and *editing commands*. The address is used to locate lines of text to be operated on, and editing commands modify text. During operation, each line (that is, text separated by newline characters) of input to *sed* is processed individually and without regard to adjacent lines. If multiple editing commands are to be used (through the use of a script file or multiple *-e* options), they are all applied in order to each line before moving on to the next line.

Addressing

Addresses in *sed* locate lines of text to which commands will be applied. The addresses can be:

- A line number (note that *sed* counts lines continuously across multiple input files). The symbol $ can be used to indicate the last line of input. A range of line numbers can be given by separating the starting and ending lines with a comma (*start,end*). So, for example, the address for all input would be 1,$.

- A regular expression delimited by forward slashes (/*regex*/).

- A line number with an interval. The form is *n~s*, where *n* is the starting line number and *s* is the step, or interval, to apply. For example, to match every odd line in the input, the address specification would be 1~2 (start at line 1 and match every two lines thereafter). This feature is a GNU extension to *sed*.

If no address is given, commands are applied to all input lines by default. Any address may be followed by the ! character, applying commands to lines that *do not match* the address.

Commands

The sed command immediately follows the address specification if present. Commands generally consist of a single letter or symbol, unless they have arguments. Following are some basic sed editing commands to get you started.

d

> Delete lines.

s

> Make substitutions. This is a very popular *sed* command. The syntax is as follows:
>
> s/*pattern*/*replacement*/[*flags*]
>
> The following *flags* can be specified for the s command:
>
> *g*
>
> > Replace all instances of *pattern*, not just the first.
>
> *n*
>
> > Replace *n*th instance of *pattern*; the default is 1.
>
> *p*
>
> > Print the line if a successful substitution is done. Generally used with the *-n* command-line option.
>
> *w file*
> > Print the line to *file* if a successful substitution is done.
>
> *y*
>
> > Translate characters. This command works in a fashion similar to the *tr* command, described earlier.

Example 1

Delete lines 3 through 5 of *file1*:

```
$ sed '3,5d' file1
```

Example 2

Delete lines of *file1* that contain a # at the beginning of the line:

```
$ sed '/^#/d' file1
```

Example 3

Translate characters:

> y/abc/xyz/

Every instance of a is translated to x, b to y, and c to z.

Example 4

Write the @ symbol for all empty lines in *file1* (that is, lines with only a newline character but nothing more):

```
$ sed 's/^$/@/' file1
```

Example 5

Remove all double quotation marks from all lines in *file1*:

```
$ sed 's/"//g' file1
```

Example 6

Using *sed* commands from external file *sedcmds*, replace the third and fourth double quotation marks with (and) on lines 1 through 10 in *file1*. Make no changes from line 11 to the end of the file. Script file *sedcmds* contains:

```
1,10{
s/"/(/3
s/"/)/4
}
```

The command is executed using the *-f* option:

```
$ sed -f sedcmds file1
```

This example employs the positional flag for the s (substitute) command. The first of the two commands substitutes (for the third double-quote character. The next command substitutes) for the fourth double-quote character. Note, however, that the position count is interpreted *independently* for each subsequent command in the script. This is important because each command operates on the results of the commands preceding it. In this example, since the third double quote has been replaced with (, it is no longer counted as a double quote by the second command. Thus, the second command will operate on the *fifth* double quote character in the original *file1*. If the input line starts out with the following:

```
""""""
```

after the first command, which operates on the third double quote, the result is this:

```
""(""""
```

At this point, the numbering of the double-quote characters has changed, and the fourth double quote in the line is now the fifth character. Thus, after the second command executes, the output is as follows:

```
""(")"
```

As you can see, creating scripts with sed requires that the sequential nature of the command execution be kept in mind.

If you find yourself making repetitive changes to many files on a regular basis, a sed script is probably warranted. Many more commands are available in sed than are listed here.

Examples

Now that the gory details are out of the way, here are some examples of simple regular expression usage that you may find useful.

Anchors

Description

Anchors are used to describe position information. Table 6-8, shown earlier, lists anchor characters.

Example 1

Display all lines from *file1* where the string Linux appears at the start of the line:

```
$ grep '^Linux' file1
```

Example 2

Display lines in *file1* where the last character is an x:

```
$ grep 'x$' file1
```

Display the number of empty lines in *file1* by finding lines with nothing between the beginning and the end:

```
$ grep -c '^$' file1
```

Display all lines from *file1* containing only the word null by itself:

```
$ grep '^null$' file1
```

Groups and ranges

Description

Characters can be placed into groups and ranges to make regular expressions more efficient, as shown in Table 6-10, previously.

Example 1

Display all lines from *file1* containing Linux, linux, TurboLinux, and so on:

```
$ grep '[Ll]inux' file1
```

Example 2

Display all lines from *file1* that contain three adjacent digits:

```
$ grep '[0-9][0-9][0-9]' file1
```

Example 3

Display all lines from *file1* beginning with any single character other than a digit:

```
$ grep '^[^0-9]' file1
```

Example 4

Display all lines from *file1* that contain the whole word Linux or linux, but not LinuxOS or TurboLinux:

```
$ grep '\<[Ll]inux\>' file1
```

Example 5

Display all lines from *file1* with five or more characters on a line (excluding the newline character):

```
$ grep '.....' file1
```

GNU/Unix
Commands

Example 6

Display all nonblank lines from *file1* (i.e., that have at least one character):

```
$ grep '.' file1
```

Example 7

Display all lines from *file1* that contain a period (normally a metacharacter) using an escape:

```
$ grep '\.' file1
```

Modifiers

Description

Modifiers change the meaning of other characters in a regular expression. Table 6-11, shown previously, lists these modifiers.

Example 1

Display all lines from *file1* that contain ab, abc, abcc, abccc, and so on:

```
$ grep 'abc*' file1
```

Example 2

Display all lines from *file1* that contain abc, abcc, abccc, and so on, but not ab:

```
$ grep 'abcc*' file1
```

Example 3

Display all lines from *file1* that contain two or more adjacent digits:

```
$ grep '[0-9][0-9][0-9]*' file1
```

or:

```
$ grep '[0-9]\{2,\}' file1
```

Example 4

Display lines from *file1* that contain file (because ? can match zero occurrences), file1, or file2:

```
$ grep 'file[12]\?' file1
```

Example 5

Display all lines from *file1* containing at least one digit:

```
$ grep '[0-9]\+' file1
```

Example 6

Display all lines from *file1* that contain 111, 1111, or 11111 on a line by itself:

```
$ grep '^1\{3,5\}$' file1
```

Example 7

Display all lines from *file1* that contain any three-, four-, or five-digit number:

```
$ grep '\<[0-9]\{3,5\}\>' file1
```

Example 8

Display all lines from *file1* that contain Happy, happy, Sad, sad, Angry, or angry:

```
$ grep -E '[Hh]appy|[Ss]ad|[Aa]ngry' file1
```

Example 9

Display all lines of *file* that contain any repeated sequence of abc (abcabc, abcabcabc, and so on):

```
$ grep '\(abc\)\{2,\}' file
```

You may find it useful to employ the GNU option *--color* to *grep* when working with regular expressions. It prints the section of the string that matched your regular expression in a different color, so you can see exactly what *grep* was looking for.

Basic regular expression patterns

Example 1

Match any letter:

```
[A-Za-z]
```

Example 2

Match any symbol (not a letter or digit):

```
[^0-9A-Za-z]
```

Example 3

Match an uppercase letter, followed by zero or more lowercase letters:

```
[A-Z][a-z]*
```

Example 4

Match a U.S. Social Security Number (123-45-6789) by specifying groups of three, two, and four digits separated by dashes:

```
[0-9]\{3\}-[0-9]\{2\}-[0-9]\{4\}
```

Example 5

Match a dollar amount, using an escaped dollar sign, zero or more spaces or digits, an escaped period, and two more digits:

```
\$[ 0-9]*\.[0-9]\{2\}
```

GNU/Unix Commands

Example 6

Match the month of June and its abbreviation, Jun. The question mark matches zero or one instance of the e:

```
June\?
```

On the Exam

Make certain you are clear about the difference between *file globbing* and the use of regular expressions.

Using regular expressions as addresses in sed

These examples are commands you would issue to *sed*. For example, the commands could take the place of *command1* in this usage:

```
$ sed [options] 'command1'[files]
```

These commands could also appear in a standalone **sed** script.

Example 1

Delete blank lines:

```
/^$/d
```

Example 2

Delete any line that doesn't contain #keepme:

```
/#keepme/!d
```

Example 3

Delete lines containing only whitespace (spaces or Tabs). In this example, Tab means the single Tab character and is preceded by a single space:

```
/^[ Tab]*$/d
```

Because GNU *sed* also supports character classes, this example could be written as follows:

```
/^[[:blank:]]*$/d
```

Example 4

Delete lines beginning with periods or pound signs:

```
/^[\.#]/d
```

Example 5

Substitute a single space for any number of spaces wherever they occur on the line:

```
s/  */ /g
```

or:

```
s/ \{2,\}/ /g
```

Example 6

Substitute `def` for `abc` from line 11 to 20, wherever it occurs on the line:

```
11,20s/abc/def/g
```

Example 7

Translate the characters *a*, *b*, and *c* to the @ character from line 11 to 20, wherever they occur on the line:

```
11,20y/abc/@@@/
```

Objective 8: Perform Basic File Editing Operations Using vi

vi is perhaps the most ubiquitous text editor available on Linux systems. Since most system administration tasks eventually require editing text files, being able to work effectively in *vi* is essential.

This Objective concentrates on a subset of *vi* functionality. *Learning the vi and Vim Editors (http://oreilly.com/catalog/9780596529833)* (O'Reilly) is an indispensable reference for anyone interested in learning more about *vi* and the enhancements available in its various implementations. There is also a large amount of documentation available at *http://vimdoc.sourceforge.net* and *http://www.vim.org* for the popular *vi* implementation Vim, most of which is applicable to any version of *vi*.

Invoking vi

To start *vi*, simply execute it. You will be editing a temporary file. To directly edit one or more files, give the names of the files on the command line:

```
$ vi file1.txt file2.txt
```

You are presented with a main window showing the contents of *file1.txt*, or if the specified files don't already exist, a blank screen with tilde (~) characters running the length of the left column (they indicate areas of the screen containing no text, not even blank lines).

vi Basics

The *vi* editor has two modes of operation: *command* or *insert*. In command mode, *vi* allows you to navigate around your file and enter commands. To enter new text, put *vi* into insert mode. In command mode, the keyboard keys are interpreted as *vi* commands instead of text. The convenience of being able to manipulate the editor without moving your hands from the keyboard is considered one of *vi*'s strengths.

Commands are brief, case-sensitive combinations of one or more letters. For example, to switch from command to insert mode, press the "i" key. To terminate insert mode, press the Escape key (Esc), which puts you back in command mode.

Almost any command can be prefixed with a number to repeat the command that number of times. For example, `r` will replace the character at the current cursor position. To replace exactly 10 characters, use **10r**. Commonly used *vi* commands are listed in Table 6-12.

Table 6-12. vi commands

Key command	Description
h or left arrow	Move left one character.
j or down arrow	Move down one line.
k or up arrow	Move up one line.
l or right arrow	Move right one character.
H	Move to the top of the screen.
L	Move to the bottom of the screen.
G	Move to the end of the file.
w	Move forward one word.
b	Move backward one word.
0 (zero)	Move to the beginning of the current line.
^	Move to the first nonwhitespace character on the current line.
$	Move to the end of the current line.
Ctrl-B	Move up (back) one screen.
Ctrl-F	Move down (forward) one screen.
i	Insert at the current cursor position.
I	Insert at the beginning of the current line.
a	Append after the current cursor position.
A	Append to the end of the current line.
o	Start a new line after the current line.
O	Start a new line before the current line.
r	Replace the character at the current cursor position.
R	Start replacing (overwriting) at the current cursor position.
x	Delete the character at the current cursor position.
X	Delete the character immediately before (to the left) of the current cursor position.
s	Delete the character at the current cursor position and go into insert mode. (This is the equivalent of the combination xi.)
S	Delete the contents of the current line and go into insert mode.
d*X*	Given a movement command *X*, cut (delete) the appropriate number of characters, words, or lines from the current cursor position.
dd	Cut the entire current line.
D	Cut from the current cursor position to the end of the line. (This is equivalent to d$.)
c*X*	Given a movement command *X*, cut the appropriate number of characters, words, or lines from the current cursor position and go into insert mode.
cc	Cut the entire current line and go into insert mode.

Key command	Description
C	Cut from the current cursor position to the end of the line and enter insert mode. (This is equivalent to c$.)
y*X*	Given a movement command *X*, copy (yank[a]) the appropriate number of characters, words, or lines from the current cursor position.
yy or Y	Copy the entire current line.
p	Paste after the current cursor position.
P	Paste before the current cursor position.
.	Repeat the last command.
u	Undo the last command.[b]
/*regex*	Search forward for *regex*.
?*regex*	Search backward for *regex*.
n	Find the next match.
N	Find the previous match. (In other words, repeat the last search in the opposite direction.)
:n	Next file; when multiple files are specified for editing, this command loads the next file. Force this action (if the current file has unsaved changes) with :n!.
:e *file*	Load *file* in place of the current file. Force this action with :e! *file*.
:r *file*	Insert the contents of *file* after the current cursor position.
:q	Quit without saving changes. Force this action with :q!.
:w *file*	Write the current buffer to *file*. To append to an existing file, use :w >>*file*. Force the write (when possible, such as when running as *root*) with :w! *file*.
:wq	Write the file contents and quit. Force this action with :wq!.
:x	Write the file contents (if changed) and quit (the *ex* equivalent of ZZ).
ZZ	Write the file contents (if changed) and quit.
:! *command*	Execute *command* in a subshell.

[a] Emacs users should be careful not to confuse the *vi* definition of yank (copy) with that of Emacs (paste).

[b] Many of the popular *vi* implementations support multilevel undo. Vim breaks compatibility with traditional *vi* by making a repeated u perform another level of undo. Nvi uses . after u to do multilevel undo and, like traditional *vi*, uses a repeated u to redo (undo the undo, so to speak). This can cause some confusion when moving between Linux distributions that have different default implementations of *vi*.

Keep in mind that this is *not* a complete list, but it is not necessary to know every *vi* command to use it effectively. In fact, even after using *vi* as your only editor for years, you may find yourself using only a small subset of the available commands.

There is a pattern in *vi*'s keyboard commands that makes them easier to remember. For every lowercase character that has some action assigned to it, the same uppercase character *usually* has some related action assigned to it. As an example, i and I both put *vi* in insert mode, at the current cursor position and at the beginning of the line, respectively.

7

Devices, Linux Filesystems, and the Filesystem Hierarchy Standard (Topic 104)

Filesystem management is among the most critical activities that you must perform to maintain a stable Linux system. In simple situations, after a successful installation, you may never have a problem or need to manage filesystem specifics. However, understanding how to configure and maintain Linux filesystems is essential to safely manage your system and to pass Exam 101. This section contains the following Objectives:

Objective 1: Create Partitions and Filesystems
This Objective states that an LPIC 1 candidate should be able to configure disk partitions and create filesystems on media such as hard disks. It also includes using various *mkfs* commands to set up filesystems such as *ext2*, *ext3*, *reiserfs*, *vfat*, and *xfs*, in addition to managing swap partitions. Weight: 2.

Objective 2: Maintain the Integrity of Filesystems
A candidate should be able to verify the integrity of filesystems, monitor free space and inodes, and repair simple filesystem problems. This Objective includes the commands required to maintain a standard filesystem as well as the extra data associated with a *journaling* filesystem. Weight: 2.

Objective 3: Control Filesystem Mounting and Unmounting
Candidates should be able to manually mount and unmount filesystems, configure filesystem mounting on system boot, and configure user-mountable removable filesystems such as flash drives, floppies, and CDs. Weight: 3.

Objective 4: Set and View Disk Quotas
This Objective includes managing disk quotas for system users. You should be able to set up a disk quota for a filesystem, edit, check, and generate user quota reports. Weight: 1.

Objective 5: Manage File Permissions and Ownership
Candidates should be able to control file access through file permissions. This Objective includes access permissions on regular and special files as well as directories. Also included are access modes such as *suid, sgid*, and the *sticky bit*. You should also be aware of the use of the group field to grant file access to workgroups, the *immutable flag*, and the default file creation mode. Weight: 3.

Objective 6: Create and Change Hard and Symbolic Links
Candidates should be able to create and manage hard and symbolic links to a file. This Objective includes the ability to create and identify links, copy files through links, and use linked files to support system administration tasks. Weight: 2.

Objective 7: Find System Files and Place Files in the Correct Location
This Objective states that candidates should be thoroughly familiar with the FHS, including typical file locations and directory classifications. This includes the ability to find files and commands on a Linux System. Weight: 2.

Objective 1: Create Partitions and Filesystems

The term *filesystem* refers to two different things. First, it can mean the way files and directories are physically structured on a disk or other storage medium. Linux supports many different filesystems (in this sense of the word), including *ext2* and *ext3*, the nonjournaled and journaled (respectively) native filesystems; *msdos* or *vfat*, the native MS-DOS and Windows (respectively) filesystems; JFS, a filesystem used on OS/2 and AIX; XFS, the native IRIX filesystem; and many, many others.

In the second sense of the word, it refers to the structure and contents of some storage medium. To view the contents of a filesystem (in this sense of the word) on a Linux system, the device must be *mounted*, or attached to the hierarchical directory structure on the system. Much of the strength and flexibility of Linux (and Unix) comes from the ability to mount any filesystem that it supports, whether that filesystem is somewhere remote on the network or on a locally attached disk, anywhere in its directory structure, in a way that is completely transparent to users. For example, the files under */usr* will work equally well whether they are on a disk attached to the system or mounted from a master server. Even the / (root) filesystem can be located on a distant server if the system is properly configured.

Disk Drives Under Linux

Linux supports many types of disk devices and formats. Any SCSI or IDE hard disk will work with Linux, as will floppy disks, CD-ROMs, CD-Rs, USB flash drives, and other types of removable media. These media can contain the standard Linux *ext2* filesystem, FAT, FAT32, NTFS, as well as other filesystem types. This flexibility makes Linux coexist nicely with other operating systems on multiboot systems.

The most commonly found hard disks on PCs are IDE drives. These disks feature a relatively simple system interface, and most of the "smarts" of the disk are onboard the disk itself. The IDE standard allows disk manufacturers to sell their product at a very competitive price, expanding their markets to more consumers and limited-budget commercial customers.

A single IDE interface is capable of attaching two disk drives to a system. One device is named *master* and the other is the *slave*. Most PCs have a *primary* and *secondary* IDE interface. Together, these interfaces allow up to four devices (primary master, primary slave, secondary master, and secondary slave).

Also used on PCs are SCSI drives. SCSI is an older standard for connecting peripherals; however, modern SCSI versions are quite fast and flexible. Typically, SCSI devices are used for their increased speed and reliability in large-scale and high-end server environments. With the increased speeds, however, come increased prices—often two to five times the price of their IDE counterparts.

Compared to IDE, SCSI offers excellent performance, lower CPU utilization, and a much more flexible connection scheme capable of handling up to 15 devices on a single bus. These conveniences allow SCSI systems to grow as space requirements increase without major hardware reconfiguration.

A third option available on motherboards in recent years is the Serial ATA (SATA) interface. SATA is basically a newer version of the IDE standard, and allows for much faster communication between the controller and the physical disk. The Linux kernel currently uses the *SCSI emulation layer* to support SATA hard drives, so from a device standpoint, SATA disks are treated the same way as SCSI disks. It's also important to note that some Linux distributions are configured to use the SCSI emulation layer for IDE disks as well, so you may be referring to your disks via the SCSI naming conventions even if you have IDE or SATA disks.

Hard disk devices

By default, Linux defines IDE device files as follows:

/dev/hda
> Primary master IDE (often the hard disk)

/dev/hdb
> Primary slave IDE

/dev/hdc
> Secondary master IDE (often a CD-ROM)

/dev/hdd
> Secondary slave IDE

SCSI device files (or any devices using the SCSI emulation layer) are similar, except that there is no four-device limitation:

/dev/sda
> First SCSI drive

/dev/sdb
> Second SCSI drive

/dev/sdc
> Third SCSI drive (and so on)

Under Linux, a typical PC with a single hard disk on the primary IDE interface and a single CD-ROM on the secondary IDE interface would have disk drive /dev/hda and CD-ROM /dev/hdc.

On the Exam

You should be prepared to identify IDE and SCSI devices based on their device filenames.

Disk partitions

Almost every operating system supports a system for dividing a disk into logical devices, called *partitions*. Other terms for the same basic concept are *slices* and *logical volumes*, although logical volumes generally also imply the ability to span physical disks. Linux supports several different partitioning formats, but by default it uses the MS-DOS format. The MS-DOS partition table allows for up to four *primary partitions*. One of these four primary partitions can be replaced with an *extended partition*, which can contain up to 12 *logical partitions*, for a total of 15 possible usable partitions (16 if you count the extended partition "container," but it is not usable for data).

The type of partition (as well as the type of device) affects the name of the device Linux uses to access the partition.

Primary partitions
> This type of partition contains a filesystem. If all four primary partitions exist on an IDE drive, they are numbered as follows:
>
> - /dev/hda1
> - /dev/hda2
> - /dev/hda3
> - /dev/hda4
>
> One of these primary partitions may be marked *active*, in which case the PC BIOS will be able to select it for boot.

Extended partitions
> An extended partition is a variant of the primary partition but cannot contain a filesystem. Instead, it contains *logical partitions*. Only one extended partition may exist on a single physical disk. For example, the partitions on a disk with one primary partition and the sole extended partition might be numbered as follows:
>
> - /dev/hda1 (primary)
> - /dev/hda2 (extended)

Logical partitions
> Logical partitions exist *within* the extended partition. Logical partitions are numbered from 5 to 16. The partitions on a disk with one primary partition, one extended partition, and four logical partitions might be numbered as follows:

- */dev/hda1* (primary)
- */dev/hda2* (extended)
- */dev/hda5* (logical)
- */dev/hda6* (logical)
- */dev/hda7* (logical)
- */dev/hda8* (logical)

If the partitions were made on a SCSI or SATA drive, the *hda* would be replaced by *sda*, for example, */dev/sda2*.

On the Exam

Be sure that you understand how partition numbering works. In particular, pay attention to the differences in numbering between primary, extended, and logical partitions.

The root filesystem and mount points

As a Linux system boots, the first filesystem that becomes available is the top level, or *root* filesystem, denoted with a single forward slash. The root filesystem /, also known as the *root directory*, shouldn't be confused with the *root* superuser account or the superuser's home directory, */root*. The distinct directories / and */root* are unrelated and are not required to share the same filesystem. In a simple installation, the root filesystem could contain nearly everything on the system. However, such an arrangement could lead to system failure if the root filesystem fills to capacity. Instead, multiple partitions are typically defined, each containing one of the directories under /. As the Linux kernel boots, the partitions are *mounted* to the root filesystem, and together create a single unified filesystem (see "Objective 3: Control Filesystem Mounting and Unmounting" on page 161 for a discussion about mounting). Everything on the system that is not stored in a mounted partition is stored locally in the / (root) partition. The mounted filesystems are placed on separate partitions and possibly multiple disk drives.

The choice of which directories are placed into separate partitions is both a personal and technical decision. Here are some guidelines for individual partitions:

/ (the root directory)
> Since the only filesystem mounted at the start of the boot process is /, certain directories must be part of it to be available for the boot process. These include:
>
> */bin and /sbin*
>> Contains required system binary programs
>
> */dev*
>> Contains device files
>
> */etc*
>> Contains configuration information used on boot
>
> */lib*
>> Contains shared libraries

These directories are always part of the single / partition. See the description of the FHS in "Objective 7: Find System Files and Place Files in the Correct Location" on page 192 for more on the requirements for the root filesystem.

/boot

This directory holds static files used by the boot loader, including kernel images. On systems where kernel development activity occurs regularly, making */boot* a separate partition eliminates the possibility that / will fill with kernel images and associated files during development.

/home

User files are usually placed in a separate partition. This is often the largest partition on the system and may be located on a separate physical disk or disk array.

/tmp

This directory is often a separate partition used to prevent temporary files from filling the root filesystem. By default, all users have read/write access to files they create in */tmp*.

/var

Logfiles are stored here. This is similar to the situation with */tmp*, where user files can fill any available space if something goes wrong or if the files are not cleaned periodically.

/usr

This directory holds a hierarchy of directories containing user commands, source code, and documentation. It is often quite large, making it a good candidate for its own partition. Because much of the information stored under */usr* is static, some users prefer that it be mounted as read-only, making it impossible to corrupt.

In addition to the preceding six partitions listed, a *swap* partition is also necessary for a Linux system to enable virtual memory. For information on determining the size of a swap partition, see Chapter 5.

Using these guidelines at installation time, the disk partitions for an IDE-based system with two physical disks (40 GB and 200 GB) on the primary IDE controller might look as described in Table 7-1.

Table 7-1. An example partitioning scheme

Partition	Type	Mounted filesystem	Size
/dev/hda1	Primary	*/boot*	1 GB
/dev/hda2	Primary	/	5 GB
/dev/hda3	Extended	-	-
/dev/hda5	Logical	*/usr*	10 GB
/dev/hda6	Logical	*/var*	10 GB
/dev/hda7	Logical	*/opt*	10 GB
/dev/hda8	Logical	*/tmp*	2 GB

Partition	Type	Mounted filesystem	Size
/dev/hda4	Primary	(swap partition)	2 GB
/dev/hdb1	Primary	/home	200 GB

Once a disk is partitioned, it can be difficult or risky to change the partition sizes. Commercial and open source tools are available for this task, but a full backup is recommended prior to their use.

> If you are resizing your partitions, you may want to investigate setting up your system using *Logical Volume Manager* (LVM). LVM is currently not covered on the LPI exams, but its use is quickly growing. For more information, read the LVM-HOWTO at the Linux Documentation Project (*http://www.tldp .org*).

Managing partitions

Linux has two basic options for partitioning disk drives. The *fdisk* command is a text-based program that is easy to use and exists on every Linux distribution. It is also required for Exam 101. Another option you may wish to explore after mastering *fdisk* is *cfdisk*, which is still a text-mode program but uses the *curses* system to produce a GUI-style display.

---

fdisk

Syntax

```
fdisk [device]
```

Description

Manipulate or display the partition table for *device* using a command-driven interactive text interface. *device* is a physical disk such as */dev/hda*, not a partition such as */dev/hda1*. If omitted, *device* defaults to */dev/hda*. Interactive commands to *fdisk* are a single letter followed by a carriage return. The commands do not take arguments, but instead start an interactive dialog. Commands that operate on a partition will request the partition number, which is an integer. For primary and extended partitions, the partition number is from 1 to 4. For logical partitions, which are available only when the extended partition already exists to contain them, the partition number is from 5 to 16.

When making changes to the partition table, *fdisk* accumulates changes without writing them to the disk, until it receives the write command.

Frequently used commands

a

Toggle the *bootable* flag on/off for a primary partition.

d

Delete a partition. You are prompted for the partition number to delete. If you delete a logical partition when higher-numbered logical partitions exist, the partition numbers are decremented to keep logical partition numbers contiguous.

l

List the known partition types. A table of partition types is printed.

m

Display the brief help menu for these commands.

n

Add a new partition. You are prompted for the partition type (primary, extended, or logical). For primary and extended partitions, you are asked for the partition number (1–4). For logical partitions, the next logical partition number is selected automatically. You are then prompted for the starting disk cylinder for the partition and are offered the next free cylinder as a default. Finally, you are prompted for the last cylinder or a size, such as +300M. By default, new partitions are assigned as Linux *ext2*, type 83. To create another partition type, such as a swap partition, first create the partition with the *n* command, and then change the type with the *t* command.

> Note that *fdisk* displays options for extended and primary partition types if an extended partition does not yet exist. If the extended partition already exists, *fdisk* displays options for logical and primary partition types.

p

Display the partition table as it exists in memory. This depiction will differ from the actual partition table on disk if changes have not been saved.

q

Quit without saving changes.

t

Change a partition's system ID. This is a hex number that indicates the type of filesystem the partition is to contain. Linux *ext2* partitions are type 83, and Linux swap partitions are type 82.

w

Write (save) the partition table to disk and exit. No changes are saved until the *w* command is issued.

Example 1

Display the existing partition table on */dev/hda* without making any changes:

```
# fdisk /dev/hda
Command (m for help): p
Disk /dev/hda: 255 heads, 63 sectors, 1027 cylinders
Units = cylinders of 16065 * 512 bytes
   Device Boot   Start    End    Blocks   Id  System
/dev/hda1    *       1    250   2008093+   83  Linux
/dev/hda2          251    280    240975    82  Linux swap
/dev/hda3          281   1027   6000277+    5  Extended
/dev/hda5          281    293    104391    83  Linux
```

```
/dev/hda6              294      306    104391   83  Linux
/dev/hda7              307      319    104391   83  Linux
Command (m for help): q
#
```

In this configuration, */dev/hda* has two primary partitions, */dev/hda1*, which is bootable, and */dev/hda2*, which is the swap partition. The disk also has an extended partition */dev/hda3*, which contains three logical partitions, */dev/hda5*, */dev/hda6*, and */dev/hda7*. All other primary and logical partitions are Linux *ext2* partitions.

Example 2

Starting with a blank partition table, create a bootable primary partition of 300 MB on */dev/hda1*, the extended partition on */dev/hda2* containing the remainder of the disk, a logical partition of 200 MB on */dev/hda5*, a logical swap partition of 128 MB on */dev/hda6*, and a logical partition on */dev/hda7* occupying the remainder of the extended partition:

```
# fdisk /dev/hda
Command (m for help): n
Command action
   e   extended
   p   primary partition (1-4)p
Partition number (1-4): 1
First cylinder (1-1027, default 1): Enter
Using default value 1
Last cylinder or +size or +sizeM or +sizeK (1-1027, default 1027): +300M
Command (m for help): a
Partition number (1-4): 1
Command (m for help): n
Command action
   e   extended
   p   primary partition (1-4)e
Partition number (1-4): 2
First cylinder (40-1027, default 40): Enter
Using default value 40
Last cylinder or +size or +sizeM or +sizeK (40-1027, default 1027): Enter
Using default value 1027
Command (m for help): n
Command action
   l   logical (5 or over)
   p   primary partition (1-4)l
First cylinder (40-1027, default 40): Enter
Using default value 40
Last cylinder or +size or +sizeM or +sizeK (40-1027, default 1027): +200M
Command (m for help): n
Command action
   l   logical (5 or over)
   p   primary partition (1-4)l
First cylinder (79-1027, default 79): Enter
Using default value 79
Last cylinder or +size or +sizeM or +sizeK (79-1027, default 1027): +128M
Command (m for help): t
Partition number (1-6): 6
Hex code (type L to list codes): 82
Changed system type of partition 6 to 82 (Linux swap)
Command (m for help): n
```

```
Command action
   l   logical (5 or over)
   p   primary partition (1-4)l
First cylinder (118-1027, default 118): Enter
Using default value 118
Last cylinder or +size or +sizeM or +sizeK (118-1027, default 1027): Enter
Using default value 1027
Command (m for help): p
Disk /dev/hda: 255 heads, 63 sectors, 1027 cylinders
Units = cylinders of 16065 * 512 bytes
     Device Boot   Start     End   Blocks   Id  System
/dev/hda1    *         1      39   313236   83  Linux
/dev/hda2             40    1027  7936110    5  Extended
/dev/hda5             40      65   208813+  82  Linux swap
/dev/hda6             66      82   136521   83  Linux
/dev/hda7             83    1027  7590681   83  Linux
Command (m for help): w
The partition table has been altered!
Calling ioctl() to re-read partition table.
Syncing disks.
#
```

Note the use of defaults for the partition start cylinders and for end cylinder selections, indicated by Enter in this example. Other partition sizes are specified in megabytes using responses such as +128M.

If you are attempting to create partitions for other operating systems with the Linux *fdisk* utility, you could run into a few problems. As a rule, it is safest to prepare the partitions for an operating system using the native tools of that operating system.

As you might expect, using *fdisk* on a working system can be dangerous, because one errant *w* command can render your disk useless. Use extreme caution when working with the partition table of a working system, and be sure you know exactly what you intend to do and how to do it.

On the Exam

You should understand disk partitions and the process of creating them using *fdisk*.

Creating filesystems

Once a disk is partitioned, filesystems may be created in those partitions using the *mkfs* utility. *mkfs* is a frontend program for filesystem-specific creation tools such as *mkfs.ext2* and *mkfs.msdos*, which are in turn linked to *mke2fs* and *mkdosfs*, respectively. *mkfs* offers a unified frontend, while the links provide convenient names. The choice of which executable to call is up to you.

mkfs

Syntax

```
mkfs [-t fstype] [fs_options] device
```

Description

Make a filesystem of type *fstype* on *device*. If *fstype* is omitted, *ext2* is used by default. When called by *mkfs*, these programs are passed any *fs_options* included on the command line. It is common to see references to commands such as *mkfs.ext2*, *mkfs.ext4*, or *mkfs.xfs*. These are all aliases for mkfs, specifying a specific kind of filesystem you wish to create.

Frequently used options

-c

Check *device* for bad blocks before building the filesystem.

-L label

Set the volume label for the filesystem (ext-based filesystems only).

-n label

Set the 11-character volume label for the filesystem (*mkdosfs* only).

-q

Uses mkfs in quiet mode, resulting in very little output.

-v

Used to enter verbose mode.

-j

Create an *ext3* journal file (*mkfs.ext2* only). Using *-t ext3* or running *mkfs.ext3* has the same effect as using the *-j* option.

Example 1

Using defaults, quietly create an *ext2* partition on */dev/hda3*:

```
# mkfs -q /dev/hda3
mke2fs 1.14, 9-Jan-1999 for EXT2 FS 0.5b, 95/08/09
#
```

Example 2

Create an *ext2* filesystem labeled *rootfs* on existing partition */dev/hda3*, checking for bad blocks and with full verbose output:

```
# mkfs -t ext2 -L rootfs -cv /dev/hda3
mke2fs 1.27 (8-Mar-2002)
Filesystem label=rootfs
OS type: Linux
Block size=1024 (log=0)
Fragment size=1024 (log=0)
26208 inodes, 104422 blocks
5221 blocks (5.00%) reserved for the super user
First data block=1
13 block groups
8192 blocks per group, 8192 fragments per group
```

```
2016 inodes per group
Superblock backups stored on blocks:
        8193, 16385, 24577, 32769, 40961, 49153,
        57345, 65537, 73729, 81921, 90113, 98305
Running command: badblocks -b 1024 -s /dev/hda3 104422
Checking for bad blocks (read-only test): done
Writing inode tables: done
Writing superblocks and filesystem accounting information: done
This filesystem will be automatically checked every 28 mounts or
180 days, whichever comes first.  Use tune2fs -c or -i to override.
```

Additional options are available in the *mke2fs* and *mkdosfs* programs, which may be needed to fine-tune specific filesystem parameters for special situations. In most cases, the default parameters are appropriate and adequate.

Creating swap partitions

Swap partitions are necessary if you want your Linux system to have access to virtual memory. Virtual memory is a section of the hard disk designated for use as memory when the main system memory (the RAM) is all in use. The common formula for determining the amount of swap space you need has usually been twice the amount of RAM your system has. Although swap is not required by Linux, at least 128 MB is recommended for some spooling functions. On the other hand, memory-intensive applications may recommend much more, based on variables such as the number of users, database tables/sizes, or other application configuration guidelines. It is important to know what the system will be used for when considering swap space.

The command to create a swap partition is *mkswap*. This command prepares a partition for use as Linux swap space and is needed if you plan to fully configure a disk from scratch. It is also required if you need to add an additional swap partition.

mkswap

Syntax

```
mkswap device
```

Description

Prepare a partition for use as swap space. This command can also set up swap space in a file on another filesystem.

Example

On an existing partition, which should be set to type 82 (Linux swap), ready swap space:

```
# mkswap /dev/hda5
Setting up swapspace version 1, size = 139792384 bytes
#
```

Running any of the filesystem creation programs is, like *fdisk*, potentially dangerous. All data in any previously existing filesystems in the specified partition will be deleted. Since *mkfs* does not warn you prior to creating the filesystem, be certain that you are operating on the correct partition.

On the Exam

The exam is likely to contain general questions about using *mkfs* and *mkswap*, although details such as inode allocation are beyond the scope of the LPIC Level 1 exams.

Objective 2: Maintain the Integrity of Filesystems

Over the course of time, active filesystems can develop problems, such as:

- A filesystem fills to capacity, causing programs or perhaps the entire system to fail.
- A filesystem is corrupted, perhaps due to a power failure or system crash.
- A filesystem runs out of inodes, meaning that new filesystem objects cannot be created.

Carefully monitoring and checking Linux filesystems on a regular basis can help prevent and correct these types of problems.

Monitoring Free Disk Space and Inodes

A read/write filesystem isn't much good if it grows to the point where it won't accept any more files. This could happen if the filesystem fills to capacity or runs out of *inodes*.

Inodes are the data structures within filesystems that describe files on disk. Every filesystem contains a finite number of inodes, set when the filesystem is created. This number is also the maximum number of files that the filesystem can accommodate. Because filesystems are created with a huge number of inodes, you'll probably never create as many files as it would take to run out of inodes. However, it is possible to run out of inodes if a partition contains many small files.

It is important to prevent space and inode shortages from occurring on system partitions. The *df* command gives you the information you need on the status of both disk space utilization and inode utilization.

---

df

Syntax

```
df [options] [file [file...]]
```

Description

Display overall disk utilization information for mounted filesystems on *file*. Usually, *file* is a device file for a partition, such as */dev/hda1*. The *file* may also be the mount point or any file beneath the mount point. If *file* is omitted, information for mounted filesystems on all devices in */etc/fstab* are displayed.

Frequently used options

-*h*

> Displays results in a human-readable format, including suffixes such as M (megabytes) and G (gigabytes).

-*i*

> Displays information on remaining inodes rather than the default disk space information.

Example 1

Check disk space utilization on all filesystems:

```
# df -h
Filesystem       Size  Used Avail Use% Mounted on
/dev/sda1        387M   56M  311M  15% /
/dev/sda5        296M  5.2M  276M   2% /boot
/dev/sda9        1.9G  406M  1.4G  22% /home
/dev/sda6         53M   12M   39M  23% /root
/dev/sda10        99M  104k   93M   0% /tmp
/dev/sda8        972M  507M  414M  55% /usr
/dev/sda7        296M  9.3M  272M   3% /var
```

This example shows that of the seven filesystems mounted by default, none exceeds 55 percent capacity.

Example 2

Check the same filesystems for inode utilization:

```
# df -i
Filesystem       Inodes   IUsed   IFree IUse% Mounted on
/dev/sda1        102800    7062   95738   7% /
/dev/sda5         78312      29   78283   0% /boot
/dev/sda9        514000     934  513066   0% /home
/dev/sda6         14056     641   13415   5% /root
/dev/sda10        26104      60   26044   0% /tmp
/dev/sda8        257040   36700  220340  14% /usr
/dev/sda7         78312     269   78043   0% /var
```

Among these partitions, the largest consumption of inodes is a mere 14 percent. It is clear that none of the filesystems is anywhere near consuming the maximum number of inodes available. Note that the */usr* partition (with 14 percent of inodes used) has used 55 percent of the disk space. With utilization like this, the */usr* volume will most likely fill to capacity long before the inodes are exhausted.

Example 3

Quickly determine which partition the current working directory (represented simply by a single dot) is located:

```
# df .
Filesystem          1k-blocks     Used Available Use% Mounted on
/dev/sda1             102800       7062    95738   7% /
```

When a filesystem is nearing capacity, files may simply be deleted to make additional space available. However, in the rare case in which an inode shortage occurs, the filesystem must be recreated with a larger number of inodes unless a significant number of files can be deleted.

Monitoring Disk Usage

Have you ever found yourself wondering, "Where did all the disk space go?" Some operating systems make answering this question surprisingly difficult using only native tools. On Linux, the *du* command can help display disk utilization information on a per-directory basis and perhaps answer that question. *du* recursively examines directories and reports detailed or summarized information on the amount of space consumed.

du

Syntax

```
du [options] [directories]
```

Description

Display disk utilization information for *directories*. If *directories* are omitted, the current working directory is searched.

Frequently used options

-a

Shows all files, not just directories.

-c

Produces a grand total for all listed items.

-h

Displays results in a human-readable format, including suffixes such as M (megabytes) and G (gigabytes).

-s

Prints a summary for each of the *directories* specified, instead of totals for each subdirectory found recursively.

-S

Excludes subdirectories from counts and totals, limiting totals to *directories*.

Example 1

Examine disk utilization in */etc/rc.d*:

```
# du /etc/rc.d
882     /etc/rc.d/init.d
1       /etc/rc.d/rc0.d
1       /etc/rc.d/rc1.d
```

```
1      /etc/rc.d/rc2.d
1      /etc/rc.d/rc3.d
1      /etc/rc.d/rc4.d
1      /etc/rc.d/rc5.d
1      /etc/rc.d/rc6.d
904    /etc/rc.d
```

Example 2

Display utilization by files in */etc*, including subdirectories beneath it:

```
# du -s /etc
13002   /etc
```

Example 3

Display utilization by files in */etc*, but not in subdirectories beneath it:

```
# du -Ss /etc
1732    /etc
```

Example 4

Show a summary of all subdirectories under */home*, with human-readable output:

```
# du -csh /home/*
42k     /home/bsmith
1.5M    /home/httpd
9.5M    /home/jdean
42k     /home/jdoe
12k     /home/lost+found
1.0k    /home/samba
11M     total
```

This result shows that 11 MB of total disk space is used.

Example 5

Show the same summary, but sort the results to display in order of largest to smallest disk utilization:

```
# du -cs /home/* | sort -nr
11386   total
9772    jdean
1517    httpd
42      jdoe
42      bsmith
12      lost+found
1       samba
```

This result shows that user *jdean* is consuming the largest amount of space. Note that the human-readable format does not sort in this way, since *sort* is unaware of the human-readable size specifications.

Modifying a Filesystem

There are many cases where an administrator might want to make changes to an existing filesystem. For example, if the purpose of a particular filesystem changes, the volume label should be changed to match. This and many other *ext2* filesystem settings can be viewed and modified using the *tune2fs* command.

tune2fs

Syntax

```
tune2fs [options] device
```

Description

Modify tunable parameters on the *ext2* or *ext3* filesystem on *device*.

Frequently used options

-l device
> List the tunable parameters on *device*.

-c n
> Set the maximum mount count to *n*. When the filesystem has been mounted this many times, the kernel will warn that the filesystem has exceeded the maximum mount count when the filesystem is mounted, and *e2fsck* will automatically check the filesystem. See the discussion of *e2fsck* in the next section, "Checking and Repairing Filesystems" on page 157.
>
> Setting this value to 0 tells the kernel and *e2fsck* to ignore the mount count.

-i n
> Set the maximum time between two filesystem checks to *n*. If *n* is a number or is followed by d, the value is in days. A value followed by w specifies weeks. A value followed by m specifies months.
>
> The time since the last filesystem check is compared to this value by the kernel and *e2fsck -p*, much like the maximum mount count. A value of 0 disables this check.

-L label
> Sets the volume label of the filesystem to *label*. The volume label can also be set with the *e2label* command.

-j
> Adds an *ext3* journal file to the filesystem and sets the has_journal feature flag.

-m n
> Sets the reserved block percentage to *n*. By default, *ext2* filesystems reserve 5 percent of the total number of available blocks for the *root* user. This means that if a filesystem is more than 95 percent full, only *root* can write to it. (It also means that *df* will report the filesystem as 100 percent full when it is really only 95 percent full.)
>
> On very large filesystems, or filesystems where only user data will be written, the reserved block percentage can be safely reduced to make more of the filesystem available for writing by regular users.

-r n
> Sets the number of reserved blocks to *n*. This is similar to the *-m* option, except it specifies a number instead of a percentage.

Example 1

List the contents of the superblock on /dev/sda1:

```
# tune2fs -l /dev/sda1
tune2fs 1.41.4 (27-Jan-2009)
Filesystem volume name:   /boot
Last mounted on:          <not available>
Filesystem UUID:          35f8a3e0-9257-4b71-913d-407bef4eeb90
Filesystem magic number:  0xEF53
Filesystem revision #:    1 (dynamic)
Filesystem features:      has_journal ext_attr resize_inode \
                              dir_index filetype needs_recovery sparse_super
Filesystem flags:         signed_directory_hash
Default mount options:    user_xattr acl
Filesystem state:         clean
Errors behavior:          Continue
Filesystem OS type:       Linux
Inode count:              50200
Block count:              200780
Reserved block count:     10039
Free blocks:              158854
Free inodes:              50152
First block:              1
Block size:               1024
Fragment size:            1024
Reserved GDT blocks:      256
Blocks per group:         8192
Fragments per group:      8192
Inodes per group:         2008
Inode blocks per group:   251
Filesystem created:       Mon Dec 15 14:43:58 2008
Last mount time:          Fri Jul 24 10:25:08 2009
Last write time:          Fri Jul 24 10:25:08 2009
Mount count:              23
Maximum mount count:      20
Last checked:             Mon Dec 15 14:43:58 2008
Check interval:           31536000 (12 months, 5 days)
Reserved blocks uid:      0 (user root)
Reserved blocks gid:      0 (group root)
First inode:              11
Inode size:               128
Journal inode:            8
Default directory hash:   half_md4
Directory Hash Seed:      92b218b8-9e1f-4aab-b481-08bec3ea2946
Journal backup:           inode blocks
```

Example 2

Turn off the maximum mount count and check interval tests on /dev/sda1:

```
# tune2fs -i 0 -c 0 /dev/sda1
tune2fs 1.41.4 (27-Jan-2009)
Setting maximal mount count to -1
Setting interval between checks to 0 seconds
```

xfs_info

Syntax

```
xfs_info device
```

Description

XFS is a filesystem type that was originally designed for use on the IRIX operating system. It has been ported to Linux and is a popular choice among Linux users for its large filesystem capacity and robust feature set. The *xfs_info* program will print out information about the XFS partition.

Examples

Create an XFS filesystem on */dev/sdb1*:

```
# mkfs.xfs -q /dev/sdb1
```

Query the filesystem for information:

```
# xfs_info /dev/sdb1
meta-data=/dev/sdb1          isize=256    agcount=4, agsize=490108 blks
         =                   sectsz=512   attr=2
data     =                   bsize=4096   blocks=1960432, imaxpct=25
         =                   sunit=0      swidth=0 blks
naming   =version 2          bsize=4096   ascii-ci=0
log      =internal           bsize=4096   blocks=2560, version=2
         =                   sectsz=512   sunit=0 blks, lazy-count=0
realtime =none               extsz=4096   blocks=0, rtextents=0
```

Checking and Repairing Filesystems

No matter how stable, computers do fail, even due to something as simple as a power cable being accidentally unplugged. Unfortunately, such an interruption can make a mess of a filesystem. If a disk write operation is aborted before it completes, the data in transit could be lost, and the portions of the disk that were allocated for it are left marked as used. In addition, filesystem writes are cached in memory, and a power loss or other crash prevents the kernel from synchronizing the cache with the disk. Both of these scenarios lead to inconsistencies in the filesystem and must be corrected to ensure reliable operation.

Filesystems are checked with *fsck*. Like *mkfs*, *fsck* is a frontend to filesystem-specific utilities, including *fsck.ext2*, which is a link to the *e2fsck* program. (See its manpage for detailed information.)

 e2fsck can also check *ext3* filesystems. When it finds an *ext3* filesystem that was not cleanly unmounted, it first commits the journal, then checks the filesystem as it normally would with *ext2*.

Part of the information written on disk to describe a filesystem is known as the *superblock*, written in block 1 of the partition. If this area of the disk is corrupted, the filesystem is inaccessible. Because the superblock is so important, copies of it are made in the filesystem at regular intervals, by default every 8192 blocks. The first superblock copy is located at block 8193, the second copy is at block 16385, and so on. As you'll see, *fsck* can use the information in the superblock copies to restore the main superblock.

fsck

Syntax

```
fsck [options] [-t type] [fs-options] filesystems
```

Description

Check *filesystems* for errors and optionally correct them. By default, *fsck* assumes the *ext2* filesystem type and runs interactively, pausing to ask for permission before applying fixes.

Frequently used options for fsck

-A

> Run checks on all filesystems specified in */etc/fstab*. This option is intended for use at boot time, before filesystems are mounted.

-N

> Don't execute, but show what would be done.

-t type

> Specify the type of filesystem to check; the default is *ext2*. The value of *type* determines which filesystem-specific checker is called.

Frequently used options for e2fsck

-b superblock

> Use an alternative copy of the superblock. In interactive mode, *e2fsck* automatically uses alternative superblocks. Typically, you'll try **-b 8193** in noninteractive mode to restore a bad superblock.

-c

> Check for bad blocks.

-f

> Force a check, even if the filesystem looks clean.

-p

> Automatically repair the filesystem without prompting.

-y

> Answers "yes" to all interactive prompts, allowing *e2fsck* to be used noninteractively.

Example 1

Check the *ext3* filesystem on */dev/sda1*, which is not mounted:

```
# fsck /dev/sda1
fsck 1.41.4 (27-Jan-2009)
```

```
e2fsck 1.41.4 (27-Jan-2009)
/boot: clean, 48/50200 files, 41926/200780 blocks
```

The partition was clean, so *fsck* didn't really check it.

Example 2

Force a check:

```
# fsck -f /dev/sda1
fsck 1.41.4 (27-Jan-2009)
e2fsck 1.41.4 (27-Jan-2009)
Pass 1: Checking inodes, blocks, and sizes
Pass 2: Checking directory structure
Pass 3: Checking directory connectivity
Pass 4: Checking reference counts
Pass 5: Checking group summary information
/boot: 48/50200 files (22.9% non-contiguous), 41926/200780 blocks
```

Example 3

Force another check, this time with verbose output:

```
# fsck -fv /dev/sda1
fsck 1.41.4 (27-Jan-2009)
e2fsck 1.41.4 (27-Jan-2009)
Pass 1: Checking inodes, blocks, and sizes
Pass 2: Checking directory structure
Pass 3: Checking directory connectivity
Pass 4: Checking reference counts
Pass 5: Checking group summary information

       48 inodes used (0.10%)
       11 non-contiguous files (22.9%)
        0 non-contiguous directories (0.0%)
          # of inodes with ind/dind/tind blocks: 22/12/0
    41926 blocks used (20.88%)
        0 bad blocks
        0 large files

       32 regular files
        6 directories
        0 character device files
        0 block device files
        0 fifos
        0 links
        1 symbolic link (1 fast symbolic link)
        0 sockets
--------
       39 files
```

Example 4

Allow *fsck* to automatically perform all repairs on a damaged filesystem by specifying the *-y* option to run the command automatically:

```
# fsck -y /dev/sda1
fsck 1.41.4 (27-Jan-2009)
```

Devices, Filesystems, FHS

```
e2fsck 1.41.4 (27-Jan-2009)
Couldn't find ext2 superblock, trying backup blocks...
/dev/sda1 was not cleanly unmounted, check forced.
Pass 1: Checking inodes, blocks, and sizes
Pass 2: Checking directory structure
Pass 3: Checking directory connectivity
Pass 4: Checking reference counts
Pass 5: Checking group summary information
Block bitmap differences:  +1 +2 +3 +4
Fix? yes
Inode bitmap differences:  +1 +2 +3 +4 +5 +6
Fix? yes
/dev/sda1: ***** FILE SYSTEM WAS MODIFIED *****
/dev/sda1: 1011/34136 files (0.1% non-contiguous), 4360/136521 blocks
```

When Linux boots, the kernel performs a check of all filesystems in */etc/fstab* using the *-A* option to *fsck* (unless the */etc/fstab* entry contains the *noauto* option). Any filesystems that were not cleanly unmounted are checked. If that check finds any significant errors, the system drops into single-user mode so you can run *fsck* manually. Unfortunately, unless you have detailed knowledge of the inner workings of the filesystem, there's little you can do other than to have *fsck* perform all of the repairs. As a result, it is common to use the *-y* option and hope for the best.

In some cases, a filesystem may be beyond repair or may even trigger a bug in *e2fsck*. In these (thankfully *very* rare) situations, there are a few commands that can help an *ext2* filesystem wizard debug the problem. These commands are *e2image*, *dumpe2fs*, and *debugfs*. For more information on these tools, read their appropriate manpages.

xfs_metadump

Syntax

```
xfs_metadump [options] device
```

Description

xfs_metadump is a debugging tool that copies the metadata from an XFS filesystem to a file. This is useful as a debugging tool when you suspect filesystem problems, or as a backup tool. Images created by *xfs_metadump* can be restored to a filesystem using the command *xfs_mdrestore*.

Frequently used options

-e

Stops the dump on a read error. Normally, it will ignore read errors and copy all the metadata that is accessible.

-g

Shows dump progress.

-w

Prints warnings of inconsistent metadata to *stderr*. Bad metadata is still copied.

Objective 3: Control Filesystem Mounting and Unmounting

As discussed in "Objective 1: Create Partitions and Filesystems" on page 140, the Linux directory hierarchy is usually made up of multiple partitions, each joined to the root filesystem. Filesystems on removable media, such as CD-ROMs, USB flash drives, and floppy disks, are joined in the same way, but usually on a temporary basis. Each of these separate filesystems is *mounted* to the parent filesystem as a directory (or *mount point*) in the unified hierarchy.

Directories intended as mount points usually don't contain files or other directories. Instead, they're just empty directories created solely to mount a filesystem. If a directory that already contains files is used as a mount point, its files are obscured and unavailable until the filesystem is unmounted. Typical mount points include the directories */usr*, */home*, */var*, and others.

Managing the Filesystem Table

Since the Linux filesystem hierarchy is spread across separate partitions and/or multiple drives, it is necessary to automatically mount those filesystems at boot time. In addition, removable media and filesystems on remote NFS servers may be used regularly with recurring mount properties. All of this information is recorded in the */etc/fstab* file. Filesystems defined in this file are checked and mounted when the system boots. Entries in this file are consulted for default information when users wish to mount removable media.

The */etc/fstab* file (see Example 7-1) is plain text and consists of lines with six fields:

Device
> This field specifies the device file of the partition holding the filesystem (for example, */dev/hda1*). This may either be the device name (like */dev/hda1*), the UUID of the device (like *UUID=35f8a3e0-9257-4b71-913d-407bef4eeb90*), or the partition label (like *LABEL=/boot*).

Mount point
> This field specifies the directory on which the filesystem is to be mounted. For example, if */dev/hda1* contains the root filesystem, it is mounted at /. The root filesystem will contain additional directories intended as mount points for other filesystems. For example, */boot* may be an empty directory intended to mount the filesystem that contains kernel images and other information required at boot time.

Filesystem type
> Next, the type of filesystem is specified. These may include *ext2* filesystems, *swap*, *nfs*, *iso9660* (CD-ROM), and others.

Mount options

This field contains a comma-separated list of options. Some options are specific to particular filesystem types. Options are described later in this Objective.

Dump frequency

The *dump* program, a standard Unix backup utility, will consult */etc/fstab* for information on how often to dump each filesystem. This field holds an integer, usually set to 1 for native Linux filesystems such as *ext2*, and to 0 for others.

Pass number for fsck

This field is used by the *fsck* utility when the *-A* option is specified, usually at boot time. It is a flag that may contain only the values 0, 1, or 2.

- A 1 should be entered for the root filesystem and instructs *fsck* to check that filesystem first.

- A 2 instructs *fsck* to check corresponding filesystems after those with a 1.

- A 0 instructs *fsck* not to check the filesystem.

Example 7-1. Sample /etc/fstab file

```
/dev/sda1     /              ext2      defaults         1 1
/dev/sda5     /boot          ext2      defaults         1 2
/dev/sda9     /home          ext2      defaults         1 2
/dev/sda6     /root          ext2      defaults         1 2
/dev/sda10    /tmp           ext2      defaults         1 2
/dev/sda8     /usr           ext2      defaults         1 2
/dev/sda7     /var           ext2      defaults         1 2
/dev/sda11    swap           swap      defaults         0 0
/dev/fd0      /mnt/floppy    ext2      noauto,users     0 0
/dev/hdc      /mnt/cdrom     iso9660   noauto,ro,users  0 0
/dev/hdd      /mnt/zip       vfat      noauto,users     0 0
fs1:/share    /fs1           nfs       defaults         0 0
```

The *fstab* in Example 7-1 depicts a system with a single SCSI disk, */dev/sda*. The first partition, */dev/sda1*, contains an *ext2* root filesystem. Partition */dev/sda11* is swap. Partitions */dev/sda5* through */dev/sda10* contain *ext2* filesystems for */boot*, */home*, */root*, */tmp*, */usr*, and */var*, respectively. All of the local *ext2* partitions are to be checked by *fsck* and dumped. Entries for the floppy disk (*/dev/fd0*), CD-ROM (*/dev/hdc*), and IDE Zip drive (*/dev/hdd*) hold appropriate mount properties, making manual mounting of these devices simple. Finally, this example shows a remote NFS mount of directory */share* of system fs1. It is mounted locally at */fs1*.

The */etc/fstab* file is automatically created when Linux is installed and is based on the partitioning and mount point configuration specified. This file can be changed at any time to add devices and options, tailoring the filesystem to meet your specific needs.

On the Exam

You should memorize the functions of each column in */etc/fstab* and be prepared to answer questions on each.

Mounting Filesystems

Filesystems are mounted using the *mount* command. At boot time, those filesystems with a nonzero pass number in */etc/fstab* are checked and automatically mounted. Later, you can run *mount* manually to add other filesystems to the filesystem hierarchy.

mount

Syntax

```
mount [options] device
mount [options] directory
mount [options] device directory
```

Description

Used to mount filesystems into the filesystem hierarchy. The first and second forms consult */etc/fstab* and mount the filesystem located on **device** or intended to be attached to **directory**, respectively. In both cases, information necessary to complete the mount operation is taken from */etc/fstab*. The third form is independent of */etc/fstab* and mounts the filesystem on **device** at mount point **directory**.

The *mount* command accepts two kinds of options: *command-line* and *mount*. The command-line options provide general direction for the *mount* command. The mount options are used to specify additional information about the device being mounted.

Command-line options

-a
  Mounts all of the partitions specified in */etc/fstab*, except those with the noauto option.

-h
  Displays help on the *mount* command.

-o mount_options
  Specifies mount options on the command line.

-r
  Mounts the filesystem as read-only.

-t fstype
  Specifies that the filesystem to be mounted is of type **fstype**. This option is typically used interactively when no entry for the mount exists in */etc/fstab*.

-v
  Sets verbose mode.

-w
  Mounts the filesystem in read/write mode.

Mount options

A number of parameters are available as options for mounting filesystems. These options may be specified in */etc/fstab* or as arguments of the *-o* command-line *mount* argument. These options modify the way *mount* configures the mounted filesystem. Some of the options can provide added security by controlling some operations on the filesystem. Others protect the filesystem from damage. Here is a partial list:

async

> Establishes asynchronous I/O to the mounted filesystem. The opposite is *sync*.

auto

> Enables a mount specification in */etc/fstab* to be processed with the *-a* command-line option, as needed at boot time. The opposite is *noauto*.

defaults

> Implies *rw*, *suid*, *dev*, *exec*, *auto*, *nouser*, and *async*. It is commonly found on */etc/fstab* entries for *ext2* and *ext3* mount points.

dev

> Interprets character or block special devices on the filesystem.

exec

> Enables the execution of programs contained on the mounted partition. The opposite is *noexec*.

noauto

> Prohibits automatic mounting with the *-a* option. This is usually specified for removable media.

noexec

> Prohibits the execution of executable programs, a potential security measure.

nosuid

> Disables the effect of suid or sgid bits on executable files.

nouser

> Forbids nonroot users from mounting and unmounting the filesystem. See *user* and *users* for the opposite effect.

ro

> Equivalent to specifying the command-line option *-r*.

rw

> Equivalent to specifying the command-line option *-w*.

suid

> Enables the effect of suid and sgid bits on executable files.

sync

> Establishes synchronous I/O to the mounted filesystem. The opposite is *async*.

user

> Allows an ordinary user to mount the filesystem but prohibits other ordinary users from unmounting it. This is useful for removable media that an individual requires control over. See also *users*.

users

> Allows any user to mount and unmount the filesystem.

Note that the *user* and *users* options make the *mount* and *umount* commands available to nonroot users. This may be important for some systems where end users must have the ability to mount removable media.

The prevalence of removable media such as USB flash drives has caused the majority of Linux distributions to be configured by default to mount these devices automatically when they are plugged into a USB port. These devices are usually mounted under the directory */media* and are given a directory name that matches the label name of the partition. For example, if the partition on my USB flash drive is labeled "USBDISK", it will be automatically mounted under the directory */media/USBDISK* when I plug it into a USB slot. Although the device is mounted automatically, there is no way to *unmount* it automatically, and you must be careful of potential data loss if you remove a device like this before Linux is done writing data to it. The *umount* command (described later in this chapter) is required in order to detach this device from the filesystem, flush all pending disk writes, and allow it to be safely removed. Most Linux distributions also have some sort of GUI tool to handle the unmounting of removable media.

Filesystem types

When mounting a filesystem, the *filesystem type* should be specified either by using the *-t* option to *mount* or in the third field in */etc/fstab*. (If *-t* is omitted or *auto* is specified, the kernel will attempt to probe for the filesystem type. This can be convenient for removable media, where the filesystem type may not always be the same or even known.) Linux can mount a variety of filesystems. The following are some of the more popular ones:

ext2
> The standard Linux filesystem.

ext3
> A journaling filesystem that is backward-compatible with *ext2*.

msdos
> The MS-DOS FAT filesystem, limited to "8.3" filenames (eight characters, a dot, and a three-character extension).

vfat
> Virtual FAT, used instead of *msdos* when long filenames must be preserved. For example, you may wish to have access to Windows partitions on systems configured to boot both Linux and Windows.

ntfs
> The native MS Windows partition since Windows 2000.

iso9660
> The CD-ROM format.

nfs
> Remote servers.

swap
> Swap partitions.

proc
> This type represents the *proc* filesystem, which is not really a filesystem at all. The virtual files found in this virtual filesystem provide a window into the kernel. It is usually mounted on */proc*.

Example 1

Display filesystems currently mounted on the system:

```
# mount
/dev/sda1 on / type ext2 (rw)
```

```
none on /proc type proc (rw)
/dev/sda5 on /boot type ext2 (rw)
/dev/sda9 on /home type ext2 (rw)
/dev/sda6 on /root type ext2 (rw)
/dev/sda10 on /tmp type ext2 (rw)
/dev/sda8 on /usr type ext2 (rw)
/dev/sda7 on /var type ext2 (rw)
none on /dev/pts type devpts (rw,mode=0622)
/dev/hdd on /mnt/zip type vfat (rw,noexec,nosuid,nodev)
```

In this example, you can see that most of the filesystems specified in the */etc/fstab* from Example 7-1 are already mounted.

Example 2

Mount the IDE CD-ROM device found on */dev/hdc* to the existing directory */mnt/cdrom* (read-only, of course):

```
# mount -rt iso9660 /dev/hdc /mnt/cdrom
```

Note that without the *-r* option, you will receive a warning but still get appropriate results:

```
# mount -t iso9660 /dev/hdc /mnt/cdrom
mount: block device /dev/hdc is write-protected,
mounting read-only
```

Another option would be to add the following to */etc/fstab*:

```
/dev/hdc   /mnt/cdrom   iso9660   ro   0 0
```

Then the device can be mounted with just `mount /mnt/cdrom`.

Example 3

Mount an MS-DOS floppy in the first floppy disk drive */dev/fd0* (A: in MS-DOS) to the existing directory */mnt/floppy*:

```
# mount -t msdos /dev/fd0 /mnt/floppy
```

Example 4

The filesystems mounted at */home* and */opt* have been unmounted for some kind of maintenance and are now remounted using the *-a* option:

```
# mount -av
mount: /dev/hda5 already mounted on /root
mount: /dev/hda9 already mounted on /usr
mount: /dev/hda7 already mounted on /var
mount: none already mounted on /proc
mount: none already mounted on /dev/pts
/dev/hda10 on /home type ext2 (rw)
/dev/hda8 on /opt type ext2 (rw)
```

Note that *mount* should work silently without the *-v* option. It also safely skips filesystems that have been previously mounted.

Unmounting Filesystems

Filesystems can be unmounted using the *umount* command. When a filesystem is unmounted, the buffers of the filesystem are synchronized with the actual contents on disk and the filesystem is made unavailable, freeing the mount point. If the filesystem is busy, *umount* yields an error. This will happen, for example, when the filesystem contains open files or when a process has a working directory within the filesystem. Other less obvious errors can occur when removable media are exchanged without being unmounted first.

umount

Syntax

```
umount [options] device
umount [options] directory
```

Description

Unmount the filesystem on *device* or mounted on *directory*.

-a

Unmounts all of the filesystems described in */etc/mtab*. This file is maintained by the *mount* and *umount* commands and contains an up-to-date list of mounted filesystems. This option is typically used at shutdown time.

-t fstype

Unmounts only filesystems of type *fstype*.

Example 1

Unmount the CD-ROM mounted on */dev/hdc* at */mnt/cdrom*:

```
# umount /mnt/cdrom
```

or:

```
# umount /dev/hdc
```

Example 2

Unmount all NFS filesystems:

```
# umount -at nfs
```

On the Exam

Be sure that you understand how to use *mount* and mount points and how */etc/fstab* is used when mounting files.

Objective 4: Set and View Disk Quotas

Managing disk space can be a difficult problem. The available space is a finite resource and is often consumed at an alarming rate, turning today's carefully sized filesystem into tomorrow's expansion requirement. On multiuser systems—no matter how big the filesystem—users will find a way to fill it. The last thing you want is for a filesystem to fill to capacity too early. One way to prevent this from happening is to enforce *disk quotas*, which allow you to assign a limit to the amount of space individual users or groups have on a filesystem.

A typical quota size is usually much smaller than the filesystem it is configured on, thus preventing the user or group from consuming too much space. Quotas can be configured for each filesystem mentioned in */etc/fstab*, though they are usually applied only where multiple end users store files (e.g., */home/username*). There is no need for a quota on */usr*, for example, since end users cannot store files there. Quotas may be configured for individual users listed in */etc/passwd* and for groups listed in */etc/group*.

Quota Limits

Each filesystem has up to five types of quota limits that can be enforced on it. These limits are specified in disk *blocks*, usually 1,024 bytes each:

Per-user hard limit
> The *hard limit* is the maximum amount of space an individual user can have on the system. Once the user reaches his quota limit, he won't be allowed to write files to the disk.

Per-user soft limit
> Each user is free to store data on the filesystem until reaching her *soft limit*. The soft limit implements a sort of warning zone, instructing the user to clean up while still allowing her to work. When the amount of data exceeds this limit but does not exceed the hard limit, a message is printed on the user's terminal, indicating that her quota has been exceeded; however, the write operation will succeed.

Per-group hard limit
> This is the final limit set for a group by the quota system. Once this limit has been reached, none of the users within that group will be allowed to write files to the disk—even if the user's individual limits are not exceeded.

Per-group soft limit
> This limit behaves in the same way as a user's soft limit but is enforced based on group ownership instead of individual ownership.

Grace period
> Once a soft limit is reached, the user or group enters the *grace period*. After the grace period expires, the soft limit becomes a hard limit until enough files are deleted to eliminate the over-quota situation. The grace period may be specified for any number of months, weeks, days, hours, minutes, or seconds. A typical value is seven days.

These limits are set using the *edquota* command, detailed in the next section.

When a disk write exceeds a hard limit or an expired soft limit, only part of the write operation will complete, leaving a truncated and probably useless file. The messages reported to the user when a quota is exceeded may be lost if the shell he is using is hidden (for example, if the user is writing to the disk through an SMB share from a Windows system). This could confuse the user because the error message generated by the application indicates that the disk is full or write-protected.

Quota Commands

Linux offers a host of commands to manage, display, and report on filesystem quotas. Some of the setup required to initially enable quotas is done manually and without specific quota commands, a process that is covered in the next section.

quota

Syntax

```
quota [-u] [options] user
quota -g [options] group
```

Description

Displays quota limits on *user* or *group*. The *-u* option is the default. Only the superuser may use the *-u* flag and *user* to view the limits of other users. Other users can use the *-g* flag and *group* to view only the limits of groups of which they are members, provided that the *quota.group* files are readable by them.

Frequently used options

-q

Sets quiet mode, which shows only over-quota situations.

-v

Enables verbose mode to display quotas even if no storage space is allocated.

Example 1

As *root*, examine all quotas for user *jdoe*:

```
# quota -uv jdoe
Disk quotas for user jdoe (uid 500):
Filesystem  blks  quota limit grace  files quota limit grace
/dev/sda9   9456  10000 10200         32    0    0
/dev/hda1    23      0     0          17    0    0
```

This example shows that *jdoe* is barely within her soft limit of 10,000 blocks, with a corresponding hard limit of 10,200 blocks on */dev/sda9*, and has no quota on */dev/hda1*. The entry for */dev/hda1* is displayed in response to the *-v* option. No values are shown for the grace periods, because the soft limit has not been exceeded.

Example 2

As user *jdoe*, examine quotas for the *finance* group, of which he is a member:

```
$ quota -gv finance
Disk quotas for group finance (gid 501):
Filesystem  blks  quota  limit grace  files quota limit grace
/dev/sda9   1000* 990    1000  6days     34  3980  4000
/dev/hda1      0    0       0            0     0     0
```

Here, the *finance* group has exceeded its meager soft limit of 990 blocks and has come up against its hard limit of 1,000 blocks. (The write operation that wrote the 1,000th block was probably incomplete.) The original grace period in this example was set to seven days and has six days remaining, meaning that one day has elapsed since the soft limit was exceeded.

quotaon

Syntax

```
quotaon [options] [filesystems]
quotaon [options] -a
```

Description

Enable previously configured disk quotas on one or more *filesystems*.

Frequently used options

-a

Turns quotas on for all filesystems in */etc/fstab* that are marked read-write with quotas. This is normally used automatically at boot time to enable quotas.

-g

Turns on group quotas. This option is not necessary when using the *-a* option, which includes both user and group quotas.

-u

Turns on user quotas; this is the default.

-v

Enables verbose mode to display a message for each filesystem where quotas are turned on.

Example 1

Turn on all quotas as defined in */etc/fstab*:

```
# quotaon -av
/dev/sda9: group quotas turned on
/dev/sda9: user quotas turned on
/dev/hda1: group quotas turned on
/dev/hda1: user quotas turned on
```

Example 2

Turn on user quotas only on the */home* filesystem:

```
# quotaon -gv /home
/dev/sda9: group quotas turned on
```

quotaoff

Syntax

```
quotaoff [options] [filesystems]
quotaoff [options] -a
```

Description

Disables disk quotas on one or more *filesystems*.

Frequently used options

-a

Turns quotas off for all filesystems in *etc/fstab*.

-g

Turns off group quotas. This option is not necessary when using the *-a* option, which includes both user and group quotas.

-u

Turns off user quotas; this is the default.

-v

Enables verbose mode to display a message for each filesystem where quotas are turned off.

Example

Turn off all quotas:

```
# quotaoff -av
/dev/sda9: group quotas turned off
/dev/sda9: user quotas turned off
/dev/hda1: group quotas turned off
/dev/hda1: user quotas turned off
```

quotacheck

Syntax

```
quotacheck [options] filesystems
quotacheck [options] -a
```

Description

Examine filesystems and compile quota databases. This command is not specifically called out in the LPI Objectives for Exam 101, but is an important component of the Linux quota system. You should run the *quotacheck -a* command on a regular basis (perhaps weekly) via *cron*.

Frequently used options

-a

Checks all of the quotas for the filesystems mentioned in *etc/fstab*. Both user and group quotas are checked as indicated by the *usrquota* and *grpquota* options.

-g group

> Compiles information only on *group*.

-u user

> Compiles information only on *user*; this is the default action. However, if the *-g* option is specified, then this option also should be specified when both group and user quotas are to be processed.

-v

> Enables verbose mode to display information about what the program is doing. This option shows activity by displaying a spinning character in the terminal. This is nice but could be a problem if you are logged in over a slow modem link.

Example 1

Initialize all quota files:

```
# quotaoff -a
# quotacheck -aguv
Scanning /dev/sda9 [/home] done
Checked 237 directories and 714 files
Using quotafile /home/quota.user
Using quotafile /home/quota.group
Scanning /dev/hda1 [/mnt/hd] done
Checked 3534 directories and 72673 files
Using quotafile /mnt/hd/quota.user
Using quotafile /mnt/hd/quota.group
# quotaon -a
```

By turning off quotas during the update, the quota database files are updated.

Example 2

With quotas active, update the user quotas in memory for */home*:

```
# quotacheck -v /home
Scanning /dev/sda9 [/home] done
Checked 237 directories and 714 files
Using quotafile /home/quota.user
Updating in-core user quotas
```

edquota

Syntax

```
edquota [-p proto-user] [options] names
edquota [options] -t
```

Description

Modify user or group quotas. This interactive command uses a text editor to configure quota parameters for users or groups. The *vi* editor is used by default unless either the EDITOR or VISUAL environment variables are set to another editor, such as *emacs*. When the command is issued, the editor is launched with a temporary file containing quota settings. When the temporary file is saved and the editor is terminated, the changes are saved in the quota databases.

In the first form, a space-separated list of users or groups specified in *names* is modified. If *proto-user* is specified with the *-p* option, quotas of that user or group are copied and used for *names* and no editor is launched. In the second form with the *-t* option, the soft limit settings are edited interactively for each filesystem.

Frequently used options

-g

> Modify group quotas. If *-g* is specified, all *names* are assumed to be groups and not users, even if *-u* is also specified.

-p proto-user

> Duplicate the quotas of the prototypical user or group *proto-user* for each user or group specified. This is the normal mechanism used to initialize quotas for multiple users or groups at the same time.

-t

> Modify soft limits. Time units of *sec*(onds), *min*(utes), *hour*(s), *day*(s), *week*(s), and *month*(s) are understood.

-u

> Modify user quotas. This is the default action. This option is ignored if *-g* is also specified.

 The following examples use the *vi* editor. The contents of the edit buffer, not program output, are shown after each example.

Example 1

Modify the user quotas for *jdoe*:

```
# edquota -u jdoe
Quotas for user jdoe:
/dev/sda9: blocks in use: 87, limits (soft = 99900, hard = 100000)
        inodes in use: 84, limits (soft = 0, hard = 0)
/dev/hda1: blocks in use: 0, limits (soft = 0, hard = 0)
        inodes in use: 0, limits (soft = 0, hard = 0)
~
~
"/tmp/EdP.auHTZJO" 5 lines, 241 characters
```

Here, *jdoe* has been allocated a soft limit of 99,900 blocks (which on a default Linux *ext2* or *ext3* filesystem with a 4k block size means 390 MB), a hard limit of 100,000 blocks (only 400 KB higher than the soft limit), and no limit on the number of files on */dev/sda9*. She has no limits on */dev/hda1*.

Example 2

Modify soft limits for users on all filesystems:

```
# edquota -tu
Time units may be: days, hours, minutes, or seconds
Grace period before enforcing soft limits for users:
/dev/sda9: block grace period: 7 days,
    file grace period: 3 days
```

Devices, Filesystems, FHS

```
/dev/hda1: block grace period: 7 days,
    file grace period: 3 days
~
~
"/tmp/EdP.aiTShJB" 5 lines, 249 characters
```

Here, the user grace periods have been set to seven days for blocks (disk space) and three days for files (inodes).

repquota

Syntax

```
repquota [options] filesystems
repquota -a [options]
```

Description

Used to report on the status of quotas. In the first form, repquota displays a summary report on the quotas for the given *filesystems* on a per-user or per-group basis. In the second form, the *-a* option causes a summary for all filesystems with quotas to be displayed. This command fails for nonroot users unless the quota database files are world-readable. The current number of files and the amount of space utilized are printed for each user, along with any quotas created with *edquota*.

Frequently used options

-a

Report on all of the quotas for the read-write filesystems mentioned in */etc/fstab*. Both user and group quotas are reported as indicated by the *usrquota* and *grpquota* options.

-g

Report quotas for groups.

-u

Report quotas for users; this is the default action.

-v

Enable verbose mode, which adds a descriptive header to the output.

Example

Report user quotas for */home*:

```
# repquota -v /home
*** Report for user quotas on /dev/sda9 (/home)
                        Block limits      File limits
User          used  soft    hard grace used soft hard grace
root      --  418941    0       0        269    0    0
328       --    1411    0       0         20    0    0
jdean     --    9818 99900  100000       334    0    0
u1        --      44    0       0         43    0    0
u2        --      44    0       0         43    0    0
u3        --     127  155     300        124    0    0
jdoe      --      87 99900  100000        84    0    0
bsmith    --      42 1990    2000         41    0    0
```

Enabling Quotas

To use quotas, they must first be enabled. Quota support must also be compiled into the kernel. In the unlikely event that your kernel does not contain quota support, you will need to recompile the kernel. This is not a difficult process, but unfortunately it is not completely straightforward either. To clarify the procedure, this section provides a brief tutorial on how to enable user and group quotas for a filesystem on */dev/sda9* mounted under */home*. Note that you may enable user quotas only, group quotas only, or both, as your needs dictate.

1. Set options in */etc/fstab*. On the line containing the */home* filesystem, add the `usrquota` and `grpquota` options to the existing `default` option, like this:

   ```
   /dev/sda9    /home    ext2    defaults,usrquota,grpquota  1  2
   ```

   These options tell quota configuration utilities which partitions should be managed when the utilities reference */etc/fstab*.

2. Create the *quota.user* and *quota.group* files at the top of the */home* filesystem and set their protection bits for root access only:

   ```
   # touch /home/quota.user /home/quota.group
   # chmod 600 /home/quota.user /home/quota.group
   ```

   These two files are the databases for user and group quotas. Each filesystem with quotas uses its own quota databases. When quotas are enabled, these files will contain binary data (that is, they're not text files). Note that if you want end users to be able to examine quotas on groups to which they belong, *quota.group* will need a protection mode of 644 instead of 600.

3. Run *quotacheck* to initialize the databases:

   ```
   # quotacheck -avug
   Scanning /dev/sda9 [/home] done
   Checked 236 directories and 695 files
   Using quotafile /home/quota.user
   Using quotafile /home/quota.group
   ```

4. Then, verify that your quota database files have been initialized by noting that they are no longer of size zero (here they are 16,192 bytes each):

   ```
   # ls -al /home/quota.*
   -rw-------  1 root  root 16192 Dec 27 19:53 /home/quota.group
   -rw-------  1 root  root 16192 Dec 27 19:53 /home/quota.user
   ```

5. Run *quotaon* to enable the quota system:

   ```
   # quotaon -a
   ```

6. Verify that your system's initialization script (*/etc/rc.d/rc.sysinit* or similar) will turn on quotas when your system boots. Something along these lines is appropriate, although your system may be very different:

   ```
   if [ -x /sbin/quotacheck ]; then
       echo "Checking quotas."
       /sbin/quotacheck -avug
       echo " Done."
   fi
   ```

```
if [ -x /sbin/quotaon ]; then
    echo "Turning on quotas."
    /sbin/quotaon -avug
fi
```

7. Add a command script to a system *crontab* directory (such as the directory */etc/crontab.weekly*) to execute *quotacheck* on a routine basis. An executable script file like the following will work:

```
#!/bin/bash
exec /sbin/quotacheck -avug
```

If you prefer, you could instead put */sbin/quotacheck* in *root*'s *crontab* file (using the *crontab -e* command) for weekly execution, like this:

```
# run quotacheck weekly
0 3 * * 0   /sbin/quotacheck -avug
```

At this point, the */home* filesystem is ready to accept quotas on a per-user and per-group basis, enforce them, and report on them.

On the Exam

A general understanding of quotas is necessary for the exam. In particular, you should know the function of each command. Also remember that quotas are set on a per-filesystem basis.

Objective 5: Manage File Permissions and Ownership

Filesystem security is a fundamental requirement for any multiuser operating system. The system's files, such as the kernel, configuration files, and programs, must be protected from accidents and tampering by unauthorized people. Users' files must be protected from modification by other users and sometimes must be kept completely private. In general, a form of *access control* must be implemented to allow secure operations.

Linux Access Control

Native Linux filesystem access control is implemented using a set of properties, maintained separately for each file. These properties are collectively called the *access mode*, or simply the *mode*, of the file. The mode is a part of the file's inode, the information retained in the filesystem that describes the file. A file's mode controls access by these three classes of users:

User
    The user who owns the file

Group
    The group that owns the file

Other
    All other users on the system

Like the mode, user and group ownership properties are a part of the inode, and both are assigned when a file is created. Usually, the owner is the user who created the file. The file's group is usually set to its creator's default group. Group ownership adds flexibility in situations in which a team shares files. The "other" users are those who aren't members of the file's group and are not the file's owner. For each of these three user classes, the access mode defines three types of permissions, which apply differently for files and directories. The permissions are listed in Table 7-2.

Table 7-2. File permissions

Permission	Mnemonic	File permission	Directory permission
Read	r	Examine the contents of the file.	List directory contents.
Write	w	Write to or change the file.	Create and remove files in the directory.
Execute	x	Run the file as a program.	Access (cd into) the directory.

These three permissions apply to the three different classes of users: *user, group*, and *other*. Each has *read, write*, and *execute* permissions, as shown in Figure 7-1.

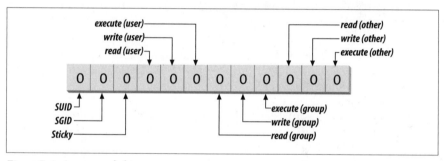

Figure 7-1. Access mode bits

All of the permissions are binary (either granted or not granted) and are thought of as single binary bits in the access mode. When displayed by commands such as *ls*, the permissions use the mnemonic in Table 7-2 for the true state and a hyphen for the false state. To represent only the read permission, for example, r-- would be used. Read and execute together, typical for directories, would be denoted r-x. These notations are usually offered in sets of three, such as:

    rw-rw-r--

A file with this setting would give read/write permission to the user and group, and read-only permission to everyone else.

In addition to the nine bits for user, group, and other, the access mode contains three more bits, which control special attributes for executable files and directories:

SUID

The SUID property is for executable files only and has no effect on directories. Normally the user who launches a program owns the resulting process. However, if an executable file has its SUID bit set, the file's owner owns the resulting process, no matter who launched it. When SUID is used, the file's owner is usually root. This offers anyone temporary root access for the duration of the command. An example of an SUID program is *passwd*. This command needs special access to manipulate the shadow password file (*/etc/shadow*), and runs as user *root*.

Using the SUID bit in cases like *passwd* enhances security by allowing access to secure functions without giving away the root password. On the other hand, SUID can be a security risk if access is granted unwisely. For example, consider a situation where */bin/vi* was set to SUID mode. Any user would be able to edit any file on the system!

SGID

The SGID property works the same way as SUID for executable files, setting the process group owner to the file's group. In addition, the SGID property has a special effect on directories. When SGID is set on a directory, new files created within that directory are assigned the same group ownership as the directory itself. For example, if directory */home/fin* has the group *finance* and has SGID enabled, then all files under */home/fin* are created with group ownership of *finance*, regardless of the creator's group. This is an important attribute for teams, ensuring that shared files all have the same group ownership.

Sticky

At one time, the *sticky bit* applied to executable programs, flagging the system to keep an image of the program in memory after the program finished running. This capability increased performance for subsequent uses by eliminating the programs' load phase, and was applied to programs that were large or were run frequently. Modern virtual memory techniques have made this use unnecessary, and under Linux there is no need to use the sticky bit on executable programs.

When applied to a directory, the sticky bit offers additional security for files within the directory. Regardless of file permissions, the only users who can rename or delete the files from a directory with the sticky bit set are the file owner, the directory owner, and *root*. When used in a team environment, the sticky bit allows groups to create and modify files but allows only file owners the privilege of deleting or renaming them. The */tmp* directory on Linux systems usually has the sticky bit set, to allow any user to write to it, but allow only the file owner to delete files or directories.

Like the other access controls, these special properties are binary and are considered bits in the access mode.

The mode bits

The *special, user, group*, and *other* permissions can be represented in a string of 12 binary bits, as shown in Figure 7-2.

It is common to refer to these bits in four sets of three, translated into four octal (base-8) digits. The first octal digit represents the special permissions SUID, SGID, and sticky. The other three represent the read, write, and execute permissions, respectively, in each of the user, group, and other user classes. Octal notation is used

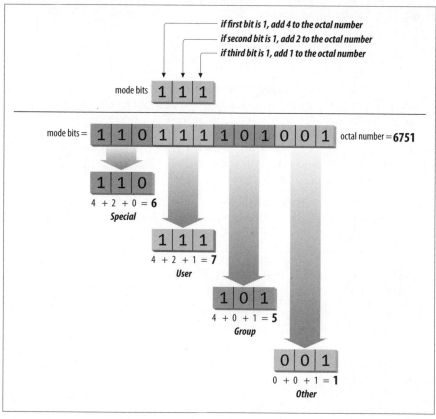

Figure 7-2. Changing permission bits to an octal number

as shorthand for binary strings such as the access mode, and each group of three bits has $2^3 = 8$ possible values, listed in Table 7-3.

The read permission by itself is `r--`, which can be thought of as binary 100, or octal 4. Adding the write permission yields `rw-`, or binary 110, which is octal 6. Figure 7-2 shows how to total bit values into the octal equivalents. Memorizing, or even writing, the binary-to-octal equivalents may be easier on the exam than adding bit values. Use the technique that works best for you.

Table 7-3. Octal numbers

Octal value	Binary equivalent
0	000
1	001
2	010
3	011
4	100
5	101

Octal value	Binary equivalent
6	110
7	111

To turn the mode bits 110111101001 into an octal representation, first separate them into chunks of three bits: 110, 111, 101, and 001. The first group, representing the special permissions, is 110. This can be thought of as 4 + 2 + 0 = 6. The second group, representing user permissions, is 111, or 4 + 2 + 1 = 7. The third group, representing group permissions, is 101, or 4 + 0 + 1 = 5. The last group, representing other permissions, is 001, or 0 + 0 + 1 = 1. The mode string for this example can then be written as the octal 6751.

This is the form used to display the file mode in the output from the *stat* command. Here, the octal access mode for the *mount* command is 4755:

```
# stat /bin/mount
  File: `/bin/mount'
  Size: 69100          Blocks: 144        IO Block: 4096    regular file
Device: fd00h/64768d   Inode: 14671934    Links: 1
Access: (4755/-rwsr-xr-x) Uid: (    0/    root)  Gid: (    0/    root)
Access: 2009-08-07 15:40:29.000000000 -0500
Modify: 2009-06-01 06:17:46.000000000 -0500
Change: 2009-06-29 14:37:58.000000000 -0500
```

The special permissions are represented in this example by octal 4, or binary 100, indicating that the SUID permission is set (-rws). The user permission is octal 7, or binary 111, indicating read, write, and execute for the file's owner (in this case, *root*). Both the group and other permissions are set to octal 5, or binary 101, indicating read and execute, but not write.

The mode string

As mentioned earlier, the user, group, and other permissions are often spelled out in symbolic mode descriptions such as rwxr-xr-x. This notation is found in the output of the *ls -l* and *stat* commands. As you can see in the access mode for *mount*, this scheme is modified slightly in the presence of special permissions. Instead of adding three more bits to the left of rwxr-xr-x, the SUID permission is indicated in the string by changing the user execute position from x to s. SGID permission is handled the same way. The sticky permission is indicated by replacing x in the other execute position with T. For example, an executable program with mode 6755 would have the following equivalent symbolic mode:

```
rwsr-sr-x
```

A directory with mode 1774 would have this equivalent string:

```
rwxr-xr-T
```

While this layering of special permissions may appear to obscure the underlying execute permissions, it makes sense. The special permissions are relatively rare in the filesystem, so depicting the three extra bits would waste space on your terminal or terminal window. When the executable bits are set, the setuid and setgid bits are represented with s. When the executable bits are not set, the setuid and setgid bits are represented with S. Similarly, the sticky bit is represented with either t or T.

Setting Access Modes

New files are created with a default access mode to automatically set the permission levels. Regardless of your default umask, access modes on existing files can be changed or modified at will.

New files

When new files are created, the protection bits are set according to the user's default setting. That default is established using the *umask* command, probably in a startup script. This command accepts only one argument, which is a three-digit octal string that masks the user, group, and other permission bits for newly created files and directories. Without a value, *umask* reports the current value:

```
$ umask
0022
```

When provided with an integer, *umask* sets the value for the current shell:

```
$ umask 2
$ umask
0002
```

A *umask* of 22 can be rewritten as 022, or as 000010010 in binary.

The process of creating the initial mode for newly created files begins with a raw initial mode string, as defined in Table 7-4.

Table 7-4. Initial access modes

Form	For files	For directories
Symbolic	rw-rw-rw-	rwxrwxrwx
Binary	110110110	111111111
Octal	666	777

The special bits are always turned off and are not masked by the *umask*. When a file is created, the *umask* is subtracted from 666; for directories, it is subtracted from 777. This calculation yields the effective protection mode for the file or directory. For example, a *umask* of 22 (022) is applied to a new file, masking the write permission for group and other user classes:

```
  110 110 110
- 000 010 010
-------------
  110 100 100
```

This is the same as mode 644, or rw-r--r--.

Using the same mask on a directory yields a similar result:

```
  111 111 111
- 000 010 010
-------------
  111 101 101
```

This is the same as mode 755, or `rwxr-xr-x`, which is appropriate for directories. A umask of 002 or 022 is typical, although if you wish to ensure maximum privacy, a umask of 077 blocks all access except for the superuser. To set a custom umask, enter the *umask* command in a startup script, such as *~/.bash_profile*. Here's an example of the *umask* in action:

```
$ umask 27
$ touch afile
$ mkdir adir
$ ls -ld adir afile
drwxr-x---  2 jdean    jdean        1024 Jan  2 20:31 adir
-rw-r-----  1 jdean    jdean           0 Jan  2 20:31 afile
```

In this case, the *umask* of 27 makes the file *afile* read-only to members of the group and disallows access to the file to all others.

As you can see in the output of the previous example, *ls* adds an extra letter at the beginning of the mode string for the *adir* directory. This symbol indicates the type of file being listed and is not part of the access mode. The letter d indicates a directory, a - indicates a file, the letter l indicates a symbolic link, a b indicates a block device (such as a disk), and a c indicates a character device (such as a terminal).

Changing access modes

Access modes can be changed with the *chmod* command, which accepts either *octal* or *symbolic* access mode specifications. Octal bits, as shown in the previous section, are specified explicitly. However, some people prefer to use symbolic forms because they usually modify an existing mode instead of completely replacing it. Symbolic mode specifications have three parts, made up of individual characters, as shown in Table 7-5.

Table 7-5. Symbolic modes for the chmod command

Category	Mode	Description
User class	u	User
	g	Group
	o	Other
	a	All classes
Operation	-	Take away permission
	+	Add permission
	=	Set permission exactly
Permissions	r	Read permission
	w	Write permission

Category	Mode	Description
	x	Execute permission
	X	Execute permission for directories and files with another execute permission, but not plain files
	s	SUID or SGID permissions
	t	Sticky bit

The individual user class characters and permissions characters may be grouped to form compound expressions, such as ug for user and group combined or rw for read and write. Here are some examples of symbolic mode specifications:

u+x

> Add execute permission for the user.

go-w

> Remove write permission from group and other classes.

o+t

> Set the sticky bit.

a=rw

> Set read and write, but not execute, permissions for everyone.

a+X

> Give everyone execute permission for directories and for those files with any existing execute permission.

The *chmod* command is used to modify the mode.

chmod

Syntax

```
chmod [options] symbolic_mode[,symbolic_mode]...files
chmod [options] octal_mode files
chmod [options] --reference=rfile files
```

Description

Modify the access mode on *files*. In the first form, use one or more comma-separated *symbolic_mode* specifications to modify *files*. In the second form, use an *octal_mode* to modify *files*. In the third form, use the mode of *rfile* as a template to be applied to *files*.

Frequently used options

-c

> Like verbose mode, but report only changes.

-R

> Use recursive mode, descending through directory hierarchies under *files* and making modifications throughout.

-v

> Use verbose behavior, reporting actions for all *files*.

Devices, Filesystems, FHS

Example 1

Set the mode for a file to `rw-r--r--`, using an octal specification:

```
$ chmod 644 afile
$ ls -l afile
-rw-r--r--   1 jdean    jdean              0 Jan  2 20:31 afile
```

Example 2

Set the same permission using a symbolic specification, using the verbose option:

```
$ chmod -v u=rw,go=r afile
mode of afile retained as 0644 (rw-r--r--)
```

Example 3

Recursively remove all permissions for *other* on a directory:

```
$ chmod -R -v o-rwx adir
mode of adir retained as 0770 (rwxrwx---)
mode of adir/file1 changed to 0660 (rw-rw----)
mode of adir/file2 changed to 0660 (rw-rw----)
mode of adir/file3 changed to 0660 (rw-rw----)
mode of adir/file4 changed to 0660 (rw-rw----)
mode of adir/dir1 changed to 0770 (rwxrwx---)
mode of adir/dir1/file6 changed to 0660 (rw-rw----)
mode of adir/dir1/file5 changed to 0660 (rw-rw----)
mode of adir/dir2 changed to 0770 (rwxrwx---)
```

Example 4

Set the sticky bit on a directory:

```
$ chmod -v +t adir
mode of adir changed to 1770 (rwxrwx--T)
```

Modification of ownership parameters may become necessary when moving files, setting up workgroups, or working in a user's directory as *root*. This is accomplished using the *chown* command, which can change user and group ownership, and the *chgrp* command for modifying group ownership.

---

chown

Syntax

```
chown [options] user-owner files
chown [options] user-owner. files
chown [options] user-owner.group-owner files
chown [options] .group-owner files
chown [options] --reference=rfile files
```

Description

Used to change the owner and/or group of *files* to *user-owner* and/or *group-owner*. In the first form, *user-owner* is made the owner of *files* and the group is not affected. In the second form (note the trailing dot on *user-owner*), the *user-owner* is made the owner of *files*, and the group of the files is changed to *user-owner*'s default group. In the third form, both *user-owner* and *group-owner* are assigned to *files*. In the fourth form, only the *group-owner* is assigned to *files*, and the user is not affected. In the fifth form, the owner and group of *rfile* is used as a template and applied to *files*. Only the superuser may change file ownership, but group ownership may be set by anyone belonging to the target *group-owner*.

 Note that historically BSD systems have used the *user.group* syntax, but SysV-based systems have used *user:group* (: instead of .). Older versions of GNU *chown* accepted only the BSD syntax, but recent versions support both.

Frequently used options

-c

> Like verbose mode, but report only changes.

-R

> Use recursive mode, descending through directory hierarchies under *files* and making modifications throughout.

-v

> Use verbose behavior, reporting actions for all *files*.

Example 1

As root, set the user owner of a file:

```
# chown -v jdoe afile
owner of afile changed to jdoe
```

Example 2

As root, set the user and group owner of a file:

```
# chown -v jdoe.sales afile
owner of afile changed to jdoe.sales
```

chgrp

Syntax

```
chgrp [options] group-owner files
chgrp [options] --reference=rfile files
```

Description

Change the group owner of *files* to *group-owner*. In the first form, set the *group-owner* of *files*. In the second form, the group of *rfile* is used as a template and applied to *files*. Options and usage are the same as that of *chown*.

Example 1

Recursively change the group owner of the entire *sales* directory:

```
# chgrp -Rv sales sales
changed group of 'sales' to sales
```

```
changed group of 'sales/file1' to sales
changed group of 'sales/file2' to sales
...
```

Setting Up a Workgroup Directory

The steps you may use to create a useful workgroup directory for a small team of people are briefly described here. The goals of the directory are as follows:

- The workgroup is to be called *sales* and has members *jdoe*, *bsmith*, and *jbrown*.
- The directory is */home/sales*.
- Only the creators of files in */home/sales* should be able to delete them.
- Members shouldn't worry about file ownership, and all group members require full access to files.
- Nonmembers should have no access to any of the files.

The following steps will satisfy the goals:

1. Create the new group:

   ```
   # groupadd sales
   ```

2. Add the existing users to the group:

   ```
   # usermod -a -G sales jdoe
   # usermod -a -G sales bsmith
   # usermod -a -G sales jbrown
   ```

3. Create a directory for the group:

   ```
   # mkdir /home/sales
   ```

4. Set the ownership of the new directory:

   ```
   # chgrp sales /home/sales
   ```

5. Protect the directory from others:

   ```
   # chmod 770 /home/sales
   ```

6. Set the SGID bit to ensure that the *sales* group will own all new files. Also set the sticky bit to protect files from deletion by nonowners:

   ```
   # chmod g+s,o+t /home/sales
   ```

7. Test it:

   ```
   # su - jdoe
   $ cd /home/sales
   $ touch afile
   $ ls -l afile
   -rw-rw-r--   1 jdoe      sales      0 Jan  3 02:44 afile
   $ exit
   # su - bsmith
   # cd /home/sales
   # rm afile
   rm: cannot unlink 'afile': Operation not permitted
   ```

After the *ls* command, we see that the group ownership is correctly set to *sales*. After the *rm* command, we see that *bsmith* cannot delete *afile*, which was created by *jdoe*. We also note that although *afile* has mode 664, the directory containing it has mode 770, preventing other users from reading the file.

On the Exam

For the exam, you should be prepared to answer questions on file and directory permissions in both symbolic and numeric (octal) forms. You should also be able to translate between the two forms given an example.

Objective 6: Create and Change Hard and Symbolic Links

Often it is useful to have access to a file in multiple locations in a filesystem. To avoid creating multiple copies of the file, use a *link*. Links don't take up very much space, as they only add a bit of metadata to the filesystem, so they're much more efficient than using separate copies.

There are two types of links used on Linux:

Symbolic links

> A symbolic link is simply a pointer to another filename. When Linux opens a symbolic link, it reads the pointer and then finds the intended file that contains the actual data. Symbolic links can point to other filesystems, both local and remote, and they can point to directories. The *ls -l* command clearly lists them as links by displaying a special "l" (a lowercase *L*) in column one, and they have no file protections of their own (the actual file's permissions are used instead).
>
> A symbolic link can point to a filename that does not actually exist. Such a symbolic link is said to be *broken* or *stale*.

Hard links

> A hard link is not really a link at all; it is simply another directory entry for an existing file. The two directory entries have different names but point to the same inode and thus to the same actual data, ownership, permissions, and so on. In fact, when you delete a file, you are only removing a directory entry (in other words, one hard link to the file). As long as any directory entries remain, the file's inode is not actually deleted. In fact, a file is not deleted until its *link count* drops to zero (and the file is no longer open for reading or writing).
>
> Hard links have two important limitations. First, because all of the links to a file point to the same inode, any hard links must by definition reside on the same filesystem. Second, hard links cannot point to directories. However, hard links take no disk space beyond an additional directory entry.

Why Links?

To see an example of the use of links in practice, consider the directories in */etc/ rc.d* on a typical RPM-based system:

```
drwxr-xr-x  2 root    root    1024 Dec 15 23:05 init.d
-rwxr-xr-x  1 root    root    2722 Apr 15  1999 rc
-rwxr-xr-x  1 root    root     693 Aug 17  1998 rc.local
-rwxr-xr-x  1 root    root    9822 Apr 13  1999 rc.sysinit
drwxr-xr-x  2 root    root    1024 Dec  2 09:41 rc0.d
drwxr-xr-x  2 root    root    1024 Dec  2 09:41 rc1.d
drwxr-xr-x  2 root    root    1024 Dec 24 15:15 rc2.d
drwxr-xr-x  2 root    root    1024 Dec 24 15:15 rc3.d
drwxr-xr-x  2 root    root    1024 Dec 24 15:16 rc4.d
drwxr-xr-x  2 root    root    1024 Dec 24 15:16 rc5.d
drwxr-xr-x  2 root    root    1024 Dec 14 23:37 rc6.d
```

Inside *init.d* are scripts to start and stop many of the services on your system, such as *httpd*, *crond*, and *syslogd*. Some of these files are to be executed with a start argument, while others are run with a stop argument, depending on the *runlevel* of your system. To determine just which files are run and what argument they receive, a scheme of additional directories has been devised. These directories are named *rc0.d* through *rc6.d*, one for each runlevel (see Chapter 4 for a complete description of this scheme). Each of the runlevel-specific directories contains several links, each with a name that helps determine the configuration of services on your system. For example, *rc3.d* contains the following links, among many others:

```
S30syslog -> ../init.d/syslog
S40crond -> ../init.d/crond
S85httpd -> ../init.d/httpd
```

All of these links point back to the scripts in *init.d* as indicated by the arrows (->) after the script name. If these links were copies of the scripts, editing would be required for all of the runlevel-specific versions of the same script just to make a single change. Instead, links allow us to:

- Make changes to the original file once. References to the links will yield the updated contents as long as the filename doesn't change.

- Avoid wasting disk space by having multiple copies of the same file in different places for "convenience."

As another example, consider the directory for the kernel source, */lib/modules/kernel_version/build*:

```
build -> /usr/src/linux-2.4.18
```

Makefiles and other automated tools for building third-party kernel modules can refer to */lib/modules/`uname -r`/build*, but in reality they reference */usr/src/linux-2.4.18*. If a new kernel is added, say, version 2.4.20, its source would be placed into an appropriately named directory and the *build* link in the new modules directory would be set, as follows:

```
build -> /usr/src/linux-2.4.20
```

Now the appropriate directory can be selected simply by changing the link. No files need to be moved or deleted. Once created, links are normal directory entries, which may be copied, renamed, deleted, and backed up.

Symbolic and hard links are created with the *ln* command.

ln

Syntax

```
ln [options] file link
ln [options] files directory
```

Description

Create links between files. In the first form, a new `link` is created to point to `file`, which must already exist. In the second form, links are created in `directory` for all `files` specified.

Hard links are created unless the *-s* option is specified.

Frequently used options

-f

Overwrite (force) existing links or existing files in the destination `directory`.

-i

Prompt interactively before overwriting destination files.

-s

Create a symbolic link rather than a hard link.

Example 1

Note that the Bourne shell (*sh*) on a Linux system is a symbolic link to *bash*:

```
$ ls -l /bin/bash /bin/sh
-rwxr-xr-x   1 root     root       626028 Feb 11 07:34 /bin/bash
lrwxrwxrwx   1 root     root            4 Feb 23 10:24 /bin/sh -> bash
```

Example 2

Create a file named *myfile*, a symbolic link to that file named *myslink*, and a hard link to that file named *myhlink*, and then examine them:

```
$ touch myfile
$ ln -s myfile myslink
$ ln myfile myhlink
$ ls -l my*
-rw-r--r--   2 jdoe  jdoe  0 Jan  3 13:21 myfile
-rw-r--r--   2 jdoe  jdoe  0 Jan  3 13:21 myhlink
lrwxrwxrwx   1 jdoe  jdoe  6 Jan  3 13:21 myslink -> myfile
```

Using the *stat* command on my* demonstrates that *myfile* and *myhlink* both ultimately reference the same inode (the inode numbers are the same) and indicates the number of hard links to the file:

```
# stat my*
File: 'myfile'
  Size: 0           Blocks: 0          IO Block: 4096   Regular File
```

```
Device: 3a05h/14853d    Inode: 1212467     Links: 2
Access: (0644/-rw-r--r--) Uid: (    0/    root)  Gid: (    0/    root)
Access: 2009-03-15 21:36:33.000000000 -0600
Modify: 2009-03-15 21:36:33.000000000 -0600
Change: 2009-03-15 21:36:33.000000000 -0600
 File: 'myhlink'
  Size: 0               Blocks: 0         IO Block: 4096    Regular File
Device: 3a05h/14853d    Inode: 1212467     Links: 2
Access: (0644/-rw-r--r--) Uid: (    0/    root)  Gid: (    0/    root)
Access: 2009-03-15 21:36:33.000000000 -0600
Modify: 2009-03-15 21:36:33.000000000 -0600
Change: 2009-03-15 21:36:33.000000000 -0600
 File: 'myslink' -> 'myfile'
  Size: 6               Blocks: 0         IO Block: 4096    Symbolic Link
Device: 3a05h/14853d    Inode: 1213365     Links: 1
Access: (0777/lrwxrwxrwx) Uid: (    0/    root)  Gid: (    0/    root)
Access: 2009-03-15 21:36:33.000000000 -0600
Modify: 2009-03-15 21:36:33.000000000 -0600
Change: 2009-03-15 21:36:33.000000000 -0600
```

Note that the symbolic link has an inode of its own, which can also be displayed using the *-i* option to *ls*:

```
# ls -li my*
1212467 -rw-r--r--  2 root  root  0 Mar 15 21:36 myfile
1212467 -rw-r--r--  2 root  root  0 Mar 15 21:36 myhlink
1213365 lrwxrwxrwx  1 root  root  6 Mar 15 21:36 myslink -> myfile
```

Here you can see that the directory entries for *myfile* and *myhlink* both point to inode 1212467, while the directory entry for *myslink* points to inode 1213365. That inode contains the symbolic link to *myfile*.

As another example, consider the two filesystems in Figure 7-3. The root partition on */dev/sda1* holds a file intended as an example *bash* startup file, located in */etc/bashrc_user*. On the same filesystem, the *root* user has elected to use */etc/bashrc_user*. Not wanting to maintain both files individually, *root* has created a hard link, */root/.bashrc*, to the example file.

Both of the directory entries, */etc/bashrc_user* and */root/.bashrc*, point to the same text data in the same file, described by the same inode, on */dev/sda1*. User *jdoe* has also elected to link to the example file. However, since his home directory is located in */home* on */dev/sda9*, *jdoe* cannot use a hard link to the file on */dev/sda1*. Instead, he created a symbolic link, */home/jdoe/.bashrc*, which points to a small file on */dev/sda9*. This contains the pointer to directory entry */etc/bashrc_user*, which finally points at the text. The result for *root* and *jdoe* is identical, though the two styles of links implement the reference in completely different ways.

Preserving links

Programs such as *tar* and *cp* contain options that control whether symbolic links are followed during operation. In the case of a *tar* backup, this may be important if you have multiple links to large files, because you would get many redundant backups of the same data.

When a symbolic link is encountered with *cp*, the contents of the file to which the link points are copied, unless the *-d* option is specified. This "no dereference" operator causes *cp* to copy the links themselves instead. For example, consider a directory *dir1* containing a symbolic link, which is recursively copied to other directories with and without the *-d* option:

```
# ls -l dir1
total 13
lrwxrwxrwx 1 root root      19 Jan  4 02:43 file1 -> /file1
-rw-r--r-- 1 root root   10240 Dec 12 17:12 file2
# cp -r dir1 dir2
# ls -l dir2
total 3117
-rw-r--r-- 1 root root 3164160 Jan  4 02:43 file1
-rw-r--r-- 1 root root   10240 Jan  4 02:43 file2
# cp -rd dir1 dir3
# ls -l dir3
total 13
lrwxrwxrwx 1 root root      19 Jan  4 02:43 file1 -> /file1
-rw-r--r-- 1 root root   10240 Jan  4 02:43 file2
```

Directory *dir2* has a copy of the entire *file1*, which is large, probably wasting disk space. Directory *dir3*, created with *cp -rd*, is the same as *dir1* (including the symbolic link) and takes very little space.

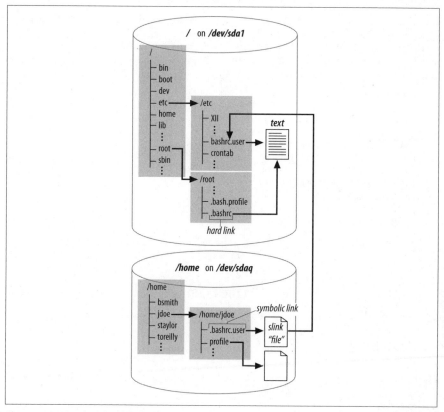

Figure 7-3. Hard and symbolic links

Finding links to a file

Finding the file pointed to by a symbolic link is simple. The *ls -l* command displays a convenient pointer notation, indicating just where links are pointing:

```
lrwxrwxrwx 1 root root      19 Jan  4 02:43 file1 -> /file1
```

Going the other way and finding symbolic links to a file is less obvious but is still relatively easy. The *-lname* option to the *find* utility locates them for you by searching for symbolic links containing the original filename. Here, the entire local filesystem is searched for *myfile*, turning up three symbolic links:

```
# find / -lname myfile
/home/world/rootsfile
/home/finance/hisfile
/root/myslink
```

Remember that symbolic links could be anywhere, which includes a remote system (if you're sharing files), so you may not be able to locate them all. (See "Objective 3: Perform Basic File Management" on page 91, for additional information on the *find* command).

Since hard links aren't really links but duplicate directory entries, you can locate them by searching directory entries for the inode, which is identical in all the links. Unlike symbolic links, you are guaranteed to find all of the links since hard links cannot cross filesystem boundaries. First, identify the inode you're interested in, as well as the filesystem that contains the links:

```
# df file1
Filesystem    1k-blocks      Used Available Use% Mounted on
/dev/sda9      1981000    451115   1427473  24% /home
# ls -i file
90469 file1file1 is on the /home filesystem, and its inode
number is 90469. Next, find is used with the -inum
option to locate all instances of inode 90469:
# find /home -inum 90469
/home/world/file1
/home/finance/file1
/home/jdoe/private/.myfile1
```

This example turns up three links to *file1*, including one that user *jdoe* appears to be hiding!

On the Exam

You should be prepared to identify the differences between hard and symbolic links, when each is used, and their limitations.

Objective 7: Find System Files and Place Files in the Correct Location

In 1993, the Linux community formed a project to provide a standardized filesystem layout for all general-purpose distributions of Linux. The intent of this standardization was to provide advice on how to reduce the proliferation of proprietary Linux filesystem layouts and their possible contribution to market fragmentation.

The project released a document describing the Linux Filesystem Standard, usually abbreviated FSSTND, in 1994. The following year, the group began to reduce Linux-specific content and to refine the standard to include other Unix or Unix-like operating systems. As the FSSTND attracted broader appeal, it was renamed the *Filesystem Hierarchy Standard*. Although the FHS is not a requirement of Linux developers and distributors, the Linux community understands the importance of standards, and all major distributions support the standard.

The full FHS specification is available at *http://www.pathname .com/fhs/*. The information in this chapter is consistent with version 2.3 of the specification.

Datatypes

To frame its recommendations, the FHS defines two categories of data use, each with two opposing subtypes:

Data sharing
:   This category defines the scope of data use in a networked environment:

    Sharable
    :   Sharable data can be used by multiple host systems on a network. Sharable files contain general-purpose information, without ties to any specific host. Examples include user data files, executable program files, and system documentation.

    Nonsharable
    :   Data is not sharable when linked to a specific host, such as a unique configuration file.

Data modification
:   This category specifies how data changes:

    Variable
    :   Data is considered variable when changed by natural, frequent processes. Examples include user files and system logfiles, such as */var/log/messages*.

    Static
    :   Static data is left alone for the most part, remaining the same from day to day or even year to year. Examples include binary programs such as *ls* and *bash*, which change only when the system administrator performs an upgrade.

Some directories in the Linux filesystem are intended to hold specific types of data. For example, the executable files in */usr* are rarely changed, and thus could be defined as *static* because they are needed by all users on a network. Before disks were as large as they are today, the files commonly found in */usr* were often mounted from remote servers to preserve local disk space. Thus, in addition to being static, */usr* is said to be *sharable*. Keeping files organized with respect to these attributes can simplify file sharing, system administration, and backup complexity, as well as reduce storage requirements. The FHS arranges the preceding data categories into a 2 × 2 matrix, as shown with a few example directories in Table 7-6.

Table 7-6. FHS datatypes

	Sharable	Nonsharable
Static	/usr	/etc
	/usr/local	/boot
Variable	/var/mail	/var/log
	/home	/proc

On many networks, */usr* and */usr/local* are mounted by individual workstations from an NFS server. This can save a considerable amount of local storage on the workstations. More importantly, placing these directories on another system can make upgrades and additions much simpler. These directories are usually shared as read-only filesystems because they are never modified by most end users. The */var/mail* and */home* directories, on the other hand, are shared but must be changed regularly by users. The */etc* and */boot* directories contain files that are static in the sense that only the administrator changes them, but sharing them is not necessary or advised, because they are local configuration files. The */var/log* and */proc* directories are very dynamic but also of local interest only.

The root Filesystem

The FHS offers a significant level of detail describing the exact locations of files, using rationale derived from the static/variable and sharable/nonsharable definitions. However, knowledge of the location of every file is not necessary or required for Exam 101. This section discusses the major portions of the FHS directory hierarchy overall, with specific example files offered as illustrations.

Although the FHS is a defining document for the Linux filesystem, it does not follow that all directories described in the FHS will be present in all Linux installations. Some directory locations cited in the FHS are package-dependent or open to customization by the vendor.

The root filesystem is located at the top of the entire directory hierarchy. The FHS defines these goals for the root filesystem:

- It must contain utilities and files sufficient to boot the operating system, including the ability to mount other filesystems. This includes utilities, device files, configuration, boot loader information, and other essential start-up data.
- It should contain the utilities needed by the system administrator to repair or restore a damaged system.

- It should be relatively small. Small partitions are less likely to be corrupted due to a system crash or power failure than large ones are. In addition, the root partition should contain nonsharable data to maximize the remaining disk space for sharable data.
- Software should not create files or directories in the root filesystem.

Although a Linux system with everything in a single root partition may be created, doing so would not meet these goals. Instead, the root filesystem should contain only essential system directories, along with mount points for other filesystems. Essential root filesystem directories include:

/bin

> The */bin* directory contains executable system commands such as *cp, date, ln, ls, mkdir*, and *more*. These commands are deemed essential to system administration in case of a problem.

/dev

> Device files, necessary for accessing disks and other devices, are stored in */dev*. Examples include disk partitions, such as *hda1*, and terminals, such as *tty1*. Devices must be present at boot time for proper mounting and configuration. The exception to this rule is systems using *devfs*, which is a relatively recent addition to the Linux kernel that makes */dev* a virtual filesystem, much like */proc*, where device-special files are created by the kernel when drivers register devices. Use of *devfs* is currently not covered by the Level 1 Objectives.

/etc

> The */etc* directory contains configuration information unique to the system and is required for boot time. No binary executable programs are stored here. Prior practice in various versions of Unix had administrative executable programs stored in */etc*. These have been moved to */sbin* under the FHS. Example files include *passwd, hosts*, and *login.defs*.

/lib

> The */lib* directory contains shared libraries and kernel modules, both essential for system initialization.

/mnt

> This directory is provided for the local system administrator's use. Generally, it is empty except for some mount points for temporary partitions, including *cdrom* and *floppy*.

/root

> The recommended default (but optional) home directory for the superuser is */root*. Although it is not absolutely essential for */root* to be on the root filesystem, it is customary and convenient, because doing so keeps root's configuration files available for system maintenance or recovery.

/sbin

> Essential utilities used for system administration are stored in */sbin*. Examples include *fdisk, fsck*, and *mkfs*.

The remaining top-level directories in the root filesystem are considered nonessential for emergency procedures:

/boot

> The /boot directory contains files for the boot loader (such as LILO or GRUB). Because it is typically small, it can be left in the root filesystem. However, it is often separated to keep the boot loader files within the first 1,024 cylinders of a physical disk.

/home

> The /home filesystem contains home directories for system users. This is usually a separate filesystem and is often the largest variable filesystem in the hierarchy.

/opt

> The /opt directory is intended for the installation of software other than that packaged with the operating system. This is often the location selected by third-party software vendors for their products.

/tmp

> The /tmp directory is for the storage of temporary files. The FHS recommends (but does not require) that its contents are deleted upon every system boot.

/usr

> The /usr filesystem contains a significant hierarchy of executable programs deemed nonessential for emergency procedures. It is usually contained in a separate partition. It contains sharable, read-only data, and is often mounted locally read-only and shared via NFS read-only. /usr is described in detail in the next section.

/var

> Like /usr, the /var filesystem contains a large hierarchy and is usually contained in a separate partition. It holds data that varies over time, such as logs, mail, and spools.

The /usr filesystem

The /usr filesystem hierarchy contains system utilities and programs that do not appear in the root partition. For example, user programs such as *less* and *tail* are found in /usr/bin. /usr/sbin contains system administration commands such as *adduser* and *traceroute*, and a number of daemons needed only on a normally operating system. No host-specific or variable data is stored in /usr. Also disallowed is the placement of directories directly under /usr for large software packages. An exception to this rule is made for X11, which has a strong precedent for this location.

The following subdirectories may be found under /usr:

/usr/X11R6

> This directory contains files for XFree86. Because X is deployed directly under /usr on many Unix systems, X breaks the rule that usually prohibits a custom /usr directory for a software package.

/usr/bin

The */usr/bin* directory is the primary location for user commands that are not considered essential for emergency system maintenance (and thus are stored here rather than in */bin*).

/usr/include

/usr/include is the standard location for *include* or *header* files, used for C and C++ programming.

/usr/lib

This directory contains shared libraries that support various programs. FHS also allows the creation of software-specific directories here. For example, */usr/lib/perl5* contains the standard library of Perl modules that implement programming functions in that language.

/usr/local

/usr/local is the top level of another hierarchy of binary files, intended for use by the system administrator. It contains subdirectories much like */usr* itself, such as */bin, /include, /lib*, and */sbin*. After a fresh Linux installation, this directory contains no files but may contain an empty directory hierarchy. Example items that may be found here are locally created documents in */usr/local/doc* or */usr/local/man*, and executable scripts and binary utilities provided by the system administrator in */usr/local/bin*.

/usr/sbin

The */usr/sbin* directory is the primary location for system administration commands that are not considered essential for emergency system maintenance (and thus are stored here rather than in */sbin*).

/usr/share

/usr/share contains a hierarchy of datafiles that are independent of, and thus can be shared among, various hardware architectures and operating system versions. This is in sharp contrast to architecture-dependent files such as those in */usr/bin*. For example, in an enterprise that uses both i386- and Alpha-based Linux systems, */usr/share* could be offered to all systems via NFS. However, since the two processors are not binary-compatible, */usr/bin* would have two NFS shares, one for each architecture.

The information stored in */usr/share* is static data, such as the GNU *info* system files, dictionary files, and support files for software packages.

/usr/src

/usr/src is an optional directory on all modern glibc-based systems. On older libc4- and libc5-based systems, */usr/src/linux* was expected to contain a copy of the kernel source, or at least the directories *include/asm* and *include/linux* for kernel header files.

On glibc-based systems, nothing should refer to the */usr/src/linux* directory. In fact, leaving kernel source at that location is generally regarded as a bad practice, since it has the potential to confuse old software.

The /var filesystem

The */var* filesystem contains data such as printer spools and logfiles that vary over time. Since variable data is always changing and growing, */var* is usually contained in a separate partition to prevent the root partition from filling. The following sub-directories can be found under */var*:

/var/account
> Some systems maintain process accounting data in this directory.

/var/cache
> */var/cache* is intended for use by programs for the temporary storage of inter-mediate data, such as the results of lengthy computations. Programs using this directory must be capable of regenerating the cached information at any time, which allows the system administrator to delete files as needed. Because it holds transient data, */var/cache* never has to be backed up.

/var/crash
> This optional directory holds crash dumps for systems that support that feature.

/var/games
> This optional directory is used to store state information, user score data, and other transient items.

/var/lock
> Lock files, used by applications to signal their existence to other processes, are stored here. Lock files usually contain no data.

/var/log
> The */var/log* directory is the main repository for system logfiles, such as those created by the syslog system. For example, the default system logfile is */var/log/messages*.

/var/mail
> This is the system mailbox, with mail files for each user. */var/mail* is a replace-ment for */var/spool/mail* and aligns FHS with many other Unix implementa-tions. You may find that your Linux distribution still uses */var/spool/mail*.

/var/opt
> This directory is defined as a location for temporary files of programs stored in */opt*.

/var/run
> */var/run* contains various files describing the present state of the system. All such files may be deleted at system boot time. This is the default location for PID files, which contain the PIDs of the processes for which they are named. For example, if the Apache web server, httpd, is running as process number 534, */var/run/httpd.pid* will contain that number:
>
> ```
> # cat /var/run/httpd.pid
> 534
> ```
>
> Such files are needed by utilities that must be able to find a PID for a running process. Also located here is the *utmp* file, used by commands such as *who* and *last* to display logged-in users.

/var/spool

The */var/spool* directory contains information that is queued for processing. Examples include print queues, outgoing mail, and *crontab* files.

/var/state

The */var/state* directory is intended to contain information that helps applications preserve state across multiple invocations or multiple instances.

/var/tmp

As with */tmp* in the root filesystem, */var/tmp* is used for storage of temporary files. Unlike */tmp*, the files in */var/tmp* are expected to survive across multiple system boots. The information found in */var/tmp* could be considered more persistent than information in */tmp*.

Although it is not specified this way in the FHS, some distributions use */var/tmp* as a more secure temporary directory for use by *root*.

/var/yp

This optional directory contains the database files of the Network Information Service (NIS), if implemented. NIS was formerly known as *yellow pages* (not to be confused with the big yellow book).

This directory shouldn't be confused with */var/nis*, which is used by NIS+. Oddly, */var/nis* is mentioned in a footnote in FHS 2.3, but it does not have an entry in the specification.

Linux annex

Since FHS migrated away from being a Linux-only document and expanded to cover other operating systems, information specific to any one operating system was moved to an *annex*. The only annex listed in v2.3 of FHS is the Linux annex, which mentions a few guidelines and makes allowances for the placement of additional program files in */sbin*. The Linux annex also mentions and supports the use of the */proc* filesystem for the processing of kernel, memory, and process information.

Where's that binary?

Compiled executable files, called *binary files*, or just *binaries*, can be located in a number of places in an FHS-compliant filesystem. However, it's easy to become a little confused over why a particular executable file is placed where it is in the FHS. This is particularly true for *bin* and *sbin* directories, which appear in multiple locations. Table 7-7 lists these directories and shows how each is used.

Table 7-7. Binary file locations

Type of file	User commands	System administration commands
Vendor-supplied, essential (root filesystem)	/bin	/sbin
Vendor-supplied, nonessential (*/usr* filesystem)	/usr/bin	/usr/sbin
Locally supplied, nonessential (*/usr* filesystem)	/usr/local/bin	/usr/local/sbin

Locating Files

FHS offers the Linux community an excellent resource that assures consistency across distributions and other operating systems. In practice, however, file location problems can be frustrating, and the need arises to find files in the system quickly. These file location tools are required for Exam 101: *which, find, locate, whereis*, and *type*.

which uses the PATH variable to locate executable files. *find* searches specified areas in the filesystem. *whereis* searches in a small subset of common directories. *locate* offers a quick alternative to *find* for filename searches and is suited for locating files that are not moved around in the filesystem. Without a fresh database to search, *locate* is not suitable for files recently created or renamed.

which

Syntax

```
which command
```

Description

Determine the location of *command* and display the full pathname of the executable program that the shell would launch to execute it. *which* searches only the user's path.

Example

Determine the shell that would be started by entering the *tcsh* command:

```
# which tcsh
/bin/tcsh
```

which is small and does only one thing: determines what executable program will be found and called by the shell. Such a search is particularly useful if you're having trouble with the setup of your PATH environment variable or if you are creating a new version of an existing utility and want to be certain you're executing the experimental version.

find

Syntax

```
find paths expression
```

Description

Locate files that match an *expression* starting at *paths* and continuing recursively. The find command has a rich set of *expression* directives for locating just about anything in the filesystem.

Example

To find files by name located in the */usr* directory hierarchy that might have something to do with the *csh* shell or its variants, you might use the *-name filename* directive:

```
# find /usr -name "*csh*"
/usr/bin/sun-message.csh
/usr/doc/tcsh-6.08.00
/usr/doc/tcsh-6.08.00/complete.tcsh
/usr/doc/vim-common-5.3/syntax/csh.vim
/usr/man/man1/tcsh.1
/usr/share/apps/ktop/pics/csh.xpm
/usr/share/apps/ktop/pics/tcsh.xpm
/usr/share/emacs/20.3/etc/emacs.csh
/usr/share/vim/syntax/csh.vim
/usr/src/linux-2.2.5/fs/lockd/svcshare.c
```

Some of these results are clearly related to *csh* or to *tcsh*, whereas others are questionable. In addition, this command may take a while because find must traverse the entire */usr* hierarchy, examining each filename for a match. This example demonstrates that if filename wildcards are used, the entire string must be quoted to prevent expansion by the shell prior to launching *find*.

find is among the most useful commands in the Linux administrator's toolkit and has a variety of useful options. *find* is handy in certain cases. For example:

- You need to limit a search to a particular location in the filesystem.

- You must search for an attribute other than the filename.

- Files you are searching for were recently created or renamed, in which case *locate* may not be appropriate.

Refer to Chapter 6, for additional information on the *find* command.

On the Exam

You should have a general understanding of *find*. Remember that by default, *find* prints matching directory entries to the screen. However, detailed knowledge of *find* options and usage are beyond the scope of LPIC Level 1 exams.

---

locate

Syntax

```
locate patterns
```

Description

Locate files whose names match one or more **patterns** by searching an index of files previously created.

Example

Locate files by name in the entire directory hierarchy that might have something to do with the *csh* shell or its variants:

```
# locate csh
/home/jdean/.tcshrc
/root/.cshrc
/root/.tcshrc
/usr/bin/sun-message.csh
```

```
/usr/doc/tcsh-6.08.00
/usr/doc/tcsh-6.08.00/FAQ
/usr/doc/tcsh-6.08.00/NewThings
/usr/doc/tcsh-6.08.00/complete.tcsh
/usr/doc/tcsh-6.08.00/eight-bit.txt
/usr/doc/vim-common-5.3/syntax/csh.vim
/usr/man/man1/tcsh.1
/usr/share/apps/ktop/pics/csh.xpm
/usr/share/apps/ktop/pics/tcsh.xpm
/usr/share/emacs/20.3/etc/emacs.csh
/usr/share/vim/syntax/csh.vim
/usr/src/linux-2.2.5/fs/lockd/svcshare.c
/etc/csh.cshrc
/etc/profile.d/kde.csh
/etc/profile.d/mc.csh
/bin/csh
/bin/tcsh
```

The *locate* command must have a recent database to search, and that database must be updated periodically to incorporate changes in the filesystem. If the database is stale, using *locate* yields a warning:

```
# locate tcsh
locate: warning: database /var/lib/slocate/slocate.db' is more \
                                         than 8 days old
```

updatedb

Syntax

```
updatedb [options]
```

Description

Refresh (or create) the *slocate* database in */var/lib/slocate/slocate.db*.

Option

-e directories
    Exclude a comma-separated list of *directories* from the database.

Example

Refresh the *slocate* database, excluding files in temporary locations:

```
# updatedb -e "/tmp,/var/tmp,/usr/tmp,/afs,/net,/proc"
```

updatedb is typically executed periodically via *cron*.

Additional options

Some Linux distributions (Debian, for example) come with a version of *updatedb* that accepts additional options that can be specified on the command line:

--netpaths='path1 path2 ... '
    Add network *paths* to the search list.

--prunepaths=‘path1 path2 ... ’
> Eliminate *paths* from the search list.

--prunefs=‘filesystems ... ’
> Eliminate entire types of *filesystems*, such as NFS.

These options modify the behavior of *updatedb* on some Linux systems by prohibiting the parsing of certain filesystem locations and by adding others. There are a few more of these options than those listed here, but these three are special in that they can also be specified through the use of environment variables set prior to *updatedb* execution. The variables are NETPATHS, PRUNEPATHS, and PRUNEFS. These variables and the options to *updatedb* are discussed here because this Objective makes specific mention of *updatedb.conf*, a sort of control file for *updatedb*. Despite its name, *updatedb.conf* isn't really a configuration file, but rather a fragment of a Bourne shell script that sets these environment variables. Example 7-2 shows a sample *updatedb.conf* file.

Example 7-2. Sample updatedb.conf file

```
# This file sets environment variables used by updatedb
# filesystems which are pruned from updatedb database:
PRUNEFS="NFS nfs afs proc smbfs autofs auto iso9660"
export PRUNEFS
# paths which are pruned from updatedb database:
PRUNEPATHS="/tmp /usr/tmp /var/tmp /afs /amd /alex"
export PRUNEPATHS
# netpaths which are added:
NETPATHS="/mnt/fs3"
export NETPATHS
```

In this example, the PRUNEFS and PRUNEPATHS variables cause *updatedb* to ignore types of filesystems and particular paths, respectively. NETPATHS is used to add network paths from remote directory */mnt/fs3*.

updatedb.conf doesn't directly control *updatedb*, but eliminates the need for lengthy options on the *updatedb* command line, which can make *crontab* files a bit cleaner.

On the Exam

Remember that *updatedb* does not require configuration to execute. On systems that provide for configuration, *updatedb.conf* can specify a few extra options to *updatedb* by way of environment variables.

---

whereis

Syntax

```
whereis [options] filename
```

Description

whereis locates source/binary and manuals sections for specified files.

Example

```
# whereis ls
ls: /bin/ls /usr/share/man/man1p/ls.1p.gz /usr/share/man/man1/ls.1.gz
```

type

Syntax

```
type [options] filename
```

Description

type is not actually a separate program, but a built-in part of the *bash* shell. *type* will tell you how a *filename* would be interpreted if used as a command name.

Example

```
# type ls
ls is aliased to `ls --color=auto'
# type grep
grep is hashed (/bin/grep)
# type foo
-bash: type: foo: not found
```

On the Exam

You must be familiar with the FHS concept and the contents of its major directories. Be careful about the differences between (and reasons for) */bin* and */sbin*, root filesystem and */usr* filesystem, and locally supplied commands. Also practice with various file location techniques and be able to differentiate among them.

8

Exam 101 Review Questions and Exercises

This section presents review questions to highlight important concepts and hands-on exercises that you can use to gain experience with the topics covered on the LPI 101 Exam. The exercises can be particularly useful if you're not accustomed to routine Linux administration and should help you better prepare for the exam. To complete the exercises, you'll need a working Linux system that is not in production use. You might also find it useful to have a pen and paper handy to write down your responses as you work your way through the review questions and exercises.

System Architecture (Topic 101)

Review Questions

1. Describe the boot process on a PC, and identify the order in which control passes as a system boots.

2. Name three files in the */proc* filesystem that contain information on system resource allocations.

3. Which of the following SCSI interfaces has the fastest data transfer rates: SCSI-1, SCSI-2, Ultra SCSI, or Fast-Wide SCSI?

4. What is the naming convention in */dev* for the different hard disk interfaces?

5. What command is used to obtain USB information on a Linux system?

6. What driver is used for USB hard drives?

7. What is your default runlevel? How can you tell?

Exercises

1. Boot your PC and enter the BIOS configuration utility. Determine how to change the boot order and how to enable and disable peripherals built into the motherboard.

2. Examine the enabled serial and parallel ports. Can you manually configure the interrupts and I/O ports assigned to them?

3. Examine your modem and sound external interfaces on your PC. Are the devices built into your motherboard or independent expansion cards?

4. If you have a SCSI controller, reboot your PC and enter the SCSI BIOS. What device number is selected, if any, for boot? How are the controller's onboard terminators configured? What data rate is the controller configured for?

5. If you have a RAID controller, reboot your PC and enter the RAID BIOS. What options do you have to configure RAID on your system?

6. Examine the kernel's interrupt assignments by executing *cat /proc/interrupts*. Are your devices reported correctly? Are any devices sharing interrupts?

7. Review output from *cat /proc/dma* and *cat /proc/ioports*.

8. Create a list of all installed PCI devices using *lspci*. Note the devices built into your motherboard.

9. Run *lsmod* and match the loaded kernel modules with hardware in your system.

10. Connect a USB device (mouse, printer, etc.) to your system. Run *lsmod* to verify that the appropriate driver loaded.

11. Run the *dmesg* command and go through the hardware your kernel recognized at boot time.

12. Reboot the system and modify the grub boot line to boot into single-user mode.

13. At the root prompt, type *kill 1*. What happens? Why?

Linux Installation and Package Management (Topic 102)

Review Questions

1. Why is the */var* directory usually located in a partition of its own?

2. As a system administrator for a network with many workstations and a central NFS file server, how can you safely share */usr* with your users while still maintaining control of its contents?

3. What is the recommended size for a swap partition, as a function of the memory in a system?

4. Describe how to create a *tar* archive and how its contents are extracted.

5. In general terms, describe the procedure used to compile and install free or open source software from source code.

6. What is a shared library? How can you determine what library dependencies exist in a compiled executable?

7. How does your system know where to look for shared libraries?

8. Briefly describe the major functional modes of *rpm*.

9. How do you add additional repositories to *yum*?

10. What are the reasons to choose LILO over GRUB as a boot loader, or vice versa?

11. Why might a Debian Linux administrator use *dpkg -iG* instead of simply *dpkg -i* to install a package?

Exercises

1. In a shell, examine your disk layout using *fdisk*. For example:

```
# fdisk /dev/sda
Command (m for help): p
Disk /dev/sda: 200.0 GB, 200049647616 bytes
255 heads, 63 sectors/track, 24321 cylinders
Units = cylinders of 16065 * 512 = 8225280 bytes
Disk identifier: 0x0003bf13

    Device Boot      Start         End      Blocks   Id  System
/dev/sda1   *            1          25      200781   83  Linux
/dev/sda2               26          89      514080   82  Linux swap / Solaris
/dev/sda3               90       24321   194643540   83  Linux
```

Is the entire disk consumed by the existing filesystems?

2. Examine how system directories are mapped to disk partitions on your system. Are */var* and */tmp* in their own partitions? Is */boot* in its own partition within cylinder 1024? Is the root filesystem relatively small?

3. Download a tarball (from *http://sourceforge.net*, for example), and install it on your system with the following steps:

    a. Unpack it using *tar -xzvf file* (or *tar –xjvf file* if it is compressed with bzip2).

    b. Configure it with *./configure*.

    c. Build the software using *make* as directed in the documentation.

    d. Install the software using the instructions provided.

    Were there any difficulties with this procedure?

4. Use *ldd* to examine library dependencies of executable programs on your system. For example:

```
# ldd `which gcc`
  linux-gate.so.1 => (0x00110000)
  libc.so.6 => /lib/libc.so.6 (0x00682000)
  /lib/ld-linux.so.2 (0x00663000)
```

5. Using a system that utilizes *dpkg*, obtain a list of all packages installed under *dpkg* management with *dpkg -l | less*. Find a package in the list that looks unfamiliar, and query information about the package using *dpkg -s pkg_name*.

6. Using a system that utilizes RPM, obtain a list of all packages installed under RPM management with *rpm -qa | less*. Find a package in the list that looks unfamiliar, and query information about the package using *rpm -qi pkg_name*.

7. Using a system that utilizes RPM, obtain a list of all available packages that you can install from the currently configured repositories with *yum list available | less*.

GNU and Unix Commands (Topic 103)

Review Questions

1. Describe the difference between shell variables and environment variables.

2. Compare and contrast built-in and explicitly defined commands and those found in $PATH.

3. After a lengthy session of file manipulation on the command line, what will *!ls* produce?

4. What files does *bash* read when you log in?

5. Explain the notion of *pipes* as they refer to shell capabilities, and illustrate using an example of two or more filter programs.

6. Explain the *-p* option to *cp* and give an example of why it is necessary.

7. Give two examples of files matched by the wildcard ??[!1-5].

8. Name the three standard I/O streams and their functions.

9. Give an example of the redirection operator, >, and describe how the outcome would be different using the >> operator.

10. What process is the parent of all system processes? Give both the PID and the program name.

11. Name three common utilities used for process monitoring.

12. What happens to a typical daemon when it receives SIGHUP? How would the behavior be different if it received SIGKILL?

13. Compare and contrast background and foreground jobs, and state the syntax to put a command in the background on the command line.

14. What two classifications of characters make up regular expressions?

15. How are the regular expressions [A-Z]* and ^[A-Z]*$ different?

16. What is the difference between executing :q versus :q! in *vi*?

17. What does it mean to put *vi* into *command mode*?

Exercises

1. Start a *bash* shell in a console or terminal window and enter the following commands:

```
$ MYVAR1="Happy"
$ MYVAR2="Birthday"
$ export MYVAR1
$ bash
$ echo $MYVAR1 $MYVAR2
```

```
$ exit
$ echo $MYVAR1 $MYVAR2
```

a. Was the behavior of the two *echo* commands identical?

b. If so, why? If not, why not?

c. What happened immediately after the *bash* command?

d. Which variable is an environment variable?

2. Continuing the previous exercise, press the up arrow until you see the last *echo* command. Press the up arrow again.

a. What do you see?

b. Why wasn't it the *exit* command?

c. Press the up arrow again so that the export command is displayed. Add a space and MYVAR2 so that the line now looks like this:

```
$ export MYVAR1 MYVAR2
```

What happens when you enter this command?

3. Still continuing the previous exercise, enter the command !echo. Does anything change as a result of the revised *export* command?

4. The *file* command is used to examine a file's contents and displays the file type. Explain the result of using *file* as follows:

```
$ cd / ; file `ls | head -10`
```

5. Execute this command on your system:

```
$ cut -d: -f1 /etc/passwd | fmt -w 20 | head -1
```

a. What was displayed?

b. How many lines of output did you see? Why?

c. What was the width of the output? Why?

6. Execute the following *sed* substitution command and explain why it might be used on */etc/passwd*:

```
$ sed 's/:[^:]*:/:---:/' /etc/passwd | less
```

7. Execute this command:

```
$ cd /sbin ; ls -li e2fsck fsck.ext2
```

a. What is the significance of the first field of the output?

b. Why is it identical for both listings?

c. Why are the file sizes identical?

8. Execute the following command sequence and explain the result at each step (this example assumes that *cp* is not aliased to *cp -i*, which is a common default alias):

```
$ cd
$ cp /etc/skel .
$ cp -r /etc/skel .
```

```
$ cp -rfv /etc/skel .
$ cp -rfvp /etc/skel .
```

9. Remove the directory created in the previous exercise, using *rmdir* and/or *rm*. Which command can complete the task in a single step?

10. Explain when the wildcard {htm,html} might be useful.

11. Give an example of how the wildcard *.[Tt][Xx][Tt] could be used with directory listings.

12. What can be said about filenames matched by the *.? wildcard?

13. Experiment with redirecting the output of *ls* as follows:

    ```
    $ cp /etc/skel . 2> info.txt
    ```

    a. How is the terminal output different than that observed in Exercise 8?

    b. What is written to *info.txt* ?

14. Experiment with *ps*, *pstree*, and *top* to monitor active processes on your system. Include *top*'s interactive commands.

15. If you have Apache running, use *ps* (and perhaps *grep*) to identify the *httpd* process and its PID, which is owned by root. Send that process the HUP signal as follows:

    ```
    $ kill -SIGHUP pid
    ```

    Using *tail*, examine the Apache error log (the location of your logfile may differ):

    ```
    $ tail /var/log/httpd/error_log
    ```

    What was the effect of HUP on Apache?

16. While running X, start some interactive processes in the background and experiment with using *jobs*, *bg*, and *fg*. For example:

    ```
    $ firefox &
    $ xterm &
    $ emacs &
    $ jobs
    $ fg 1
    $ fg 2...
    ```

    Were you able to bring each of the jobs to the foreground successfully?

17. This exercise starts a process, using various methods to view and modify the process execution priority:

    Start an editing session in the background using *nice*:

    ```
    $ nice vi &
    ```

    Observe that the process was *nice*'d using *ps*:

    ```
    $ ps -u
    ```

    Check it again using *top*:

    ```
    $ top -i
    ```

Within *top, renice* the *vi* process using the *r* command and observe the effect on priority.

Exit *top* and use *renice* to set the nice value back to zero.

18. Use a simple regular expression with *grep* to find *bash* users in */etc/passwd*.

19. Examine the difference between grep and egrep by issuing the following commands:

```
$ grep ".+:x:.+:/bin/bash$" /etc/passwd
$ egrep ".+:x:.+:/bin/bash$" /etc/passwd
```

How is the output of these commands different? Why?

20. Determine the number of empty lines in */etc/inittab*.

21. Use *vi* to create a text file. Enter *insert mode* with i and insert text. Quit insert mode with Esc and move around using h, j, k, and 1, then re-enter insert mode and add more text. End the session with ZZ. *cat* the file. Is it as expected?

Devices, Linux Filesystems, and the Filesystem Hierarchy Standard (Topic 104)

Review Questions

1. What are the three types of disk partitions found on a Linux system? Which type can contain other partitions, and which type does it contain?

2. Name the directories that must be within the / partition.

3. Describe the differences between physical disks, partitions, and filesystems.

4. What is a journaling filesystem and how does it differ from a nonjournaling filesystem?

5. What is a *swap* partition used for? Why not just use swap files?

6. What kind of output will *df -h* yield?

7. Describe a common situation that is likely to cause the automatic use of *fsck* on the next system boot.

8. Name the fields in */etc/fstab*.

9. Give the command to mount a CD-ROM drive on the secondary master IDE device, assuming that */etc/fstab* does not contain a line for the device.

10. If the ro option is used in */etc/fstab* for */usr*, what limitation is placed on that filesystem?

11. Compare and contrast hard and soft quota limits.

12. Name the symbolic permission that is equivalent to 0754.

13. Describe a situation that requires the SUID permission. What ramifications does this permission imply?

14. How do you determine what binaries on your system have the SUID bit set?

15. Compare and contrast the differences between hard and symbolic links.

16. Name the document to which Linux directory assignments should conform.

17. Compare and contrast the differences between the *locate* and *find* commands.

Exercises

1. As root, run *fdisk* on your main hard drive and enter the p command to print the partition table. Examine your system's configuration and make sure you understand everything you see. Enter the l command and review the many partition types Linux can accommodate. Enter the q command to quit without saving changes.

2. If you have available disk space, use *fdisk* to create a new *ext3* partition, and then format it with *mkfs*. Pay close attention to the output from *mkfs*.

3. Use a pager to examine */var/log/messages* and search for entries made by *fsck*. Did it find any problems?

4. If you created a new partition in the previous exercises, check it with *fsck* and observe the output:

   ```
   $ fsck -f /dev/partition
   ```

5. Check on the status of filesystems using *df*:

   ```
   $ df -h
   ```

   a. How does the *-h* flag assist you with interpreting the results?

   b. Are any of your filesystems nearly full?

   c. Which are underutilized?

6. As root, get a top-level view of disk usage by user using *du*:

   ```
   $ du -s /home/*
   ```

   Are there any surprises?

7. How could you use *sort* to make the output from the previous exercise more useful?

8. Review */etc/fstab*. Be sure you can name all six fields and their order as well as describe their function.

9. Examine the output of the *mount* command without options. Compare the output with the contents of */etc/fstab*.

10. If you created a new partition in the previous exercises, mount it on */mnt/new* or some other location of your choosing:

    ```
    $ mkdir /mnt/new
    $ mount /dev/partition /mnt/new
    $ df /mnt/new
    ```

    a. Did the filesystem mount correctly? Can you store files on it?

    Next, unmount it:

    ```
    $ umount /dev/partition /mnt/new
    ```

Add a line to */etc/fstab* for the new partition:

```
/dev/partition  /mnt/new   ext3    defaults   1 2
```

11. Test the quotas by setting them low for a particular user, and then start adding files as that user until the quota is exceeded. What is the observable consequence of exceeding the quota?

12. Practice converting these file modes from octal to symbolic form:

    a. 0777

    b. 0754

    c. 0666

    d. 1700

    e. 7777

13. Practice converting these file modes from symbolic to octal form. You can assume that x bits are set under SUID, SGID, and sticky bits:

    a. -rwxr-xr-x

    b. -r--r--r--

    c. -rwsrwsrwx

    d. -rw-rw---t

    e. -rws-w--w-

14. Create temporary files and use *chmod* with both symbolic and numeric mode modifications. Include SUID, SGID, and sticky bits.

15. As *root*, create temporary files and use *chown* to modify user ownership and group ownership.

16. Use *chgrp* to modify group ownership on the temporary files created in the previous exercise.

17. Create a temporary file and links as follows:

```
$ touch a_file
$ ln -s a_file an_slink
$ ln a_file an_hlink
```

Now verify that the file and the hard link indeed share an inode and that the symbolic link points to the original file:

```
$ ls -li a_file an_slink an_hlink
```

18. Review the latest version of the FHS at *http://www.pathname.com/fhs/*.

19. Examine your filesystem. Does it match the FHS? If you find discrepancies, is it clear why they don't?

20. Use *which* to check on the location of executable files.

21. Use *find* to search for *bash*:

```
$ find / -name bash
```

Now use *locate* for the same file:

```
$ locate bash
```

How are the results different? Describe a context in which each command would be useful.

22. Update your *locate* database using *updatedb*. Note the amount of time this command takes and the resources it consumes on your system.

9

Exam 101 Practice Test

This chapter will give you an idea of what kinds of questions you can expect to see on the LPI 101 test. All questions are either multiple-choice single answer, multiple-choice multiple answer, or fill in the blank.

The questions are not designed to trick you; they are designed to test your knowledge of the Linux operating system.

As of April 1, 2009, the exam weights for each LPI exam have been standardized to 60 weights. This means that if an Objective has a weight of 2, there will be 2 questions on the test about items under that Objective.

The answers for these sample questions are at the end of the chapter.

Questions

1. What kind of hardware is represented by the device name */dev/hda*?
    a. Sound Card
    b. Modem
    c. IDE Hard Drive
    d. SCSI Hard Drive
    e. SATA Hard Drive
2. What file should you query to determine whether there is an IRQ conflict on your system?
    a. */proc/ioports*
    b. */proc/interrupts*
    c. */proc/cpuinfo*
    d. */proc/meminfo*
    e. */proc/irqstatus*

3. Which of the following are arguments you can pass to the kernel at boot time to tell it to start in runlevel 1 (single-user mode)?

    a. *one*

    b. *1*

    c. *safe*

    d. *single*

    e. *user*

4. Which process is referred to as the "mother of all processes" and always has PID 1?

    a. mother

    b. admin

    c. administrator

    d. init

    e. bios

5. Which logfile should you examine for information about the hardware that the kernel initialized at boot time?

    a. */var/log/syslog*

    b. */var/log/messages*

    c. */var/log/lastlog*

    d. */var/log/wtmp*

    e. */var/log/cron*

6. If you want to change your system's default boot device from the hard drive to the CD-ROM drive, where would you make that configuration change?

    a. The file */boot/grub/grub.conf*

    b. The file */etc/lilo.conf*

    c. An argument passed to the kernel at boot time

    d. The BIOS

    e. The file */etc/inittab*

7. What command line would reboot a running Linux system immediately, forcing an *fsck* of every drive on reboot?

    a. */sbin/shutdown –r –F now*

    b. */sbin/shutdown –h –F now*

    c. */sbin/shutdown*

    d. */sbin/shutdown –r –f now*

    e. */sbin/shutdown –t –f*

8. Which of the following are valid ways to interactively switch a running system to runlevel 3?

    a. *chrunlevel 3*

b. *runlevel 3*

c. *init 3*

d. *telinit 3*

e. *init -3*

9. If you have created your own script that you wish to run every time your system boots, but it must run after all other processes have completed, where is the best place to reference it?

a. */etc/inittab*

b. */etc/rc.d/rc.sysinit*

c. A symlink beginning with *S* in */etc/rc.d/rc5.d/*

d. */etc/rc.d/rc.local*

e. A symlink beginning with *K* in */etc/rc.d/rc5.d/*

10. Which command is used to display the current mounted partitions, their mount points, and the available free space on each?

a. *du*

b. *df*

c. *fdisk*

d. *fsck*

e. *mount*

11. Which partition is designed to hold data that changes often and is writable by all users?

a. */var*

b. */home*

c. */tmp*

d. */opt*

e. */sys*

12. What does MBR stand for?

a. Main Booting Runlevel

b. Main Block Record

c. Master Boot Record

d. Master Block Record

e. Master Boot Resource

13. Which of the following lines in */boot/grub/grub.conf* would tell GRUB to use the first partition of the first hard drive as the root partition?

a. `root (hd0,0)`

b. `boot (hd0,0)`

c. `root (hd1,1)`

d. `boot (hd1,1)`

e. root (hd1,0)

14. What file contains a list of directories that are searched to find shared libraries when a binary program is executed?

    a. */etc/loader.conf*

    b. */etc/library/conf*

    c. */etc/ld.so.cache*

    d. */etc/ld.so.conf*

    e. */etc/ld.conf*

15. For distributions that use the Debian package management system, what command will download and update all installed packages to the latest available version?

    a. *apt-get install*

    b. *apt-cache update*

    c. *apt-get update*

    d. *apt-cache install*

    e. *dpkg –i*

16. If I download a *.deb* package (*package.deb*) and wish to install it, what's the best command to use?

    a. *dpkg –i package.deb*

    b. *apt-get install package.deb*

    c. *apt install package.deb*

    d. *dpkg package.deb*

    e. None of the above

17. For distributions that use the Red Hat package management system, what command will list all packages currently installed?

    a. *rpm –qa*

    b. *rpm –i*

    c. *rpm –Uvh*

    d. *rpm –list*

    e. *rpm –all*

18. For distributions that use the Red Hat package management system, what command will download and update all installed packages to the latest available version?

    a. *yum update*

    b. *yum install*

    c. *yum config*

    d. *yum list available*

    e. *yum download*

19. What option(s) to *rpm* will instruct *rpm* to run a verification check on all pack-ages installed on the system?

    a. *rpm –verify –all*

    b. *rpm –Va*

    c. *rpm –qa*

    d. *rpm –check*

    e. *rpm –c*

20. What command is used to display a list of directories the shell will search in to find a command that has been entered?

    a. *show $MYPATH*

    b. *echo $PATH*

    c. *echo $MYPATH*

    d. *setenv*

    e. *set $PATH*

21. Which file(s) does the bash shell read at login to set environment variables?

    a. */etc/bashrc*

    b. *~/.bashrc*

    c. *~/.bash_profile*

    d. All of the above

    e. None of the above

22. What commands can be used to view a list of the last commands typed into the shell?

    a. *history*

    b. <Ctrl-R>

    c. <up arrow>

    d. All of the above

    e. None of the above

23. If my current directory is */opt* and I wish to run the command */opt/runme*, what command(s) could I type (assuming */opt* is *not* in your $PATH)?

    a. */opt/runme*

    b. *./runme*

    c. *runme*

    d. *opt/runme*

    e. *~/runme*

24. Which of the following commands will redirect the standard output of */bin/ls* to */dev/null*, while allowing standard error to display on the screen?

    a. */bin/ls > /dev/null 2> /dev/screen*

    b. */bin/ls 1> /dev/null*

c. */bin/ls > /dev/null*

d. */bin/ls > /dev/null 2>&1*

e. */bin/ls 2> /dev/null 1>&2*

25. Which of the following command(s) will display the first 5 lines of the file */etc/passwd*?

    a. *cat -5 /etc/passwd*

    b. *more -5 /etc/passwd*

    c. *head -5 /etc/passwd*

    d. *cat /etc/passwd | head -5*

    e. *cat /etc/passwd | more -5*

26. Which commands can be used to perform a search and replace on a file or a text stream?

    a. *sed*

    b. *tr*

    c. *search*

    d. *cat*

    e. *more*

27. What command(s) can be used to copy data to and from raw devices, bypassing the filesystem?

    a. *cp*

    b. *tar*

    c. *dd*

    d. *mv*

    e. *sed*

28. What option can be passed to */bin/ls* to display every file in a directory that ends in *.txt*?

    a. *ls +.txt*

    b. *ls *.txt*

    c. *ls * txt*

    d. *ls [txt]*

    e. *ls *txt**

29. What option can be passed to */bin/ls* to display every file that starts with the letters *a*, *b*, or *c*?

    a. *ls abc**

    b. *ls a*b*c**

    c. *ls ^abc*

    d. *ls [abc]+*

    e. *ls [abc]**

30. Which file extensions are common for files or directories that have been con-catenated with *tar* and then compressed with *bzip2*?

 a. *.tar.bz2*

 b. *.tbz2*

 c. *.tbz*

 d. All of the above

 e. None of the above

31. What device should you redirect output to if you do not want to see it or save it?

 a. */dev/zero*

 b. */dev/nothing*

 c. */dev/empty*

 d. */dev/null*

 e. */dev/bitbucket*

32. Which of the following commands would list the contents of the direc-tory */tmp*, store that list in the file */root/tmp.txt*, and display the list a screen at a time?

 a. *ls –l /tmp | tee /root/tmp.txt | more*

 b. *ls –l /tmp | xargs /root/tmp.txt | more*

 c. *ls –l /tmp | more | tee /root/tmp.txt*

 d. *tee /root/tmp.txt | ls –l /tmp | more*

 e. *more /tmp | tee /root/tmp.txt*

33. What character is used after a command line to indicate that the command should run in the background and return shell control to the user?

 a. *

 b. +

 c. &

 d. –

 e. .

34. What command is used at the beginning of a command line to detach the proc-ess from a terminal, allowing it to continue running after the user has logged out?

 a. *hangup*

 b. *detach*

 c. *nohup*

 d. *background*

 e. *bg*

35. What command will display a full-screen, updated list of all running processes?
    a. *kill*
    b. *ps*
    c. *list*
    d. *top*
    e. *free*

36. If a running process is not responding to a standard terminate signal from the */bin/kill* command, what option can you pass to force the process to terminate immediately?
    a. *kill -1*
    b. *kill --HUP*
    c. *kill --stop*
    d. *kill -9*
    e. *kill --now*

37. What command can be used to kill processes by name, rather than process ID?
    a. *killproc*
    b. *killname*
    c. *killall*
    d. *kill –name*
    e. *killpath*

38. Which command line would start the program */usr/bin/top* with the highest priority possible?
    a. *nice --20 /usr/bin/top*
    b. *nice 20 /usr/bin/top*
    c. *nice 19 /usr/bin/top*
    d. *nice -20 /usr/bin/top*
    e. None of the above

39. Which command is used to modify the priority of a process already running?
    a. *nice*
    b. *renice*
    c. *priority*
    d. *chage*
    e. *ps*

40. Which command(s) would display every line in */tmp/file.txt* that begins with the letter *h* and ends with the letter *t*?
    a. *grep "^h.+t$" /tmp/file.txt*
    b. *grep –E "^h.+t$" /tmp/file.txt*
    c. *grep –E "$h.+t^" /tmp/file.txt*

d. *grep –E "$ht^" /tmp/file.txt*

e. *grep –E "^h.*t$" /tmp/file.txt*

41. Which command(s) would display every line in */tmp/file.txt* that contains at least one letter of the alphabet?

    a. *grep " [a-zA-Z] " /tmp/file.txt*

    b. *grep " [:alpha:] " /tmp/file.txt*

    c. *grep " [:letters:] " /tmp/file.txt*

    d. *grep " (a-zA-Z) " /tmp/file.txt*

    e. None of the above

42. In the *vi* editor, what command sequence given in command mode will make a copy of the current line?

    a. `yyp`

    b. `cp`

    c. `yp`

    d. `ccp`

    e. None of the above

43. In the *vi* editor, what command sequence given in command mode will save the current file and quit the editor?

    a. `:qw`

    b. `:wq`

    c. `:WQ`

    d. `:pq`

    e. None of the above

44. In the *vi* editor, what command sequence given in command mode will quit a file without saving, even if changes have been made?

    a. `:q`

    b. `:q1`

    c. `:q!`

    d. `:w`

    e. `:w!`

45. Which of the following are examples of journaling filesystems?

    a. ext2

    b. ext3

    c. xfs

    d. reiserfs

    e. vfat

46. What command will create an ext3 partition on the first partition of the first SCSI hard drive?

    a. *mkfs –t ext3 /dev/sda1*

    b. *fdisk –t ext3 /dev/sda1*

    c. *fsck –t ext3 /dev/sda1*

    d. *mkfs –s ext3 /dev/hda1*

    e. *mkfs –t ext3 /dev/hda1*

47. What command is used to convert an existing ext2 partition (*/dev/sda1*) to an ext3 (journaled) partition?

    a. *tune2fs –j /dev/sda1*

    b. *dumpe2fs –j /dev/sda1*

    c. *fsck –j /dev/sda1*

    d. *mkfs.ext2 –j /dev/sda1*

    e. None of the above

48. What command is used to display the number of free inodes on an ext2 or ext3 partition?

    a. *tune2fs*

    b. *dumpe2fs*

    c. *showe2fs*

    d. *fsck*

    e. *fdisk*

49. Which file defines what partitions are mounted at boot time?

    a. */etc/partitions*

    b. */etc/mount*

    c. */etc/mtab*

    d. */etc/fstab*

    e. */etc/filesystems*

50. Which command will mount all partitions of type nfs defined in */etc/fstab*?

    a. *mount –a –t nfs*

    b. *mount –a nfs –t*

    c. *mount –nfs*

    d. *mountall –nfs*

    e. None of the above

51. If you would like to give a normal (nonroot) user the ability to mount a device, what option should you define for that device in */etc/fstab*?

    a. *mountable*

    b. *noroot*

    c. *user*

d. *ok*

e. *mount*

52. Which option to *chmod* would assign read/write permission to the file owner, read-only permission to the group owner, and read-only permission to everyone else?

    a. *chmod 644 file.txt*

    b. *chmod 755 file.txt*

    c. *chmod 466 file.txt*

    d. *chmod 777 file.txt*

    e. None of the above

53. Which option to *umask* would set my default file permissions such that files are created with these permissions: user has read/write, group has read/write, and everyone else has read only?

    a. *umask 002*

    b. *umask 022*

    c. *umask 200*

    d. *umask 220*

    e. *umask 775*

54. Which command can be used to quickly tell you if an executable command is in any directory defined in your $PATH environment variable?

    a. *find*

    b. *locate*

    c. *which*

    d. *who*

    e. *what*

55. Which directory, according to the Filesystem Hierarchy Standard, is designed to hold essential system binaries?

    a. */sbin*

    b. */bin*

    c. */usr/bin*

    d. */opt/bin*

    e. */usr/local/bin*

56. According to the Filesystem Hierarchy Standard, what directory (or directories) must hold the system kernel?

    a. */boot*

    b. */*

    c. */opt*

    d. */sbin*

    e. */kernel*

57. What command is used to maintain the filesystem index that the command */usr/bin/locate* searches?

    a. *update*

    b. *updatelocate*

    c. *locate –update*

    d. *updatedb*

    e. *update -db*

Answers

1. **c.** IDE Hard Drive

2. **b.** */proc/interrupts*

3. **b.** *1* AND **d.** *single*. Both answers are correct.

4. **d.** init

5. **b.** */var/log/messages*. This is the default logfile that syslogd saves to.

6. **d.** The BIOS

7. **a.** */sbin/shutdown –r –F now*. This may seem like a small detail to have to remember, but this is an important command, and you should have its options memorized, particularly the difference between *–F* (force *fsck* on reboot) and *–f* (skip *fsck* on reboot).

8. **c.** *init 3* AND **d.** *telinit 3*. Both answers are correct.

9. **a.** A symlink beginning with *S* in */etc/rc.d/rc5.d/* AND **b.** */etc/rc.d/rc.local*. Both answers are correct. Note that most distributions have an */etc/rc.d/rc.local* file that runs after the default runlevel scripts are run.

10. **b.** *df*

11. **c.** */tmp*. If the question was just about a partition where data changed often, that would be both */tmp* and */var*. But */tmp* is the only partition that needs to be writable by all users.

12. **c.** Master Boot Record

13. **a.** *root (hd0,0)*. GRUB (the Grand Unified Boot Loader) starts counting drives and partitions at 0, so the first partition on the first drive is 0,0.

14. **d.** */etc/ld.so.conf*. When modifications are made to this file, the command */sbin/ldconfig* must be run.

15. **c.** *apt-get update*

16. **a.** *dpkg –i package.deb*

17. **a.** *rpm –qa*

18. **a.** *yum update*

19. **a.** *rpm –verify –all* AND **b.** *rpm –Va*. Both of these commands are equivalent.

20. **b.** *echo $PATH*

21. **d.** All of the above. Remember that the ~ key indicates a user's home directory.

22. **d.** All of the above. The *history* command will list the last commands run (how many commands are listed is configurable), <Ctrl-R> will allow you to search the history by keyword, and <up arrow> cycles through the last command typed in the order in which they were typed.

23. **a.** */opt/runme* AND **b.** *./runme*

24. **b.** */bin/ls 1> /dev/null* AND **c.** */bin/ls > /dev/null*. The syntax > and 1> are equivalent. If you don't redirect *STDERR*, it will display to the screen by default.

25. **c.** *head -5 /etc/passwd* AND **d.** *cat /etc/passwd | head -5*

26. **a.** *sed* AND **b.** *tr*

27. **b.** *tar* AND **c.** *dd*. The *tar* command is often used to talk directly to tape devices (*tar –xvf /dev/st0*), and *dd* can be used to make copies of devices. For example, to create a raw image of a 1.44 MB floppy disk, use *dd if=/dev/fd0 of=/tmp/floppy.img*

28. **c.** *ls *.txt*. Remember that the syntax for file globbing is different from the syntax for regular expressions. In particular, the behavior of the asterisk (*) is vastly different between the two.

29. **e.** *ls [abc]**. Another file globbing example.

30. **d.** All of the above. Since file extensions are not really necessary in the Linux world, there isn't one single standard that covers them all. However, *tar.bz2*, *tbz2*, and *.tbz* are all examples of file extensions you might see to indicate that a file is tarred and bzipped.

31. **d.** */dev/null*. Also referred to as the "bit bucket."

32. **a.** *ls –l /tmp | tee /root/tmp.txt | more*. It's important to remember the order of commands when you are piping multiple commands together, especially when the *tee* command is involved.

33. **c.** &

34. **c.** *nohup*. The *nohup* command is usually paired with & to put a process in the background and detach it from the current terminal. For example, *nohup /opt/long_process.sh &* would start the command */opt/long_process.sh* and allow me to log out while the process remains running.

35. **d.** *top*. There are many ways to view processes on a machine, but the *top* command is probably one of the most useful commands, giving you sort ability and process interaction capability.

36. **d.** *kill -9*. Note that this might not kill a process that is waiting on disk I/O or some other kind of blocking, noninterruptible process.

37. **c.** *killall*

38. **a.** *nice --20 /usr/bin/top*. This is a tricky one. First, you have to remember that priority values range from -20 (highest priority) to 19 (lowest priority). So if I want to pass the highest priority to a process, I have to pass *-20*. However, options to commands start with the - (dash) character, so I need to make sure I type 2 dashes, the first to indicate that the next argument is an option, and the second to indicate that I'm passing a negative number to the *nice* command.

39. **b.** *renice*

40. **e.** *grep −E "^h.*t$" /tmp/file.txt*. This command literally means, "Search for the extended regular expression that matches *h* as the first character, followed by zero or more of any other character, and having *t* as the last character." The −E option is required because the presence of the .* makes this an extended regular expression. The answer in **a.** is close, but the syntax .+ means "match 1 or more characters of any kind." The regular expression in **a.** would not match the line "ht", whereas the regular expression in **e.** would.

41. **a.** *grep " [a-zA-Z] " /tmp/file.txt* AND **b.** *grep " [:alpha:] " /tmp/file.txt*. Become familiar with the sets that are defined with the syntax *[:setname:]*; they are very useful in advanced regular expressions. You can see a complete list of them in the manpage for *grep*.

42. **a.** yyp. An easy way to remember this: Yank-Yank-Put.

43. **b.** :wq. The colon brings up the command entry line at the bottom of the *vi* screen, w stands for write, and q stands for quit.

44. **c.** :q!. The *vi* editor has many, many commands, but if you become familiar with a few dozen, you'll be able to accomplish 99 percent of what you will commonly need to accomplish in *vi*.

45. **b.** ext3 AND **c.** xfs AND **d.** reiserfs. Ext3 is ext2 with journaling support added. Vfat is a Microsoft filesystem.

46. **a.** *mkfs −t ext3 /dev/sda1*. The command *mkfs.ext3* is equivalent to *mkfs −t ext3*.

47. **a.** *tune2fs −j /dev/sda1*. Technically, the command listed in **d.** (*mkfs.ext2 −j /dev/sda1*) will create an ext3 partition on */dev/sda1*, but it will destroy whatever partition is there in the process.

48. **b.** *dumpe2fs*

49. **d.** */etc/fstab*

50. **a.** *mount −a −t nfs*

51. **c.** *user*

52. **a.** *chmod 644 file.txt*

53. **b.** *umask 022*

54. **c.** *which*

55. **a.** */sbin*

56. **a.** */boot* AND **b.** /. Both directories are correct. Most Linux distributions will store the kernel in */boot*; the presence of a kernel in / is deprecated.

57. **d.** *updatedb*

10

Exam 101 Highlighter's Index

System Architecture

Objective 101.1: Determine and Configure Hardware Settings

PC BIOS

- The BIOS is the PC's firmware.
- The BIOS sets date and time for on-board clock, storage device configuration, and so on, via menus.

Resource assignments

- Interrupts (IRQs) allow peripherals to interrupt the CPU.
- I/O addresses are locations in the processor's memory map for hardware devices.
- Useful files to query for hardware information: */proc/interrupts*, */proc/io-ports*, */proc/cpuinfo*, */proc/devices*.
- Useful commands to run for hardware information: */sbin/lspci*, */sbin/lsusb*.
- DMA allows certain devices to work directly with memory, freeing the processor (see Table 10-1).

Table 10-1. Common device settings

Device	I/O address	IRQ	DMA
ttyS0 (COM1)	3f8	4	NA
ttyS1 (COM2)	2f8	3	NA
ttyS2 (COM3)	3e8	4	NA
ttyS3 (COM4)	2e8	3	NA
lp0 (LPT1)	378-37f	7	3 (if configured in the BIOS)

Device	I/O address	IRQ	DMA
lp1 (LPT2)	278-27f	5	NA
fd0, fd1 (floppies 1 and 2)	3f0-3f7	6	2

Objective 101.2: Boot the System

Boot order

- Power on → BIOS → Boot Loader → Kernel → init → startup services → shell

Information

- The command *dmesg* can be used to view the output of the boot process.
- The *init* process is always PID 1 and is the parent of all other processes.

Objective 101.3: Change Runlevels and Shut Down or Reboot System

Runlevels

- Defaults are defined in Table 10-2.

Table 10-2. Default Runlevels

Runlevel	Description
0	Halt
1	Single-user mode
2	Multiuser, without NFS
3	Full multiuser mode, without X
4	Unused
5	Full multiuser mode, with X
6	Reboot

- Runlevels can be changed on-the-fly with *init <runlevel>* or *telinit <runlevel>*.
- The default runlevel is stored in the file */etc/inittab*.
- The *init* process will run the scripts in */etc/rc.d/rcX.d* (where X is your default runlevel) in order, sending a "stop" parameter to scripts that start with K and a "start" parameter to scripts that start with S.

Linux Installation and Package Management

Objective 102.1: Design Hard Disk Layout

- Keep / small by distributing larger parts of the directory tree to other filesystems.
- Separate a small */boot* partition below cylinder 1024 for kernels.
- Separate */var* into its own partition to prevent runaway logs from filling /.

- Separate */tmp*.
- Separate */usr* if it is to be shared read-only among other systems via NFS.
- Set swap size to be somewhere between one and two times the size of main memory.

/proc

- The */proc* filesystem includes information on interrupts, I/O ports, and DMA in */proc/interrupts*, */proc/ioports*, and */proc/dma*.

Objective 102.2: Install a Boot Manager

LILO

- LILO has historically been the default Linux boot loader.
- LILO consists of the *lilo* command, which installs the boot loader, and the boot loader itself.
- LILO is configured using */etc/lilo.conf*.
- Any modification to the */etc/lilo.conf* file requires the *lilo* command to be rerun.

GRUB

- GRUB can boot Linux as well as most other PC-based operating systems.
- GRUB relies on various files in the */boot/grub* directory to support reading from various types of filesystems.
- GRUB is configured using */boot/grub/menu.lst* (or */boot/grub/grub.conf* on some distributions).
- GRUB can be configured to present a text or graphical menu interface and also has a command-line interface.
- Modifications to the GRUB configuration files do not require the *grub* command to be re-run (unlike LILO).

Objective 102.3: Manage Shared Libraries

Concepts

- System libraries provide many of the functions required by a program.
- A program that contains executable code from libraries is *statically linked* because it stands alone and contains all necessary code to execute.
- Since static linking leads to larger executable files and more resource consumption, system libraries can be shared among many executing programs at the same time.

Commands

- A program that contains references to external, shared libraries is *dynamically linked* at runtime by the dynamic linker, *ld.so*.
- New locations for shared libraries can be added to the LD_LIBRARY_PATH variable. As an alternative, the locations can be added to */etc/ld.so.conf*, which lists library file directories. After this, you must run */sbin/ldconfig* to translate this file into the binary index */etc/ld.so.cache*.

Objective 102.4: Use Debian Package Management

Commands

- *dpkg* automates the installation and maintenance of software packages and offers a number of options.
- *dselect* uses a text-based interactive menu to select (or deselect) packages for installation.
- *alien* can convert packages to and from the RPM and Debian package format.
- *apt-get* is a powerful tool that interfaces with online repositories of Debian packages to install and upgrade packages by name and resolves each package's dependencies automatically.

Objective 102.5: Use Red Hat Package Manager (RPM)

Concepts

- RPM automates the installation and maintenance of software packages.
- Package dependencies are defined but not resolved automatically.
- *-i, -e, -U, -v, -h, --nodeps*, and *--force* are common options.
- The *yum* command is a frontend to RPM, interacting with online software repositories to download and install software automatically.
- The command *yum update* will search for updates to installed packages, download them, resolve dependencies, and install them automatically.

GNU and Unix Commands

Objective 103.1: Work on the Command Line

The interactive shell and shell variables

- A *shell* provides the command prompt and interprets commands.
- A *shell variable* holds a value that is accessible to shell programs.
- PATH is a shell variable that contains a listing of directories that hold executable programs.

- Commands must be *bash* built-ins, found in the PATH, or explicitly defined in order to succeed.
- When shell variables are *exported*, they become part of the *environment*.

Entering commands

- Commands are comprised of a valid command, with or without one or more options and arguments, followed by a carriage return.
- Interactive commands can include looping structures more often used in shell scripts.

Command history, editing, and substitution

- Shell sessions can be viewed as a conversation. History, expansion, and editing make that dialog more productive.
- Commands can be reissued, modified, and edited. Examples are shown in Table 10-3.
- Command substitution allows the *result* of a command to be placed into a shell variable.

Table 10-3. Shell expansion, editing, and substitution examples

History type	Examples
Expansion	!!
	!n
	^string1^string2
Editing	Ctrl-P, previous line
	Ctrl-K, kill to end of line
	Ctrl-Y, paste (yank) text
Substitution	VAR=$(command) or VAR='command'

Recursive execution

- Many commands contain either a *-r* or *-R* option for recursive execution through a directory hierarchy.
- The *find* command is inherently recursive, and is intended to descend through directories looking for files with certain attributes or executing commands.

Objective 103.2: Process Text Streams Using Filters

The commands

The following programs modify or manipulate text from files and standard input:

cat [file]
> Print *file* to standard output.

cut [files]
> Cut out selected columns or fields from one or more *files*.

expand [files]
> Convert Tabs to spaces in *files*.

fmt [files]
> Format text in *files* to a specified width by filling lines and removing newline characters.

head [files]
> Print the first few lines of *files*.

join file1 file2
> Print a line for each pair of input lines, one each from *file1* and *file2*, that have identical join fields.

nl [files]
> Number the lines of *files*, which are concatenated in the output.

od [files]
> Dump *files* in octal, hexadecimal, ASCII, and other formats.

paste files
> Paste together corresponding lines of one or more files into vertical columns.

pr [file]
> Convert a text file into a paginated, columnar version, with headers and page fills.

sort [file]
> Sort lines in *file* alphabetically, numerically, or other ways.

split [infile] [outfile]
> Split *infile* into a specified number of line groups; the output will go into a succession of files: *outfile*aa, *outfile*ab, and so on.

tac [file]
> Print *file* to standard output in reverse line order.

tail [files]
> Print the last few lines of one or more files.

tr [string1 [string2]]
> Translate characters by mapping from *string1* to the corresponding character in *string2*.

unexpand [files]
> Convert spaces to Tabs in *files*.

uniq [files]
> Display only unique lines in *files* that are already sorted.

wc [files]
> Print counts of characters, words, and lines for *files*.

The stream editor, sed

sed is a popular text-filtering program found on every Unix system. It has the following syntax:

```
sed command [files]
sed -e command1 [-e command2] [files]
sed -f script [files]
```

Execute *sed commands*, or those found in *script*, on standard input or *files*.

Objective 103.3: Perform Basic File Management

Concepts

- Filesystem creation prepares a disk device (or partition) for use. Linux usually uses the native *ext3* (third extended) journaling filesystem, but it supports many other filesystem types. You can see a list of all the filesystems Linux supports by using the "l" option under the *fdisk* command.

- The Linux filesystem is arranged into a hierarchical structure anchored at the *root directory*, or /. Beneath this is a tree of directories and files.

- Identification information for a filesystem object is stored in its *inode* (index node), which holds location, modification, and security information. Filesystems are created with a finite number of inodes.

File and directory management commands

The following commands are essential for the management of files and directories:

bzip2 [options] [pattern]
> Create or uncompress an archive with the bzip2 algorithm.

cp file1 file2

cp files directory
> Copy *file1* to *file2*, or copy *files* to *directory*.

cpio[options] [files]
> Create or extract a binary archive, containing either files or a recursive set of files and directories.

dd [options] [files]
> Copy and convert files. The *dd* command can also copy data from raw devices, bypassing the filesystem layer.

file [file]
> Determine the type of *file* by performing a number of tests.

find [directory] [options] [pattern]
> Search through *directory* looking for objects that match *pattern*.

gunzip [options] [file]
> Uncompress an archive created with *gzip*.

gzip [options] [pattern]
> Create a compressed archive containing files and directories that match *pattern*.

ls [options] [pattern]
> List the contents of a directory, or list only files that match *[pattern]*.

mkdir directories
> Create one or more *directories*.

mv source target
> Move or rename files and directories.

rm files
> Delete one or more *files* from the filesystem. When used recursively (with the -r option), *rm* also removes directories.

rmdir directories
> Delete *directories*, which must be empty.

tar [options] [files]
> Create or extract a Tape Archive, containing either files or a recursive set of files and directories.

touch files
> Change the access and/or modification times of *files* by default to the present time.

File-naming wildcards

Wildcards (also called *file globs*) allow the specification of many files at once. A list of commonly used wildcards can be found in Table 10-4.

Table 10-4. File-naming wildcards

Wildcard	Function
*	Match zero or more characters.
?	Match exactly one character.
[characters]	Match any single character from among *characters* listed between brackets.
[!characters]	Match any single character other than *characters* listed between brackets.
[a-z]	Match any single character from among the range of characters listed between brackets.
[!a-z]	Match any single character from among the characters not in the range listed between brackets.
{frag1,frag2,frag3,...}	Brace expansion: create strings *frag1, frag2*, and *frag3*, etc., such that file_{one,two,three} yields file_one, file_two, and file_three.

Objective 103.4: Use Streams, Pipes, and Redirects

Concepts

- A central concept for Linux and Unix systems is that *everything is a file*.
- Many system devices are represented in the filesystem using a *device file*, such as */dev/ttyS0* for a serial port.

Standard I/O

- The shell provides the *standard I/O* capability, offering three default file descriptors to running programs:
  - *Standard input (STDIN)* is a text input stream, by default attached to the keyboard.
  - *Standard output (STDOUT)* is an output stream for normal program output. By default, this is the screen.
  - *Standard error (STDERR)* is an output stream meant for error messages. By default, this is the screen.

Pipes and redirection

- It is possible to tie the output of one program to the input of another. This is known as a *pipe* and is created by joining commands using the pipe symbol (|).
- Pipes are a special form of *redirection*, which allows you to manage the origin of input streams and the destination of output streams. Redirection syntax for various shells differs slightly. See Table 10-5 for examples of common redirection operators.

Table 10-5. Common redirection operators

Redirection function	Syntax for bash
Send *STDOUT* to *file*.	$ cmd > file
	$ cmd 1> file
Send *STDERR* to *file*.	$ cmd 2> file
Send both *STDOUT* and *STDERR* to *file*.	$ cmd > file 2>&1
	$ cmd > file 2> file
Receive *STDIN* from *file*.	$ cmd < file
Append *STDOUT* to *file*.	$ cmd >> file
	$ cmd 1>> file
Append *STDERR* to *file*.	$ cmd 2>> file
Append both *STDOUT* and *STDERR* to *file*.	$ cmd >> file 2>&1
Pipe *STDOUT* from *cmd1* to *cmd2*.	$ cmd1	cmd2
Pipe *STDOUT* and *STDERR* from *cmd1* to *cmd2*.	$ cmd1 2>&1	cmd2
Pipe *STDOUT* from *cmd1* to *cmd2* while simultaneously writing it to *file1* using *tee*.	$ cmd1	tee file1	cmd2

Objective 103.5: Create, Monitor, and Kill Processes

Concepts

- Processes have:
  - A lifetime
  - A PID
  - A UID
  - A GID
  - A parent process
  - An environment
  - A current working directory

Monitoring commands

ps
  Generate a one-time snapshot of the current processes on standard output.

pstree
  Display a hierarchical list of processes in a tree format.

top
  Generate a continuous, formatted, real-time process activity display on a terminal or in a terminal window.

Signaling processes

- Processes listen for *signals* sent by the kernel or users using the *kill* command:

      kill -*sigspec* [*pids*]

  Send *sigspec* to *pids*.
- The *killall* command is used to send signals to processes by program name instead of PID.
- Common *kill* signals are listed in Table 10-6.

Table 10-6. Common signals

Signal	Number	Meaning
HUP	1	Hangup, reread configuration.
INT	2	Interrupt, stop running.
KILL	9	Exit immediately.
TERM	15	Terminate nicely.
TSTP	18	Stop executing.

Shell job control

Shells can run processes in the *background*, where they execute on their own, or in the *foreground*, attached to a terminal. Each process handled in this way is known as a *job*. Jobs are manipulated using job control commands:

bg [jobspec]
> Place *jobspec* in the background as if it had been started with **&**.

fg [jobspec]
> Place *jobspec* in the foreground, making it the current job.

jobs [jobspecs]
> List *jobspecs* on standard output.

nohup [command] &
> Execute *command*, detach it from the terminal, and allow it to continue running after the user logs out.

Objective 103.6: Modify Process Execution Priorities

Concepts

- A process's *execution priority* is managed by the kernel.
- You can bias the execution priority by specifying a *nice number* in the range of −20 to +19 (default is 0).
- Positive nice numbers reduce priority; negative nice numbers increase priority and are reserved for the superuser.

Commands

nice -adjustment [command]
> Apply nice number *adjustment* to the process created to run *command*.

renice [+|-]nicenumber targets
> Alter the *nicenumber*, and thus the scheduling priority, of one or more running *target* processes.

Objective 103.7: Search Text Files Using Regular Expressions

Concepts

- *Regular expressions* are used to match text. The term is used to describe the loosely defined text-matching language as well as the patterns themselves. A regular expression is often called a *regex* or a *regexp*.
- Regular expressions are made up of *metacharacters* (with special meaning) and *literals* (everything that is not a metacharacter).
- The backslash character (\) turns off (escapes) the special meaning of the character that follows, turning metacharacters into literals. For nonmetacharacters, it often turns on some special meaning.

Position anchors

The operators in Table 10-7 match line position.

Table 10-7. Regular expression position anchors

Regular expression	Description
^	Match the beginning of a line.
$	Match the end of a line.
\< \>	Match word boundaries. Word boundaries are defined as whitespace, start of a line, end of a line, or punctuation marks. The backslashes are required and enable this interpretation of < and >.

Character sets

The operators in Table 10-8 match text.

Table 10-8. Regular expression character sets

Regular expression	Description
[abc] [a-z]	Match any single character from among listed characters (*abc*) or from among the characters comprising a range (*a–z*).
[^abc] [^a-z]	Match any single character not among listed characters or ranges.
.	Match any single character except a newline.

Modifiers

The operators in Table 10-9 modify the way other operators are interpreted.

Table 10-9. Regular expression modifiers

Basic regular expression	Extended regular expression	Description
*	*	Match zero or more of the character that precedes it.
\?	?	Match zero or one instance of the preceding *regex*.
\+	+	Match one or more instances of the preceding *regex*.
\{n,m\}	{n,m}	Match a range of occurrences of the single character or regex that precedes this construct. \{n\} matches *n* occurrences, \{n,\} matches at least *n* occurrences, and \{n,m\} matches any number of occurrences between *n* and *m*, inclusively.
|			Match the character or expression to the left or right of the vertical bar.
\(regex\)	(regex)	Matches *regex*, but it can be modified as a whole and used in back-references. (\1 expands to the contents of the first \(\) and so on up to \9.)

Commands

- Many commands support the regular expression syntax, but the most commonly used is the command *grep*, which is designed to display lines from a file or files matching a given regular expression.
- There are multiple ways to call *grep* to change its behavior:

grep
> Treat the pattern as a basic regular expression.

egrep
> Treat the pattern as an extended regular expression. Same as *grep –E*.

fgrep
> Treat the pattern as a list of fixed strings, any of which may be matched. Same as *grep –F*.

Objective 103.8: Perform Basic File Editing Operations Using vi

Subcommands

- Start *vi* with *vi file1 [file2 [...]]*. See Table 10-10.

Table 10-10. Basic vi editing commands

Command	Description
Esc	Exit insert mode and put the editor into command mode.
h or left arrow	Move left one character.
j or down arrow	Move down one line.
k or up arrow	Move up one line.
l or right arrow	Move right one character.
H	Move to the top of the screen.
L	Move to the bottom of the screen.
G	Move to the end of the file.
W	Move forward one word.
B	Move backward one word.
0 (zero)	Move to the beginning of the current line.
^	Move to the first nonwhitespace character on the current line.
$	Move to the end of the current line.
Ctrl-B	Move up (back) one screen.
Ctrl-F	Move down (forward) one screen.
i	Insert at the current cursor position.
I	Insert at the beginning of the current line.

Command	Description
a	Append after the current cursor position.
A	Append to the end of the current line.
o	Start a new line after the current line.
O	Start a new line before the current line.
r	Replace the character at the current cursor position.
R	Start replacing (overwriting) at the current cursor position.
x	Delete the character at the current cursor position.
X	Delete the character immediately before (to the left) of the current cursor position.
s	Delete the character at the current cursor position and go into insert mode. (This is the equivalent of the combination xi.)
S	Delete the contents of the current line and go into insert mode.
d*X*	Given a movement command *X*, cut (delete) the appropriate number of characters, words, or lines from the current cursor position.
dd	Cut the entire current line.
D	Cut from the current cursor position to the end of the line. (This is equivalent to d$.)
c*X*	Given a movement command *X*, cut the appropriate number of characters, words, or lines from the current cursor position and go into insert mode.
cc	Cut the entire current line and go into insert mode.
C	Cut from the current cursor position to the end of the line and enter insert mode. (This is equivalent to c$.)
y*X*	Given a movement command *X*, copy (yank) the appropriate number of characters, words, or lines from the current cursor position.
yy or Y	Copy the entire current line.
p	Paste after the current cursor position.
P	Paste before the current cursor position.
.	Repeat the last command.
u	Undo the last command.
/*regex*	Search forward for *regex*.
?*regex*	Search backward for *regex*.
n	Find the next match.
N	Find the previous match. (In other words, repeat the last search in the opposite direction.)
:n	Next file; when multiple files are specified for editing, this command loads the next file. Force this action (if the current file has unsaved changes) with :n!.
:e *file*	Load *file* in place of the current file. Force this action with :e! *file*.
:r *file*	Insert the contents of *file* after the current cursor position.
:q	Quit without saving changes. Force this action with :q!.
:w *file*	Write the current buffer to *file*. To append to an existing file, use :w >>*file*. Force the write (when possible, such as when running as root) with :w! *file*.
:wq	Write the file contents and quit. Force this action with :wq!.

Command	Description
:x	Write the file contents (if changed) and quit (the ex equivalent of ZZ).
ZZ	Write the file contents (if changed) and quit.
:! command	Execute command in a subshell.

Devices, Linux Filesystems, and the Filesystem Hierarchy Standard

Objective 104.1: Create Partitions and Filesystems

Disk drives and partitions

- IDE disks are known as *dev/hda*, *dev/hdb*, *dev/hdc*, *dev/hdd*, and so on.

- Any disks using the SCSI emulation layer are known as *dev/sda*, *dev/sdb*, *dev/sdc*, and so on. These include SCSI disks, SATA disks, and, in newer kernels, IDE disks.

- Three types of partitions:

  Primary
  > Filesystem container. At least one must exist, and up to four can exist on a single physical disk. They are identified with numbers 1 to 4, such as */dev/hda1*, */dev/hda2*, and so on.

  Extended
  > A variant of a primary partition, but it cannot contain a filesystem. Instead, it contains one or more *logical partitions*. Only one extended partition may exist, and it takes one of the four possible spots for primary partitions.

  Logical
  > Created *within* the extended partition. From 1 to 12 logical partitions may be created. They are numbered from 5 to 16, such as */dev/hda5*, */dev/hda6*, and so on.

- Up to 15 partitions with filesystems may exist on a single physical disk.

Filesystems

- The Linux kernel supports many different kinds of filesystems:

  ext3
  > The third extended filesystem. A journaling filesystem, this has been the default for most Linux distributions since the early 2000s.

  ext2
  > The second extended filesystem. This was the initial default Linux filesystem. *ext3* is basically *ext2* with journaling support.

  xfs
  > Journaling filesystem created by Silicon Graphics for IRIX and ported to Linux.

reiserfs
> This was the first journaling filesystem introduced in the standard Linux kernel.

vfat
> A Microsoft Windows filesystem for Windows 95, 98, and ME systems.

The root filesystem and mount points

- The top of the filesystem tree is occupied by the *root filesystem*. Other filesystems are mounted under it, creating a unified filesystem.
- */etc*, */lib*, */bin*, */sbin*, and */dev* must be part of the root filesystem.

Partition and filesystem management commands

The following commands are commonly used to repair and manage filesystems:

fdisk [device]
> Manipulate or display the partition table for *device* using a command-driven interactive text interface. *device* is a physical disk such as */dev/hda*, not a partition such as */dev/hda1*.

mkfs device
> Make a filesystem on *device*, which must be a partition.

mkswap device
> Prepare a partition for use as swap space.

Objective 104.2: Maintain the Integrity of Filesystems

Filesystem commands

df [directories]
> Display overall disk utilization information for mounted filesystems on *directories*.

du [directories]
> Display disk utilization information for *directories*.

fsck filesystems
> Check *filesystems* for errors and optionally correct them.

dumpe2fs filesystem
> Display the detailed information about the *ext2* or *ext3* filesystem at *filesystem*.

tune2fs filesystem
> Modify filesystem variables for the *ext2* or *ext3* filesystem at *filesystem*.

Objective 104.3: Control Filesystem Mounting and Unmounting

Managing the filesystem table

- */etc/fstab* contains mount information for filesystems. Each line contains a single filesystem entry made up of six fields, shown in Table 10-11.

- The */media* directory is often used by distributions as a place to automount hotplug devices, such as USB drives.

Table 10-11. Fields found in the /etc/fstab file

Entry	Description
Device	The device file for the partition holding the filesystem.
Mount point	The directory upon which the filesystem is to be mounted.
Filesystem type	A filesystem type, such as *ext3*.
Mount options	A comma-separated list.
Dump frequency	For use with dump.
Pass number for `fsck`	Used at boot time.

Mounting and unmounting

The following commands are used to mount and unmount filesystems:

mount *device*

mount *directory*

mount *device directory*

  Mount filesystems onto the hierarchy. The first and second forms consult */etc/fstab* for additional information.

umount *device*

umount *directory*

  Unmount the filesystem on *device* or mount it on *directory*.

Filesystem types

Common filesystem types compatible with Linux include:

ext2

  The standard Linux filesystem.

ext3

  A journaling filesystem that is backward-compatible with *ext2*.

iso9660

  The standard CD-ROM format.

vfat

  The Microsoft Windows FAT filesystem.

nfs

  Remote servers.

proc

  A system abstraction for access to kernel parameters.

swap

  Swap partitions.

Objective 104.4: Set and View Disk Quotas

Quota types

Per-user hard
> The maximum size for an individual.

Per-user soft
> A warning threshold.

Per-group hard
> The maximum size for a group.

Per-group soft
> A warning threshold.

Grace period
> A time restriction on the soft limit.

Commands

quota user

quota -g group
> Display quota limits on *user* or *group*.

quotaon [filesystems]
> Enable previously configured disk quotas on one or more *filesystems*.

quotaoff [filesystems]
> Disable disk quotas on one or more *filesystems*.

quotacheck [filesystems]
> Examine filesystems and compile quota databases. Usually run via *cron*.

edquota names
> Modify user or group quotas by spawning a text editor.

repquota filesystems
> Display a summary report of quota status for *filesystems*, or use *-a* for all filesystems.

 Enabling quotas requires usrquota and/or grpquota options in */etc/fstab*, creation of *quota.user* and *quota.group* files at the top of the filesystem, a *quotacheck*, and a *quotaon*.

Objective 104.5: Manage File Permissions and Ownership

Access control

- Access control is implemented using a set of properties called the *access mode*, stored in the inode. Three classes of user are defined:

User
> The user who owns the file.

Group
> The group that owns the file.

Other
> All other users on the system.

- Three permissions are either granted or not granted to each class of user:

Read (r)
> Allows access to file contents and listing of directory contents.

Write (w)
> Allows writing a file or creating files in a directory.

Execute (x)
> Allows execution of a file and ability to read/write files in a directory.

- These comprise nine bits in the mode User rwx, Group rwx, and Other rwx.
- Three additional mode bits are defined:

SUID
> To grant processes the rights of an executable file's owner.

SGID
> To grant processes the rights of an executable file's group.

Sticky bit
> Prohibits file deletion by nonowners.

- These 12-mode bits are often referred to in octal notation as well as with mnemonic constructs.
- Mode bits are displayed using such commands as *ls* and *stat*.

Setting access modes

- New files receive initial access mode as described by the *umask*.
- The *umask* strips specified bits from the initial mode settings. Typical umasks are 002 and 022.
- Existing file modes are changed using *chmod* with either symbolic or octal mode specifications:

— Symbolic:

```
[ugoa][-+=][rwxXst]
```

— Octal bits:

```
user r, w, x, group r, w, x, other r, w, x
rwxrwxrwx = 111111111 = 777
rwxr-xr-- = 111101100 = 751
```

chmod uses the following syntax:

chmod mode files
> Modify the access mode on *files* using a symbolic or octal *mode*.

Commands for file ownership

chown user-owner.group-owner files
> Change the owner and/or group of *files* to *user-owner* and/or *group-owner*.

chgrp group-owner files
> Change the group ownership of *files* to *group-owner*.

> *chgrp* functionality is included in *chown*.

Objective 104.6: Create and Change Hard and Symbolic Links

Concepts

- A link is a pseudonym for another file.
- Links take up very little space in the filesystem.
- A *symbolic link* is a tiny file that contains a pointer to another file. Symbolic links can span filesystems.
- A *hard link* is a copy of a file's directory entry. Both directory entries point to the same inode and thus the same data, ownership, and permissions.

ln

ln has the following syntax:

> *ln file link*
> *ln files directory*

Create *link* to *file* or in *directory* for all *files*. Symbolic links are created with the *-s* option.

Objective 104.7: Find System Files and Place Files in the Correct Location

File Hierarchy Standard (FHS)

- The FHS is used by Linux distributions to standardize filesystem layout. It defines two categories of data use, each with opposing subtypes:

  Data sharing
  > Sharable data can be used by multiple host systems on a network. Non-sharable data is unique to one particular host system.

  Data modification
  > Variable data is changed continually by naturally occurring (i.e., frequent) processes. Static data is left alone, remaining unchanged over extended periods of time.

- The FHS seeks to define the filesystem contents in these terms and locate information accordingly.

The directory hierarchy

- The root filesystem (/):

  — Must contain utilities and files sufficient to boot the operating system, including the ability to mount other filesystems.

  — Should contain the utilities needed by the system administrator to repair or
  restore a damaged system.

  — Should be relatively small.

- */usr* contains system utilities and programs that do not appear in the / (root)
  filesystem. It includes directories such as *bin*, *lib*, *local*, and *src*.

- */var* contains varying data such as printer spools and logfiles, including directories such as *log*, *mail*, and *spool*.

Locating files

- Various methods can be used to locate files in the filesystem:

  which command
  > Determine the location of *command* and display the full pathname of the
  > executable program that the shell would launch to execute it.

  find paths expression
  > Search for files that match *expression*, starting at *paths* and continuing
  > recursively.

  locate patterns
  > Locate files whose names match one or more *patterns* by searching an
  > index of files previously created.

  updatedb
  > Refresh (or create) the *slocate* database, usually via *cron*.

  whatis keywords

  apropos keywords
  > Search the *whatis* database for *keywords*. *whatis* finds only exact matches,
  > whereas *apropos* finds partial word matches.

11

Exam 102 Overview

LPI Exam 102 is the second of two exams required for the LPI's Level 1 certification (officially referred to as LPIC 1). This exam tests your knowledge on 6 of the 10 major Topic areas specified for LPIC Level 1. Each section details certain Objectives, which are described here and on the LPI website (*http://www.lpi.org/eng/certifica tion/the_lpic_program/lpic_1/exam_102_detailed_objectives*).

Each Topic contains a series of Objectives covering specific areas of expertise. Each of these Objectives is assigned a numeric weight, which acts as an indicator of the importance of the Objective. Weights run between 1 and 8, with higher numbers indicating more importance. An Objective carrying a weight of 1 can be considered relatively unimportant and isn't likely to be covered in much depth on the exam. Objectives with larger weights are sure to be covered on the exam, so you should study these Topics closely. The weights of the Objectives are provided at the beginning of each Topic section.

Exam Topics are numbered using the *topic.objective* notation (e.g., 101.1, 101.2, 102.1). The 100 series topics represent LPI Level 1 certification topics, which are unique to all levels of LPI exams (e.g., 101, 102, 201, 202, etc.). The objective number represents the objectives that are associated with the Topic area (e.g., 1, 2, 3, 4, and so on).

The Level 1 Topics are distributed between the two exams to create tests of similar length and difficulty without subject matter overlap. As a result, there's no requirement or advantage to taking the exams in sequence, the only caveat being that you cannot be awarded an LPIC 2 or higher certifications until you pass the requirements for the lower level certification.

The Topics for Exam 102 are listed in Table 11-1.

Table 11-1. LPI Topics for Exam 102

Name	Number of objectives	Description
Shells, Scripting, and Data Management	3	Covers the shell and its startup files and writing *bash* scripts, querying databases, and manipulating data using basic SQL commands.
User Interfaces and Desktops	3	The X-based Objectives cover only subjects that every Level 1 sysadmin is expected to encounter. Some of these tasks include installing and configuring X11, setting up a display manager such as XDM, GDM, or KDM, and installing and understanding basic accessibility tools.
Administrative Tasks	3	Covers all of the basic administrative tasks done by a junior level Linux sysadmin, including managing users and groups, user environment variables, job scheduling, and data backup.
Essential System Services	4	Covers administering system services that must be configured, including maintaining system time, system logs, basic understanding of mail transfer agents, and managing printing.
Networking Fundamentals	3	Explores TCP/IP, network interfaces, DHCP, and client-side DNS; includes troubleshooting commands.
Security	3	Covers security issues such as SUID issues, *ssh* client use, GPG for data encryption, and user limits.

Exam 102 lasts a maximum of 90 minutes and contains exactly 60 questions. The exam is administered using a custom application on a PC in a private room with no notes or other reference material. The majority of the exam is made up of multiple-choice single-answer questions. These questions have only one correct answer and are answered using radio buttons. A few of the questions present a scenario needing administrative action. Others seek the appropriate commands for performing a particular task or for proof of understanding of a particular concept. Some people may get an exam with an additional 20 items. These items are used to test new questions and don't count as part of the score. An additional 30 minutes is provided in this case, and there is no indication of which items are unscored.

The exam also includes a few multiple-choice multiple-answer questions, which are answered using checkboxes. These questions can have multiple correct responses, each of which must be checked. These are probably the most difficult type of question to answer because the possibility of multiple answers increases the likelihood of mistakes. An incorrect response on any one of the possible answers causes you to miss the entire question.

The exam also has some fill-in-the-blank questions. These questions provide a one-line text area input box for you to fill in your answer. These questions check your knowledge of concepts such as important files, commands, or well-known facts that you are expected to know.

12

Exam 102 Study Guide

The second part of this book contains a section for each of the six Topics found on Exam 102 for LPIC Level 1 certification. Each of the following tables details the Objectives described for the corresponding Topic on the LPI website (*http://www.lpi.org/eng/certification/the_lpic_program/lpic_1/exam_102_detailed_objectives*).

Exam Preparation

LPI Exam 102 is thorough, but if you have a solid foundation in Linux concepts as described here, you should find it straightforward. If you've already taken Exam 101, you'll find that Exam 102 covers a broader range of Linux administration skills. Included are user interfaces, printing, documentation, shells and scripting, administrative tasks, networking fundamentals, system services, and security. Exam 102 is quite specific on some Topics, such as network applications (for example, Sendmail), but you won't come across questions intended to trick you, and you're unlikely to find questions that you feel are ambiguous.

For clarity, this material is presented in the same order as the LPI Topics and Objectives. To assist you with your preparation, Table 12-1 through 12-9 provide a complete listing of the Topics and Objectives for Exam 102. Because of changes made during test development, the final Objectives are not always in exact numerical order. After you complete your study of each Objective, simply check it off here to measure and organize your progress.

Table 12-1. Shells, Scripting, and Data Management (Topic 105)

Objective	Weight	Description
1	4	Customize and Use the Shell Environment
2	4	Customize or Write Simple Scripts
3	2	SQL Data Management

Table 12-2. The X Window System (Topic 106)

Objective	Weight	Description
1	2	Install and Configure X11
2	2	Set Up a Display Manager
3	1	Accessibility

Table 12-3. Administrative Tasks (Topic 107)

Objective	Weight	Description
1	5	Manage User and Group Accounts and Related System Files
2	4	Automate System Administration Tasks by Scheduling Jobs
3	3	Localization and Internationalization

Table 12-4. Essential System Services (Topic 108)

Objective	Weight	Description
1	3	Maintain System Time
2	2	System Logging
3	3	Mail Transfer Agent (MTA) Basics
4	2	Manage Printers and Printing

Table 12-5. Networking Fundamentals (Topic 109)

Objective	Weight	Description
1	4	Fundamentals of Internet Protocols
2	4	Basic Network Configuration
3	4	Basic Network Troubleshooting
4	2	Configuring Client Side DNS

Table 12-6. Security (Topic 110)

Objective	Weight	Description
1	3	Perform Security Administration Tasks
2	3	Set Up Host Security
3	3	Securing Data with Encryption

13

Shells, Scripting, and Data Management (Topic 105)

Depending upon the computing environments you're used to, the concepts of shells and shell programs (usually called *scripts*) may be a little foreign. On Linux systems, the shell is a full programming environment that can be scripted or used interactively.

This chapter covers Topic 105 and its three Objectives:

Objective 1: Customize and Use the Shell Environment
This Objective covers your shell and basic scripting concepts, including environment variables, functions, and script files that control the login environment. Weight: 4.

Objective 2: Customize or Write Simple Scripts
Customization of the many scripts found on a Linux system is important for its management and automation. Topics for this Objective include shell syntax, checking the status of executed programs, and issues surrounding the properties of script files. Weight: 4.

Objective 3: SQL Data Management
This objective covers the basic use of SQL databases to store and query data. Topics for this Objective include communicating with a SQL database, basic queries, basic database concepts, and the relationship between data and tables. Weight: 2.

It is important for Linux administrators to become comfortable with at least one shell and its programming language. This can be an area of some concern to those used to graphics-only environments, where the use of a command interpreter is not a daily activity. As you'll see, becoming adept at working with your favorite shell will allow you to customize many trivial tasks and become a more efficient system administrator.

Objective 1: Customize and Use the Shell Environment

This Objective could be considered a brief "getting started with shells" overview because it details many of the basic concepts necessary to utilize the shell environment on Linux. These concepts are fundamental and very important for system administrators working on Linux systems. If you're new to shells and shell scripting, take heart. You can think of it as a combination of computer interaction (conversation) and computer programming (automation). It is nothing more than that, but the result is far more than this simplicity implies. If you're an old hand with shell programming, you may want to skip ahead to brush up on some of the particulars necessary for Exam 102.

If you've never taken a computer programming course before, don't be too discouraged. Shell programming is mostly automating repetitive tasks. Your shell scripts can conceivably become relatively complicated programs in their own right, but shell scripting does not have the learning curve of a "conventional" programming language such as C or C++.

An Overview of Shells

A shell is a fundamental and important part of your Linux computing environment. Shells are user programs not unlike other text-based programs and utilities. They offer a rich, customizable interface to your system. Some of the main items provided by your shell are:

An interactive textual user interface to the operating system
> In this role, the shell is a command interpreter and display portal to the system. It offers you a communications channel to the kernel and is often thought of as the "shell around the kernel." That's where the name *shell* originates and is a good metaphor for conceptualizing how shells fit into the overall Linux picture.

An operating environment
> Shells set up an *environment* for the execution of other programs, which affects the way some of them behave. This environment consists of any number of *environment variables*, each of which describes one particular environment property by defining a `name=value` pair. Other features such as *aliases* enhance your operating environment by offering shorthand notations for commonly used commands.

A facility for launching and managing commands and programs
> Shells are used not only by users but also by the system to launch programs and support those programs with an operating environment.

A programming language
> Shells offer their own programming languages. At its simplest, this feature allows user commands to be assembled into useful sequences. At the other end of the spectrum, complete programs can be written in shell languages, with loop control, variables, and all of the capabilities of Linux's rich set of operating system commands.

All of the shells share some common concepts:

- They are all distinct from the kernel and run as user programs.
- Each shell can be customized by tuning the shell's operating environment.
- Shells are run for both interactive use by end users and noninteractive use by the system.
- A shell can be run from within another shell, enabling you to try a shell other than your default shell. To do this, you simply start the other shell from the command line of your current shell. In fact, this happens constantly on your system as scripts are executed and programs are launched. The new shell does not replace the shell that launched it; instead, the new shell is a process running with the original shell as a parent process. When you terminate the child shell, you go back to the original one.
- Shells use a series of *configuration files* in order to establish their operating environment.
- Shells pass on environment variables to child processes.

The Bash Shell

bash is the GNU Project implementation of the standard Unix shell *sh*. Since the original *sh* was the "Bourne shell," *bash* is the "Bourne again shell". As the *bash* home page (*http://www.gnu.org/software/bash*) says:

> Bash is an *sh*-compatible shell that incorporates useful features from the Korn shell (*ksh*) and C shell (*csh*). It is intended to conform to the IEEE POSIX P1003.2/ISO 9945.2 Shell and Tools standard. It offers functional improvements over *sh* for both programming and interactive use.

While there are a number of shells available to choose from on a Linux system, *bash* is very popular and powerful, and it is the default shell for new accounts. Bash has become popular enough that it is available on many other Unix flavors as well, including Sun's Solaris and Hewlett-Packard's HP/UX. Exam 102 concentrates on its use and configuration. The next few sections deal with common shell concepts, but the examples are specific to *bash*.

Shells and environment variables

Many programs running under Linux require information about you and your personal preferences to operate sensibly. Although you could manually provide this information to each program you run, much of the information you'd convey would be redundant because you'd be telling every command you enter the same ancillary information at each invocation. For example, you'd need to tell your paging program about the size and nature of your terminal or terminal window each time you use it. You would also need to give fully qualified directory names for the programs you run.

Rather than force users to include so much detail to issue commands, the shell handles much of this information for you automatically. You've already seen that the shell creates an operating environment for you. That environment is made up of a series of *variables*, each of which has a value that is used by programs and other shells. The two types of variables used by most shells are:

Environment variables

These variables can be thought of as *global variables* because they are passed on to all processes started by the shell, including other shells. This means that child processes inherit the environment. By convention, environment variables are given uppercase names. *bash* doesn't require the case convention; it is just intended for clarity to humans. However, variable names are case-sensitive. Your shell maintains many environment variables, including the following examples:

PATH

A colon-delimited list of directories through which the shell looks for executable programs as you enter them on the command line. All of the directories that contain programs that you'll want to execute are stored together in the PATH environment variable. Your shell looks through this list in sequence, from left to right, searching for each command you enter. Your PATH may differ from the PATHs of other users on your system because you may use programs found in different locations or you may have a local directory with your own custom programs that need to be available. The PATH variable can become quite long as more and more directories are added.

HOME

Your home directory, such as */home/adamh*.

USERNAME

Your username.

TERM

The type of terminal or terminal window you are running. This variable is likely to have a value such as `xterm` or `xterm-color`. If you are running on a physical VT100 (or compatible) terminal, TERM is set to `vt100`.

Shell variables

These variables can be thought of as *local* because they are specific only to the current shell. Child processes do not inherit them. Some shell variables are automatically set by the shell and are available for use in shell scripts. By convention, shell variables are given lowercase names.

To create a new *bash* shell variable, simply enter a *name=value* pair on the command line:

```
# pi=3.14159
```

To see that this value is now assigned to the local variable `pi`, use the *echo* command to display its contents:

```
# echo $pi
3.14159
```

The dollar sign preceding the variable name indicates that the name will be replaced with the variable's value. Without the dollar sign, *echo* would just return the text that was typed, which in this case is the variable name `pi`. At this point, `pi` is a local variable and is not available to child shells or programs. To make it available to other shells or programs, the variable must be exported to the environment:

```
# export pi
```

Aliases

Among the features missing from *sh* was the ability to easily make new commands or modify existing commands. *bash* has the ability to set an alias for commonly used commands or sequences of commands. For example, if you habitually call for the older pager *more* but actually prefer *less*, an alias can be handy to get the desired behavior, regardless of the command you use:

```
$ alias more='less'
```

This has the effect of intercepting any command entries for *more*, substituting *less*. The revised command is passed along to the shell's command interpreter.

Another common use for an alias is to modify a command slightly so that its default behavior is more to your liking. Many people, particularly when operating with superuser privileges, will use this alias:

```
$ alias cp='cp -i'
```

With this alias in effect, the use of the *cp* (copy) command becomes safer, because with the *-i* option always enforced by the alias, *cp* prompts you for approval before overwriting a file of the same name. Additional options you enter on the command line are appended to the end of the new command, such that *cp -p* becomes *cp -i -p*, and so on.

If the righthand side of the aliased command is bigger than a single word or if it contains multiple commands (separated by semicolons, *bash*'s command terminator), you probably need to enclose it in single quotation marks to get your point across. For example, suppose you wished to use a single alias to pair two simple commands:

```
$ alias lsps=ls -l; ps
```

Your current *bash* process will interpret this command not as a single alias but as two separate commands. First the alias *lsps* will be created for *ls -l*, and then a *ps* command will be added for immediate execution. What you really want is:

```
$ alias lsps='ls -l; ps'
```

Now, entering the command *lsps* will be aliased to *ls -l; ps*, and will correctly generate `ls` output immediately followed by `ps` output, as this example shows:

```
$ lsps
total 1253
drwx------  5 root  root   1024 May 27 17:15 dir1
drwxr-xr-x  3 root  root   1024 May 27 22:41 dir2
-rw-r--r--  1 root  root  23344 May 27 22:44 file1
drwxr-xr-x  2 root  root  12288 May 25 16:13 dir3
  PID TTY          TIME CMD
```

```
  892 ttyp0    00:00:00 bash
 1388 ttyp0    00:00:00 ps
```

Admittedly, this isn't a very useful command, but it is built upon in the next section.

After adding aliases, it may become easy to confuse which commands are aliases or native. To list the aliases defined for your current shell, simply enter the *alias* command by itself. This results in a listing of all the aliases currently in place:

```
$ alias
alias cp='cp -i'
alias lsps='ls -l;ps'
alias mv='mv -i'
alias rm='rm -i'
```

Note that aliases are local to your shell and are not passed down to programs or to other shells. You'll see how to ensure that your aliases are always available in the section "Configuration files" on page 261.

Aliases are mainly used for simple command replacement. The shell inserts your aliased text in place of your alias name before interpreting the command. Aliases don't offer logical constructs and are limited to a few simple variable replacements. Aliases can also get messy when the use of complicated quoting is necessary, usually to prevent the shell from interpreting characters in your alias.

Functions

In addition to aliases, *bash* also offers *functions*. They work in much the same way as aliases, in that some function name of your choosing is assigned to a more complex construction. However, in this case that construction is a small program rather than a simple command substitution. Functions have a simple syntax:

```
[ function ] name () { command-list; }
```

This declaration defines a function called *name*. *function* is optional, and the parentheses after *name* are required if *function* is omitted. The body of the function is the *command-list* between the curly brackets ({ and }). This list is a series of commands, separated by semicolons or by newlines. The series of commands is executed whenever *name* is specified as a command. The simple `lsps` alias shown earlier could be implemented as a function like this:

```
$ lsps () { ls -l; ps; }
```

Using this new function as a command yields exactly the same result the alias did. However, if you implement this command as a function, parameters can be added to the command. Here is a new version of the same function, this time entered on multiple lines (which eliminates the need for semicolons within the function):

```
$ lsps () {
> ls -l $1
> ps aux | grep `/bin/basename $1`
> }
```

The > characters come from *bash* during interactive entry, indicating that *bash* is awaiting additional function commands or the } character, which terminates the function definition (this is called the secondary shell prompt). This new function allows us to enter a single *argument* to the function, which is inserted everywhere $1 is found in the function. These arguments are called *positional parameters* because each one's number denotes its position in the argument list. This example uses only one positional parameter, but there can be many, and the number of parameters is stored for your use in a special variable $#.

The command implemented in the previous example function now prints to *STDOUT* a directory listing and process status for any program given as an argument. For example, if the Apache web server is running, the command:

```
$ lsps /usr/sbin/httpd
```

yields a directory listing for */usr/sbin/httpd* and also displays all currently running processes that match httpd:

```
-rwxr-xr-x 1 root root 317072 2010-01-22 14:31 /usr/sbin/httpd
root      1882  0.0  1.5  22664  8088 ?       Ss   Aug10   0:14 /usr/sbin/httpd
apache   20869  0.0  0.6  22664  3560 ?       S    04:27   0:00 /usr/sbin/httpd
apache   20870  0.0  0.6  22664  3560 ?       S    04:27   0:00 /usr/sbin/httpd
apache   20872  0.0  0.6  22664  3560 ?       S    04:27   0:00 /usr/sbin/httpd
apache   20874  0.0  0.6  22664  3560 ?       S    04:27   0:00 /usr/sbin/httpd
apache   20875  0.0  0.6  22664  3560 ?       S    04:27   0:00 /usr/sbin/httpd
apache   20876  0.0  0.6  22664  3560 ?       S    04:27   0:00 /usr/sbin/httpd
apache   20877  0.0  0.6  22664  3560 ?       S    04:27   0:00 /usr/sbin/httpd
apache   20878  0.0  0.6  22664  3560 ?       S    04:27   0:00 /usr/sbin/httpd
```

Configuration files

It's a good assumption that every Linux user will want to define a few aliases, functions, and environment variables to suit his or her needs. However, it's undesirable to manually enter them upon each login or for each new invocation of *bash*. To set up these things automatically, *bash* uses a number of configuration files to set its operating environment when it starts. Some of these files are used only upon initial login, whereas others are executed for each instance of *bash* you start, including at login time. Some of these configuration files are system-wide files for all users to use, whereas others reside in your home directory for your use alone.

bash configuration files important to Exam 102 are listed in Table 13-1.

Table 13-1. bash configuration files

File	Description
/etc/profile	This is the system-wide initialization file executed during login. It usually contains environment variables, including an initial PATH, and startup programs.
/etc/bashrc	This is another system-wide initialization file that may be executed by a user's *.bashrc* for each *bash* shell launched. It usually contains functions and aliases.
~/.bash_profile	If this file exists, it is executed automatically after */etc/profile* during login.
~/.bash_login	If *.bash_profile* doesn't exist, this file is executed automatically during login.
~/.profile	If neither *.bash_profile* nor *.bash_login* exists, this file is executed automatically during login. Note that this is the original Bourne shell configuration file.

File	Description
~/.bashrc	This file is executed automatically when *bash* starts. This includes login, as well as subsequent interactive and noninteractive invocations of *bash*.
~/.bash_logout	This file is executed automatically during logout.
~/.inputrc	This file contains optional key bindings and variables that affect how *bash* responds to keystrokes. By default, *bash* is configured to respond like the Emacs editor.

 The syntax ~ (the tilde) refers to the current user's "home directory" (usually */home/username*). Although this shortcut may not represent much of a savings in typing, some Linux configurations may place users' directories in various and sometimes nonobvious places in the filesystem. Using the tilde syntax reduces the need for you to know exactly where a user's home directory is located.

In practice, users will generally (and often unknowingly) use the system-wide */etc/profile* configuration file to start. In addition, they'll often have three personal files in their home directory: *~/.bash_profile*, *~/.bashrc*, and *~/.bash_logout*. The local files are optional, and *bash* does not mind if one or all of them are not available in your directory.

Each of these configuration files consists entirely of plain text. They are typically simple, often containing just a few commands to be executed in sequence to prepare the shell environment for the user. Since they are evaluated by *bash* as lines of program code, they are said to be *sourced*, or interpreted, when *bash* executes them.

Like most programming languages, shell programs allow the use of comments. Most shells, including *bash*, consider everything immediately following the hash mark (#) on a single line to be a comment. An important exception is the $# *variable*, which has nothing to do with comments but contains the number of positional parameters passed to a function. Comments can span an entire line or share a line by following program code. All of your shell scripts and configuration files should use comments liberally.

Files sourced at login time are created mainly to establish default settings. These settings include such things as where to search for programs requested by the user (the PATH) and creation of shortcut names for commonly used tasks (aliases and functions). After login, files sourced by each subsequent shell invocation won't explicitly need to do these things again, because they *inherit* the environment established by the login shell. Regardless, it isn't unusual to see a user's *.bashrc* file filled with all of their personal customizations. It also doesn't hurt anything, provided the *.bashrc* file is small and quick to execute.

Although it is not necessary to have detailed knowledge of every item in your shell configuration files, Exam 102 requires that you understand them and that you can edit them to modify their behavior and your resulting operating environment. The following examples are typical of those found on Linux systems and are annotated with comments. Example 13-1 shows a typical Linux systemwide *profile*. This file is executed by every user's *bash* process at login time. A few environment variables and other parameters are set in it.

Example 13-1. An example system-wide bash profile

```
#!/bin/bash
# /etc/profile

pathmunge () {
 if ! echo $PATH | /bin/egrep -q "(^|:)$1($|:)" ; then
   if [ "$2" = "after" ] ; then
     PATH=$PATH:$1
   else
     PATH=$1:$PATH
   fi
 fi
}

# ksh workaround
if [ -z "$EUID" -a -x /usr/bin/id ]; then
 EUID=`id -u`
 UID=`id -ru`
fi

# Path manipulation
if [ "$EUID" = "0" ]; then
 pathmunge /sbin
 pathmunge /usr/sbin
 pathmunge /usr/local/sbin
fi

# No core files by default
ulimit -S -c 0 > /dev/null 2>&1

if [ -x /usr/bin/id ]; then
 USER="`id -un`"
 LOGNAME=$USER
 MAIL="/var/spool/mail/$USER"
fi

HOSTNAME=`/bin/hostname`
HISTSIZE=1000

if [ -z "$INPUTRC" -a ! -f "$HOME/.inputrc" ]; then
 INPUTRC=/etc/inputrc
fi

export PATH USER LOGNAME MAIL HOSTNAME HISTSIZE INPUTRC

for i in /etc/profile.d/*.sh ; do
 if [ -r "$i" ]; then
   . $i
 fi
done
```

```
unset i
unset pathmunge
```

Example 13-2 shows a system-wide *.bashrc* file. This file is not executed by default when *bash* starts. Instead, it is optionally executed by users' local *.bashrc* files.

Example 13-2. An example system-wide .bashrc file

```
# /etc/bashrc
# System wide functions and aliases
# Environment stuff goes in /etc/profile

# By default, we want this to get set.
# Even for non-interactive, non-login shells.
if [ $UID -gt 99 ] && [ "`id -gn`" = "`id -un`" ]; then
 umask 002
else
 umask 022
fi

# are we an interactive shell?
if [ "$PS1" ]; then
 case $TERM in
 xterm*)
  if [ -e /etc/sysconfig/bash-prompt-xterm ]; then
   PROMPT_COMMAND=/etc/sysconfig/bash-prompt-xterm
  else
   PROMPT_COMMAND='echo -ne "\033]0;${USER}@${HOSTNAME%%.*}:\
                                   ${PWD/#$HOME/~}"; echo -ne "\007"'
  fi
 ;;
 screen)
  if [ -e /etc/sysconfig/bash-prompt-screen ]; then
   PROMPT_COMMAND=/etc/sysconfig/bash-prompt-screen
  else
   PROMPT_COMMAND='echo -ne "\033_${USER}@${HOSTNAME%%.*}:\
                                   ${PWD/#$HOME/~}"; echo -ne "\033\\"'
  fi
 ;;
 *)
  [ -e /etc/sysconfig/bash-prompt-default ] && PROMPT_COMMAND=\
                                   /etc/sysconfig/bash-prompt-default
 ;;
 esac
 # Turn on checkwinsize
 shopt -s checkwinsize
 [ "$PS1" = "\\s-\\v\\\$ " ] && PS1="[\u@\h \W]\\$ "
fi

if ! shopt -q login_shell ; then # We're not a login shell
 # Need to redefine pathmunge, it gets undefined at the end of /etc/profile
 pathmunge () {
  if ! echo $PATH | /bin/egrep -q "(^|:)$1($|:)" ; then
   if [ "$2" = "after" ] ; then
    PATH=$PATH:$1
   else
```

```
    PATH=$1:$PATH
  fi
 fi
}

for i in /etc/profile.d/*.sh; do
 if [ -r "$i" ]; then
   . $i
 fi
done
unset i
unset pathmunge
fi
# vim:ts=4:sw=4
alias more='less'                    # prefer the "less" pager
alias lsps='ls -l;ps'                # a dubious command
```

Example 13-3 shows an example user's local *.bash_profile*. Note that this file sources the user's *.bashrc* file (which in turn sources the system-wide */etc/bashrc*), and then goes on to local customizations.

Example 13-3. An example user's .bash_profile file

```
# .bash_profile
# Get the aliases and functions
if [ -f ~/.bashrc ]; then
 . ~/.bashrc
fi

# User specific environment and startup programs
PATH=$PATH:$HOME/bin
export PATH
unset USERNAME
```

Example 13-4 shows an individual's *.bashrc* file.

Example 13-4. An example user's .bashrc file

```
# .bashrc

# User specific aliases and functions

alias rm='rm -i'
alias cp='cp -i'
alias mv='mv -i'

# Source global definitions
if [ -f /etc/bashrc ]; then
 . /etc/bashrc
fi
lsps() {   # Define a personal function
 ls -l $1
 ps aux | grep `/bin/basename $1`
}
```

Example 13-5 shows a short, simple, and not uncommon *.bash_logout* file. Probably the most likely command to find in a logout file is the *clear* command. Including a *clear* in your logout file is a nice way of being certain that whatever you were doing just before you log out won't linger on the screen for the next user to ponder. This file is intended to execute commands for a logout from a text session, such as a system console or terminal. In a GUI environment where logout and login are handled by a GUI program, *.bash_logout* might not be of much value.

Example 13-5. A simple .bash_logout file

```
# .bash_logout
# This file is executed when a user logs out of the system
/usr/bin/clear          # Clear the screen
/usr/games/fortune      # Print a random adage
```

On the Exam

Make certain that you understand the difference between execution at login and execution at shell invocation, as well as which of the startup files serves each of those purposes.

.inputrc

Among the many enhancements added to *bash* is the ability to perform as if your history of commands is the buffer of an editor. That is, your command history is available to you, and you may cut, paste, and even search among command lines entered previously. This powerful capability can significantly reduce typing and increase accuracy. By default, *bash* is configured to emulate the Emacs editor, but a *vi* editing interface is also available.

The portion of *bash* that handles this function, and in fact handles all of the line input during interactive use, is known as *readline*. Readline may be customized by putting commands into an initialization file, which by default is in your home directory and called *.inputrc*. For example, to configure *bash* to use *vi*-style editing keys, add this line to *.inputrc*:

```
set editing-mode vi
```

 You may also set the INPUTRC variable to the name of another file if you prefer. On your system, this variable may be set to */etc/initrc* by default, which would override any settings you put into a local *.initrc*. To use your own file, you must first explicitly place the command unset INPUTRC in your *.bash_profile*.

The default editing facilities enabled in *bash* are extensive and are beyond the scope of this section and Exam 102. However, you need to understand the concepts of adding your own custom key bindings to the *.inputrc* file and how they can help automate common keystrokes unique to your daily routine for the test.

For example, suppose you often use *top* to watch your system's activity (*top* is a useful process-monitoring utility that is described in Chapter 6):

```
$ top -Ssd1
```

If you do this often enough, you'll get tired of typing the command over and over and will eventually want an alias for it. To create the alias, simply alias this command to *top*:

```
$ alias top='/usr/bin/top -Ssd1'
```

Better yet, you can use *.inputrc* to create a key binding that will enter it for you. Here's how the *.inputrc* file would look if you were to bind your *top* command to the key sequence Ctrl-T:

```
# my .inputrc file
Control-t: "top -Ssd1 \C-m"
```

The lefthand side of the second line indicates the key combination you wish to use (Ctrl-T). The righthand side indicates what you wish to bind to that key sequence. In this case, *bash* outputs *top -Ssd1* and a carriage return, denoted here by \C-m (Ctrl-M), when Control-T is pressed.

Through modifications of your local configuration files, you can customize your environment and automate many of your daily tasks. You may also override system-wide settings in your personal files simply by setting variables, aliases, and functions.

On the Exam

You won't need to have detailed knowledge of this key-binding syntax, but be aware of the *.inputrc* file and the kinds of things it enables *bash* to do.

Objective 2: Customize or Write Simple Scripts

You've seen how the use of *bash* configuration files, aliases, functions, variables, and key bindings can customize and make interaction with your Linux system efficient. The next step in your relationship with the shell is to use its natural programming capability, or *scripting language*. The scripting language of the original Bourne shell is found throughout a Linux system, and *bash* is fully compatible with it. This section covers essential *bash* scripting language concepts as required for Exam 102.

In order to have a full appreciation of shell scripting on Linux, it's important to look at your Linux system as a collection of unique and powerful tools. Each of the commands available on your Linux system, along with those you create yourself, has some special capability, and by combining them, you are able to have a productive and maintainable environment.

Script Files

Just as the configuration files discussed in the last section are plain text files, so are the scripts for your shell. In addition, unlike compiled languages such as C or Pascal, no compilation of a shell program is necessary before it is executed. You can use any editor to create script files, and you'll find that many scripts you write are portable from Linux to other Unix systems.

Creating a simple bash script

The simplest scripts are those that string together some basic commands and perhaps do something useful with the output. Of course, this can be done with a simple alias or function, but eventually you'll have a requirement that exceeds a one-line request, and a shell script is the natural solution. Aliases and functions have already been used to create a rudimentary new command, *lsps*. Now let's look at a shell script (Example 13-6) that accomplishes the same thing.

Example 13-6. The lsps script

```
# A basic lsps command script for bash
ls -l $1
ps -aux | grep `/bin/basename $1`
```

As you can see, the commands used in this simple script are identical to those used in the alias and in the function created earlier. To make use of this new file, instruct your currently running *bash* shell to source it, giving it an option for the $1 positional parameter:

> $ **source ./lsps /usr/sbin/httpd**

If you have */usr/sbin/httpd* running, you should receive output similar to that found previously for the alias. By replacing the word source with a single dot, you can create an alternate shorthand notation to tell *bash* to source a file, as follows:

> $ **. ./lsps /usr/sbin/httpd**

Another way to invoke a script is to start a new invocation of *bash* and tell that process to source the file. To do this, simply start *bash* and pass the script name and argument to it:

> $ **/bin/bash ./lsps /usr/sbin/httpd**

This last example gives us the same result; however, it is significantly different from the alias, the function, or the sourcing of the *lsps* file. In this particular case, a new invocation of *bash* was started to execute the commands in the script. This is important, because the environment in which the commands are running is distinct from the environment in which the user is typing. This is described in more detail later in this section.

> The ./ syntax indicates that the file you're referring to is in the current working directory. For security reasons, it is not advisable to add . to a user's $PATH variable. Instead, either type the relative path to the command (./lsps) or the full path (/usr/bin/ lsps).

Thus far, a shell script has been created and invoked in a variety of ways, but it hasn't been made into a command. A script really becomes useful when it can be called by name like any other command.

Executable files

On a Linux system, programs are said to be executable if they have content that can be run by the processor (native execution) or by another program such as a shell (interpreted execution). However, in order to be eligible for execution when called at the command line, the files must have attributes that indicate to the shell that they are executable. To make a file executable, it must have at least one of its *executable bits* set. To turn the example script from a plain text file into an executable program, that bit must be set using the *chmod* command:

```
$ chmod a+x lsps
```

More information on *chmod* can be found in Chapter 7.

Once this is done, the script is executable by its owner, group members, and everyone else on the system. At this point, running the new command from the *bash* prompt yields the familiar output:

```
$ ./lsps /usr/sbin/httpd
```

When *lsps* is called by name, the commands in the script are interpreted and executed by the *bash* shell. However, this isn't ultimately what is desired. In many cases, users will be running some other shell interactively but will still want to program in *bash*. Programmers also use other scripting languages such as Perl or Python. To have the scripts interpreted correctly, the system must be told which program should interpret the commands in the scripts.

Shebang!

Many kinds of script files are found on a Linux system, and each interpreted language comes with a unique and specific command structure. There needs to be a way to tell Linux which interpreter to use for each script. This is accomplished by using a special line at the top of the script naming the appropriate interpreter. Linux examines this line and launches the specified interpreter program, which then reads the rest of the file. The special line must begin with #!, a construct often called *shebang*, often thought of as being short for **Sh**arp (#) **Bang** (!). For *bash*, the shebang line is:

```
#!/bin/bash
```

This command explicitly states that the program named *bash* can be found in the */bin* directory and designates *bash* to be the interpreter for the script. You'll also see other types of lines on script files, including:

```
#!/bin/sh
```
    The Bourne shell
```
#!/bin/csh
```
    The C-shell

```
#!/bin/tcsh
```
    The enhanced C-shell
```
#!/bin/sed
```
    The stream editor
```
#!/usr/bin/awk
```
    The awk programming language
```
#!/usr/bin/perl
```
    The Perl programming language

Each of these lines specifies a unique command interpreter for the script lines that follow. (*bash* is fully backward-compatible with *sh*; *sh* is just a link to *bash* on Linux systems.). Note that the full paths given here are the default; some distributions might have slight differences. For example, Perl is often in */bin/perl* or even */usr/local/bin/perl*.

On the Exam

An incorrectly stated shebang line can cause the wrong interpreter to attempt to execute commands in a script.

The shell script's environment

When running a script with `#!/bin/bash`, a new invocation of *bash* with its own environment is started to execute the script's commands as the parent shell waits. Exported variables in the parent shell are copied into the child's environment; the child shell executes the appropriate shell configuration files (such as *.bash_profile*). Because configuration files will be run, additional shell variables may be set and environment variables may be overwritten. If you are depending upon a variable in your shell script, be sure that it is either set by the shell configuration files or exported into the environment for your use, but not both.

Another important concept regarding your shell's environment is known as *unidirectional* or *one-way inheritance*. Although your current shell's environment is passed *into* a shell script, that environment is *not passed back* to the original shell when your program terminates. This means that changes made to variables during the execution of your script are not preserved when the script exits. Instead, the values in the parent shell's variables are the same as they were before the script executed. This is a basic Unix construct; inheritance goes from parent process to child process, and not the other way around.

On the Exam

It is important to remember how variables are set, how they are inherited, and that they are inherited only from parent process to child process.

Location, ownership, and permissions

The ability to run any executable program, including a script, under Linux depends in part upon its location in the filesystem. Either the user must explicitly specify the location of the file to run or it must be located in a directory known by the shell to contain executables. Such directories are listed in the PATH environment variable. For example, the shells on a Linux system (including *bash*) are located in */bin*. This directory is usually in the PATH, because you're likely to run programs that are stored there. When you create shell programs or other utilities of your own, you may want to keep them together and add the location to your own PATH. If you maintain your own *bin* directory, you might add the following line to your *.bash_profile*:

```
PATH=$PATH:$HOME/bin
```

This statement modifies your path to include your */home/username/bin* directory. If you add personal scripts and programs to this directory, *bash* finds them automatically.

Execute permissions (covered in the section "Objective 5: Manage File Permissions and Ownership" on page 176) also affect your ability to run a script. Since scripts are just text files, execute permission must be granted to them before they are considered executable, as shown earlier.

You may wish to limit access to the file from other users with the following:

```
$ chmod 700 ~/bin/lsps
```

This prevents anyone but the owner from making changes to the script.

The issue of file ownership is dovetailed with making a script executable. By default, you own all of the files you create. However, if you are the system administrator, you'll often be working as the superuser and will be creating files with username *root* as well. It is important to assign the correct ownership and permission to scripts to ensure that they are secured.

SUID and SGID rights

On rare occasions, it may become necessary to allow a user to run a program under the name of a different user. This is usually associated with programs run by non-privileged users that need special privileges to execute correctly. Linux offers two such rights: SUID and SGID.

When an executable file is granted the SUID right, processes created to execute it are owned by the user who owns the file instead of the user who launched the program. This is a security enhancement, in that the delegation of a privileged task or ability does not imply that the superuser password must be widely known. On the other hand, any process whose file is owned by *root* and that has the SUID set will run as *root* for everyone. This could represent an opportunity to break the security of a system if the file itself is easy to attack (as a script is). For this reason, Linux systems will ignore SUID and SGID attributes for script files. Setting SUID and SGID attributes is detailed in "Objective 5: Manage File Permissions and Ownership" on page 176.

Basic Bash Scripts

Now that some of the requirements for creating and using executable scripts are established, some of the features that make them so powerful can be introduced. This section contains basic information needed to customize and create new *bash* scripts.

Return values

As shell scripts execute, it is important to confirm that their constituent commands complete successfully. Most commands offer a *return value* to the shell when they terminate. This value is a simple integer and has a meaning specific to the program you're using. Almost all programs return the value 0 when they are successful and return a nonzero value when a problem is encountered. The value is stored in the special *bash* variable $?, which can be tested in your scripts to check for successful command execution. This variable is reset for every command executed by the shell, so you must test it immediately after execution of the command you're verifying. As a simple example, try using the *cat* program on a nonexistent file:

```
$ cat bogus_file
cat: bogus_file: No such file or directory
```

Then immediately examine the status variable twice:

```
$ echo $?
1
$ echo $?
0
```

The first *echo* yielded 1 (failure) because the *cat* program failed to find the file you specified. The second *echo* yielded 0 (success) because the first *echo* command succeeded. A good script makes use of these status flags to exit gracefully in case of errors.

If it sounds backward to equate zero with success and nonzero with failure, consider how these results are used in practice:

Error detection

Scripts that check for errors include `if-then` code to evaluate a command's return status:

```
command
if (failure_returned) ; then
   ...error recovery code...
fi
```

In a *bash* script, `failure_returned` is examining the value of the `$?` variable, which contains the result of the command's execution.

Error classification

Since commands can fail for multiple reasons, many return more than one failure code. For example, *grep* returns 0 if matches are found and 1 if no matches are found; it returns 2 if there is a problem with the search pattern or input files. Scripts may need to respond differently to various error conditions.

On the Exam

Make certain you understand the meaning of return values in general and that they are stored in the `$?` variable.

File tests

During the execution of a shell script, specific information about a file—such as whether it exists, is writable, is a directory or a file, and so on—may sometimes be required. In *bash*, the built-in command *test* performs this function. (There is also a standalone executable version of *test* available in */usr/bin* for non-bash shells.) *test* has two general forms:

test *expression*

In this form, *test* and an *expression* are explicitly stated.

[*expression*]

In this form, *test* isn't mentioned; instead, the *expression* is enclosed inside brackets.

The *expression* can be formed to look for such things as empty files, the existence of files, the existence of directories, equality of strings, and others. (See the more complete list with their operators in section, "Abbreviated bash command reference" on page 274. The bash manpage also details all the *test* options that are available.)

When used in a script's `if` or `while` statement, the brackets ([and]) may appear to be grouping the test logically. In reality, [is simply another form of the *test* command, which requires the trailing]. A side effect of this bit of trickery is that the spaces around [and] are mandatory, a detail that is sure to get you into trouble eventually.

Command substitution

bash offers a handy ability to do *command substitution* with the `$(command)` or `` `command` `` syntax. Wherever `$(command)` is found, its output is substituted prior to interpretation by the shell. For example, to set a variable to the number of lines in your *.bashrc* file, you could use *wc -l*:

```
$ RCSIZE=$(wc -l ~/.bashrc)
```

Another form of command substitution encloses *command* in *backquotes* or *backticks* (`):

```
$ RCSIZE=`wc -l ~/.bashrc`
```

The result is the same, except that the backquote syntax allows the backslash character to escape the dollar symbol ($), the backquote (`), and another backslash (\). The $(*command*) syntax avoids this nuance by treating all characters between the parentheses literally.

Mailing from scripts

The scripts you write will often be rummaging around your system at night when you're asleep or at least while you're not watching. Since you're too busy to check on every script's progress, a script will sometimes need to send some mail to you or another administrator. This is particularly important when something big goes wrong or when something important depends on the script's outcome. Sending mail is as simple as piping into the *mail* command:

```
echo "Backup failure 5" | mail -s "Backup failed" root
```

The *-s* option indicates that a quoted subject for the email follows. The recipient could be yourself, *root*, or if your system is configured correctly, any Internet email address. If you need to send a logfile, redirect the input of *mail* from that file:

```
mail -s "subject" recipient < log_file
```

or:

```
cat log_file | mail -s "subject" recipient
```

Sending email from scripts is easy and makes tracking status easier than reviewing logfiles every day. On the downside, having an inbox full of "success" messages can be a nuisance too, so many scripts are written so that mail is sent only in response to an important event, such as a fatal error.

Abbreviated bash command reference

This section lists some of the important *bash* built-in commands used when writing scripts. Please note that not all of the *bash* commands are listed here; for a complete overview of the *bash* shell, see *Learning the bash Shell (http://oreilly.com/catalog/9780596009656/)* by Cameron Newham (O'Reilly).

break

Syntax
```
break [n]
```

Description

Exit from the innermost (most deeply nested) for, while, or until loop or from the *n* innermost levels of the loop.

case

Syntax

```
case string in
    pattern1)
        commands1
        ;;
    pattern2)
        commands2
        ;;
    ...
esac
```

Description

Choose *string* from among a series of possible patterns. These patterns use the same form as file globs (wildcards). If *string* matches pattern *pattern1*, perform the subsequent *commands1*. If string matches *pattern2*, perform *commands2*. Proceed down the list of patterns until one is found. To catch all remaining strings, use *) at the end.

continue

Syntax

```
continue [n]
```

Description

Skip remaining commands in a for, while, or until loop, resuming with the next iteration of the loop (or skipping *n* loops).

echo

Syntax

```
echo [options] [string]
```

Description

Write *string* to standard output, terminated by a newline. If no string is supplied, echo only a newline. Some Linux distributions have a version of *echo* at */bin/echo*. If that is the case, the built-in *bash* version of *echo* will usually take precedence.

Frequently used options

-*e*

Enable interpretation of escape characters.

-*n*

Suppress the trailing newline in the output.

Useful special characters

\a

Sound an audible alert.

\b

Insert a backspace.

\c

Suppress the trailing newline (same as -n).

\f

Form feed.

exit

Syntax

```
exit [n]
```

Description

Exit a shell script with status *n*. The value for *n* can be 0 (success) or nonzero (failure). If *n* is not given, the exit status is that of the most recent command.

Example

```
if ! test -f somefile
then
   echo "Error: Missing file somefile"
   exit 1
fi
```

for

Syntax

```
for x in list
do
    commands
done
```

Description

Assign each word in *list* to *x* in turn and execute *commands*. If *list* is omitted, it is assumed that positional parameters from the command line, which are stored in $@, are to be used.

Example

```
for filename in bigfile* ; do
   echo "Compressing $filename"
   gzip $filename
done
```

function

Syntax

```
function name
{
    commands
}
```

Description

Define function *name*. Positional parameters ($1, $2, ...) can be used within *commands*.

Example

```
# function myfunc
{
    echo "parameter is $1"
}
# myfunc 1
parameter is 1
# myfunc two
parameter is two
```

getopts

Syntax

```
getopts string name [args]
```

Description

Process command-line arguments (or *args*, if specified) and check for legal options. The *getopts* is used in shell script loops and is intended to ensure standard syntax for command-line options. The *string* contains the option letters to be recognized by *getopts* when running the script. Valid options are processed in turn and stored in the shell variable *name*. If an option letter is followed by a colon, the option must be followed by one or more arguments when the command is entered by the user.

if

Syntax

```
if expression1
then
    commands1
elif expression2
then
    commands2
else
    commands
fi
```

Description

The *if* command is used to define a conditional statement. There are three possible formats for using the *if* command:

```
if-then-fi
if-then-else-fi
if-then-elif-then-...fi
```

kill

Syntax

```
kill [options] IDs
```

Description

Send signals to each specified process or job ID, which you must own unless you are a privileged user. The default signal sent with the *kill* command is TERM, instructing processes to shut down.

Options

-l

   List the signal names.

-s signal or -signal

   Specify the signal number or name.

read

Syntax

```
read [options] variable1 [variable2...]
```

Description

Read one line of standard input, and assign each word to the corresponding variable, with all remaining words assigned to the last variable.

Example

```
echo -n "Enter last-name, age, height, and weight > "
read lastname everythingelse
echo $lastname
echo $everythingelese
```

The name entered is placed in variable $lastname; all of the other values, including the spaces between them, are placed in $everythingelse.

return

Syntax

```
return [n]
```

Description

This command is used inside a function definition to exit the function with status *n*. If *n* is omitted, the exit status of the previously executed command is returned.

seq

Syntax

```
seq [OPTION]... LAST
seq [OPTION]... FIRST LAST
seq [OPTION]... FIRST INCREMENT LAST
```

Description

Print a sequence of numbers. This is useful in for and while loops.

Frequently used options

-w

Equalize the output's width by padding with leading zeros.

-f or --format=FORMAT

Use the printf-style floating-point FORMAT.

Example

```
year=$(date +%Y) # get current year
for month in $(seq -w 1 12)
{
 monthname=$(date -d "${year}-${month}-01" +%B)
 echo "Month $month is $monthname"
}
Month 01 is January
Month 02 is February
Month 03 is March
Month 04 is April
Month 05 is May
Month 06 is June
Month 07 is July
Month 08 is August
Month 09 is September
Month 10 is October
Month 11 is November
Month 12 is December
```

shift

Syntax

```
shift [n]
```

Description

Shift positional parameters down *n* elements. If *n* is omitted, the default is 1, so $2 becomes $1, $3 becomes $2, and so on.

source

Syntax

```
source file [arguments]
. file [arguments]
```

Description

Read and execute lines in *file*. The *file* does not need to be executable but must be in a directory listed in PATH. The dot syntax is equivalent to stating source.

test

Syntax

```
test expression
[ expression ]
```

Description

Evaluate the conditional expression and return a status of 0 (true) or 1 (false). The first form explicitly calls out the *test* command. The second form implies the *test* command. The spaces around *expression* are required in the second form. *expression* is constructed using options. Some Linux distributions have a version of *test* at */usr/bin/test*. If that is the case, the built-in *bash* version of *test* will usually take precedence.

Frequently used options

-d file
> True if *file* exists and is a directory

-e file
> True if *file* exists

-f file
> True if *file* exists and is a regular file

-L file
> True if *file* exists and is a symbolic link

-n string
> True if the length of *string* is nonzero

-r file
> True if *file* exists and is readable

-s file
> True if *file* exists and has a size greater than zero

-w file
> True if *file* exists and is writable

-x file
> True if *file* exists and is executable

-z string
> True if the length of *string* is zero

file1 -ot file2
> True if *file1* is older than *file2*

string1 = string2
> True if the strings are equal

string1 != string2
> True if the strings are not equal

Example

To determine if a file exists and is readable, use the *-r* option:

```
if test -r file
then
    echo "file exists"
fi
```

Using the [ ] form instead, the same test looks like this:

```
if [ -r file ]
then
    echo "file exists"
fi
```

until

Syntax

```
until
    test-commands
do
    commands
done
```

Description

Execute *test-commands* (usually a *test* command), and if the exit status is nonzero (that is, the test fails), perform commands and repeat. Opposite of while.

while

Syntax

```
while
    test-commands
do
    commands
done
```

Description

Execute *test-commands* (usually a *test* command), and if the exit status is nonzero (that is, the test fails), perform `commands` and repeat. Opposite of `until`.

Example

Example 13-7 shows a typical script from a Linux system. This example is */etc/rc.d/init.d/ sendmail*, which is the script that starts and stops Sendmail. This script demonstrates many of the built-in commands referenced in the last section.

Example 13-7. Sample sendmail startup script

```
#!/bin/bash
#
# sendmail      This shell script takes care of starting and stopping
#               sendmail.
#
# chkconfig: 2345 80 30
# description: Sendmail is a Mail Transport Agent, which is the program \
#              that moves mail from one machine to another.
# processname: sendmail
# config: /etc/mail/sendmail.cf
# pidfile: /var/run/sendmail.pid

# Source function library.
. /etc/rc.d/init.d/functions

# Source networking configuration.
[ -f /etc/sysconfig/network ] && . /etc/sysconfig/network

# Source sendmail configureation.
if [ -f /etc/sysconfig/sendmail ] ; then
        . /etc/sysconfig/sendmail
else
        DAEMON=no
        QUEUE=1h
fi
[ -z "$SMQUEUE" ] && SMQUEUE="$QUEUE"
[ -z "$SMQUEUE" ] && SMQUEUE=1h

# Check that networking is up.
[ "${NETWORKING}" = "no" ] && exit 0

[ -f /usr/sbin/sendmail ] || exit 0
```

```
RETVAL=0
prog="sendmail"

start() {
        # Start daemons.

        echo -n $"Starting $prog: "
        if test -x /usr/bin/make -a -f /etc/mail/Makefile ; then
          make all -C /etc/mail -s > /dev/null
        else
          for i in virtusertable access domaintable mailertable ; do
            if [ -f /etc/mail/$i ] ; then
                makemap hash /etc/mail/$i < /etc/mail/$i
            fi
          done
        fi
        /usr/bin/newaliases > /dev/null 2>&1
        daemon /usr/sbin/sendmail $([ "x$DAEMON" = xyes ] && echo -bd) \
                      $([ -n "$QUEUE" ] && echo -q$QUEUE) $SENDMAIL_OPTARG
        RETVAL=$?
        echo
        [ $RETVAL -eq 0 ] && touch /var/lock/subsys/sendmail

        if ! test -f /var/run/sm-client.pid ; then
        echo -n $"Starting sm-client: "
        touch /var/run/sm-client.pid
        chown smmsp:smmsp /var/run/sm-client.pid
        if [ -x /usr/sbin/selinuxenabled ] && /usr/sbin/selinuxenabled; then
            /sbin/restorecon /var/run/sm-client.pid
        fi
        daemon --check sm-client /usr/sbin/sendmail -L sm-msp-queue -Ac \
                      -q$SMQUEUE $SENDMAIL_OPTARG
        RETVAL=$?
        echo
        [ $RETVAL -eq 0 ] && touch /var/lock/subsys/sm-client
        fi

        return $RETVAL
}

reload() {
        # Stop daemons.
        echo -n $"reloading $prog: "
        /usr/bin/newaliases > /dev/null 2>&1
        if [ -x /usr/bin/make -a -f /etc/mail/Makefile ]; then
          make all -C /etc/mail -s > /dev/null
        else
          for i in virtusertable access domaintable mailertable ; do
            if [ -f /etc/mail/$i ] ; then
                makemap hash /etc/mail/$i < /etc/mail/$i
            fi
          done
        fi
        daemon /usr/sbin/sendmail $([ "x$DAEMON" = xyes ] && echo -bd) \
            $([ -n "$QUEUE" ] && echo -q$QUEUE)
        RETVAL=$?
```

```
        killproc sendmail -HUP
        RETVAL=$?
        echo
        if [ $RETVAL -eq 0 -a -f /var/run/sm-client.pid ]; then
                echo -n $"reloading sm-client: "
                killproc sm-client -HUP
                RETVAL=$?
                echo
        fi
        return $RETVAL
}

stop() {
        # Stop daemons.
        if test -f /var/run/sm-client.pid ; then
                echo -n $"Shutting down sm-client: "
                killproc sm-client
                RETVAL=$?
                echo
                [ $RETVAL -eq 0 ] && rm -f /var/run/sm-client.pid
                [ $RETVAL -eq 0 ] && rm -f /var/lock/subsys/sm-client
        fi
        echo -n $"Shutting down $prog: "
        killproc sendmail
        RETVAL=$?
        echo
        [ $RETVAL -eq 0 ] && rm -f /var/lock/subsys/sendmail
        return $RETVAL
}

# See how we were called.
case "$1" in
  start)
        start
        ;;
  stop)
        stop
        ;;
  reload)
        reload
        RETVAL=$?
        ;;
  restart)
        stop
        start
        RETVAL=$?
        ;;
  condrestart)
        if [ -f /var/lock/subsys/sendmail ]; then
            stop
            start
            RETVAL=$?
        fi
        ;;
  status)
        status sendmail
```

```
        RETVAL=$?
        ;;
    *)
        echo $"Usage: $0 {start|stop|restart|condrestart|status}"
        exit 1
esac

exit $RETVAL
```

Objective 3: SQL Data Management

Up until this point, we have focused on data and code stored in text files, the standard method of data storage in the Unix world. This has worked well for many years. However, limitations of this format have required that Linux system administrators become familiar with basic database concepts. Specifically, the Structured Query Language (SQL) syntax that is shared among most database systems is an important tool to have in your sysadmin arsenal.

There are many SQL database options available in the Linux world. Arguably, the most popular are MySQL, PostgreSQL, and SQLite. Like the flamewars that often arise around the merits of various text editors (*vi* versus *emacs* being the historical Unix equivalent of the Hatfields versus the McCoys), the choice of a SQL database tends to bring out very strong feelings in Linux users. Due to its popularity among many database-backed open source projects, MySQL tends to be the SQL database that is most often seen on Linux systems (although the smaller footprint and rich API set of SQLite are making it a more popular choice every day). PostgreSQL is often touted as the only "real" Relational Database Management System (RDBMS) in the list of popular databases, and although that technically may be true, the ubiquity of MySQL means that PostgreSQL, at least for now, will continue to play a supporting role in the Linux database world.

For the sake of simplicity, this section will use MySQL as an example. However, the SQL commands given here should work across the majority of SQL databases.

Accessing a MySQL Server

MySQL is popular enough that it is distributed by default with most modern Linux distributions. Like many client-server applications, MySQL is usually distributed as multiple packages. Most often this means there are separate packages for the server binaries and the client binaries, although there may also be a third package that includes "common" code. Be sure to familiarize yourself with your distribution's package management system so you can effectively determine what software is installed on your system. Refer to Chapter 5 for more information on the common Linux package managers.

Assuming that the MySQL server package is installed, the server is started the same way that most Linux services are started:

```
# /etc/rc.d/init.d/mysqld start
Starting MySQL:             [  OK  ]
```

You should now have a running mysqld process, listening on TCP port 3306 by default. You can verify both of these with the *ps* and *netstat* commands, respectively:

```
# ps aux | grep -i mysqld
root 1865 0.0 0.2 4656 1132 pts/0 S 22:20 0:00 /bin/sh \
            /usr/bin/mysqld_safe --datadir=/var/lib/mysql \
            --socket=/var/lib/mysql/mysql.sock --log-error=\
            /var/log/mysqld.log --pidfile=\
            /var/run/mysqld/mysqld.pid
mysql 1989 0.3 3.6 161508 19012 pts/0 Sl 22:20 0:00 \
            /usr/libexec/mysqld --basedir=/usr --datadir=\
            /var/lib/mysql --user=mysql --pid-file=\
            /var/run/mysqld/mysqld.pid --skipexternal-locking \
            --socket=/var/lib/mysql/mysql.sock
# netstat -anp | grep "LISTEN" | grep "mysqld"
tcp 0 0 0.0.0.0:3306 0.0.0.0:* LISTEN \
            1989/mysqld
```

By default, communication with the MySQL server takes place over the TCP port that the server listens on (normally tcp/3306). This communication can be either through the *mysql* command-line client program, a programming language such as PHP or Perl, or a GUI application. A number of useful GUI applications are available as free downloads from *http://dev.mysql.com/downloads/gui-tools*. This section will focus on using the *mysql* command-line program, both interactively and in shell scripts.

To access the MySQL server, use the *mysql* command-line program:

```
# mysql -uroot -p -hlocalhost
Enter password:
Welcome to the MySQL monitor. Commands end with ; or \g.
Your MySQL connection id is 14
Server version: 5.0.45 Source distribution

Type 'help;' or '\h' for help. Type '\c' to clear the buffer.

mysql>
```

The options passed on the command line are:

-u

Username to connect as. This is not the same as the Linux username; MySQL uses its own username and password combinations. They are often similar to the Linux usernames (root, for example), but they bear no relation to them.

-p

Prompt for the password. The password can also be given on the command line, but this is considered insecure and is not recommended.

-h

What hostname (or IP address) to connect to. Useful if you are connecting to another server on your network. It is not recommended that you connect to MySQL servers over an unsecured network (such as the Internet) without using SSL or some other form of encryption. MySQL offers some basic SSL options, but that level of security is outside the scope of what will appear on the LPI 102 exam.

Now that we have successfully connected to our database, it's time to review basic database concepts.

Database Overview

A full understanding of database management recommendations and design methodology is outside the scope of this book and outside the scope of the LPI 102 exam. However, you will need to know the basics of storing data in a MySQL table, managing that data (adding, updating, and deleting), and performing relatively complex queries on that data.

A MySQL server instance allows the creation and access of multiple databases simultaneously. The MySQL server actually creates a directory in the filesystem for each new database created. Each database may contain many tables, the layout of which is set upon initial table creation, but can be modified later. Although there are many options and pros and cons regarding database formats and storage engines, for the purposes of the LPI 102 exam we will assume the default storage engine (MyISAM) and concern ourselves more with table layout and querying. For more information on storage engines and other advanced MySQL topics, visit *http://dev .mysql.com/doc/*.

A table is made up of a number of columns, each given a certain datatype that defines what data may be stored in this column. Table 13-2 describes some of the more common MySQL datatypes.

Table 13-2. Common MySQL datatypes

Datatype	Description
INTEGER	A normal-size integer. The signed range is −2147483648 to 2147483647. The unsigned range is 0 to 4294967295.
FLOAT	A floating-point number.
BOOLEAN	Stored as a single character integer. A value of zero is considered false. Nonzero values are considered true.
DATE	A date in the range of '1000-01-01' to '9999-12-31'. Dates are displayed as YYYY-MM-DD by default.
DATETIME	A date and time combination in the range of '1000-01-01 00:00:00' to '9999-12-31 23:59:59'.
CHAR	A fixed-length string in the range of 0–255 characters.
VARCHAR	A variable-length string. Before MySQL 5.0.3, the maximum length of a VARCHAR was 255 characters. Since 5.0.3, the maximum length is 65535.

Datatype	Description
BLOB	A binary format with a maximum size of 65535 bytes.
TEXT	A text format with a maximum size of 65535 characters.

Why are datatypes important? Wouldn't it be easier if we had only two datatypes, ASCII and binary? It is important to specify datatypes because MySQL queries are datatype-aware. For example, if I want to create a query that says, "Give me all the records earlier than a certain date," I can use the less-than operator (<) on a column that has a datatype of DATE. MySQL will know that less-than in this case means "on a date earlier than the one given." This would be much more difficult to accomplish if we did not have strongly defined datatypes.

Let's start with an example table and walk through the creation steps. For our example, we will create a database called *community*. In this database, our first table will be *families*, which will store names and birthdates for the members of a family:

```
# mysql -uroot -p -hlocalhost
Welcome to the MySQL monitor.  Commands end with ; or \g.
Your MySQL connection id is 53
Server version: 5.0.45 Source distribution

Type 'help;' or '\h' for help. Type '\c' to clear the buffer.

mysql> create database community;
Query OK, 1 row affected (0.02 sec)

mysql> use community;
Database changed
mysql> CREATE TABLE families (
    ->    id INTEGER UNSIGNED NOT NULL AUTO_INCREMENT,
    ->    father_name VARCHAR(100),
    ->    father_dob DATE,
    ->    mother_name VARCHAR(100),
    ->    mother_dob DATE,
    ->    number_of_children INTEGER UNSIGNED,
    ->    child1_name VARCHAR(100),
    ->    child1_dob DATE,
    ->    child2_name VARCHAR(100),
    ->    child2_dob DATE,
    ->    child3_name VARCHAR(100),
    ->    child3_dob DATE,
    ->    notes TEXT,
    ->    PRIMARY KEY (id)
    -> );
Query OK, 0 rows affected (0.05 sec)
```

The *CREATE TABLE* command is used to create a table in an existing database. Each column of the table is named and given a datatype. In addition, options can be given to columns to change their behavior. For example, we gave the *id* column the option *AUTO_INCREMENT*. This means that MySQL will automatically increment this integer value for every row added to the table. This is a common practice and ensures that every row will be unique, because even if all the other columns have the same data, the *id* field will always be different. This is enforced by the line "PRI-MARY KEY (id)". By naming the *id* field as the primary key, we're instructing MySQL to enforce the uniqueness of this value for each row. This means that if we tried to add a row of data that included an *id* value that already existed, MySQL would display an error and the data would not be added.

The other fields added are names, which we defined as a varchar with an upper limit of 100 characters (more than enough to hold a first name, middle name and last name), dates of birth (denoted by the DATE datatype), and a notes field, which we defined as type TEXT.

To add data to this table, we use the *INSERT* command:

```
mysql> INSERT into families
    -> (father_name, father_dob, mother_name, mother_dob,
    -> number_of_children, child1_name, child1_dob,
    -> child2_name, child2_dob, notes)
    -> VALUES
    -> ("Joe Smith", "1970-04-01", "Jan Smith", "1970-05-10",
    -> "2", "Jimmy Smith","2000-08-10", "Janey Smith",
    -> "2002-12-12", "This is the smith family
    -> of Chicago, IL");
Query OK, 1 row affected, 0 warnings (0.02 sec)
```

Notice that we did not insert data into every column of the table. By identifying the fields we wished to use and then the values for each, we're able to insert exactly the data we wish into the table. To view the data we just added, use the *SELECT* command:

```
mysql> SELECT id, father_name, mother_name, number_of_children from families;
+----+-------------+-------------+--------------------+
| id | father_name | mother_name | number_of_children |
+----+-------------+-------------+--------------------+
|  1 | Joe Smith   | Jan Smith   |                  2 |
+----+-------------+-------------+--------------------+
1 row in set (0.00 sec)
```

In this case, we instructed the *SELECT* statement to show us only the columns *id*, *father_name*, *mother_name*, and *number_of_children*. If we had wished to see all of the columns, the command would have been **SELECT * from families**.

Notice that the *id* column has a value of 1. We did not insert this value; it was set by the MySQL server when we inserted our first record. Subsequent inserts will continue to increment this number. Let's add one more row of data:

```
mysql> INSERT into families set
    -> father_name = "Ken Anderson",
    -> father_dob = "1971-06-06",
    -> mother_name = "Mary Anderson",
    -> mother_dob = "1971-01-29",
    -> number_of_children = "3",
    -> child1_name = "Shawn Anderson",
    -> child1_dob = "1999-10-17",
    -> child2_name = "Kyle Anderson",
    -> child2_dob = "2001-10-12",
    -> child3_name="Lillie Anderson",
```

```
       -> child3_dob = "2004-11-12",
       -> notes = "This is the Anderson family of Omaha, NE";
Query OK, 1 row affected (0.02 sec)
```

In this example, we accomplished the same goal as our original *INSERT* statement, but we used an alternate syntax.

Now repeat our *SELECT* query to verify that the table contains two rows:

```
mysql> SELECT id, father_name, mother_name, number_of_children from families;
+----+--------------+---------------+--------------------+
| id | father_name  | mother_name   | number_of_children |
+----+--------------+---------------+--------------------+
|  1 | Joe Smith    | Jan Smith     |                  2 |
|  2 | Ken Anderson | Mary Anderson |                  3 |
+----+--------------+---------------+--------------------+
2 rows in set (0.01 sec)
```

Now that we know how to add data to our table, the next step is modifying existing data. In our initial insert, we didn't capitalize the last name "smith" in the *notes* column. Use the *UPDATE* command with a *WHERE* clause to correct this:

```
mysql> UPDATE families set
    -> notes = "This is the Smith family of Chicago, IL"
    -> WHERE id = "1";
Query OK, 1 row affected (0.01 sec)
Rows matched: 1  Changed: 1  Warnings: 0
```

The *UPDATE* command is used to modify values in rows that already exist. In order to identify what rows to modify (assuming you don't want to update all rows in the table), you need to give a *WHERE* clause that uniquely identifies the rows you wish to modify. In this instance, we took advantage of the fact that the *id* field is unique among rows to ensure that our modification affected only the row we wanted it to affect. Use the *SELECT* command again to verify our change took place:

```
mysql> select id, notes from families;
+----+-----------------------------------------+
| id | notes                                   |
+----+-----------------------------------------+
|  1 | This is the Smith family of Chicago, IL |
|  2 | This is the Anderson family of Omaha, NE |
+----+-----------------------------------------+
2 rows in set (0.00 sec)
```

To remove data from the table, the *DELETE* command is used. The syntax is similar to the *UPDATE* command:

```
mysql> delete from families where id = "2";
Query OK, 1 row affected (0.03 sec)

mysql> select id, notes from families;
+----+-----------------------------------------+
| id | notes                                   |
+----+-----------------------------------------+
|  1 | This is the Smith family of Chicago, IL |
+----+-----------------------------------------+
1 row in set (0.00 sec)
```

The *SELECT* command shows us that we're back to one record in the table.

It is possible to alter the layout of a table after it has been created. You can either modify the datatype of an existing column or add/delete columns from the table. Be careful when you modify a datatype on a column that already contains data because you run the risk of losing your data! For example, if you change a column from varchar(255) to char(1), you will lose all but the first character of any data you had in that column.

The *ALTER TABLE* command is used to modify a table after it has been created. Let's add two new columns to our table to track the city and state where the families live:

```
mysql> ALTER TABLE families
    -> ADD COLUMN city VARCHAR(100) AFTER notes,
    -> ADD COLUMN state CHAR(2) AFTER city;
Query OK, 1 row affected (0.00 sec)
Records: 1  Duplicates: 0  Warnings: 0
```

Reinsert our second family that we previously deleted:

```
mysql> insert into families set father_name = "Ken Anderson",
-> father_dob = "1971-06-06", mother_name = "Mary Anderson",
-> mother_dob = "1971-01-29", number_of_children = "3", child1_name =
-> "Shawn Anderson", child1_dob = "1999-10-17", child2_name =
-> "Kyle Anderson", child2_dob = "2001-10-12", child3_name=
-> "Lillie Anderson", child3_dob = "2004-11-12", notes =
-> "This is the Anderson family of Omaha, NE";
```

Use *UPDATE* to add city and state values:

```
mysql> update families set city = "Chicago", state = "IL" where id = "1";
Query OK, 1 row affected (0.01 sec)
Rows matched: 1  Changed: 1  Warnings: 0

mysql> update families set city = "Omaha", state = "NE" where id = "3";
Query OK, 1 row affected (0.00 sec)
Rows matched: 1  Changed: 1  Warnings: 0

mysql> select id, city, state, notes from families;
+----+---------+-------+-------------------------------------------+
| id | city    | state | notes                                     |
+----+---------+-------+-------------------------------------------+
|  1 | Chicago | IL    | This is the Smith family of Chicago, IL   |
|  3 | Omaha   | NE    | This is the Anderson family of Omaha, NE  |
+----+---------+-------+-------------------------------------------+
2 rows in set (0.00 sec)
```

Notice that the Anderson family is now *id* "3" instead of "2". ID 2 was removed by our *DELETE* command. The autoupdate option of MySQL will never use the number 2 again in this column.

Aggregate Functions

Aggregate functions allow you to group queried data in meaningful ways. SQL databases are more than just simple data stores; the complex functionality of SQL allows you to extract meaningful data very easily.

A common aggregate function is *GROUP BY*. This function allows you to perform operations on groups of data. Let's add some more data to our example database and see what options *GROUP BY* gives us.

```
mysql> insert into families set father_name = "Adam White",
-> father_dob = "1969-06-08", mother_name = "Tina White",
-> mother_dob = "1969-01-30", number_of_children = "1",
-> child1_name = "Ed White", child1_dob = "1998-11-17",
-> notes = "This is the White family of Bellevue, NE",
-> city = "Bellevue", state = "NE";
Query OK, 1 row affected, 0 warnings (0.00 sec)
mysql> insert into families set father_name = "Bill Carpenter",
-> father_dob = "1968-06-01", mother_name = "Linda Carpenter",
-> mother_dob = "1970-02-30", number_of_children = "4",
-> child1_name = "Joe Carpenter", child1_dob = "1998-12-17",
-> child2_name = "Bob Carpenter", child2_dob = "1996-01-01",
-> child3_name = "Luke Carpenter", child3_dob = "2004-08-08",
-> notes = "This is the Carpenter family of Lincoln, NE",
-> city = "Lincoln", state = "NE";
Query OK, 1 row affected, 0 warnings (0.00 sec)

mysql> select id, father_name, city, state from families;
+----+----------------+----------+-------+
| id | father_name    | city     | state |
+----+----------------+----------+-------+
|  1 | Joe Smith      | Chicago  | IL    |
|  3 | Ken Anderson   | Omaha    | NE    |
|  4 | Adam White     | Bellevue | NE    |
|  5 | Bill Carpenter | Lincoln  | NE    |
+----+----------------+----------+-------+
4 rows in set (0.01 sec)

mysql> select count(state),state from families GROUP BY state;
+--------------+-------+
| count(state) | state |
+--------------+-------+
|            1 | IL    |
|            3 | NE    |
+--------------+-------+
2 rows in set (0.00 sec)
```

We've added two new families, so our table now contains four rows. The last query is an example of using the *GROUP BY* syntax. We asked MySQL, "How many different states are represented in our table?" You also could have achieved the same result with a combination of the *mysql* command-line program and some shell scripting knowledge:

```
# echo "select state from families" |\
> mysql -s -uroot -ppassword -hlocalhost community |\
```

```
> sort | uniq -c
      1 IL
      3 NE
```

If you are more familiar with the Linux command-line text processing tools, you can oftentimes depend on them to parse the data that a SQL query will return. As you can see from this example, the *mysql* command-line program can process queries on standard input and return results on standard output. The *-s* option tells *mysql* to be "silent," meaning not to return any column names and only return data, which is usually what you want if you're going to be passing the results to another program for processing.

Another option MySQL gives you for outputting data is the *ORDER BY* function. This simply changes the sort order of the results. Let's sort our families by the father's date of birth, from youngest to oldest:

```
mysql> select id,father_name,father_dob from families ORDER BY father_dob asc;
+----+----------------+------------+
| id | father_name    | father_dob |
+----+----------------+------------+
|  5 | Bill Carpenter | 1968-06-01 |
|  4 | Adam White     | 1969-06-08 |
|  1 | Joe Smith      | 1970-04-01 |
|  3 | Ken Anderson   | 1971-06-06 |
+----+----------------+------------+
4 rows in set (0.00 sec)
```

MySQL understands that the *father_dob* column is type DATE and sorts accordingly. The modifiers to *ORDER BY* can be *asc* (ascending) or *desc* (descending).

Multitable Queries

The final concept to describe in our basic SQL overview is that of *JOIN*. So far, we have concerned ourselves with querying only one table. This is fine for simple data storage requirements, but as data complexity grows, so does the need for multiple tables. As long as there is a relationship between data elements in the tables, the table values can be *JOIN*ed in a query.

To see an example of this, we need to create another table that has a relationship with the first table. We will use this second table to store pet information for each family.

```
mysql> CREATE TABLE pets (
    ->    id INTEGER UNSIGNED NOT NULL AUTO_INCREMENT,
    ->    family_id INTEGER UNSIGNED NOT NULL,
    ->    type VARCHAR(45) NOT NULL,
    ->    name VARCHAR(45) NOT NULL,
    ->    PRIMARY KEY (id)
    -> );
Query OK, 0 rows affected (0.02 sec)

mysql> show tables;
+---------------------+
| Tables_in_community |
```

```
+---------------------+
| families            |
| pets                |
+---------------------+
2 rows in set (0.00 sec)

mysql> describe pets;
+-----------+------------------+------+-----+---------+----------------+
| Field     | Type             | Null | Key | Default | Extra          |
+-----------+------------------+------+-----+---------+----------------+
| id        | int(10) unsigned | NO   | PRI | NULL    | auto_increment |
| family_id | int(10) unsigned | NO   |     |         |                |
| type      | varchar(45)      | NO   |     |         |                |
| name      | varchar(45)      | NO   |     |         |                |
+-----------+------------------+------+-----+---------+----------------+
4 rows in set (0.02 sec)

mysql> insert into pets (family_id,type,name) VALUES ("1","dog","Max");
Query OK, 1 row affected (0.01 sec)

mysql> insert into pets (family_id,type,name) VALUES ("3","cat","Paws");
Query OK, 1 row affected (0.01 sec)

mysql> insert into pets (family_id,type,name) VALUES ("4","cat","Muffy");
Query OK, 1 row affected (0.01 sec)

mysql> insert into pets (family_id,type,name) VALUES ("4","dog","Rover");
Query OK, 1 row affected (0.00 sec)
```

The important column in this second table is *family_id*. We need to ensure that as we add data to this table, we associate the data with the correct ID from the *families* table. This expresses the relationship between the families and their pets, and allows us to query against them. We have added four pets to our table: family ID #1 (the Smiths) have a dog named Max, family ID #3 (the Andersons) have a cat named Paws, and family ID #4 (the Whites) have a cat named Muffy and a dog named Rover. Here is a simple example of a join that queries values from both tables:

```
mysql> select a.id, a.father_name, a.mother_name, b.type, b.name
from families a, pets b where a.id = b.family_id;
+----+---------------+----------------+------+-------+
| id | father_name   | mother_name    | type | name  |
+----+---------------+----------------+------+-------+
|  1 | Joe Smith     | Jan Smith      | dog  | Max   |
|  3 | Ken Anderson  | Mary Anderson  | cat  | Paws  |
|  4 | Adam White    | Tina White     | cat  | Muffy |
|  4 | Adam White    | Tina White     | dog  | Rover |
+----+---------------+----------------+------+-------+
4 rows in set (0.02 sec)
```

This syntax is slightly different from our previous *SELECT* statements. First, notice that we have to qualify the column names with a table identifier. In this case, we're using a and b. After the *FROM* statement, we are aliasing the *families* table as a and the *pets* table as b. This is common shorthand that makes our SQL statements shorter; otherwise, we'd have to use *families.id*, *families.father_name*, etc. Finally, the *WHERE* clause of a.id = b.family_id expresses the relationship between the tables. This ensures that we know which pet belongs to which family. As you can see, the *family_id* column is not a primary key, because it does not need to be unique. Families can have multiple pets, as the White family does in our example.

Although this *SELECT* statement did not actually use the *JOIN* syntax, it is an example of the simplest kind of join. Notice that we are missing a family from our results, however: the Carpenter family does not have any pets, so our *SELECT* statement did not select them. If we want families to display in the output even if they do not have pets, we need to use the *LEFT JOIN* syntax. This is functionally very similar to the previous join of two tables, but it differs in two important ways: the syntax is quite a bit different, and because special consideration is given to the table on the LEFT, each item present in the left table will display in the results, *even if* there is not a match with the other joined table. Compare the output of this *LEFT JOIN* statement with the previous join output:

```
mysql> select families.id, families.father_name, families.mother_name,
    -> pets.type, pets.name from families
    -> LEFT JOIN pets on families.id = pets.family_id;
+----+----------------+----------------+------+-------+
| id | father_name    | mother_name    | type | name  |
+----+----------------+----------------+------+-------+
|  1 | Joe Smith      | Jan Smith      | dog  | Max   |
|  3 | Ken Anderson   | Mary Anderson  | cat  | Paws  |
|  4 | Adam White     | Tina White     | cat  | Muffy |
|  4 | Adam White     | Tina White     | dog  | Rover |
|  5 | Bill Carpenter | Linda Carpenter| NULL | NULL  |
+----+----------------+----------------+------+-------+
5 rows in set (0.01 sec)
```

The Carpenter family now appears in the query results, but with NULL values for *type* and *name*, since they did not have a corresponding record in the *pets* table. We used the more detailed *SELECT* syntax in this example, keeping the full table names instead of aliasing them with **a** and **b** but the queries are the same; the aliasing is just for readability.

On the Exam

SQL can be a complicated subject, but the LPI 102 exam will test you only on the basic syntax of adding and querying data. Make sure you are familiar with the common elements of *INSERT* and *SELECT* statements, and can describe the various datatypes available in MySQL.

14

The X Window System (Topic 106)

Unix has a long history that predates the popular demand for a graphical user interface (GUI). However, a GUI is an essential part of running desktop systems today, and the standard GUI on Linux systems is the X Window System, or more simply, X. Originally developed at MIT and Digital Equipment Corporation, X's Version 11 Release 7 is the version most commonly seen in Linux distributions. This version is more commonly referred to as *X11R7.4*, or just *X11*. X is a complete windowing GUI and is distributable under license without cost. The implementation of X for Linux is X.Org Foundation (*http://www.x.org*), which is available for multiple computer architectures and is released under the GNU Public License. This section covers the following three Objectives on X.Org Foundation for LPI Exam 102:

Objective 1: Install and Configure X11
> An LPIC 1 candidate should be able to configure and install X and an X font server. This Objective includes verifying that the video card and monitor are supported by an X server as well as customizing and tuning X for the video card and monitor. It also includes installing an X font server, installing fonts, and configuring X to use the font server (which may require manually editing */etc/X11/xorg.conf*). Weight: 2.

Objective 2: Set Up a Display Manager
> This Objective states a candidate should be able to set up and customize a display manager. This includes turning the display manager on or off and changing the display manager greetings. It also includes changing default bitplanes for the display manager and configuring display managers for use by X stations. This Objective covers the display managers: X Display Manager (*xdm*), Gnome Display Manager (*gdm*), and KDE Display Manager (*kdm*). Weight: 2.

Objective 3: Accessibility
> Demonstrate knowledge and awareness of accessibility technologies. This objective requires the candidate to be familiar with the various technologies and how they may be configured in the X Window System. Topics include keyboard

shortcuts, controlling visual settings and themes, and assistive technologies. Weight: 1.

An Overview of X

X is implemented using a client/server model. X servers and clients can be located on the same computer or separated across a network, so that computation is handled separately from display rendering. While X servers manage hardware, they do not define the look of the display, and they offer no tools to manipulate clients. The X server is responsible for rendering various shapes and colors on screen. Examples of X Servers include:

- Software from X.Org, which controls your Linux PC's video cardX.Org software on a separate networked system, displaying output from a program running on your system

- Other networked Unix systems running their own X server software

- X implementations for other operating systems, such as Microsoft Windows

- An *X Terminal*, which is a hardware device with no computational ability of its own, built solely for display purposes

X clients are user programs, such as spreadsheets or CAD tools, which display graphical output. Examples of X clients are:

- A browser, such as Firefox or Opera

- A mail program, such as Evolution or Kmail

- Office applications, such as OpenOffice, Gnumeric, or AbiWord

- A terminal emulator, such as `xterm`, running within an X window

A special client program called a *window manager* is responsible for these functions and provides windows, window sizing, open and close buttons, and so forth. The window manager controls the other clients running under an X server. Multiple window managers are available for the X Window System, allowing you to choose an interface style that suits your needs and personal taste.

A few complete graphical *desktop environments* are also available. These packages can include a window manager and additional applications that work together to create a complete, unified working environment. Most Linux distributions ship with either the KDE or GNOME, or both, along with a number of standalone window managers. There is no standard window manager or environment for Linux. The selection is entirely up to the user.

Objective 1: Install and Configure X11

Most Linux distributions install and automatically configure X.Org, freeing users from much of its installation and configuration. However, Exam 102 requires specific knowledge of some of the underpinnings of X configuration.

Be careful about installing an X server on a system that already has X installed. A backup should be made prior to the installation.

Selecting and Configuring an X Server

X.Org is the standard X Window System implementation for most distributions of Linux. X.Org is released and maintained by X.Org Foundation, which is a nonprofit community of developers and documentation writers. The X11 environment from X.Org is based on the code developed by XFree86, which was used as the X Windows implementation in many Linux distributions. Freedesktop.org (*http://www.freedesktop.org/wiki/*) is a collaborative project to develop software for X Window System computers. Get distribution files for X.Org at *http://freedesktop.org*.

The X.Org project provides support for an amazing array of graphics hardware. This outcome is possible partly due to cooperation by manufacturers through public release of graphics device documentation and driver software, and partly due to the tenacity of the X.Org developers. Fortunately, many manufacturers who were historically uninterested in offering technical information to the X.Org project have become cooperative. The result is that most recent video hardware is well-supported by X.Org.

Supported video hardware

To avoid problems, it is important to verify XFree86 compatibility with your hardware prior to installation. At the very least, you should be aware of these items:

Your X.Org version
> As with any software, improvements in X.Org are made over time, particularly in support for hardware devices. You should choose a version of X.Org that offers a good balance between the video support and stability you require. To determine which version of X you're running, simply issue the following command:

```
$ X -version
X.org X Server 1.6.1.901 (1.6.2 RC1)
Release Date 2009-5-8
X Protocol Version 11, Revision 0
```

The video chipset
> X.Org video drivers are written for graphics chipsets, not the video cards on which they're installed. Multiple video cards from a variety of manufacturers can carry the same chipset, making those cards nearly identical in function. You must verify that the chipset on your video card is supported by X.Org to use advanced graphics features. Supported chipsets are listed on the X.Org wiki.

Monitor type
> X.Org can be configured to handle just about any monitor, particularly the newer and very flexible multisync monitors sold today, which can handle preset configurations provided in the X.Org Foundation configuration utilities.

However, if you have a nonstandard monitor, you need to know some parameters describing its capabilities before configuring X, including your monitor's horizontal sync frequency (in kHz), vertical refresh frequency (in Hz), and resolution (in pixels). These items can usually be found in your monitor's documentation, but since most monitors conform to standard display settings such as *XGA* (1024 × 768 pixels at 60 Hz vertical refresh), you should be able to use a preset configuration.

Installing X.Org

It is rare that you'll actually need to install X.Org by hand, as X.Org is typically installed during initial system installation for systems that plan to use X. Most Linux distributions include X.Org packages on the installation media so you can install them from there using your distribution's choice of package managers.

Some applications might require that you install a new release or development version of X.Org that is not available as a package. In these cases, you can download the source files or precompiled binaries from X.Org mirror websites (*http://www.x .org*). Refer to Chapter 5 for more information on installing applications from packages or source files.

Configuring an X server and the xorg.conf file

X.Org configuration differs slightly among versions and among Linux distributions, but essentially involves the creation of the *xorg.conf* file customized for your system. The file is created during the system install as devices are automatically detected and configured. Typically there is no further need for modification to the file, as it will be managed by the system. The X server uses this configuration file when it starts to set such things as keyboard and mouse selections, installed fonts, and screen resolutions.

Example 14-1 contains an *xorg.conf* file. (Note that the *xorg.conf* file shown contains example settings and is not intended for use on your system.)

Example 14-1. A sample xorg.conf file for XFree86 v3.3.3

```
# /etc/X11/xorg.conf (xorg X Window System server configuration file)
# This file was generated by dexconf, the Debian X Configuration tool, using
# values from the debconf database.
# Edit this file with caution, and see the /etc/X11/xorg.conf manual page.
# (Type "man /etc/X11/xorg.conf" at the shell prompt.)
#
# This file is automatically updated on xserver-xorg package upgrades *only*
# if it has not been modified since the last upgrade of the xserver-xorg
# package.
#
# If you have edited this file but would like it to be automatically updated
# again, run the following command:
# sudo dpkg-reconfigure -phigh xserver-xorg

Section "Files"
FontPath "/usr/share/X11/fonts/misc"
FontPath "/usr/share/X11/fonts/cyrillic"
```

```
FontPath "/usr/share/X11/fonts/100dpi/:unscaled"
FontPath "/usr/share/X11/fonts/75dpi/:unscaled"
FontPath "/usr/share/X11/fonts/Type1"
FontPath "/usr/share/X11/fonts/100dpi"
FontPath "/usr/share/X11/fonts/75dpi"
FontPath "/usr/share/fonts/X11/misc"
# path to defoma fonts
FontPath "/var/lib/defoma/x-ttcidfont-conf.d/dirs/TrueType"
EndSection

Section "Module"
Load "i2c"
Load "bitmap"
Load "ddc"
Load "dri"
Load "extmod"
Load "freetype"
Load "glx"
Load "int10"
Load "type1"
Load "vbe"
EndSection

Section "InputDevice"
Identifier "Generic Keyboard"
Driver "kbd"
Option "CoreKeyboard"
Option "XkbRules" "xorg"
Option "XkbModel" "pc105"
Option "XkbLayout" "us"
Option "XkbOptions" "lv3:ralt_switch"
EndSection

Section "InputDevice"
Identifier "Configured Mouse"
Driver "mouse"
Option "CorePointer"
Option "Device" "/dev/input/mice"
Option "Protocol" "ExplorerPS/2"
Option "ZAxisMapping" "4 5"
Option "Emulate3Buttons" "true"
EndSection

Section "InputDevice"
Driver "wacom"
Identifier "stylus"
Option "Device" "/dev/wacom" # Change to
# /dev/input/event
# for USB
Option "Type" "stylus"
Option "ForceDevice" "ISDV4" # Tablet PC ONLY
EndSection

Section "InputDevice"
Driver "wacom"
Identifier "eraser"
```

```
Option "Device" "/dev/wacom" # Change to
# /dev/input/event
# for USB
Option "Type" "eraser"
Option "ForceDevice" "ISDV4" # Tablet PC ONLY
EndSection

Section "InputDevice"
Driver "wacom"
Identifier "cursor"
Option "Device" "/dev/wacom" # Change to
# /dev/input/event
# for USB
Option "Type" "cursor"
Option "ForceDevice" "ISDV4" # Tablet PC ONLY
EndSection

Section "Device"
Identifier "VMWare Inc [VMware SVGA II] PCI Display Adapter"
Driver "vmware"
BusID "PCI:0:15:0"
EndSection

Section "Monitor"
Identifier "Generic Monitor"
Option "DPMS"
HorizSync 28-51
VertRefresh 43-60
EndSection

Section "Screen"
Identifier "Default Screen"
Device "VMWare Inc [VMware SVGA II] PCI Display Adapter"
Monitor "Generic Monitor"
DefaultDepth 24
SubSection "Display"
Depth 1
Modes "1024x768" "800x600" "640x480"
EndSubSection
SubSection "Display"
Depth 4
Modes "1024x768" "800x600" "640x480"
EndSubSection
SubSection "Display"
Depth 8
Modes "1024x768" "800x600" "640x480"
EndSubSection
SubSection "Display"
Depth 15
Modes "1024x768" "800x600" "640x480"
EndSubSection
SubSection "Display"
Depth 16
Modes "1024x768" "800x600" "640x480"
EndSubSection
SubSection "Display"
```

```
Depth 24
Modes "1024x768" "800x600" "640x480"
EndSubSection
EndSection

Section "ServerLayout"
Identifier "Default Layout"
Screen "Default Screen"
InputDevice "Generic Keyboard"
InputDevice "Configured Mouse"
InputDevice "stylus" "SendCoreEvents"
InputDevice "cursor" "SendCoreEvents"
InputDevice "eraser" "SendCoreEvents"
EndSection

Section "DRI"
Mode 0666
EndSection
```

Distribution-specific tools

Various Linux distributors provide their own configuration utilities. For example, *system-config-display* is distributed by Red Hat Software. It is an X-based GUI tool that can probe graphics chipsets and features. In Red Hat Fedora 10, the *xorg.conf* file was dropped. Instead, the operating system detects system components and configures the X system accordingly every time the system boots. If you necd to configure a system component manually, you first need to create the *xorg.conf* file. This can be accomplished using different tools, such as the *system-config-display* package if it is installed. This can be run interactively as root from the command line, or it may be run from the display command in the System → Administration → Display menu. In either case, the graphical interactive control for video driver and monitor selection will open. You can install the *system-config-display* package using a package controller such as *yum*. Refer to Chapter 5 for more information about installing packages. To run the *system-config-display* package from the terminal, type the following:

```
# system-config-display
```

The alternative is to manually create and edit the *xorg.conf* file. This may be done using the *xorg –configure* command, which will create a basic new *xorg.conf* file using information that is autodetected from the system. The file will be created in the local directory.

Example 14-2 shows the creation of the *xorg.conf* file using the *–configure* option in Fedora Linux.

Example 14-2. Creating the xorg.conf file in Fedora Linux

```
# Xorg -configure
X.Org X Server 1.6.1.901 (1.6.2 RC 1)
Release Date: 2009-5-8
X Protocol Version 11, Revision 0
Build Operating System: Linux 2.6.18-128.1.6.el5 i686
Current Operating System: Linux Suffolk 2.6.29.6-213.fc11.i686.PAE #1 \
```

SMP Tue Jul 7 20:59:29 EDT 2009 i686
Kernel command line: ro root=/dev/mapper/vg_suffolk-lv_root rhgb quiet
Build Date: 18 May 2009 02:47:59PM
Build ID: xorg-x11-server 1.6.1.901-1.fc11
Before reporting problems, check http://wiki.x.org
to make sure that you have the latest version.
Markers: (--) probed, (**) from config file, (==) default setting,
(++) from command line, (!!) notice, (II) informational,
(WW) warning, (EE) error, (NI) not implemented, (??) unknown.
(==) Log file: "/var/log/Xorg.1.log", Time: Wed Aug 12 06:32:31 2009
List of video drivers:
glint
nv
vmware
voodoo
radeon
mach64
geode
sisusb
intel
s3virge
siliconmotion
ati
mga
amd
savage
ast
v4l
i128
neomagic
sis
r128
dummy
rendition
nouveau
ztv
trident
tdfx
cirrus
i740
openchrome
apm
fbdev
vesa
(++) Using config file: "/root/xorg.conf.new"

Xorg detected your mouse at device /dev/input/mice.
Please check your config if the mouse is still not
operational, as by default Xorg tries to autodetect
the protocol.

Your xorg.conf file is /root/xorg.conf.new

To test the server, run 'X -config /root/xorg.conf.new'

The resulting *xorg.conf.new* file will need to be modified and then copied to the */etc/X11/* directory so it can be used the next time the system starts:

```
# cp /root/xorg.conf.new /etc/X11/xorg.conf
```

The default location for the *xorg.conf* file is in */etc/X11*. The file contains a number of sections, listed next, that describe various parameters of devices attached to the system. The sections may be in any order.

Files
>   This section is used to specify the default font path and the path to the RGB database. Using the `FontPath` *"path"* directive multiple times creates a list of directories that the X server will search for fonts. The RGB database is an equivalence table of numeric red/green/blue color values with names. Here's a short excerpt of the RGB database:
>
> ```
> 255 228 196        bisque
> 255 218 185        peach puff
> 255 218 185        PeachPuff
> 255 222 173        navajo white
> ```
>
>   Hundreds of these names are defined and may be used in the configuration of X applications where color names are required.

ServerFlags
>   This section allows customization of X server options such as the handling of hotkeys.

InputDevice
>   This section may be used multiple times in the configuration file, depending on the types of devices connected to the system. Normally it will appear at least twice: once for the keyboard and again for the mouse.

Monitor
>   Multiple `Monitor` sections are used to define the specifications of monitors and a list of the video modes they can handle.

Device
>   Multiple `Device` sections are used to define the video hardware (cards) installed.

Screen
>   The `Screen` section ties together a `Device` with a corresponding `Monitor` and includes some configuration settings for them.

ServerLayout
>   This section ties together a `Screen` with one or more `InputDevice`s. Multiple `ServerLayout` sections may be used for multiheaded configurations (i.e., systems with more than one monitor).

X Fonts

X.Org is distributed with a collection of fonts for most basic purposes, including text displays in terminal windows and browsers. For many users, the default fonts are adequate, but others may prefer to add additional fonts to their system. A variety of fonts are available, both free and commercially, from many sources, such as Adobe. Some very creative fonts are created by individuals and distributed on the Internet (a search should return some useful links to a query such as "*X.org* fonts").

X.Org makes fonts that it finds in the *font path* available to client programs. A basic font path is compiled into the X server, but you can specify your own font path using the `FontPath` directive in the `Files` section of *xorg.conf*. The simple syntax is:

```
FontPath "path"
```

For example:

```
Section "Files"
FontPath "/usr/share/X11/fonts/misc"
FontPath "/usr/share/X11/fonts/cyrillic"
FontPath "/usr/share/X11/fonts/100dpi/:unscaled"
FontPath "/usr/share/X11/fonts/75dpi/:unscaled"
FontPath "/usr/share/X11/fonts/Type1"
FontPath "/usr/share/X11/fonts/100dpi"
FontPath "/usr/share/X11/fonts/75dpi"
FontPath "/usr/share/fonts/X11/misc"
# path to defoma fonts
FontPath "/var/lib/defoma/x-ttcidfont-conf.d/dirs/TrueType"
EndSection
```

This group of `FontPath` directives creates a font path consisting of eight directories, all under */usr/share/X11/fonts*. When X starts, it parses these font directories and includes their contents in the list of fonts available during the X session.

Installing fonts

Adding new fonts is straightforward. (For this brief discussion, we assume that we're working with Type 1 fonts. Other types, such as TrueType fonts, may require additional configuration, depending on your version of XFree86.) First, a suitable directory should be created for the new fonts, such as */usr/share/X11/fonts/local* or */usr/local/fonts*. You may wish to separate your own fonts from the default X.Org directories to protect them during upgrades. After the fonts are installed in the new directory, the *mkfontdir* utility is run to catalog the new fonts in the new directory. New entries are added to the *xorg.conf* file to include the path for new fonts. For example:

```
FontPath    "/usr/local/fonts"
```

At this point, the X server can be restarted to recognize the new fonts, or the fonts can be dynamically added using the *xset* command:

```
# xset fp+ /usr/local/fonts
```

xset is beyond the scope of the LPIC Level 1 exams.

On the Exam

Be sure you understand how the X font path is created and how to extend it to include additional directories. Knowledge of the internal details of font files is not necessary.

The X font server

On a network with multiple workstations, managing fonts manually for each system can be time consuming. To simplify this problem, the administrator can install all of the desired fonts on a single system and then run *xfs*, the X fonts server, on that system. On a local system, *xfs* off-loads the work of rendering fonts from the X server, which means the X server can do other tasks while fonts are being rendered. This is especially noticeable on slower systems or systems without a Floating Point Unit (FPU).

The X font server is a small daemon that sends fonts to clients on both local and remote systems. Some Linux distributions use *xfs* exclusively, without a list of directories in the manually created font path. To include *xfs* in your system's font path, add a FontPath directive like this:

```
Section "Files"
        RgbPath      "/usr/share/X11/fonts/rgb"
        FontPath     "unix/:-1"
    EndSection
```

If you install *xfs* from a package from your distribution, it is probably automatically configured to start at boot time and run continually, serving fonts to local and remote client programs. To start *xfs* manually, simply enter the *xfs* command. For security purposes, you may wish to run *xfs* as a nonroot user. *xfs* is configured using its configuration file, */etc/X11/fs/config*.

On the Exam

Fonts are administered primarily through the local machine, reducing network services that need to be enabled on the remote server. Coverage here is for awareness that fonts may be administered remotely via *xfs*.

Controlling X Applications with .Xresources

The X Window System also has many built-in customization features. Many X applications are programmed with a variety of *resources*, which are configuration settings that can be externally manipulated. Rather than have a configuration utility built into each application, applications can be written to examine the contents of a file in the user's home directory. The *.Xresources* file contains a line for each configured resource in the following form:

```
program*resource: value
```

This line can be translated as follows:

- *program* is the name of a configurable program, such as emacs or xterm.
- *resource* is one of the configurable settings allowed by the program, such as colors.
- *value* is the setting to apply to the resource.

For example, the following is an excerpt from *.Xresources* that configures colors for an xterm:

```
xterm*background: Black
xterm*foreground: Wheat
xterm*cursorColor: Orchid
xterm*reverseVideo: false
```

On the Exam

You should be aware of X resources and the function of the *.Xresources* file. In particular, you should understand that X applications will look in the *.Xresources* file for settings. You should also be able to construct a resource setting given a particular example, but you do not need to be able to generate a configuration file from scratch.

Objective 2: Set Up a Display Manager

The display manager is the tool to manage X sessions on physical displays both locally and across the network. Part of its job is to handle user authentication through a graphical login screen, which replaces the familiar text-mode login. There are three primary display managers implemented with Linux: *xdm*, *kdm*, and *gdm*.

Configuring xdm

The X display manager (*xdm*) is a program that allows for a graphical session to begin on an X server.

xdm is distributed as part of X.Org and is configured by a series of files located in */etc/X11/xdm*. These files include:

Xaccess
    This file controls inbound requests from remote hosts.

Xresources

This file is similar to *.Xresources*, discussed earlier. It holds configuration information for some *xdm* resources, including the graphical login screen. This file can be edited to modify the appearance of the *xdm* login screen.

Xservers

This file associates the X display names (`:0`, `:1`, ...) with either the local X server software or a foreign display, such as an X terminal.

Xsession

This file contains the script *xdm* launches after a successful login. It usually looks for *.Xsession* in the user's home directory and executes the commands found there. If such a file doesn't exist, *Xsession* starts a default window manager (or environment) and applications.

Xsetup_0

This file is a script started before the graphical login screen. It often includes commands to set colors, display graphics, or run other programs. This script is executed as *root*.

xdm-config

This file associates *xdm* configuration resources with the other files in this list. It usually isn't necessary to make changes in this file unless an expert administrator plans to customize *xdm* configuration.

Running xdm manually

xdm uses the X server to run on your local display. Therefore, you must have a working X configuration prior to using a display manager. Then, to start *xdm*, simply enter it as *root*:

```
# xdm
```

xdm launches the X server and displays the graphical login, and you can log in as usual. *xdm* then starts your graphical environment. After you log out, *xdm* resets and again displays the login screen.

Most Linux distributions enable virtual consoles. You can switch among them using the key combinations Ctrl-Alt-F1, Ctrl-Alt-F2, and so on. (The Ctrl is required only when switching from an X console to a text or other X console.) Typically, the first six consoles are set up as text-mode screens, and X launches on console 7 (Ctrl-Alt-F7) or the first TTY not running *mingetty* or some other *getty* process. This means that, as with *startx*, your original text-mode console remains unchanged after you manually start *xdm*. Therefore, you must log out of your text-mode console if you plan to leave the system unattended with *xdm* running manually.

If you want to stop *xdm*, you first must be sure that all of the X sessions under its management are logged out. Otherwise, they'll die when *xdm* exits and you could lose data. Simply stop the *xdm* process using *kill* or *killall* from a text console:

```
# killall xdm
```

The X Window System

Of course, *xdm* isn't very useful for your local system if you must always start it manually. That's why most Linux distributions include a boot-time option to start *xdm* for you, eliminating the text-mode login completely.

Running xdm automatically

For Linux systems using the System V–style initialization, a runlevel is usually reserved for login under *xdm*. This line at the bottom of */etc/inittab* instructs *init* to start *xdm* for runlevel 5:

```
# Run xdm in runlevel 5
x:5:respawn:/usr/X11R6/bin/xdm -nodaemon
```

Using this configuration, when the system enters runlevel 5, *xdm* starts and presents the graphical login as before. See Chapter 4 for more information on runlevels.

It's also possible to automatically start *xdm* simply by adding it to the end of an initialization script, such as *rc.local*. This method offers less control over *xdm* but may be adequate for some situations and for Linux distributions that don't offer runlevels.

Basic xdm customization

You may wish to personalize the look of *xdm* for your system. The look of the graphical login screen can be altered by manipulating the resources in */etc/X11/xdm/Xresources*. (Note that *Xresources* uses ! to start comments.) For example, the following excerpt shows settings to control the greeting (*Welcome to Linux on smp-pc*), other prompts, and colors:

```
! Xresources file
xlogin*borderWidth: 10
xlogin*greeting: Welcome to Linux on CLIENTHOST
xlogin*namePrompt: Login:\040
xlogin*fail: Login incorrect - try again!
xlogin*failColor: red
xlogin*Foreground: Yellow
xlogin*Background: MidnightBlue
```

You can also include command-line options to the X server in */etc/X11/xdm/Xservers* if you wish to override those found in */etc/X11/xorg.conf*. For example, to change the default color depth, add the *-bpp* (bits per pixel) option for the local display:

```
# Xservers file
:0 local /usr/X11R6/bin/X -bpp 24
```

To include additional X programs or settings on the graphical login screen, put them in */etc/X11/xdm/Xsetup_0*. In this example, the background color of the X display is set to a solid color (in hexadecimal form), and a clock is added at the lower-righthand corner of the screen:

```
#!/bin/sh
# Xsetup
/usr/X11R6/bin/xsetroot -solid "#356390"
/usr/X11R6/bin/xclock -digital -update 1 -geometry -5-5 &
```

Note that in this example, *xsetroot* exits immediately after it sets the color, allowing the *Xsetup_0* script to continue. *xclock*, however, does not exit and must be put into the background using an **&** at the end of the command line. If such commands are not placed into the background, the *Xsetup_0* script hangs, and the login display does not appear.

X Terminals

X terminals are a breed of low-cost display devices for X. They are usually diskless systems that implement an X server and drive a monitor. Such devices can be configured to access a remote host to find an *xdm* daemon or will broadcast to the entire network looking for a "willing host" to offer *xdm* services. The selected system will run an X session across the network with the X terminal as the target display. With this setup, a large number of relatively inexpensive X terminals can make use of a few high-powered host systems to run graphical clients.

xdm for X terminals

To use an X terminal with your host, *xdm* must first be running on the host machine. The host listens for inbound connections from the X terminals using *XDMCP*, the *xdm* Control Protocol (the default port for *xdmcp* is 177). When a request is received, *xdm* responds with the same graphical login screen that's used on the local system. The difference is that the X server is implemented in the X terminal hardware, not in the XFree86 software on the *xdm* host, and all of the graphics information is transmitted over the network.

> ## On the Exam
>
> You should be aware of the configuration files for *xdm*, how they are used, and where they are located. In particular, remember that the *Xresources* file controls graphical login properties. Also remember that *xdm* can be started using a special runlevel and that *xdm* must be running for X terminals to connect via XDMCP.

You can configure access to your system's *xdm* daemon in the */etc/X11/xdm/Xaccess* file. This file is a simple list of hosts that are to be restricted or enabled. To enable a host, simply enter its name. To restrict a host, enter its name with an exclamation point (!) before it. The * wildcard is also allowed to handle groups of devices.

The following example allows access to all X terminals on the local domain but prohibits access from `xterm1` on an outside domain:

```
*.example.com
!xterm1.anotherexample.com
```

Configuring KDM

KDM is built off the XDM design and is responsible for the graphical login screen that handles user authentication to the system and starts a user session. The *KDM* is the display manager for the *KDE* desktop environment.

KDM is distributed by KDE.org and is configured by a series of files located in */etc/X11/kdm*. To see the version that is available for install, use the package manager to find this information and to install the package:

```
# yum info kdm
Loaded plugins: refresh-packagekit
Available Packages
Name       : kdm
Arch       : i586
Version    : 4.2.4
Release    : 5.fc11
Size       : 1.5 M
Repo       : updates
Summary    : The KDE login manager
URL        : http://www.kde.org/
License    : GPLv2
Description: KDM provides the graphical login screen, shown shortly after boot
           : up, log out, and when user switching.
```

Use the *yum* package manager to install the *KDM* interface.

```
# yum install kdm
Loaded plugins: refresh-packagekit
Setting up Install Process
Resolving Dependencies
--> Running transaction check
---> Package kdm.i586 0:4.2.4-5.fc11 set to be updated
--> Processing Dependency: kdelibs4(x86-32) >= 4.2.4 for package: \
                                 kdm-4.2.4-5.fc11.i586
--> Processing Dependency: kde-settings-kdm for package: kdm-4.2.4-5.fc11.i586
--> Processing Dependency: libkdeui.so.5 for package: kdm-4.2.4-5.fc11.i586
--> Processing Dependency: libkio.so.5 for package: kdm-4.2.4-5.fc11.i586
--> Processing Dependency: libknewstuff2.so.4 for package: kdm-4.2.4-5.fc11.i586
--> Processing Dependency: libkde3support.so.4 for package: kdm-4.2.4-5.fc11.i586
--> Processing Dependency: libkdecore.so.5 for package: kdm-4.2.4-5.fc11.i586
--> Processing Dependency: libqimageblitz.so.4 for package: kdm-4.2.4-5.fc11.i586
--> Running transaction check
---> Package kde-settings-kdm.noarch 0:4.2-10.20090430svn.fc11 set to be updated
--> Processing Dependency: kde4-macros(api) = 2 for package: kde-settings-kdm-4.2-
10.20090430svn.fc11.noarch
--> Processing Dependency: leonidas-kde-theme for package: kde-settings-kdm-4.2-
10.20090430svn.fc11.noarch
--> Processing Dependency: xterm for package: \
                         kde-settings-kdm-4.2-10.20090430svn.fc11.noarch
--> Processing Dependency: xorg-x11-xdm for package: kde-settings-kdm-4.2-
10.20090430svn.fc11.noarch
---> Package kdelibs.i586 6:4.2.4-6.fc11 set to be updated
--> Processing Dependency: soprano(x86-32) >= 2.2 for package: \
                         6:kdelibs-4.2.4-6.fc11.i586
--> Processing Dependency: strigi-libs(x86-32) >= 0.6.3 for package: \
                         6:kdelibs-4.2.4-6.fc11.i586
--> Processing Dependency: libsoprano.so.4 for package: \
                         6:kdelibs-4.2.4-6.fc11.i586
--> Processing Dependency: kde-settings for package: \
                         6:kdelibs-4.2.4-6.fc11.i586
--> Processing Dependency: libsopranoclient.so.1 for package: \
```

```
                                        6:kdelibs-4.2.4-6.fc11.i586
--> Processing Dependency: libstreams.so.0 for package: \
                                        6:kdelibs-4.2.4-6.fc11.i586
--> Processing Dependency: kdelibs-common for package: \
                                        6:kdelibs-4.2.4-6.fc11.i586
--> Processing Dependency: libstreamanalyzer.so.0 for package: \
                                        6:kdelibs-4.2.4-6.fc11.i586
---> Package qimageblitz.i586 0:0.0.4-0.5.svn706674.fc11 set to be updated
--> Running transaction check
---> Package kde-filesystem.noarch 0:4-25.fc11 set to be updated
---> Package kde-settings.noarch 0:4.2-10.20090430svn.fc11 set to be updated
--> Processing Dependency: oxygen-icon-theme for package: kde-settings-4.2-
10.20090430svn.fc11.noarch
---> Package kdelibs-common.i586 6:4.2.4-6.fc11 set to be updated
---> Package leonidas-kde-theme.noarch 0:11.0.1-1.fc11 set to be updated
--> Processing Dependency: leonidas-backgrounds-kdm >= 11.0.0-1 \
                for package: leonidas-kde-theme-11.0.1-1.fc11.noarch
---> Package soprano.i586 0:2.2.3-1.fc11 set to be updated
--> Processing Dependency: libclucene.so.0 for package: \
                                        soprano-2.2.3-1.fc11.i586
---> Package strigi-libs.i586 0:0.6.5-2.fc11 set to be updated
--> Processing Dependency: libexiv2.so.5 for package: \
                                        strigi-libs-0.6.5-2.fc11.i586
---> Package xorg-x11-xdm.i586 1:1.1.6-10.fc11 set to be updated
---> Package xterm.i586 0:242-3.fc11 set to be updated
--> Running transaction check
---> Package clucene-core.i586 0:0.9.21-3.fc11 set to be updated
---> Package exiv2-libs.i586 0:0.18.2-2.fc11 set to be updated
---> Package leonidas-backgrounds-kdm.noarch 0:11.0.0-1.fc11 \
                                                set to be updated
---> Package oxygen-icon-theme.noarch 0:4.2.2-1.fc11 set to be updated
--> Finished Dependency Resolution

Dependencies Resolved

================================================================================
 Package                  Arch     Version                   Repository  Size
================================================================================
Installing:
 kdm                      i586     4.2.4-5.fc11              updates   1.5 M
Installing for dependencies:
 clucene-core             i586     0.9.21-3.fc11             fedora    350 k
 exiv2-libs               i586     0.18.2-2.fc11             updates   889 k
 kde-filesystem           noarch   4-25.fc11                 fedora     22 k
 kde-settings             noarch   4.2-10.20090430svn.fc11   fedora     38 k
 kde-settings-kdm         noarch   4.2-10.20090430svn.fc11   fedora     25 k
 kdelibs                  i586     6:4.2.4-6.fc11            updates    14 M
 kdelibs-common           i586     6:4.2.4-6.fc11            updates   367 k
 leonidas-backgrounds-kdm noarch   11.0.0-1.fc11             fedora    4.6 M
 leonidas-kde-theme       noarch   11.0.1-1.fc11             fedora    1.1 M
 oxygen-icon-theme        noarch   4.2.2-1.fc11              fedora     15 M
 qimageblitz              i586     0.0.4-0.5.svn706674.fc11  fedora     59 k
 soprano                  i586     2.2.3-1.fc11              fedora    692 k
 strigi-libs              i586     0.6.5-2.fc11              updates   476 k
 xorg-x11-xdm             i586     1:1.1.6-10.fc11           updates   139 k
 xterm                    i586     242-3.fc11                fedora    368 k
```

The X Window System

Objective 2: Set Up a Display Manager | 313

```
Transaction Summary
===============================================================================
Install      16 Package(s)
Update        0 Package(s)
Remove        0 Package(s)

Total download size: 39 M
Is this ok [y/N]:
```

This installation will also install the *KDE* window manager. Once this has been installed, you can select the session you wish to boot into at startup using the session menu. The main configuration file to control the way the *KDM* operates is called *kdmrc*, which is located in */etc/kde/kdm*. The following is an example of the contents of this file:

```
# KDM master configuration file
#
# Definition: the greeter is the login dialog, i.e., the part of KDM
# which the user sees.
#
# You can configure every X-display individually.
# Every display has a display name, which consists of a host name
# (which is empty for local displays specified in {Static|Reserve}Servers),
# a colon, and a display number. Additionally, a display belongs to a
# display class (which can be ignored in most cases; the control center
# does not support this feature at all).
# Sections with display-specific settings have the formal syntax
# "[X-" host [":" number [ "_" class ]] "-" sub-section "]"
# You can use the "*" wildcard for host, number, and class. You may omit
# trailing components; they are assumed to be "*" then.
# The host part may be a domain specification like ".inf.tu-dresden.de".
# It may also be "+", which means non-empty, i.e. remote displays only.
# From which section a setting is actually taken is determined by these
# rules:
```

Configuring GDM

GDM is the window manager for the GNOME desktop environment. GNOME is the default graphical desktop environment for Fedora and Ubuntu. The *GDM* window manager will be loaded automatically during the graphical installation of these operating systems. If you need to install the GNOME environment and the *GDM* manager, you can use the package manager by issuing a command similar to:

```
# yum groupinstall "GNOME Desktop Environment"
```

The main configuration file for *GDM* is either *gdm.conf* or *custom.conf*, depending on the distribution of Linux. The configuration file will be located in *etc/gdm/gdm.conf*. This file contains sections for configuring the way the login process operates, the session environments, and the look and feel of the manager or "greeter" that the user is presented with at the initial login screen. The file is heavily commented for each section of the sections. The following is an example of this configuration file's contents:

```
# For full reference documentation see the GNOME help browser under
# GNOME|System category.  You can also find the docs in HTML form on
# http://www.gnome.org/projects/gdm/
#
# NOTE: Some values are commented out, but show their default values.  Lines
# that begin with "#" are considered comments.
#
# Have fun!

[daemon]
# Automatic login, if true the first local screen will automatically logged
# in as user as set with AutomaticLogin key.
AutomaticLoginEnable=false
AutomaticLogin=

# Timed login, useful for kiosks.  Log in a certain user after a certain
# amount of time.
TimedLoginEnable=false
TimedLogin=
TimedLoginDelay=30

# The GDM configuration program that is run from the login screen, you
# should probably leave this alone.
#Configurator=/usr/sbin/gdmsetup --disable-sound --disable-crash-dialog

# The chooser program.  Must output the chosen host on stdout, probably you
# should leave this alone.
#Chooser=/usr/lib/gdm/gdmchooser

# The greeter for local (non-xdmcp) logins.  Change gdmlogin to gdmgreeter
# to get the new graphical greeter.
Greeter=/usr/lib/gdm/gdmgreeter

# The greeter for xdmcp logins, usually you want a less graphically
# intensive greeter here so it's better to leave this with gdmlogin
#RemoteGreeter=/usr/lib/gdm/gdmlogin
```

Switching display managers

More than one desktop environment may be run on the Linux system at any time. If both the KDE and GNOME environments are installed, you may switch between them during the graphical login by selecting the environment from the session menu. Both the *KDM* and *GDM* managers will have the session menu available at startup. It is possible to run only one of the display managers, but you can change which display manager is presented during startup. In order to change from the default *GDM* manager, you will need to update the */etc/sysconfig/desktop* file by editing the following:

```
desktop= "kde"
displaymanager= "kdm"
```

Another way to switch between the *KDM* and *GDM* managers is to install the *switchdesk* tool using a package manager and then execute the application. *switchdesk* allows users to simply switch between various desktop environments installed on the system. Not all display managers are supported; however, it does support KDE and GNOME:

```
$ switchdesk kde
Red Hat Linux switchdesk 4.0
Copyright (C) 1999-2004 Red Hat, Inc
Redistributable under the terms of the GNU General Public License
Desktop now set up to run KDE.
```

On the Exam

Remember that you may run more than one desktop environment at a time with Linux. You will need to know how you can switch environments and possibly make either the KDM or GDM the default window manager.

Objective 3: Accessibility

There are a wide range of physical disabilities that can impair a user's ability to interact with computers and applications. Most of the Linux distributions come with some assistive technology tools built in for visually and physically challenged users. One of the earliest tools was Emacspeak (currently at version 31), a free screen reader that allows users to interact independently with the computer. It is available for most versions of Linux. The Emacspeak desktop works with a variety of applications, including browsers.

Screen readers are software applications that provide translation of the information on the computer screen to an audio output format. The translation is passed to the speech synthesizer, and the words are spoken out loud. Currently, fully functional screen readers are available for Linux only in console mode. The following are some of the most common screen readers:

Emacspeak
> This tool is classified as a screen reader, but the creator calls it an "audio desktop." It is an excellent nongraphical, text-based interface for users who are visually impaired. This application can be used as a screen reader in conjunction with a hardware synthesizer or IBM ViaVoice® Run-time text-to-speech application.

Jupiter Speech System
> An older screen reader for Linux in console mode. This package also includes the ability to read logfiles of an interactive session and contains customizable speech commands.

Speakup
> A screen review package for the Linux operating system. It requires a hardware speech synthesizer such as the DecTalk Express. It allows computer interaction by verbal commands, in addition to synthesized voice feedback from the console.

Orca

> A screen reader designed to work with applications and toolkits that support the assistive technology service provider interface (AT-SPI). This includes the GNOME desktop and its applications, OpenOffice, Firefox, and the Java platform. Orca may be enabled under the system/preferences menu from the GNOME environment. Orca includes support for assistive tools for speech, Braille, and screen magnification.

Here are some other products that serve as screen magnifiers, which enable users who are partially blind to view selected areas of the screen, similar to using a magnifying glass:

SVGATextmode

> This product enlarges or reduces the font size for users who prefer to work in console mode. The normal text screen that Linux provides is 80 characters across and 25 vertically. After SVGATextmode is installed, the text can be displayed much larger, for example, 50 characters across and 15 vertically. The program does not offer the ability to zoom in and out, but the user can resize when necessary. Do not run try to run SVGATextmode from an X Windows terminal; you must be in console mode for the display to function properly.

Xzoom

> A screen magnifier that allows the user to magnify, rotate, or mirror a portion of the screen.

Some additional applications that may be used to support Braille devices in conjunction with the computer include:

BrLTTY

> Supports parallel port and USB Braille displays and provides access to the Linux console. It drives the terminal and provides complete screen review capabilities. It is available at *http://dave.mielke.cc/brltty/*.

Blind + Linux = BLINUX

> Provides documentation, downloads, and a mailing list that focus on users who are blind. Information and software packages are available at *http://leb.net/blinux*.

The Linux operating system also has built-in features that allow for additional keyboard configuration. In some of the X Windows desktops, these settings can be changed from the preferences menu. An application developed for X Windows called AccessX provides a graphical user interface for configuring all of the following AccessX keyboard settings:

StickyKeys

> Enables the user to lock modifier keys (for example, Ctrl and Shift), allowing single-finger operations in place of multiple key combinations.

MouseKeys

> Provides alternative keyboard sequences for cursor movement and mouse button operations.

SlowKeys

> This setting requires the user to hold the key down for a specified period of time before the keystroke is accepted. This prevents keystrokes that are pressed accidentally from being sent.

ToggleKeys

> Sounds an audio alert that warns the user that a keystroke created a locking state for keys, such as Caps Lock and Num Lock.

RepeatKeys

> Allows a user with limited coordination additional time to release keys before multiple key sequences are sent to the application.

BounceKeys or Delay Keys

> These settings have a delay between keystrokes. This function can help prevent the system from accepting unintentional keystrokes.

Onscreen keyboards enable a user to select keys using a pointing device, such as a mouse, trackball, or touch pad, and can be used in place of a standard keyboard.

GTkeyboard

> An onscreen, graphical keyboard that can be downloaded at *http://opop.nols .com/gtkeyboard.html*.

GNOME Onscreen Keyboard (GOK)

> An onscreen, graphical keyboard that enables users to control their computers without relying on a standard keyboard or mouse. More information is available at *http://www.gok.ca*.

Remember that most Linux distributions will have some form of assistive technology built into the GUI, accessible through system settings or preferences. Most of these include at least the ability to modify mouse and keyboard actions and to add a screen reader or magnification. Some, as with GNOME and the Orca project, will have more support, including the ability to add an onscreen keyboard.

On the Exam

You should be aware of the various assistive technology tools that are available for use in Linux. Many of the tools may be installed already in the operating system and just need to be enabled from the system settings or preferences menu. More information about assistive technology for Linux users may be found at Ability Net Gate (*http://abilitynet.wetpaint.com*).

15

Administrative Tasks (Topic 107)

As a system administrator in a multiuser environment, much of your activity is related to users and their system accounts, the automation of routine tasks, and internationalization. This chapter covers these administrative aspects of Linux as required for Exam 102. This chapter has three Objectives:

Objective 1: Manage User and Group Accounts and Related System Files
Candidates should be able to add, remove, suspend, and change user accounts. Tasks to adding and removing groups, and changing user/group info in password/group databases. This Objective also includes creating special-purpose and limited accounts. Weight: 5.

Objective 2: Automate System Administration Tasks by Scheduling Jobs
Candidates should be able to use *cron* or *anacron* to run jobs at regular intervals and to use *at* to run jobs at a specific time. Tasks include managing *cron* and *at* jobs and configuring user access to *cron* and *at* services. Weight. 4.

Objective 3: Localization and Internationalization
Candidates should be able to localize a system in a language other than English. Additionally, candidates should understand why LANG=C is useful when scripting. Weight: 3.

Objective 1: Manage User and Group Accounts and Related System Files

Whether on a corporate server or personal desktop machine, managing user accounts is an important aspect of running a Linux system. The *root*, or superuser, account is established when you first install Linux. Unlike single-user systems (such as MS-DOS), multiuser systems require the notion of an *owner* for files, processes, and other system objects. An owner may be a human system user or a system service, such as a web server. Each of these owners is differentiated from others by a unique *user account*, which is assigned to it by the system administrator.

User Accounts and the Password File

When a new user account is added to a Linux system, an entry is added to a list of users in the *password file*, which is stored in */etc/passwd*. This file gets its name from its original use, which was to store user information, including an encrypted form of the user's password. The password file is in plain text and is readable by everyone on the system. Each line in the password file contains information for a single user account, with fields separated by colons, as illustrated in Figure 15-1.

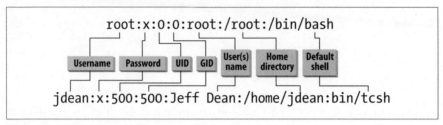

Figure 15-1. Sample lines from a password file

Each line in the file contains information for a single system account and includes the following pieces of information in colon-separated fields:

Username
> The first field on a line is a unique *username* for the person or service using the account.

Password
> Each username has an associated *password*. The password stored in this field is in a hashed (unreadable and unrecoverable) form. Despite the hash, for security reasons, most systems now store user passwords in a separate */etc/shadow* file that has restricted permissions. If the password is not included, its field is filled by the letter x, which indicates that the shadow password system is in use.

User ID
> Each username requires a unique *user identifier*, or UID. The UID is simply a nonnegative integer. The *root* account is assigned the UID of 0, which gives it global privilege on the system. By convention, the UID values from 0 to 99 are reserved for administrative use; those over 99 are for regular system users. It's not unusual for new system accounts to start at 500.

Group ID
> Each username has a default *group identifier*, or GID. The GID is also a nonnegative integer. Groups are a way of allowing users to share files through mutual group membership. Group numbers and their associated names are specified in the */etc/group* file. The GID stored for each user in */etc/passwd* is its default group ID, though a user may belong to many groups.

Full name (or other comment)
> The user's full name or other information is stored as plain text. This field may contain spaces.

Home directory
> The *home directory* is the default directory in the filesystem for the user's account. If a new account is meant for a person, a home directory will probably be created in the filesystem with standard configuration files that the user may then personalize. The full path to that home directory is listed here.

Default shell
> This field specifies the default shell for the user or service, which is the shell that runs when the user logs in or opens a shell window. In most cases, the shell will be */bin/bash*, but it can be any shell, or even another executable program. (Non-shell entries may be seen in the case of some services that should own files but never log in interactively. You may see the shell field filled with */bin/false*, a small program that does nothing but yield an error and terminate. This ensures that a service account is secured from login.)

Looking back at Figure 15-1, the first line shows the definition of the *root* account with UID and GID of 0, a name of *root*, a home directory of */root*, and a default shell of */bin/bash*. The second line shows a standard user account for Jeff Dean, with UID and GID of 500. The home directory is */home/jdean*, and the default shell is */bin/tcsh*.

More detailed information about */etc/passwd* can be found in Chapter 22.

Groups and the Group File

In addition to ownership by individual system users, filesystem objects have separate ownership settings for groups of users. This *group ownership* allows an additional level of user-specific access control beyond that of a file's individual owner. Groups are similar to users in their administration and are defined in the file */etc/group*. Like the *passwd* file, the *group* file contains colon-separated fields:

Group name
> Each group must have a unique name.

Group password
> Just as user accounts have passwords, groups can have passwords for their membership. If the password field is empty, the group does not require a password.

Group ID
> Each group requires a unique GID. Like a UID, a GID is a nonnegative integer.

Group member list
> The last field is a list of group members by username, separated by commas.

Together, these pieces of information define a group; colons separate the fields. Here are a few sample lines from a group file:

```
root:x:0:root
pppusers:x:230:jdean,jdoe
finance:x:300:jdean,jdoe,bsmith
jdean:x:500:
jdoe:x:501:
bsmith:x:502:
```

In this example, both *jdean* and *jdoe* are members of the *pppusers* group (GID 230), and *jdean*, *jdoe*, and *bsmith* are all members of the *finance* group (GID 300). The remaining groups, *root*, *jdean*, *jdoe*, and *bsmith*, are single-user groups. These groups are not intended for multiple users and do not contain additional members. For security purposes, it is common to create new users with their own personal single-user group. Doing this enhances security because new files and directories will not have group privileges for other users. (Although the GID of these single-user groups may match the UID of the user for which they're created, there is no direct relationship between the UID and GID.)

The Shadow Password and Shadow Group Systems

Encrypted passwords must be secure from all users on the system, while leaving the remainder of the information in */etc/passwd* world-readable. To do this, the encrypted password is moved to a new file that *shadows* the password file line for line. The file is aptly called */etc/shadow* and is generally said to contain *shadow passwords*. Here are a couple of example lines from a shadow file:

```
root:$1$oxEaSzzdXZESTGTU:10927:0:99999:7:-1:-1:134538444
jdean:$1$IviLopPn461z47J:10927:0:99999:7::11688:134538412
```

The first two fields contain the username and the encrypted passwords. The remaining fields contain optional additional information on password aging information.

Group passwords and shadow groups

Just as user accounts listed in */etc/passwd* are protected by encrypted passwords, groups listed in */etc/group* can also be protected by passwords. A group password can be used to allow access to a group by a user account that is not actually a member of the group. Account users can use the *newgrp* command to change their default group and enter the group password. If the password is correct, the account is granted the group privileges, just as a group member would be.

The group definition file, like the password file, is readable by everyone on the system. If group passwords are stored there, a dictionary attack could be made against them. To protect against such attacks, passwords in */etc/group* can be shadowed. The protected passwords are stored in */etc/gshadow*, which is readable only by *root*. Here are a few sample lines from a *gshadow* file:

```
root:::root
pppusers:!::
finance:Ocf7ipLtpSBGg::
jdean:!::
jdoe:!::
bsmith:!::
```

In this example, the groups *pppusers*, *jdean*, *jdoe*, and *bsmith* do not have group passwords, as indicated by the ! in the password field. The *finance* group is the only one with a password, which is hashed.

More detailed information about shadow passwords can be found in Chapter 22.

On the Exam

A major contrast between *passwd/group* and *shadow/gshadow* is the permissions on the files. The standard files are readable by everyone on the system, but the shadow files are readable only by *root*, which protects encrypted passwords from theft and possible cracking.

User and Group Management Commands

Although possible, it is rarely necessary (or advised) to manipulate the account and group definition files manually with a text editor. Instead, a family of convenient administrative commands is available for managing accounts, groups, password shadowing, group shadowing, and password aging. Password aging (rules governing change intervals and automated expiration of passwords) is not an explicit Objective for the LPIC Level 1 Exams.

useradd

Syntax

```
useradd [options] user
```

Description

Create the account *user* on the system. Both system defaults and specified *options* define how the account is configured. All system account files are updated as required. An initial password must subsequently be set for new users using the *passwd* command. It is the user's responsibility to go back and change that password when he first logs into the system.

Frequently used options

-c comment
>   Define the comment field, probably the user's name.

-d homedir
>   Use *homedir* as the user's home directory.

-m
>   Create and populate the home directory.

-s shell
>   Use *shell* as the default for the account.

-D
>   List (and optionally change) system default values.

Example

Add a new user, *bsmith*, with all default settings:

```
# useradd bsmith
```

Administrative Tasks

Add a new user, *jdoe*, with a name, default home directory, and the *tcsh* shell:

```
# useradd -mc "Jane Doe" -s /bin/tcsh jdoe
```

usermod

Syntax

```
usermod [options] user
```

Description

Modify an existing user account. The *usermod* command accepts many of the same options *useradd* does.

Frequently used options

-L

Lock the password, disabling the account.

-U

Unlock the user's password, enabling the user to once again log in to the system.

Examples

Change *jdoe*'s name in the comment field:

```
# usermod -c "Jane Deer-Doe" jdoe
```

Lock the password for *bsmith*:

```
# usermod -L bsmith
```

userdel

Syntax

```
userdel [-r] user
```

Description

Delete an existing user account. When combined with the *-r* option, the user's home directory is deleted. Note that completely deleting accounts may lead to confusion when files owned by the deleted user remain in other system directories. For this reason, it is common to disable an account rather than delete it. Accounts can be disabled using the *chage*, *usermod*, and *passwd* commands.

Example

Delete the user *bsmith*, including the home directory:

```
# userdel -r bsmith
```

groupadd

Syntax

```
groupadd group
```

Description

Add *group* to the system. In the rare case that a group password is desired on *group*, it must be added using the *gpasswd* command after the group is created.

groupmod

Syntax

```
groupmod [option] group
```

Description

Modify the parameters of *group*.

Option

-n name
> Change the name of the group to *name*.

groupdel

Syntax

```
groupdel group
```

Description

Delete *group* from the system. Deleting groups can lead to the same confusion in the filesystem as described previously for deleting a user (see *userdel*).

passwd

Syntax

```
passwd [options] username
```

Description

Interactively set the password for *username*. The password cannot be entered on the command line.

Option

-l
> Available only to the superuser, this option locks the password for the account.

gpasswd

Syntax

```
gpasswd groupname
```

Description

Interactively set the group password for *groupname*. The password cannot be entered on the command line.

Objective 2: Automate System Administration Tasks by Scheduling Jobs

There is a surprising amount of housekeeping that must be done to keep a complex operating system such as Linux running smoothly. Logfile rotation, cleanup of temporary files and directories, system database rebuilds, backups, and other tasks should be done routinely. Clearly such mundane things should be automated by the system, freeing weary system administrators for more interesting work. Fortunately, any system task that can be accomplished without real-time human intervention can be automated on Linux using the *cron* and *at* facilities. Both have the ability to execute system commands, which may start any executable program or script, at selectable times. Further, *cron* and *at* can execute these commands on behalf of any authorized system user. *cron* is intended mainly for regularly scheduled recurring activities, and *at* is most useful for scheduling single commands for execution in the future.

Using cron

The *cron* facility consists of two programs. (There is no individual program called *cron*, which is the overall name given to the facility. If you execute *man cron*, however, you will see the manpage for *crond*.)

crond
> This is the *cron* daemon, which is the process that executes your instructions. It starts at system initialization time and runs in the background thereafter.

crontab
> This is the *cron* table manipulation program. This program gives you access to your *cron* table or *crontab* file. Each authorized user may have his own *crontab* file to run commands and processes on a regular basis.

The *cron* daemon wakes up every minute and examines all *crontab* files, executing any commands scheduled for that time.

User crontab files

To use the *cron* facility, users do not need to interact directly with the *crond* daemon. Instead, each system user has access to the *cron* facility through her *crontab* file.

These files are stored together in a single directory (usually */var/spool/cron*) and are created and maintained using the *crontab* utility.

crontab

Syntax

```
crontab [options]
```

Description

View or edit *crontab* files.

Frequently used options

-e

Interactively edit the *crontab* file. Unless otherwise specified in either the EDITOR or VISUAL environment variables, the editor is vi.

-l

Display the contents of the *crontab* file.

-r

Remove the *crontab* file.

-u user

Operate on *user*'s *crontab* file instead of your own. Only *root* can edit or delete the *crontab* files of other users.

Example

Display the *crontab* file for user *jdoe*:

```
# crontab -l -u jdoe
```

Edit your own *crontab* file:

```
$ crontab -e
```

crontab files use a flexible format to specify times for command execution. Each line contains six fields:

```
minute hour day month dayofweek command
```

These fields are specified as follows:

- Minute (0 through 59)
- Hour (0 through 23)
- Day of the month (1 through 31)
- Month (1 through 12 or jan through dec)
- Day of the week (0 through 7—where 0 or 7 is Sunday—or sun through sat)
- Command (any valid command, including spaces and standard Bourne shell syntax)

For example, to execute *myprogram* once per day at 6:15 a.m., use this *crontab* entry:

```
# run myprogram at 6:15am
15 6 * * *    myprogram
```

Lines that begin with the pound sign (#) are comment lines and are ignored by *crond*. Comments must begin on a new line and may not appear within commands. The asterisks in this *crontab* are placeholders and match any date or time for the field where they're found. Here, they indicate that *myprogram* should execute at 6:15 a.m. on all days of the month, every month, all days of the week.

Each of the time specifications may be single, list (1,3,5), or range (1-5 or wed-fri) entries or combinations thereof. To modify the previous example to execute at 6:15 and 18:15 on the 1st and 15th of the month, use:

```
# run myprogram at 6:15am and 6:15pm on the 1st and 15th
15 6,18 1,15 * *   myprogram
```

As you can see, the time specifications are very flexible.

Because the *cron* daemon evaluates each *crontab* entry when it wakes up each minute, it is not necessary to restart or reinitialize *crond* when *crontab* entries are changed or new files are created.

System crontab files

In addition to *crontab* files owned by individual users, *crond* also looks for the system *crontab* files */etc/crontab* and files in the directory */etc/cron.d*. The format for these system *crontabs* differs slightly from user *crontabs*. System *crontabs* have an additional field for a username between the time specifications and the command. For example:

```
# /etc/crontab
# run myprogram at 6:15am as root
15 6 * * *   root   myprogram
```

In this example, myprogram will be executed by *cron* as the *root* user.

System *crontab* files located in */etc/cron.d* are of the same form as */etc/crontab*, including the extra user field. These files are usually associated with some package or service that includes a system *crontab*. Allowing a collection of files in */etc/cron.d* allows software installation and upgrade procedures to keep the *cron* configuration up-to-date on an individual package basis. In most cases, however, you won't need to change the *crontab* files in */etc/cron.d*.

On the Exam

Memorize the sequence of time/date fields used in *crontab* files.

On most Linux distributions, */etc/crontab* contains some standard content to enable the execution of programs and scripts on the minute, hour, week, and month. These arrangements allow you to simply drop executable files into the appropriate directory (such as */etc/cron.hourly*), where they are executed automatically. This eliminates *cron* configuration altogether for many tasks and avoids cluttering the root *crontab* file with common commands.

Using at

The *cron* system is intended for the execution of commands on a regular, periodic schedule. When you need to simply delay execution of a command or a group of commands to some other time in the future, you should use *at*. The *at* facility accepts commands from standard input or from a file.

at

Syntax

```
at [-f file] time
at [options]
```

Description

In the first form, enter commands to the *at* queue for execution at `time`. *at* allows fairly complex time specifications. It accepts times of the form `HH:MM` to run a job at a specific time of day. (If that time is already past, the next day is assumed.) You may also specify `midnight`, `noon`, or `teatime` (4 p.m.), and you suffix a time of day with `AM` or `PM` for running in the morning or evening. You can also say what day the job will be run by giving a date in month-day form, with the year being optional, or by giving a date in `MMDDYY`, `MM/DD/YY`, or `DD.MM.YY` form. The date specification must follow the time-of-day specification. You can also give times such as `now + count time-units`, where `time-units` can be minutes, hours, days, or weeks. You can tell *at* to run the job today by suffixing the time with `today`, and you can tell it to run the job tomorrow by suffixing the time with `tomorrow`.

If *-f file* is given, commands are taken from the `file`; otherwise, *at* will prompt the user for commands.

In the second form, list or delete jobs from the *at* queue.

Frequently used options

-d job1 [, *job2*, ...]
> Delete jobs from the *at* queue by number (same as the *atrm* command).

-l
> List items in the *at* queue (same as the *atq* command).

Example1

Run `myprogram` once at 6:15 p.m. tomorrow:

```
$ at 6:15pm tomorrow
at> myprogram
at> ^D
```

In the previous code listing, `^D` indicates that the user typed Ctrl-D on the keyboard, sending the end-of-file character to terminate the *at* command.

Example2

Run commands that are listed in the file *command_list* at 9 p.m. two days from now:

```
$ at -f command_list 9pm + 2 days
```

List items in the *at* queue (*root* sees all users' entries):

```
$ at -l
```

Remove job number 5 from the *at* queue:

```
$ at -d 5
```

Using *at* to schedule jobs for delayed execution, such as while you're asleep or on vacation, is simple and doesn't require creation of a recurring *cron* entry.

Controlling User Access to cron and at

In most cases, it is safe to allow users to use the *cron* and *at* facilities. However, if your circumstances dictate that one or more users should be prohibited from using these services, two simple authorization files exist for each:

- *cron.allow, cron.deny*
- *at.allow, at.deny*

These files are simply lists of account names. If the *allow* file exists, only those users listed in the *allow* file may use the service. If the *allow* file does not exist but the *deny* file does, only those users not listed in the *deny* file may use the service. For *cron*, if neither file exists, all users have access to *cron*. For *at*, if neither file exists, only *root* has access to *at*. An empty *at.deny* file allows access to all users and is the default.

Objective 3: Localization and Internationalization

In computing, internationalization and localization are means of adapting computer software to different languages and regional differences. Internationalization is the process of designing a software application so that it can be adapted to various languages and regions without engineering changes. Localization is the process of adapting internationalized software for a specific region or language by adding locale-specific components and translating text.

The terms are frequently abbreviated to the numeronyms i18n (where 18 stands for the number of letters between the first "i" and last "n" in internationalization, a usage coined at Digital Equipment Corporation in the 1970s or 1980s) and L10n respectively, due to the length of the words. The capital "L" in L10n helps to distinguish it from the lowercase "i" in i18n.

Since open source software can generally be freely modified and redistributed, it is more amenable to internationalization. The KDE project, for example, has been translated into over 100 languages.

The time zone under Linux is set by a symbolic link from */etc/localtime* to a file in the */usr/share/zoneinfo* directory that corresponds to your specific time zone. Generally this is defined during the installation process in order to provide the correct information to the system. However, manually running the command *tzconfig* can also do the job, and you won't have to remember the path to the time zones.

The *tzselect* program is a menu-based script that asks the user for information about the current location, and then sends the resulting time zone description to standard output. The output is suitable as a value for the *TZ* environment variable:

```
$ tzselect

Please identify a location so that time zone rules can be set correctly.
Please select a continent or ocean.

 1) Africa

 2) Americas

 3) Antarctica

 4) Arctic Ocean

 5) Asia

 6) Atlantic Ocean

 7) Australia

 8) Europe

 9) Indian Ocean

10) Pacific Ocean

11) none - I want to specify the time zone using the Posix TZ format.

#?
```

The *date* command can be used to print the current Coordinated Universal Time (UTC):

```
$ date -u
```

and also to show the time zone abbreviation:

```
$ date +%Z
CET
```

A locale is a set of information that most programs use for determining country- and language-specific settings. The following environment variables are used to store locale settings:

LANG
Defines all locale settings at once, while allowing further individual customization via the *LC_** settings described next.

LC_COLLATE
Defines alphabetical ordering of strings. This affects the output of sorted directory listings, for example.

LC_CTYPE

Defines the character-handling properties for the system. This determines which characters are seen as alphabetic, numeric, and so on. This also determines the character set used, if applicable.

LC_MESSAGES

This defines the programs' localizations for applications that use a message-based localization scheme. This includes the majority of GNU programs.

LC_MONETARY

Defines currency units and the formatting of currency type numeric values.

LC_NUMERIC

Defines formatting of numeric values that aren't monetary. This affects things such as the thousands separator and decimal separator.

LC_TIME

Defines the formatting of dates and times.

LC_PAPER

Defines the default paper size.

LC_ALL

A special variable for overriding all other settings.

The *locale* utility writes information about the current locale environment, or all public locales, to the standard output. For the purposes of this section, a public locale is one provided by the implementation that is accessible to the application. Issuing the *locale* command without any flags will output the current configuration:

```
$ locale
LANG=
LC_CTYPE="POSIX"
LC_NUMERIC="POSIX"
LC_TIME="POSIX"
LC_COLLATE="POSIX"
LC_MONETARY="POSIX"
LC_MESSAGES="POSIX"
LC_PAPER="POSIX"
LC_NAME="POSIX"
LC_ADDRESS="POSIX"
LC_TELEPHONE="POSIX"
LC_MEASUREMENT="POSIX"
LC_IDENTIFICATION="POSIX"
LC_ALL=
```

The C locale, also known as the POSIX locale, is the POSIX system default locale for all POSIX-compliant systems.

The *iconv* utility converts the encoding of characters in a file from one codeset to another and writes the results to standard output.

The following example converts the contents of the file *in.txt* from the ISO/IEC 6937:1994 standard codeset to the ISO/IEC 8859-1:1998 standard codeset, and stores the results in the file *out.txt*:

```
$ iconv -f IS6937 -t IS8859 in.txt > out.txt
```

16

Essential System Services (Topics 108.1 and 108.2)

As a system administrator in a multiuser environment, much of your activity is related to maintaining various system services. These services include accurate system time and logging of system events. The following two Objectives are covered in this chapter:

Objective 1: Maintain System Time
   Candidates should be able to properly maintain the system time and synchronize the clock over NTP. Tasks include setting the system date and time, setting the hardware clock to the correct time in UTC, configuring the correct time zone for the system, and configuring the system to correct clock drift to match the NTP clock. Weight: 3.

Objective 2: System Logging
   Candidates should be able to configure system logs. This Objective includes managing the type and level of information logged, manually scanning logfiles for notable activity, monitoring logfiles, arranging for automatic rotation and archiving of logs, and tracking down problems noted in logs. Weight: 2.

Objective 1: Maintain System Time

An accurate system clock is important on a Linux system for a variety of reasons. Log entries need to be accurate so you can accurately determine what system events occurred. Programs such as *make* and *anacron* require accurate modification times on files. Network file sharing (such as NFS) requires both client and server to keep accurate time so file operations are kept in sync.

The most popular way to keep accurate time on an Internet-connected Linux system is to use the Network Time Protocol (NTP) and the NTP software package from *http://www.ntp.org*.

NTP Concepts

NTP is used to set and synchronize the internal clocks of network-connected systems. When properly configured, systems running the NTP daemon can be synchronized within a few milliseconds (or better), even over relatively slow WAN connections.

The NTP daemon also supports synchronization with an external time source, such as a GPS receiver. Systems directly connected to an external time source (and properly configured) are the most accurate, so they are designated *stratum 1* servers. Systems synchronizing to stratum 1 servers are designated *stratum 2*, and so on, down to stratum 15.

> The NTP software package has support for cryptographic key-based authentication, although setting this up is outside the scope of the LPI Level 1 Exams and will not be covered here.

The NTP Software Package Components

The NTP software package consists of several programs, including the NTP daemon and a number of programs used to configure and query NTP servers. The more commonly used programs from the package are listed here.

ntpd

Syntax

```
ntpd [options]
```

Description

ntpd is the heart of the NTP software package. It performs the following functions:

- Synchronizes the PC clock with remote NTP servers
- Allows synchronization from other NTP clients
- Adjusts (skews) the rate of the kernel's clock tick so that it tracks time accurately
- Reads time synchronization data from hardware time sources such as GPS receivers

Frequently used options

-c file
> This option tells *ntpd* to use *file* as its configuration file instead of the default */etc/ntpd.conf*.

-g
> This option will let *ntpd* start on a system with a clock that is off by more than the panic threshold (1,000 seconds by default).

-n

> Normally *ntpd* runs as a daemon, in the background. This option disables that behavior.

-q

> This option tells *ntpd* to exit after setting the time once.

-N

> When this option is specified, *ntpd* attempts to run at the highest priority possible.

ntpd is configured using the file */etc/ntp.conf*. The file is fully documented in a series of files linked to from the *ntpd* documentation, found in the software distribution or at *http://www.eecis .udel.edu/~mills/ntp/html/ntpd.html*.

The most important configuration options are `restrict`, which is used to implement access controls, and `server`, which is used to direct *ntpd* to an NTP server. Another often-used configuration option (not mentioned in the sample *ntp.conf* in Example 16-1) is `peer`, which is used much like `server`, but implies that the system is both a client and a server. A `peer` is usually a system that is nearby on the network, but uses different time sources than the local system.

Example 16-1. Sample /etc/ntp.conf

```
# Prohibit general access to this service.
restrict default ignore

# Permit all access over the loopback interface.  This could
# be tightened as well, but to do so would affect some of
# the administrative functions.
restrict 127.0.0.1

# -- CLIENT NETWORK -------
# Permit systems on this network to synchronize with this
# time service.  Do not permit those systems to modify the
# configuration of this service.  Also, do not use those
# systems as peers for synchronization.
restrict 192.168.1.0 mask 255.255.255.0 notrust nomodify notrap

# --- OUR TIMESERVERS -----
# Permit time synchronization with our time source, but do not
# permit the source to query or modify the service on this system.

# time.nist.gov
restrict 192.43.244.18 mask 255.255.255.255 nomodify notrap noquery
server 192.43.244.18

# time-b.nist.gov
restrict 129.6.15.29 mask 255.255.255.255 nomodify notrap noquery
server 129.6.15.29

# --- GENERAL CONFIGURATION ---
#
# Undisciplined Local Clock. This is a fake driver intended for backup
# and when no outside source of synchronized time is available.
#
server       127.127.1.0      # local clock
fudge        127.127.1.0 stratum 10

#
```

```
# Drift file.  Put this in a directory which the daemon can write to.
# No symbolic links allowed, either, since the daemon updates the file
# by creating a temporary in the same directory and then renaming
# it to the file.
#
driftfile /etc/ntp/drift
broadcastdelay          0.008
```

Example

Normally *ntpd* consistently adjusts the time, depending on how far out-of-sync the server is from the stratum source, to the correct time. To force the system time to the right time (for example, when occasionally setting the correct time from *cron*), use the following:

```
# ntpd -g -n -q
```

Why are IP addresses used in the configuration file instead of fully qualified domain names? The answer is security. System time is an extremely important service, and as a system administrator, you must always be very careful trusting data you are receiving from an outside system. When you query a time server, you need to make sure that you're querying the correct time server. If you are querying a fully qualified domain name instead of an IP address, you are potentially vulnerable to a domain name poisoning attack. If someone has compromised the DNS server of the time server in question, they could be relaying your request to any system on the Internet. By querying directly to an IP address, you are eliminating the possibility of this kind of spoofing.

ntpdate

Syntax

```
ntpdate [options] server [server [...]]
```

Description

ntpdate is used to set the time of the local system to match a remote NTP host.

The maintainers of the ntp code intend to drop *ntpdate* in the future since *ntpd* can perform essentially the same function when used with the *-q* option.

Frequently used options

-b

Using this option, the system time is set instead of being slowly adjusted, no matter how far off the local time is.

-d

This option enables debugging mode. *ntpdate* goes through the motions and prints debugging information, but does not actually set the local clock.

-p n

Use this option to specify the number of samples (where *n* is from 1 to 8) to get from each server. The default is 4.

-q

This option causes *ntpdate* to query the servers listed on the command line without actually setting the clock.

-s

> This option causes all output from *ntpdate* to be logged via syslog instead of being printed to *stdout*.

-t n

> This option sets the timeout for a response from any server to *n* seconds. *n* may be fractional, in which case it will be rounded to the nearest 0.2 second. The default value is 1 second.

-u

> Normally *ntpdate* uses a privileged port (123/tcp) as the source port for outgoing packets. Some firewalls block outgoing packets from privileged ports, so with this option, *ntpdate* uses an unprivileged port above 1024/tcp.

-v

> This option makes *ntpdate* more verbose.

-B

> Using this option, the system time is slowly adjusted to the proper time, even if the local time is off by more than 128 ms. (Normally the time is forcibly set if it is off by more than 128 ms.)
>
> If the time is off by very much, it can take a very long time to set it with this option.

Example

Quietly sync the local clock with two stratum 1 NTP servers:

```
# ntpdate -s time.nist.gov time-b.nist.gov
```

---

ntpq

Syntax

```
ntpq [options] [host]
```

Description

ntpq is the standard NTP query program. It is used to send NTP control messages to *host* (or *localhost* if no *host* is specified), which can be used to check the status of *ntpd* on *host* or change its configuration.

The commands that can be used with *ntpq* are documented in the NTP software documentation included with the distribution and at *http://www.eecis.udel.edu/~mills/ntp/html/ntpq.html*.

Frequently used options

-c command
> Execute *command* as if it were given interactively.

-i

> Enter interactive mode. This is the default.

-n

> Suppress reverse DNS lookups. Addresses are printed instead of hostnames.

-p

Query the server for a list of peers. This is equivalent to the *peers* interactive command or *-c peers* on the command line.

Example

Print the list of peers known to the server by IP address:

```
# ntpq -p -n pool.ntp.org
```

or:

```
# ntpq -c peers -n pool.ntp.org
```

or:

```
# ntpq -n pool.ntp.org
ntpq> peers
     remote           refid      st t when poll reach   delay   offset  jitter
==============================================================================
*64.90.182.55    .ACTS.          1 u    - 1024  377    2.983    3.253   0.014
+209.51.161.238  .CDMA.          1 u    - 1024  377    2.456   -2.795   0.096
-128.118.25.3    147.84.59.145   2 u    - 1024  377   18.476   -2.586   0.446
+67.128.71.75    172.21.0.13     2 u    - 1024  377    8.195   -2.626   0.194
-66.250.45.2     192.5.41.40     2 u    - 1024  377    8.119   -6.491   0.421
ntpq>
```

The system *pool.ntp.org* is a pointer to a collection of systems that have volunteered to be publicly available time servers. Round robin DNS is used to share the request load among these servers. This kind of setup is usually sufficient for end users, but in a corporate environment, it's usually advisable to query a stratum 2 time server from a designated server on your network, and then have your other servers query that server. More information on pooling is available at *http://support.ntp.org/bin/view/Servers/WebHome*.

ntpdc

Syntax

```
ntpdc [options] [host]
```

Description

ntpdc is much like *ntpq*, except that it supports some extended commands. For this reason, it is likely to work only when talking to *ntpd* from the same version of the NTP software package.

For the most part, the command-line options it supports are the same as those of *ntpq*. Full documentation for *ntpdc* can be found in the NTP software distribution or at *http://www.eecis.udel.edu/~mills/ntp/html/ntpdc.html*.

ntptrace

Syntax

```
ntptrace [options] server [server [...]]
```

Description

Traces a chain of NTP servers back to the primary source.

Frequently used options

-n

> Turn off reverse DNS lookups.

Examples

To see where the local system is synchronizing its lock to, run *ntptrace* with no options:

```
$ /usr/sbin/ntptrace
localhost: stratum 4, offset 0.000109, synch distance 0.16133
ntp1.example.net: stratum 3, offset 0.004605, synch distance 0.06682
ntp-1.example.edu: stratum 2, offset 0.001702, synch distance 0.01241
stratum1.example.edu:        *Timeout*
```

In this example, the stratum 1 server is not directly accessible.

ntptrace can also be used on any arbitrary NTP server, assuming it is accessible. This example queries two publicly accessible stratum 2 NTP servers:

```
$ /usr/sbin/ntptrace ntp0.cornell.edu
cudns.cit.cornell.edu: stratum 2, offset -0.004214, synch distance 0.03455
dtc-truetime.ntp.aol.com: stratum 1, offset -0.005957, synch distance
0.00000, refid 'ACTS'
$ /usr/sbin/ntptrace ntp-2.mcs.anl.gov
mcs.anl.gov: stratum 2, offset -0.004515, synch distance 0.06354
clepsydra.dec.com: stratum 1, offset 0.002045, \
                   synch distance 0.00107, refid 'GPS'
```

The Hardware Clock

Computer motherboards all contain a small battery that is used to power the hardware clock. This ensures that the computer can successfully keep track of the time even when it is powered off. In Linux, you can configure this hardware clock and synchronize your system clock to it (or vice versa). The importance of the hardware clock has been somewhat minimized with the widespread use of NTP and easily available, reliable time servers. However, for systems that aren't always connected to the Internet, an accurate hardware clock is an important thing to have. Syncing a hardware clock is also required when working with old hardware that suffers from time issues, such as BIOSes that are not Y2K-aware.

Hardware clocks can suffer from the same drifts that system clocks experience, causing them to slowly lose (or gain) time over a certain period. The *hwclock* command is used in Linux to control the hardware clock.

hwclock

Syntax

```
hwclock --show
hwclock --systohc
hwclock --hctosys
hwclock --adjust
hwclock --version
```

Description

Query and/or set the hardware clock.

Examples

Query the system's hardware clock:

```
# /sbin/hwclock --show
Sat 12 Sep 2009 12:49:43 PM CDT  -0.216537 seconds
```

Set the hardware clock to the current value of the system clock:

```
# /sbin/hwclock --systohc
```

All time values in the hardware clock are stored as the number of seconds since January 1, 1970. This number is then converted to the output format desired. Time is represented as either Coordinated Universal Time (UTC) or local time. UTC is a universal time standard that is the same across all time zones. Local time is simply UTC combined with either a positive or negative offset to reflect the current time zone. For example, in the United States, the Central Time Zone is actually UTC-6 (six hours behind Coordinated Universal Time).

As a system administrator, you have the option of setting your hardware clock to either UTC or your own local time. Some administrators prefer to use UTC for this, and then reflect their current time zone in the system software. The *hwclock* command allows you to indicate how your hardware clock is set. Compare the output of these two commands:

```
# /sbin/hwclock -show --localtime
Sat Sep 12 13:33:35 2009  -0.766111 seconds
# /sbin/hwclock --show --utc
Sat Sep 12 08:33:37 2009  -0.048881 seconds
```

Telling *hwclock* that our hardware clock was set to UTC time resulted in a different answer when we asked to show the time.

Time Zones

As stated previously, a time zone is just a positive or negative value combined with UTC. Once you set the time zone on a Linux system, applications will honor that positive or negative offset when they need to use a timestamp. The time zone on a Linux system is identified by the file */etc/localtime*. This can be either a data file itself or a symbolic link to a data file in the directory */usr/share/zoneinfo*.

/usr/share/zoneinfo contains files that represent every time zone. In order to set the time zone on your Linux system, you must either copy one of these files to */etc/localtime* or create a symbolic link from */etc/localtime* to one of these files. For

example, if your system is in the United States in the Central time zone, your */etc/localtime* file would look like this:

```
$ ls -l /etc/localtime
lrwxrwxrwx 1 root root 30 Sep 12 13:56 \
        /etc/localtime -> /usr/share/zoneinfo/US/Central
```

On the Exam

Make sure you understand the difference between system time and the hardware clock, and the importance of keeping good system time. Also remember the difference between local time and UTC, and how it affects the time configuration on your Linux system.

Objective 2: System Logging

Many events occur on your Linux system that should be logged for administrative purposes. Linux uses the *syslogd* service to display and record messages describing these events. This system allows finely controlled logging of messages from the kernel as well as processes running on your system and remote systems. Messages can be placed on the console display, in logfiles, and on the text screens of users logged into the system.

What are the advantages of the *syslogd* service over applications maintaining their own logfiles?

- All logfiles are centralized, either in one directory or on one server.
- The client/server nature of *syslogd* allows for machines to log events to a centralized log server for easier monitoring and reporting.
- *Syslogd* allows multiple processes to write to the same logfile, while avoiding file-locking issues.

There are a number of different applications available for Linux that implement the *syslogd* functionality and offer additional functionality. Some examples are *rsyslog* (native database logging support) and *syslog-ng* (regular expression matching). For the purposes of the LPI exam, we cover only the basic *syslogd* server.

Configuring syslogd

The behavior of *syslogd* is controlled by its configuration file, */etc/syslog.conf*. This text file contains lines indicating what is to be logged and where. Each line contains directives in this form:

```
facility.level action
```

The directives are defined as follows:

facility
>   This represents the creator of the message (that is, the kernel or a process) and is one of the following: auth (the facility security is equivalent to auth, but its

use is deprecated), authpriv, cron, daemon, kern, lpr, mail, mark (the mark facility is meant for *syslogd*'s internal use only), news, syslog, user, uucp, or local0 through local7. The use of these facility designators allows you to control the destination of messages based on their origin. Facilities local0 through local7 are for any use you may wish to assign to them in your own programs and scripts. It's possible that your distribution has assigned one or more of the local facilities already. Check your configuration before using a local facility.

level

Specifies a severity threshold beyond which messages are logged, and is one of the following (from lowest to highest severity): debug, info, notice, warning (or warn), err (or error), crit, alert, or emerg (or panic). (warn, error, and panic are all deprecated, but you might see them on older systems.) There is also a special level called none that will disable a facility. The level defines the amount of detail recorded in the logfile. A single period separates the facility from the level, and together they comprise the *message selector*. The asterisk (*) can be used to describe all facilities or all levels.

action

The *action* directive is arguably misnamed. It represents the destination for messages that correspond to a given selector (*facility.level*). The action can be a filename (including the full pathname), a hostname preceded by the @ sign, or a comma-separated list of users or an asterisk (this means all logged-in users will receive the logged line on their consoles).

For example, if you wanted to create a separate logfile for activity reported by the scripts you write, you might include a line like this in */etc/syslog.conf*:

```
# Define a new log file for the local5 facility
local5.*                        /var/log/local5
```

You could then use the *logger* utility to write messages to the facility from your shell script (*syslogd* must be restarted or signaled to reinitialize before the new logfile is created):

```
$ logger -p local5.info "Script terminated normally"
```

The message "Script terminated normally" would be placed into */var/log/local5*, along with a timestamp and the hostname that sent the message. Example 16-2 contains an example */etc/syslog.conf* file.

Example 16-2. Sample /etc/syslog.conf file

```
# Log everything except mail & authpriv of level info
# or higher to messages.
*.info;mail.none;authpriv.none     /var/log/messages
# The authpriv file has restricted access.
authpriv.*                         /var/log/secure
# Log all the mail messages in one place.
mail.*                             /var/log/maillog
# Everybody gets emergency messages.
*.emerg                            *
# Save boot messages also to boot.log
local7.*                           /var/log/boot.log
```

If you examine this *syslog.conf* file, you'll see that nearly all system messages are sent to the */var/log/messages* file via the `*.info` message selector. In this case, the asterisk directs *syslogd* to send messages from all facilities except `mail` and `authpriv`, which are excluded using the special `none` level. The */var/log/messages* file is the default system message destination, and you will consult it frequently for information on processes running (or failing to run) and other events on your system. In this example, the low severity level of `info` is used for the *messages* file, which logs all but debugging messages. On heavily loaded servers, this may result in an unwieldy file size due to message volume. Depending upon your available disk space, you may choose to save less information by raising the level for the *messages* file.

The *syslogd* server keeps the file handles open for all files defined in */etc/syslog.conf*. This means that the only process that can write to these files is *syslogd*. Do not configure your programs to write directly to these files! Instead, call a program such as *logger*, or use one of the many syslog API interfaces available for your language of choice.

The syslog service is actually made up of two processes, *syslogd* and *klogd*. *Syslogd* is used to log events from user process, whereas *klogd* is used to log events from kernel processes. They work in tandem and use the same configuration file, so you really just need to make sure they are both running:

```
$ ps ax | egrep -i "(syslogd|klogd)"
2078 ?    Ss   0:04 syslogd -m 0
2081 ?    Ss   0:00 klogd -x
```

Client/Server Logging

Syslogd also has the ability to log messages across the network. If a syslogd process is started with the *-r* option, it will listen on the network for incoming *syslogd* messages. By default, *syslogd* uses UDP port 514 for this communication. A common practice is to set up one master logging server that receives all *syslogd* messages from all clients. On the client side, you would configure the local *syslogd* service to log events locally, and to log everything to the master logging server. This would be accomplished by adding the following line to the example *syslog.conf* file shown in Example 16-2:

```
*.*      @10.0.0.1
```

This means that messages matching all facilities and levels should be sent to the IP address 10.0.0.1.

You can determine whether a *syslogd* server is listening for remote log entries by running *netstat*:

```
# netstat -anp | grep -i ":514"
udp        0      0 0.0.0.0:514          0.0.0.0:*           26645/syslogd
```

Logfile Rotation

Most distributions will install a default *syslog* configuration for you, including logging to *messages* and other logfiles in */var/log*. To prevent any of these files from growing unattended to extreme sizes, a logfile rotation scheme should be installed as well. The *cron* system issues commands on a regular basis (usually once per day) to establish new logfiles; the old files are renamed with numeric suffixes. With this kind of rotation, yesterday's */var/log/messages* file becomes today's */var/log/ messages.1*, and a new */var/log/messages* file is created. The rotation is configured with a maximum number of files to keep, and the oldest logfiles are deleted when the rotation is run.

The utility that establishes the rotation is *logrotate*. This privileged command is configured using one or more files, which are specified as arguments to the *logrotate* command. These configuration files can contain directives to include other files as well. The default configuration file is */etc/logrotate.conf*. Example 16-3 depicts a sample *logrotate.conf* file.

Example 16-3. Sample /etc/logrotate.conf file

```
# global options
# rotate log files weekly
weekly
# keep 4 weeks worth of backlogs
rotate 4
# send errors to root
errors root
# create new (empty) log files after rotating old ones
create
# compress log files
compress
# specific files
/var/log/wtmp {
    monthly
    create 0664 root utmp
    rotate 1
}
/var/log/messages {
    postrotate
        /usr/bin/killall -HUP syslogd
    endscript
}
```

This example specifies rotations for two files, */var/log/wtmp* and */var/log/messages*. Your configuration will be much more complete, automatically rotating all logfiles on your system. A complete understanding of *logrotate* configuration is not necessary for LPIC Level 1 Exams, but you must be familiar with the concepts involved. See the *logrotate* manpages for more information.

Examining Logfiles

You can learn a lot about the activity of your system by reviewing the logfiles it creates. At times, it will be necessary to debug problems using logged information. Since most of the logfiles are plain text, it is very easy to review their contents with tools such as *tail*, *less*, and *grep*.

Syslogd stores the messages it creates with the following information, separated by (but also including) spaces:

- Date/time
- Origin hostname
- Message sender (such as `kernel`, `sendmail`, or a username)
- Message text

Typical messages will look like this:

```
Aug  3 18:45:16 moya kernel: Partition check:
Aug  3 18:45:16 moya kernel: sda: sda1 sda2 sda3 < sda5 sda6 sda7 \
                                       sda8 sda9 sda10 > sda4
Aug  3 18:45:16 moya kernel: SCSI device sdb: 195369520 512-byte \
                                       hdwr sectors (100029 MB)
Aug  3 18:45:16 moya kernel:  sdb: sdb1
Aug  3 18:45:16 moya kernel: Journalled Block Device driver loaded
Aug  3 18:45:16 moya kernel: kjournald starting.  Commit interval 5 seconds
Aug  3 18:45:16 moya kernel: EXT3-fs: mounted filesystem with ordered data
                                       mode.
Aug  3 18:45:16 moya kernel: Freeing unused kernel memory: 116k freed
Aug  3 18:45:16 moya kernel: Adding Swap: 1044216k swap-space (priority -1)
```

In this case, moya is the hostname, and the messages are coming from the kernel. At any time, you can review the entire contents of your logfiles using *less*:

```
# less /var/log/messages
```

You can then page through the file. This is a good way to become familiar with the types of messages you'll see on your system. To actively monitor the output to your messages file, you could use *tail*:

```
# tail -f /var/log/messages
```

This might be useful, for example, to watch system activity as an Internet connection is established via modem. To look specifically for messages regarding your mouse, you might use *grep*:

```
# grep '[Mm]ouse' /var/log/messages
Dec  8 00:15:28 smp kernel: Detected PS/2 Mouse Port.
Dec  8 10:55:02 smp gpm: Shutting down gpm mouse services:
```

Often, if you are using *grep* to look for a particular item you expect to find in */var/log/messages*, you will need to search all of the rotated files with a wildcard. For example, to look for all messages from *sendmail*, you can issue a command like this:

```
# grep 'sendmail:' /var/log/messages*
```

Or, if you've enabled compression for the rotated logfiles:

```
# zgrep 'sendmail:' /var/log/messages*
```

When you note problems in logfiles, look at the hostname and sender of the message first, and then the message text. In many cases, you will be able to determine what is wrong from the message. Sometimes the messages are only clues, so a broader review of your logs may be necessary. In this case, it may be helpful to temporarily turn on more messaging by using the debug level in */etc/syslog.conf* to help yield additional information that can lead you to the problem.

On the Exam

If you're not yet familiar with *syslogd*, spend some time with it, modifying */etc/syslog.conf* and directing messages to various files. An understanding of *syslogd* is critical because so many programs depend on it. It is also the first place to look when troubleshooting problems you are having with your system.

17

Mail Transfer Agent (MTA) Basics (Topic 108.3)

Mail Transfer Agents (MTAs) are a crucial part of an Internet-enabled system. The delivery and sending of email has been a key part of the Internet since its inception. For the LPI 102 exam, you must be familiar with the common MTAs available on modern Linux distributions, and some basic configuration of each. MTAs are complicated programs, but the LPI 102 exam will only question you on the basics.

This chapter covers Objective 3 of Topic 108:

Objective 3: Mail Transfer Agent (MTA) Basics
    Candidates should be aware of the commonly available MTA programs and be able to perform basic forward and alias configuration on a client host. Other configuration files are not covered. Weight: 3.

Objective 3: Mail Transfer Agent (MTA) Basics

The four main MTAs commonly available on Linux systems are sendmail, postfix, qmail, and exim. Each has its own differences, mainly with regard to the format of configuration files. Each MTA performs the basic functions of a mail transfer agent: the sending and receiving of Internet mail.

Sendmail
    Sendmail was one of the first MTAs used on Unix systems. It was derived from the original program "delivermail," which shipped with an early version of BSD Unix in 1979. Sendmail has grown over the years into quite a complicated program—as evidenced by the O'Reilly book *sendmail*, Fourth Edition (*http://oreilly.com/catalog/9780596510299/*), which weighs in at a whopping 1,312 pages—and is often quite challenging to configure correctly. That fact, combined with the history of security vulnerabilities that have plagued sendmail over the years, has caused its popularity to decrease over the last decade.

Although most major Linux distributions provide a package for sendmail, none of them currently ship with sendmail as the default MTA.

Postfix

Postfix was originally designed in the late 1990s as a more secure alternative to sendmail. It shares many of the same configuration options as sendmail, but does not share any code. At the time of this writing, postfix is currently very popular in the Linux world, and is the default MTA shipped with the most popular Linux distributions.

Qmail

In response to the increasing number of security incidents involving MTAs, qmail was developed in the mid 1990s to be as secure as a mail transfer agent can be. Qmail is small, efficient, and secure, making it a popular choice for resource-strapped systems. However, qmail has not been actively developed since 1997, and its lack of support for modern options such as IPv6 has limited its usefulness. Qmail still enjoys an active following, but is not commonly seen on newer Linux distributions.

Exim

Exim is another example of an MTA that was developed in direct response to the security issues with sendmail. For this reason, it is essentially a drop-in replacement for sendmail. It is designed to be a general-purpose mailer for Unix-like systems, and is widely used in relatively high-volume environments. It was originally written in 1995 and still enjoys active development to this day. Exim is currently the default MTA for the Debian GNU/Linux distribution.

Configuration of Sendmail

The overall configuration of sendmail is beyond the scope of this book and the LPI 102 test. We will instead focus on email address aliasing and mail forwarding, in addition to monitoring logfiles and basic troubleshooting.

Sendmail is a monolithic tool, with a single binary handling the sending and receiving of Internet email. For the purposes of this chapter, we will assume Simple Mail Transport Protocol (SMTP) email, but sendmail supports many other types of mail relaying.

By default, sendmail will listen for an incoming SMTP connection (on TCP port 25). When a connection is received, sendmail starts the SMTP conversation and accepts the email. It checks addresses and domains for validity, honors aliasing and mail forwards, and then hands the mail off to a local delivery agent for local processing. Sendmail logs all activity through the *syslog* service, which is normally configured to store mail-related logs in the file */var/log/maillog*. Here is an example of verifying a sendmail instance and sending a test mail.

```
# netstat -anpl --tcp | grep sendmail
tcp 0 0 127.0.0.1:25 0.0.0.0:* LISTEN \
                    1847/sendmail: accepting connections
# ls -l /var/spool/mail/adamh
-rw-rw---- 1 adamh mail 0 2009-04-24 01:23 /var/spool/mail/adamh
# echo "This is a test email" | mail adamh
```

```
# ls -l /var/spool/mail/adamh
-rw-rw---- 1 adamh mail 689 2010-02-07 13:21 /var/spool/mail/adamh
# tail /var/log/maillog
Feb 7 13:22:42 server sendmail[5387]: o17JMgbMO05387: from=root, \
size=32, class=0, nrcpts=1, msgid=<201002071922.o17JMgbMO05387\
@server>, relay=root@localhost
Feb 7 13:22:42 server sendmail[5388]: o17JMghcO05388: \
from=<root@server>, size=353, class=0,nrcpts=1, \
msgid=<201002071922.o17JMgbMO05387@server>, proto=ESMTP, \
daemon=MTA, relay=server [127.0.0.1]
Feb 7 13:22:42 server sendmail[5387]: o17JMgbMO05387: to=adamh, \
ctladdr=root (0/0), delay=00:00:00, xdelay=00:00:00, mailer=relay, \
pri=30032, relay=[127.0.0.1] [127.0.0.1], dsn=2.0.0, stat=Sent \
(o17JMghcO05388 Message accepted for delivery)
Feb 7 13:22:42 server sendmail[5389]: o17JMghcO05388: \
to=<adamh@server>, ctladdr=<root@server> (0/0), \
delay=00:00:00, xdelay=00:00:00, mailer=local, pri=30607, \
dsn=2.0.0, stat=Sent
# cat /var/spool/mail/adamh
From root@server  Sun Feb  7 13:22:42 2010
Return-Path: <root@server>
Received: from server (server [127.0.0.1])
        by server (8.14.2/8.14.2) with ESMTP id o17JMghcO05388
        for <adamh@server>; Sun, 7 Feb 2010 13:22:42 -0600
Received: (from root@localhost)
        by server (8.14.2/8.14.2/Submit) id o17JMgbMO05387
        for adamh; Sun, 7 Feb 2010 13:22:42 -0600
Date: Sun, 7 Feb 2010 13:22:42 -0600
From: root <root@server>
Message-Id: <201002071922.o17JMgbMO05387@server>
To: adamh@server

This is a test email
```

In this example, we verified that sendmail was listening on TCP port 25, and we used the standard Linux command *mail* to send an email address through sendmail. Sendmail saves mail to */var/spool/mail/$username* by default, so we saw the size of */var/spool/mail/adamh* increase from 0 bytes to 689 bytes. Viewing this file shows us the mail header information that sendmail stores in this file, which is in "mbox" format. Finally, we saw what mail logging looks like by examining the file */var/log/ maillog*.

The *mail* command can be used to both send mail and read mail that is stored in mbox format. The easiest way to send mail is by piping it to the *mail* command, as shown in the previous example. The *mail* command has many other options, and is a useful command to have in your arsenal. This command is not sendmail-specific, and is designed to work with any standards-compliant MTA.

mail

Syntax

```
mail [options]
```

Description

A mail processing system that can be used to both send and read Internet mail.

Example

Start mail in interactive mode to read your mail:

```
# mail
Send an email from the command line:
# mail -s "This is the subject" -c "root" adamh
Hello
.
Cc: root
```

This example shows some command-line options of *mail*, specifically the ability to indicate a subject and Cc: list. In this example, the body of the message was given interactively, ending with a "." on a line by itself. You could also *cat* an existing file and redirect *STDOUT* to the *mail* program to make this noninteractive:

```
# echo "Message body" > /tmp/body.msg
# cat /tmp/body.msg | mail -s "This is the subject" -c "root" adamh
```

This email was delivered successfully because there was a user account named *adamh* on this system. What if we want to create aliases for this user so he can get email to the same inbox via a number of different email addresses? Sendmail handles aliasing with the file */etc/aliases*:

```
# cat /etc/aliases
#
#  Aliases in this file will NOT be expanded in the header from
#  Mail, but WILL be visible over networks or from /bin/mail.
#
#       >>>>>>>>>      The program "newaliases" must be run after
#       >> NOTE >>     this file is updated for any changes to
#       >>>>>>>>>      show through to sendmail.
#

# Basic system aliases -- these MUST be present.
mailer-daemon:  postmaster
postmaster:     root

# General redirections for pseudo accounts.
bin:            root
daemon:         root
adm:            root
lp:             root

# User maintained aliases
adam:           adamh
adam.haeder:    adamh
haeder:         adamh
```

The lines in this file take the format "alias: user account". After you make modifications to this file, you must run the command *newaliases* as root. The *newaliases* command will take the */etc/aliases* file and convert it to a hashed Berkeley DB file. This is a standard method of configuration for sendmail; changes are made to text-based configuration files, and are then converted to Berkeley DB files for quicker parsing. Emails that are sent to *adam*, *adam.haeder*, or *haeder* will all be delivered to the user *adamh*.

What if you want to forward all emails sent to a specific user account to another account, either on the same system or to a different email address? The easiest way to accomplish this is with the file ~/.forward. This is simply a text file that lives in a user's home directory and contains one or more email addresses to forward all mail to. These can be either local addresses (usernames) or complete Internet email addresses (user@hostname.com). The advantage of the ~/.forward file is that the user can maintain it himself, whereas the /etc/aliases file must be maintained by the root user.

Mail queuing

Description

Sendmail is an intelligent mail agent, and it tries to deliver mail even when failures occur. For example, if a user attempts to send email to user@hostname.com, and the mail server for hostname.com is turned off, sendmail will be unable to make a connection to TCP port 25 on the mail server for hostname.com and consequently won't be able to deliver the mail. Instead of giving up, sendmail will place the email in a queue and attempt redelivery. The default action of sendmail is to attempt redelivery of queued mail every 4 hours for 5 days before giving up and sending a "Delivery Failure" notification to the original sender. Queued mail is stored in the directory /var/spool/mqueue and is managed by the program mailq.

mailq

Syntax

```
mailq [options]
```

Description

Displays the items in the mail queue.

Example

Attempt to send mail to a host that is not currently accepting email:

```
# echo "Failure Test" | mail user@unknown.com

View the mail queue
# mailq
o1591AmX005615    7182 Fri Feb  5 03:01 MAILER-DAEMON
     8BITMIME   (Deferred: Connection refused by unknown.com.)
                <user@unknown.com>
```

This mail will remain in the queue for a default time of 5 days, with retry attempts every 4 hours. You can force sendmail to attempt a resend of every item in the mail queue with the command sendmail −q −v.

Configuration of Postfix

Postfix was created as a replacement for sendmail, and therefore it maintains a mostly "sendmail-compatible" interface. In most cases, postfix can act as a drop-in replacement for sendmail, and scripts that had called sendmail directly with various command-line options will continue to work. Postfix accomplishes this by including with its distribution a program called /usr/sbin/sendmail, which exists to act as a "bridge" between calls to sendmail and the postfix utility. Because of this, many of the commands you are used to in sendmail will work with postfix:

```
# which sendmail
/usr/sbin/sendmail
# for file in /usr/sbin/sendmail /usr/bin/mailq /usr/bin/newaliases; { echo -n
"$file: " && rpm -q --whatprovides ${file}; }
/usr/sbin/sendmail: postfix-2.3.2-32
/usr/bin/mailq: postfix-2.3.2-32
/usr/bin/newaliases: postfix-2.3.2-32
```

The postfix system is made up of a number of different applications, as opposed to the monolithic nature of sendmail. The main program is */usr/lib/postfix/master*, which is the daemon that listens on TCP port 25 for incoming SMTP connections and accepts mail. Other applications are listed in Table 17-1. These applications live in */usr/lib/postfix/* unless otherwise indicated.

Table 17-1. Postfix programs

Program name	Description
anvil	Maintains statistics about client connection counts or client request rates. This information can be used to defend against clients that hammer a server with either too many simultaneous sessions or too many successive requests within a configurable time interval (hence the name "anvil"). Run by the Postfix master server.
bounce	Maintains per-message log files with delivery status information. Run by the Postfix master server.
cleanup	Processes inbound mail, inserts it into the incoming mail queue, and informs the queue manager of its arrival.
discard	Processes delivery requests from the queue manager that should be discarded.
error	Processes delivery requests from the queue manager that should be logged as errors.
flush	Maintains a record of deferred mail by destination.
lmtp	Implements the SMTP and LMTP mail delivery protocols to deliver mail.
local	Processes delivery requests from the queue manager that should be delivered locally.
pickup	Moves mail from the *maildrop* directory to the cleanup process.
pipe	Handles delivery of mail to an external command.
proxymap	Handles lookup tables between the postfix programs.
qmgr	Waits for incoming mail from the master server and hands it to the delivery process.
qmqpd	Daemon for the "Quick Mail Queueing Protocol." Designed to be a centralized mail queue for a number of hosts. This prevents having to run a full-blown mail server on each and every host.
scache	Maintains a shared multisession cache that can be used by the different postfix programs.
showq	Emulates the sendmail *mailq* command.
smtp	Alias for *lmtp*.
smtpd	The actual process that handles incoming mail. Can be run as a standalone process instead of being called by the master program.
spawn	Postfix version of *inetd*.
tlsmgr	Handles caching of TLS connections.

Program name	Description
trivial-rewrite	Handles address rewriting and domain resolving before mail is delivered.
verify	Email address verification.
virtual	Handles virtual domain name mail hosting.
/usr/bin/new-aliases	Backward-compatible with the sendmail *newaliases* command. Converts the text file */etc/aliases* into a binary file that is parsable by postfix.

Configuration of Qmail

Qmail is similar to postfix in that it was designed as a sendmail replacement and is a collection of smaller programs instead of one large one. The design goal behind Qmail is security, so often the smaller programs will run as lower-privileged users. Some of the more common Qmail programs are listed in Table 17-2.

Table 17-2. Qmail programs

Program name	Description
tcpserver	Listens for incoming TCP connections and hands them off to the appropriate program. Similar to *inetd* or *xinetd*.
qmail-smtpd	Handles incoming email.
qmail-inject	Injects outgoing email into the mail queue.
qmail-send	Delivers mail messages currently in the queue.
qmail-queue	Formats mail correctly and places it in the queue for delivery.
qmail-lspawn	Invokes *qmail-local* to handle local delivery.
qmail-rspawn	Invokes *qmail-remote* to handle remote delivery.
qmail-local	Delivers email locally.
qmail-remote	Delivers email remotely.
qmail-qmqpd	Receives mail via the Quick Mail Queueing Protocol and invokes *qmail-queue* to put mail in the outgoing queue.
qmail-qstat	Summarizes the current contents of the mail queue.
qmail-qread	Lists messages and recipients of emails in the outgoing queue.
qmail-tcpto	Lists hosts that have timed out on mail delivery attempts.
qmail-tcpok	Clears the host timeout list.
qmail-showctl	Analyzes the current qmail configuration files and explains the setup.
qmail-start	A wrapper program that starts *qmail-send*, *qmail-lspawn*, *qmail-rspawn*, and *qmail-clean* with the appropriate user IDs so mail delivery can happen.

Qmail also handles sendmail compatibility in ways similar to postfix. Qmail comes with the program */var/qmail/bin/sendmail*, which is designed to take the same command-line options that sendmail takes and pass them to qmail. The program *dot-forward* is used to read a user's *.forward* file, and the program *fastforward* will

MTA Basics

read the sendmail */etc/aliases* file. More information on qmail can be found at the author's site (*http://cr.yp.to/qmail.html*).

Configuration of Exim

Exim, like postfix and qmail, was designed to be a sendmail replacement. Therefore, it has helper programs and supports command-line options to enable a smooth transition from sendmail. Exim is monolithic like sendmail, in that the exim program handles the acceptance of email on TCP port 25 and the delivery of mail. There are a number of helper programs that come with exim, however. Some of the more common ones are listed in Table 17-3.

Table 17-3. Exim programs

Program name	Description
/usr/bin/mailq.exim	Drop-in replacement for sendmail's *mailq* command.
/usr/bin/newaliases.exim	Drop-in replacement for sendmail's *newaliases* command.
/usr/bin/runq.exim	Alias for */usr/sbin/exim*. Running this command is the same as running *exim –q*. This forces a single run through the mail queue, attempting a resend on every item.
/usr/lib/sendmail.exim	Handles sendmail command-line options and passes them to exim.
/usr/sbin/exim	The main exim binary, this process listens on TCP port 25 for incoming SMTP connections and hands incoming mail to the local delivery agent.
/usr/sbin/eximstats	Generates statistics from exim *mainlog* or *syslog* files.
/usr/sbin/exiwhat	Describes what the exim process is currently doing.
/usr/sbin/exinext	Gives specific information about retry efforts for an email address.
/usr/sbin/exipick	Displays individual messages from the exim mail queue.
/usr/sbin/exiqgrep	Searches for strings in the mail queue.
/usr/sbin/exiqsumm	Summarizes the current contents of the mail queue.

On the Exam

It is not necessary to know the detailed configuration options of each MTA for the LPI 102 exam. You need to understand the basic purpose of an MTA and know how to handle aliasing and email forwarding. You should also be familiar with the sendmail-compatibility commands included with qmail, postfix, and exim.

18

Manage Printers and Printing (Topic 108.4)

Chapter 18 contains the final Objective in Topic 108:

Objective 4: Manage Printers and Printing
  Candidates should be able to manage print queues and user print jobs using CUPS and the LPD compatibility interface. Weight: 2.

Objective 4: Manage Printers and Printing

As long as the paperless office remains a myth, printing will be an important aspect of the computing experience. Even if you don't deal with it on a daily basis, as a system administrator printing will inevitably be an important part of your job.

This topic also covers the setup, administration, and use of the Common Unix Protocol (CUPS) and the Line Printer Daemon (LPD) legacy interface (*lpr*, *lprm*, *lpq*, etc.). Although they are not covered in the current LPI Objectives, this chapter also includes an introduction to other printing systems that may be used on Linux systems.

In the current LPI exams, this objective weight was changed, the content shrank from three objectives to one, and the objective was moved to the Essential System Services topic. Bear in mind that CUPS is the main thing to know here, but CUPS's compatibility with the legacy LPD protocol are also required.

An Overview of Printing

The various printing implementations available for Linux systems have a basic architecture in common. In every printing system, a central daemon (or service) receives print jobs, via either a user command (such as *lpr*) or the network. The print job is then processed through input filters if necessary, and sent to either a local printer or another printing daemon.

Printing documents is a slow and error-prone process. Printers accept data in small amounts. They are prone to run out of paper, jam, and go offline for other reasons. Printers also must accept requests from multiple system users. As a result, by design, the end user is isolated from printing functions on most computer systems. This isolation comes in the form of a *print queue*, which holds print requests until the printer is ready for them. It also manages the order in which print jobs are processed. Feeding print jobs to printers is often called *spooling*, and the program that manages the print queues is sometimes called a *spooler*. It can also be called a *scheduler*.

BSD and System V Interfaces

Historically, there have been two competing printing implementations on Unix systems, one invented for BSD Unix and another for System V (SysV) Unix. Although the implementations are similar, they have completely different commands. The BSD printing commands include *lpd*, *lpr*, *lprm*, and *lpc*. The System V printing commands include *lp*, *enable*, *disable*, *cancel*, *lpstat*, and *lpadmin*. On System V-based systems, the *lpadmin* command manages print queues. There is no equivalent to it on BSD-based systems, other than to simply edit */etc/printcap*. Other than *lpadmin*, there is a one-to-one relationship between BSD and System V printing commands. However, the internal details, such as files used, vary considerably.

Older Linux distributions tended to use a port of the BSD *lpd* code (and related commands). Due to various security issues with the BSD code (mostly the overuse of the *root* account through SUID executables), current distributions have largely dropped the BSD code in favor of CUPS.

LPRng

LPRng is a complete rewrite of the BSD utilities. It is designed to be portable and secure. Unlike the BSD utilities, the client programs do not need to run SUID. The server (still called *lpd*) is a complete implementation of the RFC 1179 Line Printer Daemon Protocol. It also includes *lp* and *lpstat* commands for System V compatibility.

Although LPRng is a complete rewrite, configuration is still mostly the same as for the BSD utilities. It still uses */etc/printcap* (described later in this chapter). It also has two additional configuration files: */etc/lpd.conf*, which controls details of LPRng's *lpd*, and */etc/lpd.perms*, which configures access controls for *lpd*.

Sometimes it's necessary to integrate the printing server into a heterogeneous infrastructure, such as to serve systems using the LPD legacy protocol. The embedded package *cups-lpd* is the CUPS Line Printer Daemon (LPD) mini-server supporting these legacy client systems. *cups-lpd* does not act as a standalone network daemon, but instead operates using the Internet *inetd* or *xinetd* super-server.

The LPD server will listen on the default port specified in the */etc/services* file:

```
printer          515/tcp          spooler          # line printer spooler
printer          515/udp          spooler          # line printer spooler
```

LPRng is available from *http://www.lprng.com*.

CUPS

CUPS is a more recent printing system that was initially designed to support the Internet Printing Protocol (IPP) but has evolved into a drop-in replacement for both the BSD and System V utilities, including client replacements for RFC 1179 (*lpd* protocol) support.

Although it retains backward compatibility with older printing systems, the internal details of CUPS are significantly different. The server component *cupsd* handles queuing, and includes a web server for configuration and management. Nearly everything can be configured through the web interface or the included *lpadmin* command. The various configuration files in the */etc/cups* directory rarely need to be edited by hand.

The CUPS web interface, shown in Figure 18-1, is available on the machine at *http://localhost:631*.

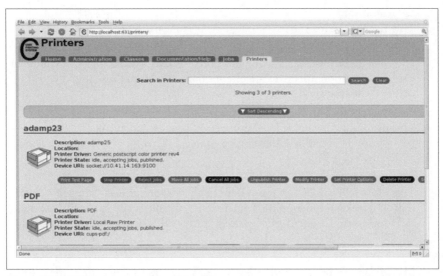

Figure 18-1. CUPS management web interface

In order to implement or troubleshoot a printing system, it's very important to understand the data flow and the steps taken on the server and client side. In the case of CUPS, these are:

1. A print job is generated by an application locally on the client side.
2. The print job is sent to the print server specified by the protocol selected for that queue (e.g., IPP or CIFS).
3. On the CUPS server, the spooler process *cupsd* fetches the data stream and saves it in the print spool directory. The default directory is */var/spool/cups*.

4. If an input filter is specified in the configuration, CUPS will pass the job to it. In any case, after any filtering, the job is sent to the backend. Many filters create formats for particular printers from generic input, such as PostScript or a PDF.

5. The backend sends the printer-specific data to the printer.

6. Once the job is completed, *cupsd* removes the respective files from the spool directory, depending on the retention time configured.

CUPS is available from *http://www.cups.org*.

CUPS printing overview

On Linux, the CUPS printing system consists of the following elements:

cupsd
> This daemon is started at boot time and runs continuously, listening for print requests directed at multiple printers. When a job is submitted to a print queue, *cupsd* handles jobs on that queue. The copy exits when the queue is emptied.

/etc/cups/cupsd.conf
> This file configures the *cupsd* daemon. It is normally located in the */etc/cups* directory.
>
> Each line in the file can be a configuration directive, a blank line, or a comment. The configuration directives are intentionally similar to those used by the popular Apache web server software.

/etc/cups/printers.conf
> This file defines available local printers. It is generated automatically by *cupsd* when printers are added, deleted, or changed. This file shouldn't be changed manually.

/etc/printcap
> This file is still present on the system to allow older printing applications that rely on it to keep functioning. Under CUPS, the file is automatically generated by *cupsd* from the */etc/cups/printers.conf* file. All changes to the file are lost if the CUPS service is restarted.

lp
> The *lp* (line print) program submits both files and information piped to its standard input to print queues.

lpq
> This program queries and displays the status and contents of print queues.

lprm
> This program removes print jobs from print queues.

lpadmin
> This program configures printer and class queues provided by CUPS. It can also be used to set the server default printer or class.

lpc
> Nowadays, *lpc* provides limited control over printer and class queues provided by CUPS. It can also be used to query the state of queues. The command *lpadmin* should be used instead.

Spool directories

The *cupsd* daemon uses */var/spool/cups* for the spooling of data awaiting printing.

Print jobs

Each print request submitted is spooled to a queue and assigned a unique number. The print jobs can be examined and manipulated as needed.

Other files are also used by particular parts of the system, such as input filters.

CUPS backends

Several backends are available for CUPS: parallel, serial, SCSI, and USB ports, as well as network backends that operate via the Internet Printing Protocol (HTTP, HTTPS, and IPP), JetDirect (AppSocket port 9100), Line Printer Daemon (LPD), CIFS (which used to be called SMB) protocols, and more. PDF generators are also available. These backends usually live in the directory */usr/lib/cups/backend*, and can be compiled programs or scripts written in any scripting language, such as Perl or Python.

The backend is always the last program executed for processing a print job. Table 18-1 lists the most popular backends.

Table 18-1. Backend processors under CUPS

Backend	URI syntax	Example URI
Parallel	`parallel:/dev/lp`*number*	`parallel:/dev/lp0`
USB	`usb://`*make/model*`?` `serial=`*number*	`usb://vendor/printer` `%201000?serial=A1B2C3`
ipp	`ipp://`*host*`/printers/` *queue*	`ipp://host/printers/` `printer1000`
LPD	`lpd://`*host*`/`*queue*	`lpd://host/printer`
socket	`socket://`*host*`:`*port*	`socket://ip:9100`
CIFS (Common Internet Filesystem, the protocol Microsoft Windows-based systems use for file and printer communication across a network)	see the *smbspool*(8) manpage	`smb://user:password@work` `group/host/share`

CUPS filters

The core of the CUPS filtering system is based on Ghostscript, part of the GNU project. It consults PPD files, which are an industry standard for representing printer capabilities (two-sided printing, four-to-a-page, etc.).

For PostScript printers, the PPD file contains the printer-specific options (and nothing else) together with the corresponding PostScript code snippets that must be sent to the PostScript interpreter in order to activate a certain option.

For non-PostScript printers, the PPD file contains additional information about which printer driver program to use and the options available for the particular driver. If several drivers can be used for a given printer, several PPD files are found on the system.

Depending on the printer-specific options set for a certain print job (e.g., -o Page Size=A4), the filter system reads the suitable PostScript code snippets (the so-called "PostScript invocation values") from the PPD file and inserts them in the PostScript data stream.

The original data has a MIME type determined by configuration options in /etc/cups/ mime.types. If the type is not application/postscript, the data is converted to Post-Script according to the /etc/cups/mime.convs configuration file. For example, text/ plain is converted to PostScript with the /usr/lib/cups/filter/texttops program.

These filter files are usually found in the directory /usr/lib/cups/filter and, like CUPS backends, can be compiled code or shell scripts.

Managing CUPS print queues

As a system administrator, you'll likely be asked to manage and manipulate printer more often. On Linux, the *lp*, *lpq*, *lpstat*, *lprm*, and *lpadmin* commands are your tools. Other tools include *lpoptions*, *accept*, *reject*, and *cancel*.

lp

Syntax

```
lp [ -E ] [ -U username ] [ -c ] [ -d destination[/instance] ]
   [ -h hostname[:port] ] [ -m ]
   [ -n num-copies ] [ -o option[=value] ] [ -q priority ] [ -s ] [ -t title ]
  [ -H handling ] [  -P page-list ] [ -- ] [ file(s) ]
```

Description

lp submits files for printing or alters a pending job.

Options

--
    Prints from standard input.

-d destination
    Prints files to the named printer.

-o "name=value [name=value ...]"
    Sets one or more job options.

Example 1

Print a double-sided legal document to a printer called "foo":

```
$ lp -d foo -o media=legal -o sides=two-sided-long-edge filename
```

Example 2

Print an image across four pages:

```
$ lp -d bar -o scaling=200 filename
```

Example 3

Print a text file with 12 characters per inch, 8 lines per inch, and a 1-inch left margin:

```
lp -d bar -o cpi=12 -o lpi=8 -o page-left=72 filename
```

---

cancel

Syntax

```
cancel [ -E ] [ -U username ] [ -a ] [ -h hostname[:port] ] [ -u username ] [ id ]
      [ destination
  ] [ destination-id ]
```

Description

cancel removes the specified print jobs from the queue.

Options

-a

    Cancels all jobs on the named destination, or all jobs on all destinations if no destination is provided.

---

lpstat

Syntax

```
lpstat [ -E ] [ -U username ] [ -h hostname[:port] ] [ -l ] [ -W which-jobs ]
      [ -a [ destination(s) ] ] [ -c [ class(es) ] ] [ -d ]
      [ -o [ destination(s) ] ]
      [ -p [ printer(s) ] ] [ -r ] [ -R ] [ -s ] [ -t ] [ -u [ user(s) ] ]
      [ -v [ printer(s) ] ]
```

Description

lpstat displays status information about the current classes, jobs, and printers. When run with no arguments, it lists jobs queued by the current user.

Options

-a [printer(s)]

    Shows the accepting state of printer queues. If no printers are specified, shows all printers.

-t

    Shows all status information. This option is very useful for troubleshooting.

lpadmin

Syntax

```
lpadmin [ -E ] [-U username ] [ -h server[:port] ] -d destination
lpadmin [ -E ] [-U username ] [ -h server[:port] ] -p printer option(s)
lpadmin [ -E ] [-U username ] [ -h server[:port] ] -x destination
```

Description

lpadmin configures printer and class queues provided by CUPS. It can also be used to set the server default printer or class.

Options

-m model
> Sets a standard System V interface script or PPD file from the model directory.

-v device-uri
> Sets the device URI attribute of the printer queue. If **device-uri** is a filename, it is automatically converted to the form **file:///file/name**. Use the *lpinfo*(8) command for a list of supported device URIs and schemes.

-E
> Enables the printer and accepts jobs; this is the same as running the *accept* and *cupsenable* programs for a specific printer.

lpq

Syntax

```
lpq [options] [users] [job#s]
```

Description

Query a print queue. If numeric **job#s** are included, only those jobs are listed. If **users** are listed, only jobs submitted by those users are listed.

Options

-l
> Long output format. This option results in a multiline display for each print job.

-P name
> This specifies the print queue *name*. In the absence of *-P*, the default printer is queried.

Example 1

Examine active jobs:

```
$ lpq
lp is ready and printing
Rank   Owner    Job  Files            Total Size
active root     193  filter           9443 bytes
1st    root     194  resume.txt       11024 bytes
2nd    root     196  (standard input) 18998 bytes
```

Here, *filter* is currently being printed. *resume.txt* is up next, followed by the 18,998 bytes of data piped into *lpr*'s standard input.

Example 2

Examine those same jobs using the long format:

```
$ lpq -l
lp is ready and printing
root: active                        [job 193AsJRzIt]
        filter                      9443 bytes
root: 1st                           [job 194AMj9lo9]
        resume.txt                  11024 bytes
root: 2nd                           [job 196A6rUGu5]
        (standard input)            18998 bytes
```

Example 3

Examine queue lp, which turns out to be empty:

```
$ lpq -Plp
no entries
```

Example 4

Examine jobs owned by *bsmith*:

```
$ lpq bsmith
Rank    Owner    Job  Files              Total Size
7th     bsmith   202  .bash_history      1263 bytes
9th     bsmith   204  .bash_profile      5676 bytes
```

Using the job numbers reported by *lpq*, any user may remove her own print jobs from the queue, or the superuser may remove any job.

lprm

Syntax

```
lprm [-Pname] [users] [job#s]
lprm -ly
```

Description

Remove jobs from a print queue. In the first form, remove jobs from queue *name* or from the default queue if -*P* is omitted. If *users* or *jobs* are specified, only those jobs will be removed. In the second form, all of a normal user's jobs will be omitted; for the superuser, the queue will be emptied.

Example 1

As a normal user, remove all of your print jobs:

```
$ lprm -
```

Example 2

As the superuser, remove all jobs from queue *ps*:

```
# lprm -Pps -
```

You may occasionally be surprised to see a no entries response from lpq, despite observing that the printer is dutifully printing a document. In such cases, the spool has probably been emptied into the printer's buffer memory, and the result is that the job is no longer under the control of the printing system. To kill such jobs, you need to use the printer's controls to stop and delete the job from memory.

---

lpr

Syntax

```
lpr [options] [files]
```

Description

Send *files* or standard input to a print queue. A copy of the input source is placed in the spool directory under */var/spool/lpr* until the print job is complete.

Frequently used options

-#*number*
> Send *number* copies of the print job to the printer.

-s
> Instead of copying a file to the print spooling area, make a symbolic link to the file, thereby eliminating transfer time and storage requirements in */var/spool/lpr*. This can relieve load on the daemon's system for very large files.

-P*name*
> Specify the print queue *name*. In the absence of -P, the default printer is queried.

Example 1

Print the file */etc/fstab* on the default print queue:

```
# lpr /etc/fstab
```

Example 2

Print a manpage by piping to *lpr*'s standard input:

```
# man -t 5 printcap | lpr
```

Example 3

Disable a print queue:

```
# lpc disable lp
```

Then, attempt to print three copies of a file to the disabled queue as superuser:

```
# lpr -#3 /etc/fstab
```

This succeeds, despite the disabled printer queue. Now try as a regular user:

```
$ lpr -#3 ~/resume.txt
lpr: Printer queue is disabled
```

As expected, normal users can't print to the disabled queue.

On the Exam

You must be familiar with *lp* and its use with both files and standard input. Also remember that *lp* doesn't send data to the printer but to the printer daemon (*cupsd* on Linux), which handles sending it to the printer backend and then to the printer.

Troubleshooting General Printing Problems

Logfiles are the first, and sometimes the best, guide to solving problems with printing. Many people still make the basic mistake of forgetting to check logfiles. These files are rotated, so that you can find recent events in the main file and older events in gzipped backup files. If you need even more detail, change the `LogLevel` line in */etc/cups/cupsd.conf* to the value `debug`. It will dump loads of extra information into the logfiles for subsequent print operations.

You should also know about the *cups-config* command, which has some options that show you information about the current state of the system.

The Error Logfile

Recent errors and related information can be found in */var/log/cups/error_log*. This file lists messages from the scheduler, which includes both errors and warnings. You can view detailed and real-time information about data transferring, filtering, etc. Sample messages generated by one typical job are:

```
I [16/Nov/2009:11:19:07 +0100] [Job 102] Adding start banner page "none".
I [16/Nov/2009:11:19:07 +0100] [Job 102] Adding end banner page "none".
I [16/Nov/2009:11:19:07 +0100] [Job 102] File of type application/postscript
queued by "brunop".
I [16/Nov/2009:11:19:07 +0100] [Job 102] Queued on "PDF" by "brunop".
I [16/Nov/2009:11:19:07 +0100] [Job 102] Started filter
/usr/libexec/cups/filter/pstops (PID 18223)
I [16/Nov/2009:11:19:07 +0100] [Job 102] Started backend
/usr/libexec/cups/backend/cups-pdf (PID 18224)
I [16/Nov/2009:11:19:07 +0100] [Job 102] Completed successfully.
I [16/Nov/2009:11:20:17 +0100] [Job ???] Request file type is
application/postscript.
I [16/Nov/2009:11:20:17 +0100] [Job 103] Adding start banner page "none".
I [16/Nov/2009:11:20:17 +0100] [Job 103] Adding end banner page "none".
I [16/Nov/2009:11:20:17 +0100] [Job 103] File of type application/postscript
queued by "brunop".
I [16/Nov/2009:11:20:17 +0100] [Job 103] Queued on "PDF" by "brunop".
I [16/Nov/2009:11:20:17 +0100] [Job 103] Started filter
/usr/libexec/cups/filter/pstops (PID 18340)
```

```
I [16/Nov/2009:11:20:17 +0100] [Job 103] Started backend
/usr/libexec/cups/backend/cups-pdf (PID 18341)
I [16/Nov/2009:11:20:17 +0100] [Job 103] Completed successfully.
```

The I that starts each line stands for "information." In this case, no errors or warnings were generated.

The Page Logfile

This logfile can be found in */var/log/cups/page_log*. It keeps information from each page sent to a printer. Each line contains the following information (when applicable):

```
printer user job-id date-time page-number num-copies job-billing \
job-originating-host-name jobname media sides
```

A sample excerpt follows:

```
Photosmart_C4500 brunop 86 [31/Oct/2009:12:48:36 +0100] 1 1 - localhost
Photosmart_C4500 brunop 86 [31/Oct/2009:12:48:52 +0100] 2 1 - localhost
adamp23 brunop 87 [02/Nov/2009:13:40:33 +0100] 1 1 - localhost
adamp23 brunop 87 [02/Nov/2009:13:40:33 +0100] 2 1 - localhost
adamp23 brunop 88 [09/Nov/2009:09:31:11 +0100] 1 1 - localhost
PDF root 100 [16/Nov/2009:11:11:52 +0100] 1 1 - localhost
PDF brunop 101 [16/Nov/2009:11:16:38 +0100] 1 1 - localhost
```

The Access Logfile

This file can be found in */var/log/cups/access_log*. It lists each HTTP resource accessed by a web browser or client. Each line is in an extended version of the so-called "Common Log Format" used by many web servers and web reporting tools. A sample follows (lines broken to fit the page of this book):

```
localhost - - [16/Nov/2009:17:28:29 +0100] "POST / HTTP/1.1" 200 138 \
            CUPS-Get-Default successful-ok
localhost - - [16/Nov/2009:17:28:29 +0100] "POST / HTTP/1.1" 200 552 \
            CUPS-Get-Printers successful-ok
localhost - root [16/Nov/2009:17:28:29 +0100] "GET /printers HTTP/1.1" \
            200 11258 - -
localhost - root [16/Nov/2009:17:28:29 +0100] "GET \
            /images/button-search.gif HTTP/1.1" 200 332 - -
localhost - root [16/Nov/2009:17:28:29 +0100] "GET \
            /images/button-clear.gif HTTP/1.1" 200 279 - -
```

Using the cups-config Utility for Debugging

The *cups-config* utility has several parameters that can be handy while troubleshooting. The options are described in Table 18-2.

Table 18-2. Options to cups-config

Option	Description
--cflags	Displays the necessary compiler options.
--datadir	Displays the default CUPS data directory.
--help	Displays the program usage message.
--ldflags	Displays the necessary linker options.
--libs	Displays the necessary libraries to link to.
--serverbin	Displays the default CUPS binary directory, where filters and backends are stored.
--serverroot	Displays the default CUPS configuration file directory.

On the Exam

Be familiar with the CUPS logfiles, and how to interpret them to troubleshoot printing issues.

Manage Printers and Printing

19

Networking Fundamentals (Topic 109.1)

Although it is not necessary for you to be a networking expert to pass the LPIC Level 1 Exams, you must be familiar with networking, network-related vocabulary, and basic Linux networking configuration. This chapter introduces fundamental networking and troubleshooting concepts specifically included in the exams. However, it is not a complete introductory treatment, and you are encouraged to review additional material for more depth. This chapter covers this Objective:

Objective 1: Fundamentals of Internet Protocols
   Candidates should demonstrate a proper understanding of network fundamentals. This Objective includes the understanding of IP addresses, network masks, and what they mean (i.e., determine a network and broadcast address for a host based on its subnet mask in *dotted quad* or abbreviated notation, or determine the network address, broadcast address, and netmask when given an IP address and number of bits). It also covers the understanding of the network classes and classless subnets (CIDR) and the reserved addresses for private network use. IPv6 is also discussed, along with how this addresses some of the limitations of IPv4. It includes the understanding of the function and application of a default route. It also includes the understanding of basic Internet protocols (IP, ICMP, TCP, UDP) and the more common TCP and UDP ports (20, 21, 23, 25, 53, 80, 110, 119, 139, 143, 161). Weight: 4.

Objective 1: Fundamentals of Internet Protocols

The TCP/IP suite of protocols was adopted as a military standard in 1983 and has since become the world standard for network communications on the Internet and on many LANs, replacing proprietary protocols in many cases. This section covers TCP/IP basics cited by the LPI Objectives.

Network Addressing

For several years IPv4 has been the standard method for assigning a unique address that identifies the host on the network and the Internet. The 32-bit IP address, also referred to as a *dotted quad*, is composed of four 8-bit fields divided by a period. These fields identify first the network and then the host for a device on the network. IPv4 provides 4.29 billion addresses.

The IP address 192.168.1.150 and the binary equivalent would be:

11000000 10101000 00000001 10010110

IPv4 addresses are categorized into classes to provide structure. There are five classifications of networks defined by IP addresses. Table 19-1 identifies the address ranges for the classes that are primarily used.

Table 19-1. IPv4 address ranges by class

Address class	IP address range
Class A	0.0.0.0 to 127.255.255.255
Class B	128.0.0.0 to 191.255.255.255
Class C	192.0.0.0 to 223.255.255.255
Class D	224.0.0.0 to 239.255.255.255
Class E	240.0.0.0 to 247.255.255.255

Every device on a network or connected to the Internet needs a unique IP address, including printers and fax machines; consequently, the supply of available IP addresses will run out eventually. There have been many technologies developed to reduce the exhaustion of available IP addresses, including network address translation (NAT), Classless Inter-Domain Routing (CIDR), and IPv6.

Private IP addresses and NAT

One of the early attempts of handling the exhaustion of IP addresses was the implementation of private IP addresses. Private IP addresses are not globally assigned, which means that different organizations may use the same private IP addresses. Private IP addresses are not routable, and therefore they are not accessible across the Internet. Organizations using private IP address internally for network connectivity use a process called network address translation (NAT) gateway or a proxy server to provide connectivity to the Internet. Each IP address class has a range of IP addresses that are reserved as private addresses. Table 19-2 lists the ranges for private IP addresses.

Table 19-2. IPv4 private network address ranges

Class	Private IP address range
Class A	10.0.0.0 to 10.255.255.255
Class B	172.16.0.0 to 172.31.255.255
Class C	192.168.0.0. to 192.168.255.255

Classless Inter-Domain Routing (CIDR)

In the 1990s it became apparent that the exhaustion of the IPv4 addresses would be reached in a few years with the ever-growing expansion of Internet technology. The move was made away from assigning IP addresses based on classes to a method that uses ranges of address. IPv4 addresses are now specified using the CIDR notation that specifies subnet masks. The CIDR notation uses the format *address/prefix*.

The *prefix* designates the number of bits that will be used by the subnet mask. Let's say we have a range of IP addresses consisting of 206.24.94.105 and a subnet mask of 255.255.255.0. We would note this address using CIDR as:

206.24.94.105/24

Using the CIDR notation allows for custom subnet masks to be created without tying them to the limitations of classes.

Internet Protocol Version 6 (IPv6)

The Internet Engineer Task Force (IETF) defined IPv6 in 1995. While IPv4 still has the majority of addressing, all network operating systems and hardware device manufacturers support IPv6. IPv6 increases the size of IP addresses from 32 bits to 128 bits, or 16 octets. This increases the possible number of available addresses to a maximum of 2^{128}, or 3.42×10^{38}, unique addresses. With the large number of available IPv6 addresses, it is not necessary to implement addressing conservation methods such as NAT and CIDR. This will help reduce the administration overhead of managing addresses.

The IPv6 address is composed of hexadecimal digits representing 4-bit sections separated by a colon. The addresses are represented by the format *xxxx:xxxx:xxxx:xxxx:xxxx:xxxx:xxxx:xxxx*. An example of the preferred format for IPv6 addresses would look like the following:

2130:0000:0000:0000:0003:0040:150c:235b

IPv6 may be abbreviated by removing the leading zeros from the address, so if applied to the previous example, the address could appear as follows:

2130:0:0:0:3:40:150c:235b

Another shorthand version of the IPv6 address uses double-colon notation, wherein address sections that consist of a series of zeros may be replaced with a double colon. In the instance of the IPv6 address 2130:0000:0000:0000:0003:0040:150c:235b, it could be shortened to:

2130::3:40:150c:235b

IPv6 address several disadvantages of IPv4 addressing, including:

Limited addresses
As mentioned previously, IPv4 has only about 10^9 available addresses, and this supply is expected to be exhausted in the near future. IPv6 has a much larger addressing capability with 10^{38} addresses.

Security

IPsec was designed to be integrated into IPv6 addressing and is mandated to be used with the protocol, whereas IPv4 treats it as an optional function. Encryption processes are also mandated to be included into IPv6 addressing.

Configuration

IPv6 devices will autoconfigure themselves when connected to an IPv6-routed network. This process is a cleaner version of the IPv4 DHCP process discussed later in this chapter. The autoconfiguration functionality also improves addressing assignments of mobile devices because these devices are assigned to a "home" address where it remains always reachable. When the mobile device is at home, it connects using the home address. When the mobile device is not at home, a home agent, typically a router, will relay messages between the mobile device and the nodes it is communicating with.

Performance

IPv6 headers have been modified to fixed widths to work with high-speed routers, increasing speed and performance when moving data packets across Internet backbones.

On the Exam

Prepare to discuss the difference between public and private IP addresses on the Internet. Also be able to discuss the major differences between IPv4 and IPv6 addressing.

Masks

The early specification of the IP recognized that it would be necessary to divide one's given allotment of IP addresses into manageable subnetworks. Such division allows for distributed management, added security (fewer hosts can potentially snoop network traffic), and the use of multiple networking technologies (Ethernet, Token Ring, ATM, etc.). IP also enables convenient partitioning of the physical portions of a network across physical and geographical boundaries. To provide the capability to locally define networks, IP addresses are considered as having two distinct parts: the part that specifies a *subnet* and the one that specifies a network interface. (Remember that IP addresses are assigned to network interfaces, not host computers, which can have multiple interfaces. For this discussion, however, we assume a one-to-one relationship between hosts and interfaces.) The boundary between the network and host portions of an IP address is delineated by a *subnet mask*, required by the TCP/IP configuration of any network interface. Like the IP address, the subnet mask is simply a 32-bit number specified in four 8-bit segments using *dotted quad* decimal notation. The familiar class A, B, and C networks have these subnet masks:

Class A: 255.0.0.0 (binary 11111111.00000000.00000000.00000000)
    8-bit network address and 24-bit host address

Class B: 255.255.0.0 (binary 11111111.11111111.00000000.00000000)
   16-bit network address and 16-bit host address

Class C: 255.255.255.0 (binary 11111111.11111111.11111111.00000000)
   24-bit network address and 8-bit host address

When logically AND'd with an IP address, the bits set to 0 in the subnet mask obscure the host portion of the address. The remaining bits represent the network address. For example, a host on a class C network might have an IP address of 192.168.1.127. Applying the class C subnet mask 255.255.255.0, the network address of the subnet would be 192.168.1.0, and the host address would be 127, as depicted in Figure 19-1.

Address	192.168.1.127	11000000.10101000.00000001.01111111
Mask	255.255.255.0	11111111.11111111.11111111.00000000
Network address	192.168.1.0	11000000.10101011.00000001.00000000
Host interface address	127	01111111

Figure 19-1. Host interface address calculation

Although it is typical to use the predefined classes (A, B, and C), the boundary can be moved left or right in the IP address, allowing for fewer or more subnets, respectively. For example, if a single additional bit were added to the class C subnet mask, its IP address would be:

255.255.255.128 (binary 11111111.11111111.11111111.10000000)
   25-bit network address and 7-bit host address

With such a subnet defined on an existing class C network such as 192.168.1.0, the 256-bit range is split into two subnets, each with 7 host bits. The first of the two subnets begins at 192.168.1.0 (the subnet address) and continues through 192.168.1.127 (the subnet broadcast address). The second subnet runs from 192.168.1.128 through 192.168.1.255. Each of the two subnets can accommodate 126 hosts. To extend this example, consider two additional bits:

255.255.255.192 (binary 11111111.11111111.11111111.11000000)
   26-bit network address and 6-bit host address

When applied to a class C network, four subnets are created, each with 6 host bits. Just as before, the first subnet begins at 192.168.1.0 but continues only through 192.168.1.63. The next subnet runs from 192.168.1.64 through 192.168.1.127, and so on. Each of the four subnets can accommodate 62 hosts. Table 19-3 shows more detail on class C subnets, considering only the host portion of the address.

Table 19-3. Class C IP subnet detail

Subnet mask	Number of subnets	Network address	Broadcast address	Minimum IP address	Maximum IP address	Number of hosts	Total hosts
128	2	0	127	1	126	126	
		128	255	129	254	126	252
192	4	0	63	1	62	62	
		64	127	65	126	62	
		128	191	129	190	62	
		192	255	193	254	62	248
224	8	0	31	1	30	30	
		32	63	33	62	30	
		64	95	65	94	30	
		96	127	97	126	30	
		128	159	129	158	30	
		160	191	161	190	30	
		192	223	193	222	30	
		224	255	225	254	30	240

On the Exam

Be prepared to define network and host addresses when provided an IP address and a subnet mask. Practice with a few subnet sizes within at least one classification (A, B, or C). Also, because the use of decimal notation can cloud human interpretation of IP addresses and masks, be ready to do binary-to-decimal conversion on address numbers.

As you can see, as the number of subnets increases, the total number of hosts that can be deployed within the original class C address range reduces. This is due to the loss of both broadcast addresses and network addresses to the additional subnets.

Protocols

TCP/IP is a suite of Internet protocols, including the Transmission Control Protocol (TCP), Internet Protocol (IP), User Datagram Protocol (UDP), and Internet Control Message Protocol (ICMP), among others. Some protocols use *handshaking* (the exchange of control information among communicating systems) to establish and maintain a connection. Such a protocol is said to be connection-oriented and reliable, because the protocol itself is responsible for handling transmission errors, lost packets, and packet arrival order. A protocol that does not exchange control information is said to be connectionless and unreliable. In this context, "unreliable" simply means that the protocol doesn't handle transmission problems itself; they must be corrected in the application or system libraries. Connectionless protocols are simpler and have fewer overheads than connection-oriented protocols. TCP/IP is a *stack* of protocols because protocols are built in a hierarchy of *layers*. Low-level protocols are used by higher-level protocols on adjacent layers of the protocol stack:

TCP

TCP is a connection-oriented transport agent used by applications to establish a network connection. TCP transports information across networks by handshaking and retransmitting information as needed in response to errors on the network. TCP guarantees packet arrival and provides for the correct ordering of received packets. TCP is used by many network services, including FTP, Telnet, and SMTP. By using TCP, these applications don't need to establish their own error-checking mechanisms, thus making their design simpler and easier to manage.

IP

IP can be thought of as the fundamental building block of the Internet. IP, which is connectionless, defines datagrams (the basic unit of transmission), establishes the addressing scheme (the IP address), and provides for the routing of datagrams between networks. IP is said to provide a *datagram delivery service*. Other higher-level protocols use IP as an underlying carrier.

UDP

UDP is a connectionless transport agent. It provides application programs direct access to IP, allowing them to exchange information with a minimum of protocol overhead. On the other hand, because UDP offers no assurance that packets arrive at destinations as intended, software must manage transmission errors and other problems such as missing and incorrectly ordered packets. UDP is used by applications such as DNS and NFS.

ICMP

ICMP is a connectionless transport agent that is used to exchange control information among networked systems. It uses IP datagrams for the following control, error-reporting, and informational functions:

Flow control

Sometimes inbound traffic becomes too heavy for a receiving system to process. In such cases, the receiving system can send a message via ICMP to the source instructing it to temporarily stop sending datagrams.

Detecting unreachable destinations

Various parts of network infrastructure are capable of detecting that a network destination is unreachable. In this case, ICMP messages are sent to the requesting system.

Redirecting routes

ICMP is used among network components to instruct a sender to use a different gateway.

Checking remote hosts

Hosts can transmit echo messages via ICMP to verify that a remote system's Internet Protocol is functioning. If so, the original message is returned. This is implemented in the *ping* command.

PPP

Point-to-Point Protocol (PPP) is used for TCP/IP dial-up network access via modem.

On the Exam

You will need a general understanding of the control messages sent via ICMP. In particular, note that ICMP does not transmit data and that it is used by *ping*.

Services

When an inbound network request is made, such as that from a web browser or FTP client, it is sent to the IP address of the server. In addition, the request carries inside it a *port number* (or just *port*), which is a 16-bit value placed near the beginning of a network packet. The port number defines the type of server software that should respond to the request. For example, by default, web browsers send requests encoded for port 80. Web servers "listen" to port 80 and respond to incoming requests. The encoded port can be considered part of the address of a request. While the IP address specifies a particular interface (or host), the port specifies a specific service available on that host. Many port numbers are predefined, and the list is expanded as needed to accommodate new technologies. The official list of port number assignments is managed by the Internet Assigned Numbers Authority (IANA). The ports known by your system are listed in */etc/services*.

Port numbers 1 through 1023 are often referred to as *privileged ports* because the services that use them often run with superuser authority. Many of these, such as ports used for FTP (21), Telnet (23), and HTTP (80), are often referred to as *well-known ports* because they are standards. Port numbers from 1024 through 65535 (the maximum) are *unprivileged ports* and can be used by applications run by ordinary system users.

During the initial contact, the client includes a local (randomly selected) unprivileged port on the client machine for the server to use when responding to the request. Client-to-server communications use the well-known port, and the server-to-client communications use the randomly selected port. This Objective requires you to be familiar with the privileged port numbers detailed in Table 19-4.

Table 19-4. Common privileged port numbers

Port number	Assigned use	Description
20 and 21	FTP data FTP control	When an FTP session is opened, the binary or ASCII data flows to the server using port 20, while control information flows on port 21. During use, both ports are managed by an FTP daemon, such as *vftpd*.
23	Telnet server	Inbound Telnet requests are sent to server port 23 and processed by *telnetd*.
25	SMTP server	This port is used by mail transfer agents (MTAs), such as Sendmail.
53	DNS server	Used by the Domain Name System (DNS) server, *named*.

Port number	Assigned use	Description
67	BOOTP/DHCP server	Hands out IP addresses to workstations dynamically.
68	BOOTP/DHCP client	The client side for BOOTP/DHCP.
80	HTTP server	Web servers, such as Apache (*httpd*), usually listen in on this port.
110	POP3	The Post Office Protocol (POP) is used by mail client programs to transfer mail from a server.
119	NNTP server	This port is used by news servers for Usenet news.
139	NetBIOS	Reserved for Microsoft's LAN Manager.
143	IMAP	An alternate to POP3, Internet Message Access Protocol (IMAP) is another type of mail protocol.
161	SNMP	Agents running on monitored systems use this port for access to the Simple Network Management Protocol (SNMP).

This list is a tiny fraction of the many well-known ports, but it may be necessary for you to know those in the list both by name and by number.

On the Exam

You should commit the list of ports in Table 19-4 to memory so you can recognize a type of network connection solely by its port number. Your exam is likely to have at least one question on how a specific port is used.

Utilities

The following popular applications, although not strictly a part of TCP/IP, are usually provided along with a TCP/IP implementation.

dig

Syntax

```
dig hostname
```

Description

dig obtains information from DNS servers. Note that additional command-line arguments and options are available for *dig* but are beyond the scope of Exam 102.

Example

```
$ dig redhat.com
; <<>> DiG 9.3.2 <<>> redhat.com
;; global options: printcmd
;; Got answer:
;; ->>HEADER<<- opcode: QUERY, status: NOERROR, id: 41163
```

```
;; flags: qr rd ra; QUERY: 1, ANSWER: 1, AUTHORITY: 0, ADDITIONAL: 0

;; QUESTION SECTION:
;redhat.com. IN A

;; ANSWER SECTION:
redhat.com. 60 IN A 209.132.177.50

;; Query time: 43 msec
;; SERVER: 68.87.68.166#53(68.87.68.166)
;; WHEN: Fri Sep 18 06:28:08 2009
;; MSG SIZE rcvd: 44
```

ftp

Syntax

```
ftp [options] host
...interactive commands...
```

Description

Establish an interactive FTP connection with *host* to transfer binary or text files. FTP creates an interactive dialog and allows for two-way file transfer. The dialog includes username/password authentication, user commands, and server responses.

Frequently used options

-i

Turn off interactive prompting during multiple file transfers (also see the *prompt* command in the next list).

-v

Set verbose mode; display server responses and transfer statistics.

Frequently used commands

ascii, binary

Establish the transfer mode for files. ASCII mode is provided to correctly transfer text among computer architectures where character encoding differs.

get file

Receive a single *file* from the server.

mget files

Receive multiple *files* from the server. *files* can be specified using normal file glob patterns.

ls [files]

Obtain a directory listing from the server, optionally listing *files*.

put file

Send a single *file* to the server.

mput files

Send multiple *files* to the server.

prompt
> Toggle on and off interactive prompting during *mget* and *mput* (also see the *-i* option in the previous list).

pwd
> Print the working remote directory.

quit, exit
> Cleanly terminate the FTP session.

Example 1

Get a file from machine *smp*:

```
$ ftp -v smp
Connected to smp.
220 smp FTP server (Version wu-2.4.2-VR17(1)
Mon Apr 19 09:21:53 EDT 1999) ready.
Name (smp:root): jdean
331 Password required for jdean.
Password:<password here>
230 User jdean logged in.
Remote system type is UNIX.
Using binary mode to transfer files.
ftp> ls myfile
200 PORT command successful.
150 Opening ASCII mode data connection for /bin/ls.
-rw-r--r--  1 jdean      jdean          29 Jan 24 01:28 myfile
226 Transfer complete.
ftp> binary
200 Type set to I.
ftp> get myfile
local: myfile remote: myfile
200 PORT command successful.
150 Opening BINARY mode data connection for myfile
(29 bytes).
226 Transfer complete.
29 bytes received in 0.000176 secs (1.6e+02 Kbytes/sec)
ftp> quit
221-You have transferred 29 bytes in 1 files.
221-Total traffic for this session was 773 bytes in 3 transfers.
221-Thank you for using the FTP service on smp.
221 Goodbye.
```

Example 2

Many FTP servers are set up to receive requests from nonauthenticated users. Such public access is said to be anonymous. Anonymous FTP is established just like any other FTP connection, except that anonymous is used as the username. An email address is commonly used as a password to let the system owner know who is transferring files:

```
# ftp -v smp
Connected to smp.
220 smp FTP server (Version wu-2.4.2-VR17(1)
Mon Apr 19 09:21:53 EDT 1999) ready.
Name (smp:root): anonymous
331 Guest login OK, send your complete e-mail address as password.
```

```
    Password: me@mydomain.com
    230 Guest login OK, access restrictions apply.
    Remote system type is UNIX.
    Using binary mode to transfer files.
    ftp> <commands follow...>
```

ping

Syntax

```
ping hostname
```

Description

The *ping* command is used to send an ICMP echo request to a host and report on how long it takes to receive a corresponding ICMP echo reply. Much as sonar systems send a pulse (or "ping") to a target and measure transit time, *ping* sends a network packet to test the availability of a network node. This technique is often used as a basic debugging technique when network problems arise.

Frequently used options

-c count
>   Send and receive *count* packets.

-q
>   Quiet output. Display only summary lines when *ping* starts and finishes.

Example

Ping a remote host and terminate using Ctrl-C after five packets are transmitted:

```
$ ping lpi.org
PING lpi.org (24.215.7.162) 56(84) bytes of data.
64 bytes from clark.lpi.org (24.215.7.162): icmp_seq=1 ttl=52 time=68.2 ms
64 bytes from clark.lpi.org (24.215.7.162): icmp_seq=2 ttl=52 time=65.8 ms
64 bytes from clark.lpi.org (24.215.7.162): icmp_seq=3 ttl=52 time=63.2 ms
64 bytes from clark.lpi.org (24.215.7.162): icmp_seq=4 ttl=52 time=65.8 ms
64 bytes from clark.lpi.org (24.215.7.162): icmp_seq=5 ttl=52 time=65.8 ms
64 bytes from clark.lpi.org (24.215.7.162): icmp_seq=6 ttl=52 time=63.6 ms
64 bytes from clark.lpi.org (24.215.7.162): icmp_seq=7 ttl=52 time=56.8 ms

--- lpi.org ping statistics ---
7 packets transmitted, 7 received, 0% packet loss, time 6016ms
rtt min/avg/max/mdev = 56.894/64.230/68.202/3.374 ms
```

telnet

Syntax

```
telnet [host] [port]
```

Description

Establish a connection to a *host* (either a system name or IP address) using *port*. If a specific port is omitted, the default port of 23 is assumed. If *host* is omitted, *telnet* goes into an interactive mode similar to FTP.

traceroute

Syntax

```
traceroute hostname
```

Description

Attempt to display the route over which packets must travel to reach a destination *hostname*. It is included here because it is mentioned in this Objective, but Objective 3 also requires *traceroute*. See Chapter 21 for more information.

whois

Syntax

```
whois target[@server]
```

Description

Pronounced, "who is," *whois* is a query/response protocol used to determine information about Internet resources. The information returned includes contact information, domain names, IP addresses, and DNS servers. Note that many websites are available for *whois* searches as well, particularly for checking on domain name availability.

Example

```
$ whois lpi.org
NOTICE: Access to .ORG WHOIS information is provided to assist persons in
determining the contents of a domain name registration record in the
Public Interest Registry registry database. The data in this record is provided
by Public Interest Registry for informational purposes only, and Public Interest
Registry does not guarantee its accuracy. This service is intended only for
query-based access. You agree that you will use this data only for lawful
purposes and that, under no circumstances will you use this data to:
(a) allow, enable, or otherwise support the transmission by e-mail, telephone,
or facsimile of mass unsolicited, commercial advertising or solicitations to
entities other than the data recipient's own existing customers; or (b) enable
high volume, automated, electronic processes that send queries or data to
the systems of Registry Operator or any ICANN-Accredited Registrar,
except as reasonably necessary to register domain names or modify existing
registrations. All rights reserved. Public Interest Registry reserves the right
to modify these terms at any time. By submitting this query, you agree
to abide by this policy.

Domain ID:D3725290-LROR
Domain Name:LPI.ORG
Created On:18-Feb-1999 05:00:00 UTC
```

```
Last Updated On:31-Oct-2008 17:00:45 UTC
Expiration Date:18-Feb-2011 05:00:00 UTC
Sponsoring Registrar:Tucows Inc. (R11-LROR)
Status:CLIENT TRANSFER PROHIBITED
Status:CLIENT UPDATE PROHIBITED
Registrant ID:tuIqxUrdqeRMHH1m
Registrant Name:DNS Admin
Registrant Organization:Linux Professional Institute Inc.
Registrant Street1:161 Bay Street, 27th Floor
Registrant Street2:
Registrant Street3:
Registrant City:Toronto
Registrant State/Province:ON
Registrant Postal Code:M5J2S1
Registrant Country:CA
Registrant Phone:+1.9163576625
Registrant Phone Ext.:
Registrant FAX:
Registrant FAX Ext.:
Registrant Email:dns@lpi.org
Admin ID:tujWL5NRmQ4MqjwW
Admin Name:DNS Admin
Admin Organization:Linux Professional Institute Inc.
Admin Street1:161 Bay Street, 27th Floor
Admin Street2:
Admin Street3:
Admin City:Toronto
Admin State/Province:ON
Admin Postal Code:M5J2S1
Admin Country:CA
Admin Phone:+1.9163576625
Admin Phone Ext.:
Admin FAX:
Admin FAX Ext.:
Admin Email:dns@lpi.org
Tech ID:tursNOD6OBDmUsSl
Tech Name:DNS Admin
Tech Organization:Linux Professional Institute Inc.
Tech Street1:161 Bay Street, 27th Floor
Tech Street2:
Tech Street3:
Tech City:Toronto
Tech State/Province:ON
Tech Postal Code:M5J2S1
Tech Country:CA
Tech Phone:+1.9163576625
Tech Phone Ext.:
Tech FAX:
Tech FAX Ext.:
Tech Email:dns@lpi.org
Name Server:NS.STARNIX.COM
Name Server:SERVER1.MOONGROUP.COM
```

20

Basic Network Configuration
(Topics 109.2 and 109.4)

A Linux system that is not connected to a network is a rare sight. Configuring a system for network access is one of the first things done within the normal installation process. This chapter covers the following Objectives:

Objective 2: Basic Network Configuration
Candidates should be able to view, change, and verify configuration settings and operational status for various network interfaces. This Objective includes manual and automatic configuration of interfaces and routing tables. This would include steps to add, start, stop, restart, delete, or reconfigure network interfaces by modifying the appropriate configuration files. It also means to change, view, or configure the routing table and to correct an improperly set default route manually. Candidates should be able to configure Linux as a DHCP client and a TCP/IP host and to debug problems associated with the network configuration. Weight: 4.

Objective 4: Configuring Client Side DNS
Candidates should be able to configure DNS on a client host. Weight: 2.

Objective 2: Basic Network Configuration and Objective 4: Configuring Client Side DNS

Linux distributions offer various automation and startup techniques for networks, but most of the essential commands and concepts are not distribution-dependent. The exam tests fundamental concepts and their relationships to one another as well as to system problems. These Objectives cover the configuration of IPv4 TCP/IP on common network interfaces, such as Ethernet.

Network Interfaces

A computer must contain at least one *network interface* to be considered part of a network. The network interface provides a communications link between the computer and external network hardware. This could mean typical network adapters such as Ethernet or Token Ring, point-to-point dial-up connections, parallel ports, wireless, or other networking forms.

Configuration files

The following files contain important information about your system's network configuration:

/etc/hosts

This file contains simple mappings between IP addresses and names and is used for name resolution. For very small private networks, */etc/hosts* may be sufficient for basic name resolution. For example, this file associates the local address 192.168.1.30 with the system *smp* and also with *smp.mydomain.com*:

```
127.0.0.1      localhost        localhost.localdomain
192.168.1.1    gate
192.168.1.30   smp smp.mydomain.com
```

/etc/nsswitch.conf

This file controls the sources used by various system library lookup functions, such as name resolution. It allows the administrator to configure the use of traditional local files (*/etc/hosts*, */etc/passwd*), an NIS server, or DNS. *nsswitch.conf* directly affects network configuration (among other things) by controlling how hostnames and other network parameters are resolved. For example, this fragment shows that local files are used for password, shadow password, group, and hostname resolution; for hostnames, DNS is used if a search of local files doesn't yield a result:

```
passwd:    files nisplus nis
shadow:    files nisplus nis
group:     files nisplus nis
hosts:     files dns nisplus nis
```

For more information, view the manpage with *man 5 nsswitch*. The *nsswitch.conf* file supersedes *host.conf*. In the majority of setups, this file does not need to be modified, as the defaults are usually sufficient.

/etc/host.conf

This file controls name resolution sources for pre-*glibc2* systems. It should contain:

```
order hosts,bind
multi on
```

This configuration has the resolver checking */etc/hosts* first for name resolution, then DNS. `multi on` enables multiple IP addresses for hosts. Newer Linux system libraries use */etc/nsswitch.conf* instead of */etc/host.conf*.

/etc/resolv.conf

This file controls the client-side portions of the DNS system, which is implemented in system library functions used by all programs to resolve system names. In particular, */etc/resolv.conf* specifies the IP addresses of DNS servers. For example:

```
nameserver 192.168.1.5
nameserver 192.168.250.2
```

Additional parameters are also available. For more information, view the man-page with *man 5 resolver*.

/etc/networks

Like */etc/hosts*, this file sets up equivalence between addresses and names, but here the addresses represent entire networks (and thus must be valid network addresses, ending in 0). The result is that you can use a symbolic name to refer to a network just as you would a specific host. This may be convenient (though not required) in NFS or routing configuration, for example, and will be shown in commands such as *netstat*. For example:

```
loopback    127.0.0.0
mylan       192.168.1.0
```

It's not unusual for */etc/networks* to be left blank.

You'll notice most of the previous configuration files concern themselves with mapping an IP address to aliases or names. This is not required for most network-enabled applications to work, as the operating system and network-enabled applications are really only concerned with the IP address for this level of data communication. The name lookups are there for us humans, who find it easier to remember names rather than numbers. Here is an example of what is going on "behind the scenes" when a web browser requests a web page from a remote server:

1. A user types *http://www.oreilly.com* into the browser address bar and hits Enter.

2. The system needs to resolve this hostname to an IP address in order to make the request. The file */etc/nsswitch.conf* (*/etc/host.conf* in pre-glibc2 systems) is consulted to determine what subsystems to ask and in what order to resolve this hostname. The default entry for hosts in */etc/nsswitch.conf* is usually:

```
hosts:   files dns
```

This tells the system to first look in files (*/etc/hosts*) and then query DNS.

3. If there is an entry in the file */etc/hosts* for *www.oreilly.com*, that IP address will be used to make this HTTP request. If not, then the second option is to query DNS.

4. The file */etc/resolv.conf* is consulted to determine the primary DNS to query. A DNS request is made to the primary DNS server. If a response is received (in the form of an IP address), that IP address is used to make the HTTP request. If a response is not received (either because the DNS server did not have an entry for that hostname or the DNS server did not respond to the request), then the next name server listed in */etc/resolv.conf* is queried. This process repeats until all name servers have been queried.

5. If all attempts at name resolution fail, the web browser will return an error.

As you can see, something as simple to the end user as typing a hostname into a web browser requires a number of steps behind the scenes. It's important to understand these steps and the order in which they occur for troubleshooting situations. It's an all too common occurrence for an end user to report, "The network is down!" when it's really just a matter of a bad entry in */etc/hosts* or a misconfigured DNS server.

On the Exam

Be familiar with all the files listed in this section; each contains specific information important for network setup. Watch for questions on */etc/host.conf*, which is not used in newer *glibc2* libraries.

Configuration commands

The commands listed in this section are used to establish, monitor, and troubleshoot a network configuration under Linux.

---

ifconfig

Syntax

```
ifconfig interface parameters
```

Description

Configure network interfaces. *ifconfig* is used to create and configure network interfaces and their parameters, usually at boot time. Without parameters, the interface and its configuration are displayed. If *interface* is also omitted, a list of all active interfaces and their configurations is displayed.

Frequently used parameters

address
  The interface's IP address.

netmask *mask*
  The interface's subnet mask.

---

up

Activate an interface (implied if *address* is specified).

down

Shut down the interface.

Example 1

Display all interfaces:

```
# ifconfig
eth0       Link encap:Ethernet   HWaddr 00:A0:24:D3:C7:21
           inet addr:192.168.1.30  Bcast:192.168.1.255  Mask:255.255.255.0
           UP BROADCAST RUNNING MULTICAST  MTU:1500  Metric:1
           RX packets:1521805 errors:37 dropped:0 overruns:0 frame:37
           TX packets:715468 errors:0 dropped:0 overruns:0 carrier:0
           collisions:1955 txqueuelen:100
           Interrupt:10 Base address:0xef00
lo         Link encap:Local Loopback
           inet addr:127.0.0.1  Mask:255.0.0.0
           UP LOOPBACK RUNNING  MTU:3924  Metric:1
           RX packets:366567 errors:0 dropped:0 overruns:0 frame:0
           TX packets:366567 errors:0 dropped:0 overruns:0 carrier:0
           collisions:0 txqueuelen:0
```

Example 2

Shut down *eth0*:

```
# ifconfig eth0 down
# ifconfig eth0
eth0       Link encap:Ethernet   HWaddr 00:A0:24:D3:C7:21
           inet addr:192.168.1.30  Bcast:192.168.1.255  Mask:255.255.255.0
           BROADCAST MULTICAST  MTU:1500  Metric:1
           RX packets:1521901 errors:37 dropped:0 overruns:0 frame:37
           TX packets:715476 errors:0 dropped:0 overruns:0 carrier:0
           collisions:1955 txqueuelen:100
           Interrupt:10 Base address:0xef00
```

Note in the emphasized line the lack of the UP indicator, which is present in Example 1. The missing UP indicates that the interface is down.

Example 3

Configure *eth0* from scratch:

```
# ifconfig eth0 192.168.1.100 netmask 255.255.255.0 broadcast 192.168.1.25
```

Although this is a perfectly valid command, network interfaces on Linux are rarely configured directly this way from the command line. It is much more common to store the network configuration options in a configuration file (often in the directory */etc/sysconfig/network-scripts*) and use a script file in */etc/init.d* to control the network interfaces. For example, on RPM-based systems such as CentOS, RedHat, or Fedora Linux, the configuration settings for *eth0* are stored in */etc/sysconfig/network-scripts/ifcfg-eth0* and the status of the network interfaces is changed by calling the script */etc/init.d/network*. The command *ifconfig* is most often used with no arguments to list information about the available network interfaces. However, it is useful to know this syntax, especially when you're working with different Linux distributions that store network configurations in different places.

ping

Syntax

```
ping [options] destination
```

Description

Send an ICMP `ECHO_REQUEST` datagram to *destination*, expecting an ICMP `ECHO_RESPONSE`. *ping* is frequently used to test basic network connectivity. See Chapter 19 for a more complete description.

route

Syntax

```
route [options]
route add [options and keywords] target
route del [options and keywords] target
```

Description

In the first form, display the IP routing table. In the second and third forms, respectively, add or delete routes to *target* from the table. *target* can be a numeric IP address, a resolvable name, or the keyword `default`. The *route* program is typically used to establish static routes to specific networks or hosts (such as the default gateway) after an interface is configured. On systems acting as routers, a potentially complex routing scheme can be established initially, but this is beyond the scope of the LPIC Level 1 Exams.

Frequently used options and keywords

-h
   Display a usage message.

-n
   Numeric mode; don't resolve hostnames.

-v
   Verbose output.

-C
   Display the kernel routing cache.

-F
   Display the kernel routing table (the default behavior without *add* or *delete* keywords).

-host
   Specify that *target* is a single host. Mutually exclusive with *-net*.

-net
   Specify that *target* is a network. Mutually exclusive with *-host*.

gw gateway
   IP packets for *target* are routed through the gateway, which must be reachable.

netmask mask
> Specify the *mask* of the route to be added. Often, the netmask is not required, because it can be determined to be class A, B, or C, depending on the *target* address.

When used to display routes, the following routing table columns are printed:

Destination
> The destination network or host.

Gateway
> The gateway address. If no gateway is set for the route, an asterisk (*) is displayed by default.

Genmask
> The netmask for the destination. 255.255.255.255 is used for a host, and 0.0.0.0 is used for the default route.

Route status flags
> ```
> ! Reject route.
> D Dynamically installed by daemon or redirect.
> G Use gateway.
> H Target is a host.
> M Modified from routing daemon or redirect.
> R Reinstate route for dynamic routing.
> U Route is up.
> ```

Metric
> The distance in hops to the target.

Ref
> Number of references to this route. This is displayed for compatibility with other route commands, but is not used in the Linux kernel.

Use
> A count of lookups for the route. Depending on the use of *-F* and *-C*, the Use is either route cache misses (*-F*) or hits (*-C*).

Iface
> The interface to which packets for this route are sent.

Example 1

Display the current routing table for a workstation:

```
# route
Kernel IP routing table
Destination  Gateway Genmask          Flags Met Ref Use Iface
192.168.1.30 *       255.255.255.255  UH    0   0     0 eth0
192.168.1.0  *       255.255.255.0    U     0   0     0 eth0
10.0.0.0     -       255.0.0.0        !     0   -     0 -
127.0.0.0    *       255.0.0.0        U     0   0     0 lo
default      gate    0.0.0.0          UG    0   0     0 eth0
```

In this example, the route to the local host 192.168.1.30 uses interface *eth0*. Note the mask 255.255.255.255 is used for host routes. The route to the local subnet 192.168.1.0 (with corresponding class C mask 255.255.255.0) is also through *eth0*. The route to 10.0.0.0 is rejected, as indicated by the ! flag. The class A loopback network route uses device *lo*. The last route shows the *default gateway* route, which is used when no others match. This default uses *eth0* to send data to router *gate*. The mask 0.0.0.0 is used for the default route.

Example 2

Display the current routing cache; the Metric (M) and Reference (R) columns are abbreviated here:

```
# route -C
Kernel IP routing cache
Source         Destination   Gateway       Flg M R Use Iface
smp            192.168.1.255 192.168.1.255 bl  0 0   1 eth0
192.168.1.102 192.168.1.255 192.168.1.255 ibl 0 0   0 lo
192.168.1.102 smp           smp           il  0 0   1 lo
192.168.1.50  smp           smp           il  0 0 224 lo
smp            192.168.1.102 192.168.1.102     0 1   0 eth0
smp            ns1.mynet.com gate              0 0   2 eth0
smp            192.168.1.50  192.168.1.50      0 1   0 eth0
localhost      localhost     localhost     1   0 0  15 lo
ns1.mynet.com  smp           smp           1   0 0   6 lo
smp            ns1.mynet.com gate              0 0   6 eth0
```

Example 3

Add the default gateway 192.168.1.1 via *eth0*:

```
# route add default gw 192.168.1.1 eth0
```

DHCP

The Dynamic Host Configuration Protocol (DHCP) is a protocol extension of the BOOTP protocol, which provides automated IP address assignment (among other things) to client systems on a network. It handles IP address allocation in one of three ways:

Dynamic allocation

In this scheme, a DHCP server maintains a preset list of IP addresses designated by the system administrator. IP addresses are assigned as clients request an address from the available addresses in the pool. The address can be used, or *leased*, for a limited period of time. The client must continually renegotiate the lease with the server to maintain use of the address beyond the allotted period. When the lease expires, the IP address is placed back into the pool for use by other requesting clients and a new IP address is assigned.

Manual allocation

The system administrator may wish to designate specific IP addresses to specific network interfaces (for example, to an Ethernet MAC address) while still using DHCP to deliver the address to the client. This allows the convenience of automated address setup and assures the same address each time.

Automatic allocation

This method assigns a permanent address to a client. Typically DHCP is used to assign a temporary address (either dynamically or statically assigned) to a client, but a DHCP server can allow an infinite lease time.

DHCP can be configured to assign not only the IP address to the client but also such things as name servers, gateways, and architecture-specific parameters. Here's an overview of how it works:

1. A DHCP client sends a broadcast message to the network to discover a DHCP server.

2. One or more DHCP servers respond to the request via their own broadcast messages, offering an IP address to the client.

3. The client chooses one of the servers and broadcasts an acknowledgment, requesting the chosen server's identity.

4. The selected server logs the connection with the client and responds with an acknowledgment and possibly additional information. All of the other servers do nothing, because the client declined their offer.

Subnets and relays

Because DHCP communications are initiated using broadcasts, they are normally confined to a single subnet. To accommodate DHCP clients and servers separated by one or more routers, a DHCP *relay* system can be established on subnets without DHCP servers. A relay system listens for DHCP client broadcasts, forwards them to a DHCP server on another subnet, and returns DHCP traffic back to the client. This configuration can centralize DHCP management in a large routed environment.

Leases

As already mentioned, when a client receives a dynamically assigned IP address from a DHCP server, the address is said to be *leased* for a finite duration. The length of a DHCP lease is configurable by the system administrator and typically lasts for one or more days. Shorter leases allow for faster turnover of addresses and are useful when the number of available addresses is small or when many transient systems (such as laptops) are being served. Longer leases reduce DHCP activity, thus reducing broadcast traffic on the network.

When a lease expires without being renegotiated by the client, it as assumed that the client system is unavailable, and the address is put back into the free pool of addresses. A lease may also be terminated by a client that no longer needs the IP address, in which case it is *released*. When this occurs, the DHCP server immediately places the IP address back in the free pool.

dhcpd

The DHCP server process is called *dhcpd*. It is typically started at boot time and listens for incoming DHCP request broadcasts. *dhcpd* can serve multiple subnets via multiple interfaces, serving a different pool of IP addresses to each.

dhcpd is configured using the text configuration file */etc/dhcpd.conf*, which contains one or more subnet declarations. These are text lines of the following form:

```
subnet network-address netmask subnet-mask {
    parameter...
    parameter...
```

```
   ...
}
```

Each subnet declaration encloses parameters for each subnet between curly braces. Parameters include one or more ranges of IP addresses to serve, lease times, and optional items such as gateways (routers), DNS servers, and so forth. Each parameter line is terminated with a semicolon. For example:

```
subnet 192.168.1.0 netmask 255.255.255.0 {
   range 192.168.1.200 192.168.1.204;
   default-lease-time 600;
   option subnet-mask 255.255.255.0;
   option broadcast-address 192.168.1.255;
   option routers 192.168.1.1;
   option domain-name-servers 192.168.1.25;
}
```

In this example, the private class C network 192.168.1.0 is served five IP addresses, 200 through 204. The default DHCP lease is 600 seconds (10 minutes). Options are also set for the subnet mask, broadcast address, router (or gateway), and DNS server. For full information on *dhcpd.conf*, see related manpages for *dhcpd(8)* and *dhcpd.conf(5)*.

The preceding option lines are not required to create a minimal DHCP setup that simply serves IP addresses. Details on the daemon follow.

dhcpd

Syntax

```
dhcpd [options] [interface [...]]
```

Description

Launch the DHCP server daemon. *dhcpd* requires that both its configuration file (*/etc/dhcpd.conf*) and its lease logfile (which by default is */var/state/dhcp/dhcpd.leases*, although many distributions use */var/lib/dhcp/dhcpd.leases*) exist. The daemon puts itself in the background and returns control to the calling shell.

Frequently used options

-cf config-file
> Use *config-file* instead of the default */etc/dhcpd.conf*.

-lf lease-file
> Use *lease-file* instead of the default to store lease information.

-q
> Use quiet mode. This option suppresses the default copyright message, keeping logfiles a little cleaner.

interface
> By default, *dhcpd* will attempt to listen for requests on every network interface that is configured up. It can be limited to specific network interfaces by including one or more interface names on the command line.

A full and detailed description of the configuration file syntax can be found in the *dhcpd.conf* manpage. When *dhcpd* runs, it sends output, including information on each transaction, to *syslogd*. For example, this series of four log entries in */var/log/messages* shows a successful exchange between *dhcpd* and a requesting DHCP client:

```
Apr 24 02:27:00 rh62 dhcpd: DHCPDISCOVER
    from 00:60:97:93:f6:8a via eth0
Apr 24 02:27:00 rh62 dhcpd: DHCPOFFER
    on 192.168.1.200 to 00:60:97:93:f6:8a via eth0
Apr 24 02:27:01 rh62 dhcpd: DHCPREQUEST
    for 192.168.1.200 from 00:60:97:93:f6:8a via eth0
Apr 24 02:27:01 rh62 dhcpd: DHCPACK
on 192.168.1.200 to 00:60:97:93:f6:8a via eth0
```

On the Exam

For the LPI Level 1 Exams, you should be familiar with both the manual and automatic network interface configuration, and how interfaces can be started, stopped, and configured.

A Standard Linux Network Configuration

A very common setup for a Linux system is to have a single Ethernet interface and be a member of a network, as either a client, a server, or both. Here are the network settings that must be configured in order for a Linux system to communicate via TCP/IP over an Ethernet network:

- A compatible Ethernet card must be installed and recognized by the kernel. See information about the commands *lsmod*, *lspci*, and *dmesg* in previous chapters for more information about hardware troubleshooting.

- An IP address and subnet mask must be assigned to the Ethernet interface (*eth0*). These can be assigned manually (static values saved in a configuration file) or assigned from a DHCP server on the local subnet. On RPM-based systems such as CentOS, Red Hat, and Fedora Linux, the network configuration file is */etc/sysconfig/network-scripts/ifcfg-eth0*. Values from this file are read by the startup script */etc/init.d/network*, which in turn calls the command *ifconfig* with the appropriate values.

- In order to communicate with other subnets, a default gateway route must be configured. This is the IP address of the device on the local network that will send your packets on to other networks. This may be a dedicated device, such as a router, or it may be a general-purpose computer (with multiple Ethernet cards) running routing software. A lower-end PC running Linux is often a good choice for a router in this instance. The default gateway route is defined in the file */etc/sysconfig/network*. This value is read by the startup script */etc/init.d/ network*, which in turn calls the *route* command to set this as the default gateway route.

- Finally, a default nameserver should be configured so applications can successfully resolve hostnames to IP addresses. As stated previously, this is defined in the file *etc/resolv.conf*.

If all of these settings are in place, your Linux system should be able to communicate successfully with other computers over a TCP/IP network.

21

Basic Network Troubleshooting (Topic 109.3)

Even the simplest of network installations will at times require troubleshooting. Every Linux system administrator needs to understand not only where to start the troubleshooting process but also what tools are available to aid in this endeavor. This chapter covers the following Objective:

Objective 3: Basic Network Troubleshooting
Candidates should be able to perform basic troubleshooting steps in diagnosing network connectivity issues and configuration. This Objective includes tools that show information about local computer configuration and the testing communication with computers on local network and remote connections. Some of these tools may also be used for network configuration, as discussed in the previous Objective. Candidates should be able to view, change, and verify configuration settings and operational status for various network interfaces. Weight: 4.

Objective 3: Basic Network Troubleshooting

One important part of an administrator's role is troubleshooting connectivity issues and tracking down sources of problems. Many of the tools introduced earlier in this book may also be used as troubleshooting tools to assist in this process. This objective revisits some of these commands and discusses how they may be used as diagnostic resources in addition to configuration resources.

ping

Syntax

```
ping [options] destination
```

Description

Send an ICMP `ECHO_REQUEST` datagram to *destination*, expecting an ICMP `ECHO_RESPONSE`. *ping* is frequently used to test basic network connectivity. See "Objective 1: Fundamentals of Internet Protocols" on page 369 for a more complete description.

host

Syntax

```
host [options] name [server]
```

Description

Look up the system with IP address or *name* on the DNS *server*.

Frequently used options

-l

List the entire domain, dumping all hosts registered on the DNS server (this can be very long).

-v

Set verbose mode to view output.

Example 1

```
$ host oreilly.com
oreilly.com has address 208.201.239.37
oreilly.com has address 208.201.239.36
```

Example 2

```
$ host -v oreilly.com
Trying "oreilly.com"
;; ->>HEADER<<- opcode: QUERY, status: NOERROR, id: 60189
;; flags: qr rd ra; QUERY: 1, ANSWER: 2, AUTHORITY: 0, ADDITIONAL: 0

;; QUESTION SECTION:
;oreilly.com.                    IN      A

;; ANSWER SECTION:
oreilly.com.           877      IN      A      208.201.239.100
oreilly.com.           877      IN      A      208.201.239.101

Received 61 bytes from 192.168.1.220#53 in 0 ms
Trying "oreilly.com"
;; ->>HEADER<<- opcode: QUERY, status: NOERROR, id: 1045
;; flags: qr rd ra; QUERY: 1, ANSWER: 0, AUTHORITY: 1, ADDITIONAL: 0

;; QUESTION SECTION:
;oreilly.com.                    IN      AAAA

;; AUTHORITY SECTION:
oreilly.com. 3577 IN SOA nsautha.oreilly.com. \
        nic-tc.oreilly.com. 86 600 1800 604800
```

```
Received 80 bytes from 192.168.1.220#53 in 0 ms
Trying "oreilly.com"
;; ->>HEADER<<- opcode: QUERY, status: NOERROR, id: 18547
;; flags: qr rd ra; QUERY: 1, ANSWER: 2, AUTHORITY: 0, ADDITIONAL: 2

;; QUESTION SECTION:
;oreilly.com.                   IN      MX

;; ANSWER SECTION:
oreilly.com.          3577      IN      MX      20 smtp1.oreilly.com.
oreilly.com.          3577      IN      MX      20 smtp2.oreilly.com.

;; ADDITIONAL SECTION:
smtp1.oreilly.com.    3577      IN      A       209.204.146.22
smtp2.oreilly.com.    3577      IN      A       216.204.211.22

Received 105 bytes from 192.168.1.220#53 in 0 ms
```

traceroute

Syntax

```
traceroute [options] destination
```

Description

Display the route that packets take to reach *destination*, showing intermediate gateways (routers). There is no direct way to make this determination, so *traceroute* uses a trick to obtain as much information as it can. By using the time-to-live (TTL) field in the IP header, *traceroute* stimulates error responses from gateways. The time-to-live field specifies the maximum number of gateway hops until the packet should expire. That number is decremented at each gateway hop, with the result that all packets will die at some point and stop roaming the Internet. To get the first gateway in the route, *traceroute* sets the time-to-live parameter to 1. The first gateway in the route to *destination* decrements the counter, and finding a zero result, reports an ICMP TIME_EXCEEDED message back to the sending host. The second gateway is identified by setting the initial time-to-live value to 2, and so on. This continues until a PORT_UNREACHABLE message is returned, indicating that the host has been contacted. To account for the potential for multiple gateways at any one hop count, each probe is sent three times.

The display consists of lines showing each gateway, numbered for the initial time-to-live value. If no response is seen from a particular gateway, an asterisk is printed. This happens for gateways that don't return "time exceeded" messages, or do return them but set a very low time-to-live on the response. Transit times for each probe are also printed.

Frequently used options

-f *ttl*
> Set the initial probe's time-to-live value to *ttl*, instead of 1.

-n
> Display numeric addresses instead of names.

-v
> Use verbose mode.

-w secs

Set the timeout on returned ICMP packets to *secs*, instead of 5.

Example

```
$ traceroute lpi.org
traceroute to lpi.org (24.215.7.162), 30 hops max, 40 byte packets
1 96.64.11.1 (96.64.11.1) 12.689 ms 5.018 ms 9.861 ms
2 ge-1-28-ur01.east.tn.knox.comcast.net (68.85.206.181) \
                              8.712 ms * 10.868 ms
3 te-8-1-ar01.bluelight.tn.knox.comcast.net (68.86.136.30) \
                              15.109 ms 6.932 ms 24.996 ms
4 * te-0-8-0-4-crs01.b0atlanta.ga.atlanta.comcast.net (68.85.232.97) \
                              41.966 ms 51.914 ms
5 pos-1-4-0-0-cr01.atlanta.ga.ibone.comcast.net (68.86.90.121) \
                              38.775 ms 26.511 ms 32.650 ms
6 68.86.86.86 (68.86.86.86) 41.428 ms 40.369 ms 46.387 ms
7 75.149.230.74 (75.149.230.74) 56.789 ms 29.051 ms 28.835 ms
8 xe-5-3-0.chi10.ip4.tinet.net (89.149.185.37) 84.556 ms \
                              123.707 ms 123.579 ms
9 peer1-gw.ip4.tinet.net (77.67.71.22) 70.550 ms 39.203 ms 39.795 ms
10 oc48-po1-0.tor-1yg-cor-1.peer1.net (216.187.114.142) \
                              52.049 ms 80.272 ms 68.667 ms
11 10ge.xe-0-0-0.tor-151f-cor-1.peer1.net (216.187.114.134) \
                              67.809 ms 45.667 ms 45.157 ms
12 oc48-po7-0.tor-151f-dis-1.peer1.net (216.187.114.149) \
                              97.586 ms 48.451 ms 45.559 ms
13 peer1-tor-gw.colosseum (66.199.142.250) \
                              56.156 ms 93.090 ms 78.800 ms
14 core-main.mountaincable.net (24.215.3.185) \
                              59.369 ms 52.889 ms 111.326 ms
15 24.215.7.110 (24.215.7.110) 50.487 ms 114.975 ms 44.655 ms
16 clark.lpi.org (24.215.7.162) 54.705 ms 84.838 ms 46.562 ms
```

In this example, there are 15 hops to *http://www.lpi.org*, reached with a time-to-live value of 16. All three probes of all time-to-live counts are successful.

netstat

Syntax

```
netstat [options]
```

Description

Depending on options, *netstat* displays network connections, routing tables, interface statistics, masqueraded connections, and multicast memberships. Much of this is beyond the scope of the LPIC Level 1 Exams, but you must be aware of the command and its basic use.

Frequently used options

-c

Continuous operation. This option yields a *netstat* display every second until interrupted with Ctrl-C.

-i

Display a list of interfaces.

-n

Numeric mode. Display addresses instead of host, port, and usernames.

-p

Programs mode. Display the process ID (PID) and process name.

-r

Routing mode. Display the routing table in the format of the *route* command.

-v

Verbose mode.

Examples

Display the interfaces table and statistics (the example output is truncated):

```
# netstat -i
Kernel Interface table
Iface MTU   Met   RX-OK RX-ERR RX-DRP RX-OVR  TX-OK
eth0  1500 0    1518801    37      0      0 713297
lo    3924 0     365816     0      0      0 365816
```

To show all current connections without resolving hostnames and protocol names:

```
# netstat -an --tcp
Active Internet connections (servers and established)

Proto Recv-Q Send-Q Local Address       Foreign Address       State
tcp        0      0 0.0.0.0:34031       0.0.0.0:*             LISTEN
tcp        0      0 0.0.0.0:6000        0.0.0.0:*             LISTEN
tcp        0      0 127.0.0.1:631       0.0.0.0:*             LISTEN
tcp        1      0 10.41.81.148:59667  10.41.0.47:3268       CLOSE_WAIT
tcp        0      0 10.41.81.148:45449  64.4.34.61:1863       ESTABLISHED
tcp        0      0 10.41.81.148:53284  10.41.0.32:143        ESTABLISHED
tcp        0      0 10.41.81.148:33722  10.41.0.38:22         ESTABLISHED
tcp        0      0 10.41.81.148:42261  74.125.77.83:443      ESTABLISHED
tcp        0      0 10.41.81.148:54879  83.85.96.153:3490     ESTABLISHED
tcp        0      0 10.41.81.148:42262  74.125.77.83:443      ESTABLISHED
tcp        0      0 10.41.81.148:34054  195.86.128.44:22      ESTABLISHED
tcp        0      0 10.41.81.148:46150  212.100.160.43:5222   ESTABLISHED
tcp        0      0 :::6000             :::*                  LISTEN
udp        0      0 127.0.0.1:46958     0.0.0.0:*
udp        0      0 0.0.0.0:34031       0.0.0.0:*
udp        0      0 0.0.0.0:631         0.0.0.0:*
```

To show the PID and name of the process to which each socket belongs, to identify what could be causing a problem:

```
$ netstat -p

(Not all processes could be identified, non-owned process info
 will not be shown, you would have to be root to see it all.)

Active Internet connections (w/o servers)
Proto Recv-Q Send-Q Local Address Foreign Address \
                        State PID/Program name
```

```
tcp 0 0 server01.domain.:60032 ew-in-f18.1e100.n:https \
                          ESTABLISHED 4698/firefox-bin
tcp 0 0 server01.domain.:40343 messaging.n:xmpp-client \
                          ESTABLISHED 4680/pidgin
tcp 0 0 server01.domain.:53533 srdc-mail-01 :imap \
                          ESTABLISHED 4679/evolution
tcp 0 0 server01.domain.:40292 195.86.25.214:http \
                          ESTABLISHED 4698/firefox-bin
tcp 0 0 server01.domain.:60209 ew-in-f147.1e100.n:http \
                          ESTABLISHED 4698/firefox-bin
tcp 0 0 server01.domain.:60031 ew-in-f18.1e100.n:https \
                          TIME_WAIT -
tcp 0 0 server01.domain.:55647 ew-in-f83.1e100.n:https \
                          ESTABLISHED 4698/firefox-bin
tcp 0 0 server01.domain.:35718 ew-in-f102.1e100.n:http \
                          ESTABLISHED 4698/firefox-bin
tcp 0 0 server01.domain.:57265 sn1msg2010707.phx.:1863 \
                          TIME_WAIT - netstat
tcp 0 0 server01.domain.:58931 195.86.25.214:http \
                          ESTABLISHED 4698/firefox-bin
tcp 0 0 server01.domain.:47146 backup2. :ssh \
                          ESTABLISHED 5113/ssh
tcp 0 0 server01.domain.:52707 g199040.upc-g.chel:4130 \
                          ESTABLISHED 4682/skype
tcp 0 0 server01.domain.:56608 bay5-terminal.bay5:1863 \
                          ESTABLISHED 4680/pidgin
tcp 1 0 server01.domain.:51980 server02 :3268 \
                          CLOSE_WAIT 4709/evolution-data
tcp 0 0 server01.domain.:36070 195.86.25.214:http \
                          ESTABLISHED 4698/firefox-bin
tcp 0 0 server01.domain.:60212 ew-in-f147.1e100.n:http \
                          ESTABLISHED 4698/firefox-bin
```

On the Exam

While the creation of complete network management scripts from scratch is beyond the scope of the LPIC Level 1 Exams, you must be familiar with these commands individually, their functions, how they are used, and when to use them.
For example, you must be familiar with *route* and its use in establishing routes to
the loopback device, the localhost, and the gateway machine, and the creation of
the default gateway route. A general understanding of the routing table display is
also required. Questions may ask you to determine the cause of a network problem
based on the routing configuration (such as a missing default route).

Common Manual Network Interface Tasks

Network interfaces are established in the kernel at boot time by probing Ethernet
hardware. As a result, these interfaces always exist unless the hardware or kernel
module is removed. The interfaces are transient and exist only when they are in use.

To list interface parameters, use *ifconfig* with the interface name:

```
# ifconfig eth0
eth0       Link encap:Ethernet  HWaddr 00:A0:24:D3:C7:21
           inet addr:192.168.1.30  Bcast:192.168.1.255  Mask:255.255.255.0
           UP BROADCAST MULTICAST  MTU:1500  Metric:1
           RX packets:1857128 errors:46 dropped:0 overruns:0 frame:46
           TX packets:871709 errors:0 dropped:0 overruns:0 carrier:0
           collisions:2557 txqueuelen:100
           Interrupt:10 Base address:0xef00
```

If you run *ifconfig* without any parameters, it displays all active interfaces, including the loopback interface *lo* and perhaps a PPP interface if a modem is dialed into a service provider or a wireless interface such as *ath0* if you have an active wireless card.

To shut down a network interface that is currently running, simply use *ifconfig* with the *down* keyword:

```
# ifconfig eth0 down
```

When the interface goes down, any routes associated with it are removed from the routing table. For a typical system with a single Ethernet interface, this means that the routes to both the interface and the default gateway will be lost. Therefore, to start a previously configured network interface, *ifconfig* is used with *up*, followed by the necessary *route* commands. For example:

```
# ifconfig eth0 up
# route add -host 192.168.1.30 eth0
# route add default gw 192.168.1.1 eth0
```

To reconfigure interface parameters, follow those same procedures and include the changes. For example, to change to a different IP address, the address is specified when bringing up the interface and adding the interface route:

```
# ifconfig eth0 down
# ifconfig eth0 192.168.1.60 up
# route add -host 192.168.1.60 eth0
# route add default gw 192.168.1.1 eth0
```

Your distribution probably supplies scripts to handle some of these chores. For example, Red Hat systems come with scripts such as *ifup* and *ifdown*, which handle all the details necessary to get an interface and its routes up and running, based on configuration files in */etc/sysconfig/network-scripts/*.

On the Exam

Be prepared to answer questions on the use of *ifconfig* and *route* for basic interface manipulation. Also remember that scripts that use these commands, both manually and automatically, are usually available at boot time.

---

dig

dig is the most complete and powerful DNS utility and is available in most Unix/Linux systems. The tool will use the default nameservers defined in the *resolv.conf* file:

```
# dig www.oreilly.com

; <<>> DiG 9.4.3-P1 <<>> www.oreilly.com
;; global options:  printcmd
;; Got answer:
;; ->>HEADER<<- opcode: QUERY, status: NOERROR, id: 17863
;; flags: qr rd ra; QUERY: 1, ANSWER: 3, AUTHORITY: 0, ADDITIONAL: 0

;; QUESTION SECTION:
;www.oreilly.com.            IN    A


;; ANSWER SECTION:
www.oreilly.com.    161    IN    CNAME    oreilly.com.
oreilly.com.        448    IN    A        100.201.239.100
oreilly.com.        448    IN    A        100.201.239.101

;; Query time: 4 msec
;; SERVER: 100.100.0.43#53(100.100.0.43)
;; WHEN: Mon Dec 14 14:48:55 2009
;; MSG SIZE  rcvd: 79
```

Sometimes it's also useful to query nameservers other than the default. This can be done without changing the default address in *resolv.conf*, by using @ plus the nameserver's IP address:

```
# dig @10.20.10.10 www.oreilly.com

; <<>> DiG 9.4.3-P1 <<>> www.oreilly.com
;; global options:  printcmd
;; Got answer:
;; ->>HEADER<<- opcode: QUERY, status: NOERROR, id: 17863
;; flags: qr rd ra; QUERY: 1, ANSWER: 3, AUTHORITY: 0, ADDITIONAL: 0

;; QUESTION SECTION:
;www.oreilly.com.            IN    A

;; ANSWER SECTION:
www.oreilly.com.    161    IN    CNAME    oreilly.com.
oreilly.com.        448    IN    A    100.201.239.100
oreilly.com.        448    IN    A    100.201.239.101

;; Query time: 4 msec
;; SERVER: 10.20.10.10#53(10.20.10.10)
;; WHEN: Mon Dec 14 14:48:55 2009
;; MSG SIZE  rcvd: 79
```

If PTR (reverse) records are missing, this can affect many network services that rely on these records, such as SSH. PTR records provide a way to map an IP address back to a fully qualified domain name. All reverse lookups should be configured when adding new addresses or changing addresses on the server. *dig* can be used to validate the presence of the PTR records:

```
# dig -x 208.201.239.100

; <<>> DiG 9.4.3-P1 <<>> -x 208.201.239.100
;; global options:  printcmd
;; Got answer:
;; ->>HEADER<<- opcode: QUERY, status: NOERROR, id: 28685
;; flags: qr rd ra; QUERY: 1, ANSWER: 1, AUTHORITY: 0, ADDITIONAL: 0

;; QUESTION SECTION:
;100.239.201.208.in-addr.arpa.     IN     PTR

;; ANSWER SECTION:
100.239.201.208.in-addr.arpa. 3600 IN     PTR     oreilly.com.

;; Query time: 298 msec
;; SERVER: 10.20.10.10#53(10.20.10.10)
;; WHEN: Mon Dec 14 15:01:01 2009
;; MSG SIZE  rcvd: 71
```

The mail exchange (MX) record for a domain defines the server that accepts SMTP email for that domain. To search for the MX records for a specific domain, use:

```
# dig mx www.oreilly.com

; <<>> DiG 9.4.3-P1 <<>> mx oreilly.com
;; global options:  printcmd
;; Got answer:
;; ->>HEADER<<- opcode: QUERY, status: NOERROR, id: 31415
;; flags: qr rd ra; QUERY: 1, ANSWER: 2, AUTHORITY: 0, ADDITIONAL: 0

;; QUESTION SECTION:
;oreilly.com.              IN     MX

;; ANSWER SECTION:
oreilly.com.        3600    IN    MX     20 smtp10.oreilly.com.
oreilly.com.        3600    IN    MX     20 smtp20.oreilly.com.

;; Query time: 153 msec
;; SERVER: 10.20.10.10#53(10.20.10.10)
;; WHEN: Mon Dec 14 15:08:19 2009
;; MSG SIZE  rcvd: 73
```

On the Exam

Be familiar with the basics of the *dig* syntax and how it's used to query DNS information.

22

Security (Topic 110.1)

A system is only as secure as the administrator. Although some operating systems may claim better security than others, this is always the "out-of-the-box" type of security. Any system, no matter how secure initially, can become insecure if poorly maintained. It is the responsibility of the system administrator to take an active hand in security, and address both active and passive threats. As with most things, the first step is knowledge. Understanding how your system works and what tools are available is fundamental to securing your system. This chapter covers the first Objective of Topic 110:

Objective 1: Perform Security Administration Tasks
 Candidates should know how to review system configuration to ensure host security in accordance with local security policies. This includes topics such as SUID/SGID bits, password aging and good password policy, discovery tools such as *nmap, netstat,* and *lsof,* limiting user actions, and giving select users elevated privileges. Weight: 3.

Objective 1: Perform Security Administration Tasks

Since everything in Linux is a file, filesystem level security is a core concept that must be understood and implemented properly. The standard Unix security model (which most Linux file systems adopt) is a relatively simple permissions-based model, but it is sufficient for most permissions needs. For more information on the details of the Unix permissions-based security model, refer to the section "Changing access modes" on page 182.

When a user executes a program in Linux, that program is spawned as a subprocess (or subshell) of the user's current shell. This subprocess is known as a *child process*, and is defined in depth in the section "Objective 5: Create, Monitor, and Kill Processes" on page 107. From a security standpoint, the important thing to remember about child processes is that they inherit the security context of the parent process. So if the user *adam* executes a program, that program will have access to the same files and directories that the user *adam* normally has (no more, and no less).

However, this is not always a desirable situation. One of the criticisms of the standard Linux security model is that it is not fine-grained enough, i.e., you're either a regular user with little or no privileges, or you are the superuser (root) with all privileges. Often, we want the ability to elevate certain users to superuser status for short periods of time, or to execute certain commands, or we want certain commands themselves to execute with elevated privileges, regardless of who executes them. There are ways to handle all of these situations in Linux: SUID and SGID bits, and the commands *sudo* and *su*.

"Changing access modes" on page 182 describes the different security modes that are available to files in Linux. These are normally read, write, or execute. One of the "special" modes available is *s*. When the mode *s* is assigned to owner permissions on an executable file, we say that file has the SUID (or SetUID) bit set. When the mode *s* is assigned to group permissions on an executable file, we say that file has the SGID (or SetGID) bit set.

SUID means that no matter the security context of the parent process running the executable, the executable will run with the security context of the owner of the executable file. This is most commonly used to give regular users the ability to run programs that require root access without actually giving them access to the root account. So if an executable file has the SUID bit set and the file is owned by root, then no matter who executes that file, the resulting process will have root-level permissions.

An example of this is the *ping* command. *ping* is used to send ICMP packets to hosts on a network and report back on replies. It is primarily a network testing tool, and is a standard part of every operating system that supports TCP/IP. *Ping* needs the ability to open a raw network socket in order to do its job, and that kind of low-level access is reserved for the root user. However, it's such a useful and ubiquitous tool, it's common to want to make it available to all users on a system. So in many Linux distributions, *ping* has the SUID bit set by default. Any user that runs the *ping* command will run it in the security context of the root user.

Here is what a directory entry for *ping* looks like:

```
$ ls -l /bin/ping
-rwsr-xr-x 1 root root 42360 2008-09-26 01:02 /bin/ping
```

The **s** in the user section of the file security setting means that the SUID bit is set.

SGID works in the same way, but for group ownership instead of user ownership.

The (In)Security of SUID

Although SUID is a useful option when it comes to delegating roles to nonroot users, its potential security vulnerabilities should not be overlooked. A program marked with the SUID bit and owned by root will run as root. Everything that that program is able to do will be done as the root user. This has large implications for the overall security of a system. Think of this example: *vi* is a common editor that is found on most Linux systems. If */bin/vi* is SUID, every user who edits any file with *vi* will have the privileges of the root user, meaning that any user could edit *any* file on the system.

This is the kind of thing that makes SUID so potentially dangerous. There is a situation worse than being able to edit any file as root: spawning a subshell from an SUID program. We can use *vi* as our example here again. The editor *vi* allows you to issue a command to spawn a subshell while you are in the editor. We know that a child process inherits the security context of the parent process. So if *vi* is SUID and it spawns an interactive shell child process, that interactive shell has a security context of *root*. So the simple act of making */bin/vi* SUID has given all users on the system an easy way to access an interactive shell prompt as the root user, completely undermining all other security protocols that might be in place.

Because of this potentially dangerous situation, a good system administrator must be aware of what programs on his system have the SUID and/or SGID bit set. The *find* command (described in depth in Chapter 6) has an option to search for files based on their permissions. Here is an example:

```
# find /bin -perm -4000 -type f
/bin/mount
/bin/su
/bin/ping
/bin/ping6
/bin/umount
/bin/fusermount
```

The *-perm -4000* option to *find* says, "Only display files that have the SUID bit set." The number 4000 is the octal representation of the security mode for a file. Reading from right to left, the first 0 is for "other" permissions, the next 0 is for "group" the third 0 is for "owner," and the 4 represents SUID. An equivalent way to write this using symbolic modes instead of the octal representation is *-perm –u=s*, as in "find all files that have the 's' bit set in the user mode section."

It is important to understand why some programs have the SUID bit set. Some programs (such as *ping*) are not required by the operating system, and it is therefore safe to remove the SUID bit from them. Some programs (such as *passwd*) need to be SUID to ensure they function correctly on the operating system (if you remove the SUID bit from the *passwd* command, then users cannot change their own passwords). If the SUID bit is not required in your situation, remove it:

```
# ls -l /bin/ping
-rwsr-xr-x 1 root root 42360 2008-09-26 01:02 /bin/ping
# chmod -s /bin/ping
# ls -l /bin/ping
-rwxr-xr-x 1 root root 42360 2008-09-26 01:02 /bin/ping
#
```

Now only the superuser will be able to use the *ping* command.

In addition to the SUID and SGID bit, the commands *su* and *sudo* can be used to elevate the privileges of a regular user.

su

Syntax

```
su [OPTION]... [-] [USER [ARG]...]
```

Description

The *su* command (short for *substitute user*) allows you to run a shell with substitute user and group IDs. It is most commonly used to allow a normal user to "become" the root user (assuming they know the root password). It is also used by the root user to "become" a regular user.

Frequently used options

-

> Make the shell that is spawned a login shell (i.e., process *.bash_profile* and set appropriate login environment variables, such as *$PATH*)

-cCOMMAND

> Pass a single command to the shell, useful for one-line commands that need to be run as *root*.

Examples

A normal user becoming root:

```
$ whoami
adam
$ su -
Password: <root password given here>
# whoami
root
```

Running a command as the root user:

```
$ wc -l /etc/shadow
wc: /etc/shadow: Permission denied
$ su -c wc -l "/etc/shadow"
Password: <root password given here>
48 /etc/shadow
```

Root becoming a regular user:

```
# whoami
root
# su - adam
$ whoami
adam
```

The - (or *-l*) option to *su* determines whether or not the new shell is a login shell. The most obvious impact of this decision is the *$PATH* variable. The most common usage of *su* is for a regular user to become the root user, to enable that user to run a command or perform a task that only *root* can do. By default, the *$PATH* environment variable contains different directories for the root user than for regular users. Specifically, the directories */sbin* and */usr/sbin* store binary programs that only the superuser should run. Regular users can read these directories, but it doesn't make sense to have those directories in a regular user's *$PATH*, because they will never need to use them.

If a regular user uses the command *su* to become root, the *$PATH* environment variable does not change, because this is not a login shell. This means that the directories */sbin* and */usr/ sbin* are not in that user's *$PATH*. This is often a source of confusion for new system administrators. Note the following example:

```
$ whoami
adam
$ su
Password: <root password given here>
# fdisk -l /dev/sda
bash: fdisk: command not found
# which fdisk
/usr/bin/which: no fdisk in
(/usr/kerberos/sbin:/usr/kerberos/bin:/usr/local/bin:/bin:/usr/bin:/home/adam/bin)
# exit
$ su -
Password: <root password given here>
# fdisk -l /dev/sda
Disk /dev/sda: 200.0 GB, 200049647616 bytes
....etc....
# which fdisk
/sbin/fdisk
# echo $PATH
/usr/kerberos/sbin:/usr/kerberos/bin:/usr/local/sbin:/usr/local/bin:\
/sbin:/bin:/usr/sbin:/usr/bin:/root/bin
```

Initially, the *fdisk* command by itself did not work because it was not in the *$PATH* variable. Once the user returned to her user shell and used *su* to become *root*, the *$PATH* environment variable then contained the */sbin* and */usr/sbin* directories, so *fdisk* was found.

sudo

Syntax

```
sudo [OPTION]... [-a auth_type] [-c class] [-p prompt] [-u username]
```

Description

sudo (substitute *u*ser *do*) allows a permitted user to execute a command as the superuser or another user, as specified in the */etc/sudoers* file.

Frequently used options

-b

Run the given command in the background.

*-u*USERNAME

Attempt to run the command as user USERNAME instead of root.

The *sudo* command lives somewhere between SUID and *su*. *sudo* is used when you want to give certain users (or groups of users) access to run certain commands with elevated privileges (usually as *root*). *Sudo* is extremely useful for a number of reasons:

- You don't have to hand out the root password to people just so they can run a few commands.
- It logs every command (completed and attempted).

- In the */etc/sudoers* file, you can limit its use by user account, by group, by machine, or by pathname.
- The design of */etc/sudoers* is such that you can replicate it across multiple systems without modification of the file.

The */etc/sudoers* configuration file is a standard text file (like most other Linux configuration files), but the syntax for the rules that define the behavior of *sudo* is formatted in Extended Backus-Naur Form (EBNF), which is a way to describe the grammar of a language. This is relatively unique to the Linux configuration file world, so your */etc/sudoers* file will look quite a bit different than other configuration files you are used to. Because of the security implications of *sudo*, and the somewhat challenging format of the file itself, it is recommended that the command *visudo* be used to edit */etc/sudoers* instead of editing the file directly. *visudo* will not only make a backup copy of the */etc/sudoers* file for editing (replacing the previous version of */etc/sudoers* when the backup copy is saved), but it also does syntax checking of the format of the file, warning you if the syntax is incorrect. If you prefer an editor other than *vi*, just make sure your *$EDITOR* environment variable contains the path to your preferred editor, and *visudo* will invoke that editor instead of *vi*.

On the Exam

The configuration options available in */etc/sudoers* can be very complicated. You will not be required to answer questions about every possible option on the LPI exams. You should know what *sudo* is for and some example command-line usage, and have a general idea of what the */etc/sudoers* file should look like.

Example 1

A simple */etc/sudoers* file:

```
# Format is:
# user     MACHINE=COMMANDS
#
# The COMMANDS section may have other options added to it.
#
Defaults     requiretty,passwd_timeout=10
# Allows members of the users group to mount and unmount the cdrom as root
%users  ALL=/sbin/mount /mnt/cdrom, /sbin/umount /mnt/cdrom
# Allow the user adam to run the dumpe2fs command on any locally attached
# disk using scsi emulation (/dev/sd*) on the computer 'fileserv',
# don't prompt for a password
adam    fileserv=NOPASSWD: /sbin/dumpe2fs /dev/sd*
```

The *NOPASSWD* option will allow the user *adam* to run the *dumpe2fs* command without being prompted for a password. Normally, *sudo* will prompt a user for his password (not the root password! If the user knew the root password, he wouldn't need *sudo*, would he?). Once the user's password is given correctly, *sudo* will cache the password and not ask again for a default of five minutes (configurable in the */etc/sudoers* file). Setting the *NOPASSWD* option allows the *sudo* command to be called from *cron* and other noninteractive, scripted situations.

The detailed logging that *sudo* offers by default is another reason why it is so popular. It is a common scenario to have multiple people acting as system administrators in a corporate environment. If all of these people log in as *root* to perform maintenance, there is no way to tell exactly which user was logged in as *root* and ran what command at a certain time. *sudo* handles this for you. It is good practice to use *sudo* to run superuser commands when you are in a shared administrator environment.

Example 2

A sample log line from *sudo*:

```
Dec 4 15:07:20 fileserv sudo: adam : TTY=pts/0 ; PWD=/sbin ; USER=root ; \
COMMAND=/sbin/dumpe2fs /dev/sda3
```

By default, *sudo* uses the *syslog* service to log all events. Depending upon your *syslog* configuration, these events will probably be logged to either */var/log/messages* or */var/log/secure*.

sudo will also log instances when a user attempts to run a command and is denied, shown next.

Example 3

Sudo denying access to user *joe*, who tried to run *sudo /bin/ls /tmp*:

```
Dec 4 15:27:29 fileserv sudo: joe : user NOT in sudoers ; TTY=pts/0 ; \
PWD=/home/joe ; USER=root ; COMMAND=/bin/ls /tmp
```

Other important things to remember about *sudo*:

- Be sure you are giving the exact path to applications in the */etc/sudoers* file. The *visudo* command will give you an error if you try to use relative path names.
- Be aware of commands that spawn subshells! This is the same issue that was discussed earlier with regards to SUID programs and subshells. A subshell (or child process) will always inherit the security context of the parent process. So if you have a line in */etc/sudoers* that looks like this:

  ```
  adam  ALL=NOPASSWD: /bin/vi
  ```

  then the user "adam" will be able to run */bin/vi* as root. By typing !bash in a *vi* session, adam will have an interactive shell as root. If you are in a situation where you need to let non-root users edit protected files, use the command *sudoedit* (an alias to "*sudo –e*"). This tells *sudo* that a file needs to be edited. The *sudo* command will make a temporary copy of the file and open an editor in the security context of the user (not root). Once the temporary file is saved, *sudo* will copy the temporarily file over the original file. This bypasses the root subshell dilemma.
- The file */etc/sudoers* can be a little daunting at first, but remember it was designed to allow you to have one copy of */etc/sudoers* work across multiple servers. If this is not your situation, you can follow the simple examples above to create and maintain an */etc/sudoers* file that is a little easier to read.

User IDs and Passwords

Users in the Unix world are most commonly referred to by their usernames, but that is not how the underlying operating system sees them. Every user on a system is assigned a user ID (UID) that uniquely identifies that user. UIDs are integers ranging from 0 to 65535. UID 0 is reserved for the superuser (commonly named *root*, but the name can in fact be anything, as long as the UID is 0). Convention dictates that "system" users (user accounts that represent system processes, not actual human beings) have UIDs below 100.

Because everything in Unix is a file, the file security permissions are of utmost importance. The owner and group owner of a file is stored in the inode (index node) at the filesystem level. This is stored as the UID integer, not as the username. To see an example of this, do a long directory listing on a directory where some files are owned by users that no longer exist on the system:

```
# cd /var/spool/mail/
# ls -l
total 1295140
-rw-rw---- 1 adamh      mail          0 Jan  6 11:04 adamh
-rw-rw---- 1 alex       mail   86311334 Jan  8 06:27 alex
-rw-rw---- 1      2047 mail          0 Dec  2  2006 alice
-rw-rw---- 1      2003 mail    1600945 Jan  7  2009 bob
-rw-rw---- 1      2080 mail      95086 Sep  9  2008 carol
```

In this example, we are looking in the directory */var/spool/mail*, where the mail spool files for each user are stored, with filenames corresponding to user account names. The files *adamh* and *alex* are owned by users *adamh* and *alex*, respectively, whereas the file *alice* is owned by UID 2047, *bob* is owned by 2003, and *carol* is owned by 2080. This reflects the fact that ownership is stored in the inode by integer (the UID). In this case, the users *alice*, *bob*, and *carol* no longer have accounts on the system, but these files still reflect that they are owned by these (now unassigned) UIDs. The *ls* command will display the username instead of the UID by default in a long directory listing (unless the *-n* option is passed to *ls*) because we human beings are better at remembering names than numbers. If *ls* is able to resolve a UID to a username, it will display the username; if not, it displays the UID.

The file */etc/passwd* acts as the source for username-to-UID mapping (unless a system such as NIS is in use, which is not covered on LPI 102). This file is the source for all user accounts on the system, and contains not only username information, but also other information about the user account, such as that user's home directory and default shell. The following is an example section from */etc/passwd*:

```
# more /etc/passwd
root:x:0:0:root:/root:/bin/bash
bin:x:1:1:bin:/bin:/sbin/nologin
daemon:x:2:2:daemon:/sbin:/sbin/nologin
adm:x:3:4:adm:/var/adm:/sbin/nologin
lp:x:4:7:lp:/var/spool/lpd:/sbin/nologin
adamh:x:500:504:Adam Haeder:/home/adamh:/bin/bash
```

Each colon-delimited line represents one user account. Table 22-1 defines these fields.

Table 22-1. Fields in /etc/passwd

Field position	Name	Description
1	Username	A human-readable name, 1–32 characters in length. Only letters, numbers, underscores, and dashes are allowed.
2	Password	Formerly stored a user's encrypted password string. If shadow passwords are in use, this field always contains the placeholder x. (Shadow passwords are covered in more depth later in this chapter.)
3	User ID (UID)	The integer from 0–65535 that identifies a user.
4	Group ID (GID)	The integer from 0–65535 that identifies the user's primary group membership.

Field position	Name	Description
5	Comments	Textual information about a user. This field usually contains a user's full name or possibly his phone number. Referred to as the GECOS field for historical reasons (early Unix machines used a General Electric Comprehensive Operating Supervisor machine for printing, so this field was created to store a Unix user's GECOS identity).
6	Home directory	The absolute path to the directory the user will be in upon successful login. This directory commonly is owned by that user.
7	Default shell	The program that runs when the user logs in. When this program is exited, the user is logged out of the system. This is usually an interactive shell program (such as */bin/ bash*) but it can be another executable program as well.

Let's take a look at the user *adamh* from our previous example:

```
adamh:x:500:504:Adam Haeder:/home/adamh:/bin/bash
```

Field 3 tells us that the UID for *adamh* is 500, and field 4 tells us that the GID for *adamh* is 504. Many Linux distributions will start "normal" user UIDs at 500, reserving UIDs from 1–499 for system accounts. Field 5 tells us that his full name is Adam Haeder, field 6 says his home directory is */home/adamh,* and finally, field 7 says that when he successfully logs in, the program */bin/bash* will be executed.

/etc/passwd is a text file, and therefore it can be edited like any other text file. However, that is a bad practice to get into because a syntax error in this file can prevent users (even *root*) from logging into the system. A much better way to maintain the */etc/passwd* file is with the command */usr/sbin/usermod*.

usermod

Syntax

```
chage [OPTIONS] [USERNAME]
```

Description

usermod is used to maintain the settings for accounts in */etc/passwd* and */etc/group* (and, by extension, */etc/shadow* and */etc/gshadow*).

Frequently used options

-c COMMENT
    Set or change the value of the Comment field (field 5).

-d HOMEDIRECTORY
    Set or change the value of the user's home directory (field 6).

-g GROUPID
    Set the primary GID (group ID) of the user.

-G comma-delimited GROUPID(S)
    Set the supplementary group ID(s) for a user.

-l USERNAME
  Change the username to *USERNAME*.

-s SHELL
  Change the user's shell to *SHELL*.

Shadow Passwords

Why is there an x in the password field (field 2) of the previous example? When Unix was originally designed, the */etc/passwd* file stored a user's encrypted password string in field 2 of */etc/passwd*. The password was encrypted using an algorithm known as a one-way hash (the *crypt* algorithm), meaning that while it was trivial to convert a string to a hashed value, it was mathematically difficult (i.e., it would take an extremely long time) to convert the hashed value back to the original string. This is a common function of algorithms used in the security world, especially for things such as passwords. If you can't determine the original password when you only know the hashed value, then we don't have to worry about the security around the hashed value itself, because it is too difficult mathematically to derive the password from the hashed value. So this hashed value can be stored in a world-readable file such as */etc/passwd* without compromising the security of the system.

If it's very difficult to derive a password from its hashed value, how does the system know I'm typing in the right password when I log in? The login process on a Linux system follows these steps:

1. Prompt user for a username and password.
2. Look in */etc/passwd* to see whether the user account exists.
3. If it does, encrypt the string given as the password using the *crypt* algorithm.
4. Compare the encrypted string given by the user with the encrypted string stored in field 2 of the */etc/passwd* entry for that username. If they match, then the user gave the correct password, and she is allowed to log in. If they did not match, present an error and ask the user for the password again.

In this way, a Linux system is able to determine whether a user provided the correct password without having to "recover" the original password from the encrypted string.

Although this solution is effective, it does pose security risks. By storing the encrypted string in the world-readable */etc/passwd* file, any user on the system has access to every other user's encrypted password. It may be extremely difficult for a user to mathematically derive the original password from the encrypted string, but she can use the same *crypt* algorithm to encrypt random strings and compare the resultant encrypted string with the encrypted strings for other users (following the same process that the login program uses). If the user is patient enough and tries enough combinations of letters and numbers, she could eventually find a string that, after encryption, exactly matches the encrypted string for a user account. This is called a *brute force attack*, because the user is forced to try every possible combination of potential passwords to determine which one is correct.

If this seems like a daunting and time-consuming task, that's because it is. Or at least it was, if we're talking about the computing power that was available to the average user in the 1960s through the 1980s. However, as the 1980s turned into the 1990s, and computers not only got much faster but also much cheaper, the average user had access to relatively powerful computational machines that could encrypt strings and compare them against other encrypted strings at the rate of thousands (or hundreds of thousands) per second. This posed a problem for the system administrators of the day; the encrypted hash was stored in a world-readable file (*/etc/passwd*), and every user could now copy this file, take it back to their personal computers, and run brute force attacks against it.

The solution to this was to move the encrypted password string to a file that is not world-readable. Thus the concept of *shadow passwords* was born, and the file */etc/ shadow* was created. This file contains not only the encrypted password but also other user account fields that are important (such as password age and account expiration dates), without requiring a modification to the format of */etc/password*. Plus, only the root user can read */etc/shadow*, preventing brute force attacks by normal users.

The */etc/shadow* file is colon-delimited, like */etc/passwd*, and contains the fields described in Table 22-2.

Table 22-2. Fields in /etc/shadow

Field position	Name	Description
1	Username	Must match a username in */etc/passwd*.
2	Password	Encrypted password string. Other special options here are:
		• *!* or *null*: This account has no password.
		• ***: Account is disabled.
		• *!<encrypted password>*: Account is locked.
		• *!!*: Password has never been set.
3	Last Changed	The number of days (since January 1, 1970) since the password was last changed.
4	Minimum	The number of days before a user may change his password. A value of 0 means the user may change his password at any time.
5	Maximum	The number of days a user can keep the same password. After this limit is reached, the user must change his password. Usually set to 99999 if password changes are not required.
6	Warn	The number of days before password expiration that a user starts to receive warnings.
7	Inactive	The number of days after password expiration that an account is automatically disabled.
8	Expire	A number indicating when the account will be disabled. This is represented as the number of days since January 1, 1970.
9	Reserved	Reserved for possible future use.

Here is the section of *etc/shadow* that corresponds to the section of */etc/passwd* listed previously:

```
root:$1$8jp/RdHb$D1x/6Xr2.puEONX3nIgdX/:14617:0:99999:7:::
bin:*:13993:0:99999:7:::
daemon:*:13993:0:99999:7:::
adm:*:13993:0:99999:7:::
lp:*:13993:0:99999:7:::
adamh:$1$IqH21LHP$BJPha9o6/XoOsSoJfWLfZO:14617:0:99999:7:::
```

 These are actual encrypted password strings. Break out your favorite brute-force password-cracking program and see if you can figure out the passwords.

We can see from this file that the root account has a password, the password was last changed 14,617 days after January 1, 1970, this user can change her password at any time, she does not have to change her password until 99,999 days after January 1, 1970, and if her password is ever set to expire, she will start getting notices 7 days before the actual expiration.

You can use the *date* command to determine the actual dates those integer values represent:

```
# echo "The password for the root account was last changed \
on `date -d "1970/01/01 +14617 days"`"
The password for the root account was last changed \
on Fri Jan 8 00:00:00 CST 2010
# echo "The password for the bin account was last changed \
on `date -d "1970/01/01 +13993 days"`"
The password for the bin account was last changed \
on Thu Apr 24 00:00:00 CDT 2008
```

The accounts for *bin*, *daemon*, *adm*, and *lp* are all examples of system accounts. These accounts are never meant to have interactive logins; they exist to run system processes and to maintain ownership of files. The * in the encrypted password fields means that these accounts are disabled from logging in interactively.

Although this file is a text file and can be edited directly to modify these values, the command */usr/bin/chage* should be used to maintain the password aging settings for accounts.

chage

Syntax

```
chage [OPTIONS] [USERNAME]
```

Description

chage (change aging) is used to maintain the password aging limits on a user account.

Frequently used options

-d LASTDAY
Set the number of days (since January 1, 1970) when the password was last changed.

-E EXPIREDATE
Set a user account to expire on a certain date.

-I INACTIVEDAYS
How many days of inactivity after a password has expired must pass before the account is locked.

-l
Show password aging information for an account. A nonprivileged user can run this to view his password aging status.

-m MINDAYS
Set the minimum number of days between password changes.

-M MAXDAYS
Set the maximum number of days a password is valid.

-W WARNDAYS
The number of days before the password expiration that the system will start warning the user.

Examples

View the password aging information for the *root* user:

```
# chage -l root
Last password change                              : Jan 08, 2010
Password expires                                  : never
Password inactive                                 : never
Account expires                                   : never
Minimum number of days between password change    : 0
Maximum number of days between password change    : 99999
Number of days of warning before password expires : 7
```

Force a user to change his password on the next login:

```
# chage -d 0 adamh
# chage -l adamh
Last password change : password must be changed
Password expires : never
Password inactive : never
Account expires : never
Minimum number of days between password change : 0
Maximum number of days between password change : 99999
Number of days of warning before password expires : 7
```

Now when the user *adamh* next logs in, he will see:

```
login as: adamh
adamh@server's password: <current password>
You are required to change your password immediately (root enforced)
Last login: Fri Jan  8 14:50:42 2010 from 10.0.0.112
WARNING: Your password has expired.
You must change your password now and login again!
Changing password for user adamh.
```

```
Changing password for adamh.
(current) UNIX password: <current password>
New UNIX password: <new password>
Retype new UNIX password: <new password>
```

On the Exam

The *chage* command can be a little confusing. Take the time to learn its different options and practice configuring different password aging settings on a test Linux system. It is likely that you will encounter questions about the syntax of the *chage* command on the LPI exams.

Setting Limits on Users

So far, the security concerns we have discussed regarding a Linux system have all revolved around the filesystem. Since everything in Linux is a file, this makes sense. However, security isn't solely concerned with which user can access what resource at what time. Security must also take into consideration the sharing of resources among users (both system and human users). A good security administrator will ensure that no insecure SUID or SGID binaries exist on his system that could give a normal user root access. But what measures are in place to ensure that a normal user doesn't run so many processes that a server is ground to a halt? What exists to make sure a user doesn't open so many network sockets that no memory is available to allocate to new connections? At first these might seem like capacity planning issues, but when we are dealing with systems that reside in a hostile environment (such as the Internet), they become the responsibility of the security administrator.

The Linux kernel has the ability to control many limits on what users can and can't do. These limits are defined in the file */etc/security/limits.conf* and are viewed or modified interactively by the *ulimit* command. *ulimit* is a command built into the bash shell, so it does not exist as a separate binary on a Linux system.

---

ulimit

Syntax

```
ulimit [OPTIONS] limit
```

Description

Provides control over the resources available to the shell and to processes started by it, on systems that allow such control.

Frequently used options

-a
>   Report all current limits.

-u NUMBER
>   The maximum number of processes available to a single user.

-x NUMBER

> The maximum number of file locks.

-v NUMBER

> The maximum amount of memory available to the shell, in kilobytes.

-H

> Indicates that a hard limit is being specified.

-S

> Indicates that a soft limit is being specified.

Example

View the current limits for a user:

```
$ ulimit -a
core file size          (blocks, -c) 0
data seg size           (kbytes, -d) unlimited
scheduling priority             (-e) 0
file size               (blocks, -f) unlimited
pending signals                 (-i) 8192
max locked memory       (kbytes, -l) 32
max memory size         (kbytes, -m) unlimited
open files                      (-n) 1024
pipe size            (512 bytes, -p) 8
POSIX message queues     (bytes, -q) 819200
real-time priority              (-r) 0
stack size              (kbytes, -s) 10240
cpu time               (seconds, -t) unlimited
max user processes              (-u) 8192
virtual memory          (kbytes, -v) unlimited
file locks                      (-x) unlimited
```

Limits are defined on Linux as being either *hard* or *soft* limits. A hard limit is set by the superuser for a user or group of users and cannot be exceeded. A soft limit is also set by the superuser, but it may be temporarily overridden by a user if the need arises (by the user calling the *ulimit* command). For example, a user may have a soft limit of 100 on the maximum number of open files, with a hard limit of 1,000. If the user is running a short-term process that needs to open 200 files, they can temporarily increase her limit in order for that program to run. That increase lasts only for the life of the user's shell. Hard and soft limits are set up by the superuser for all users in the file */etc/security/limits.conf*.

The file *limits.conf* takes four values, space- or Tab-delimited, on each line:

```
<domain> <type> <item> <value>
```

Table 22-3 describes the options for entries in *limits.conf*.

Table 22-3. Options in /etc/security/limits.conf

Field name	Possible values
Domain	• Username
	• Group name, prefixed by @
	• * to indicate the default
Type	• *hard*
	• *soft*

Field name	Possible values
Item	• *core* (limits the core file size, set in KB)
	• *data* (maximum data size in KB)
	• *fsize* (maximum file size in KB)
	• *memlock* (maximum locked-in-memory address space in KB)
	• *nofile* (maximum number of open files)
	• *rss* (maximum resident set size in KB)
	• *stack* (maximum stack size in KB)
	• *cpu* (maximum CPU time in minutes)
	• *nproc* (maximum number of processes)
	• *as* (address space limit in KB)
	• *maxlogins* (maximum number of logins for this user)
	• *maxsyslogins* (maximum number of logins on the system)
	• *priority* (the priority with which to run the user process)
	• *locks* (maximum number of file locks the user can hold)
	• *sigpending* (maximum number of pending signals)
	• *msgqueue* (maximum memory used by POSIX message queues in bytes)
	• *nice* (maximum nice priority allowed)
	• *rtprio* (maximum real-time priority)
Value	Integer

Here are some example lines from a *limits.conf* file:

```
# user adamh cannot create a file larger than 200 MB
adamh hard fsize 204800
# user adamh cannot create a file larger than 100 MB
# unless he increases his own ulimit value
adamh soft fsize 102400
# don't create core files for any user unless they
# change this ulimit value for themselves
* soft core 0
# limit all users in the group 'students' to no more
# than 20 processes running at once
@student hard nproc 20
# limit all users in the group 'faculty' to no more
# than 20 processes running at once, but allow
# them to increase their own limit temporarily
@faculty soft nproc 20
```

Let's see *ulimit* in action with the user *adamh*, given the example *limits.conf* file just shown. First, prove that user *adamh* cannot create a file larger than 102400 blocks (100 MB, assuming we're dealing with blocks that are each 1 KB in size):

```
$ whoami
adamh
$ ulimit -a
core file size          (blocks, -c) 0
data seg size           (kbytes, -d) unlimited
scheduling priority             (-e) 0
```

```
file size              (blocks, -f) 102400
pending signals              (-i) 8192
max locked memory      (kbytes, -l) 32
max memory size        (kbytes, -m) unlimited
open files                   (-n) 1024
pipe size           (512 bytes, -p) 8
POSIX message queues    (bytes, -q) 819200
real-time priority           (-r) 0
stack size             (kbytes, -s) 10240
cpu time              (seconds, -t) unlimited
max user processes           (-u) 8192
virtual memory         (kbytes, -v) unlimited
file locks                   (-x) unlimited
$ dd if=/dev/zero of=largefile bs=1M count=200
File size limit exceeded
$ ls -lh largefile
-rwxrwxrwx 1 root root 100M 2010-01-08 16:09 largefile
```

The *dd* command used in this example is attempting to create a 200 MB file by copying the contents of */dev/zero* (a special device that returns zero-valued bytes to all read requests) to the file *largefile*. It is doing this by attempting to copy 200 1-megabyte segments. After *dd* has reached 100 MB, the copy is aborted and the error "File size limit exceeded" appears. An *ls* of the file shows that user *adamh* was allowed to create a 100 MB file, but no larger. Now *adamh* will use *ulimit* to increase his file size limit to 200 MB and try the command again:

```
$ ulimit -f 204800
$ ulimit -a
core file size         (blocks, -c) 0
data seg size          (kbytes, -d) unlimited
scheduling priority          (-e) 0
file size              (blocks, -f) 204800
pending signals              (-i) 8192
max locked memory      (kbytes, -l) 32
max memory size        (kbytes, -m) unlimited
open files                   (-n) 1024
pipe size           (512 bytes, -p) 8
POSIX message queues    (bytes, -q) 819200
real-time priority           (-r) 0
stack size             (kbytes, -s) 10240
cpu time              (seconds, -t) unlimited
max user processes           (-u) 8192
virtual memory         (kbytes, -v) unlimited
file locks                   (-x) unlimited
$ dd if=/dev/zero of=largefile bs=1M count=200
200+0 records in
200+0 records out
209715200 bytes (210 MB) copied, 13.0589 s, 16.1 MB/s
$ ls -lh largefile
-rwxrwxrwx 1 root root 200M 2010-01-08 16:14 largefile
```

This time, the *dd* command completed without an error, and *adamh* was allowed to create a 200 MB file. However, if he tries to use *ulimit* to increase the limit beyond the hard limit, he is denied:

```
$ ulimit -f 204801
-bash: ulimit: file size: cannot modify limit: Operation not permitted
```

Querying System Services

Previous chapters have discussed the importance of the */bin/ps* command. It is vitally important that a system administrator knows exactly what processes are running on her machine and why. The first step toward maintaining a secure system is knowledge about that system. However, in this age of always-connected systems, understanding processes by themselves is not enough; you must also understand how they interact across the network. This can be accomplished with these Linux utilities: *netstat*, *nmap*, and *lsof*.

netstat

Description

The command */bin/netstat* is a generic, all-purpose network information tool. It will give you information about network connections, routing tables, interface statistics, and many other low-level details of your current network configuration. From a security standpoint, one of the most useful options of *netstat* is its ability to tell you what network ports are currently "open" on your system, what network connections exist, and what state those connections are in. *netstat* was defined, with examples, in Chapter 21. Here are few more examples, focusing on the security-related information provided by *netstat*.

Examples

Show protocol statistics. This is an example from a moderately busy public web server that has been up for 41 days:

```
# netstat -s
Ip:
    996714394 total packets received
    0 forwarded
    0 incoming packets discarded
    996354233 incoming packets delivered
    743668424 requests sent out
Icmp:
    308127 ICMP messages received
    488 input ICMP message failed.
    ICMP input histogram:
        destination unreachable: 669
        timeout in transit: 2
        redirects: 277573
        echo requests: 29877
        echo replies: 6
```

```
        48625 ICMP messages sent
        0 ICMP messages failed
        ICMP output histogram:
            destination unreachable: 18748
            echo replies: 29877
Tcp:
        4092366 active connection openings
        6613024 passive connection openings
        28785 failed connection attempts
        479914 connection resets received
        46 connections established
        995776060 segments received
        742269993 segments send out
        1026415 segments retransmitted
        7056 bad segments received.
        135994 resets sent
Udp:
        30804 packets received
        18657 packets to unknown port received.
        0 packet receive errors
        323385 packets sent
TcpExt:
        77483 invalid SYN cookies received
        22981 resets received for embryonic SYN_RECV sockets
        ArpFilter: 0
        6555736 TCP sockets finished time wait in fast timer
        2463 time wait sockets recycled by time stamp
        1004 packets rejects in established connections because of timestamp
        17501900 delayed acks sent
        24177 delayed acks further delayed because of locked socket
        Quick ack mode was activated 92779 times
        16609 times the listen queue of a socket overflowed
        16609 SYNs to LISTEN sockets ignored
        465508199 packets directly queued to recvmsg prequeue.
        2188914674 packets directly received from backlog
        1015042059 packets directly received from prequeue
        414843326 packets header predicted
        421778135 packets header predicted and directly queued to user
        TCPPureAcks: 52593173
        TCPHPAcks: 313477583
        TCPRenoRecovery: 3251
        TCPSackRecovery: 109485
        TCPSACKReneging: 219
        TCPFACKReorder: 409
        TCPSACKReorder: 61
        TCPRenoReorder: 287
        TCPTSReorder: 1367
        TCPFullUndo: 1433
        TCPPartialUndo: 5607
        TCPDSACKUndo: 75787
        TCPLossUndo: 60128
        TCPLoss: 93645
        TCPLostRetransmit: 31
        TCPRenoFailures: 1693
        TCPSackFailures: 44900
        TCPLossFailures: 10718
```

```
                TCPFastRetrans: 182057
                TCPForwardRetrans: 21100
                TCPSlowStartRetrans: 167274
                TCPTimeouts: 428080
                TCPRenoRecoveryFail: 2148
                TCPSackRecoveryFail: 19641
                TCPSchedulerFailed: 107692
                TCPRcvCollapsed: 0
                TCPDSACKOldSent: 89093
                TCPDSACKOfoSent: 1003
                TCPDSACKRecv: 165272
                TCPDSACKOfoRecv: 521
                TCPAbortOnSyn: 0
                TCPAbortOnData: 11898
                TCPAbortOnClose: 2165
                TCPAbortOnMemory: 0
                TCPAbortOnTimeout: 11617
                TCPAbortOnLinger: 0
                TCPAbortFailed: 0
                TCPMemoryPressures: 0
```

Display all the active TCP connections:

```
# netstat --tcp -n
Active Internet connections (w/o servers)
Proto Recv-Q Send-Q Local Address           Foreign Address         State
tcp        0      0 192.168.23.11:80        209.34.195.194:4898     SYN_RECV
tcp        0      0 192.168.23.11:80        71.126.90.107:50254     SYN_RECV
tcp        0      0 192.168.23.11:769       192.168.23.10:2049      ESTABLISHED
tcp        0      0 192.168.23.11:992       192.168.23.10:2049      ESTABLISHED
tcp        0      0 192.168.23.11:80        66.199.0.164:32211      TIME_WAIT
tcp        0      0 192.168.23.11:80        68.13.184.187:3249      ESTABLISHED
tcp        0      0 192.168.23.11:80        68.13.85.103:2972       TIME_WAIT
tcp        0      0 192.168.23.11:80        70.165.111.157:14068    TIME_WAIT
tcp        0      0 192.168.23.11:80        68.110.27.241:32808     TIME_WAIT
tcp        0      0 192.168.23.11:80        71.199.119.34:49469     TIME_WAIT
<output truncated>
```

This output shows us that there are a number of connections to TCP port 80 on our server (192.168.23.11). These connections are from many different hosts, as is typical with a busy web server. One of the interesting things about a report like this is the "State" information. A TCP connection goes through a number of different states as the connection is requested and created, data is transmitted, and the connection is completed and closed. From a security standpoint, it's a good idea to be familiar with the different states a TCP connection will be in. Some high-profile denial of service attacks in the past have taken advantage of the relatively long timeout values in TCP connections to completely exhaust the kernel memory of a system, by making thousands of TCP connections but never completing the response, and thus causing the system under attack to hold these thousands of TCP connections open until they finally time out. If you see a lot of connections in the "TIME_WAIT" state for long periods, you may be the victim of such an attack. To modify the default value, edit the file */proc/sys/net/ipv4/tcp_fin_timeout*. For more information on the */proc* filesystem and how to use it to tune your running system, refer to the text file *Documentation/filesystems/proc.txt* in your Linux kernel source.

Table 22-4 displays the different states a TCP connection goes through.

Table 22-4. States of a TCP connection

State name	Description
CLOSED	The connection is closed.
LISTEN	Listening for an incoming connection.
SYN_RCVD	SYN stands for SYNCHRONIZE, used to initiate and establish a connection. Named for the synchronization of sequence numbers that takes place throughout a TCP connection. This state indicates the connection is receiving packets.
SYN_SENT	This state indicates the connection is sending packets.
ESTABLISHED	In this state, the TCP three-way handshake has been completed, and a TCP connection is now established.
FIN_WAIT_1	FIN stands for FINISH, meaning that one of the devices wants to terminate the connection.
FIN_WAIT_2	After one end receives an acknowledgement (ACK) of a FIN, it goes into state FIN_WAIT_2.
CLOSING	The connection is in the process of closing.
CLOSE_WAIT	The state a connection is in after sending an ACK in response to an initial FIN.
LAST_ACK	One end of the connection is in the process of sending a FIN.
TIME_WAIT	After a TCP connection is closed, the kernel will keep the connection around in TIME_WAIT state, waiting for any delayed duplicate packets. This prevents another socket from using this same port and receiving data meant for an old connection.

On the Exam

netstat is an important tool that you will encounter often in your Linux career. Become familiar with the more common command-line options, and understand when it is appropriate to use the *netstat* command, because you will see a number of references to it on the LPI exams.

nmap

Syntax

```
nmap [scan type] [options] (target specifications)
```

Description

nmap (the network mapper) is a very powerful port-scanning tool. Its primary purpose is to scan a remote host (or entire subnet) and report back what TCP or UDP ports are open on each system. However, this powerful tool can do much more, including OS fingerprinting and vulnerability scanning.

Frequently used options

-sP

Don't port scan; just report what hosts respond to a ping request. This is commonly called a *ping sweep*. See the later examples.

-n

Don't do DNS resolution.

-sS
> Perform a TCP SYN scan (the default).

-sU
> Perform a UDP scan.

-p port_range
> Scan only the specified ports.

-sV
> Perform a service or version scan on open ports. This is useful when attempting to determine what software is running on the remote machine.

-O
> Attempt to determine the operating system of the system being scanned.

Example 1

Perform a "standard" TCP scan on a remote system:

```
# nmap 192.168.1.220

Starting Nmap 5.00 ( http://nmap.org ) at 2010-01-14 21:11 CST
Interesting ports on server.domain.com (192.168.1.220):
Not shown: 979 closed ports
PORT       STATE SERVICE
42/tcp     open  nameserver
53/tcp     open  domain
80/tcp     open  http
88/tcp     open  kerberos-sec
135/tcp    open  msrpc
139/tcp    open  netbios-ssn
389/tcp    open  ldap
445/tcp    open  microsoft-ds
464/tcp    open  kpasswd5
593/tcp    open  http-rpc-epmap
636/tcp    open  ldapssl
1025/tcp   open  NFS-or-IIS
1029/tcp   open  ms-lsa
1084/tcp   open  ansoft-lm-2
1090/tcp   open  unknown
1094/tcp   open  unknown
1121/tcp   open  unknown
3268/tcp   open  globalcatLDAP
3269/tcp   open  globalcatLDAPssl
3389/tcp   open  ms-term-serv
10000/tcp  open  snet-sensor-mgmt
MAC Address: 00:07:E9:82:6B:D8 (Intel)

Nmap done: 1 IP address (1 host up) scanned in 1.39 seconds
```

nmap performs its work relatively quickly, and lets us know that of the 1,700 or so common ports that were scanned, 21 ports were found open that *nmap* considers "interesting." If you want to scan every possible open TCP port (from 1 to 65535), give the *–p* option:

```
# nmap -p 1-65535 192.168.1.220

Starting Nmap 5.00 ( http://nmap.org ) at 2010-01-14 21:15 CST
```

```
Interesting ports on server.domain.com (192.168.1.220):
Not shown: 65512 closed ports
PORT       STATE SERVICE
42/tcp     open  nameserver
53/tcp     open  domain
80/tcp     open  http
88/tcp     open  kerberos-sec
135/tcp    open  msrpc
139/tcp    open  netbios-ssn
389/tcp    open  ldap
445/tcp    open  microsoft-ds
464/tcp    open  kpasswd5
593/tcp    open  http-rpc-epmap
636/tcp    open  ldapssl
1025/tcp   open  NFS-or-IIS
1029/tcp   open  ms-lsa
1084/tcp   open  ansoft-lm-2
1090/tcp   open  unknown
1094/tcp   open  unknown
1121/tcp   open  unknown
3268/tcp   open  globalcatLDAP
3269/tcp   open  globalcatLDAPssl
3389/tcp   open  ms-term-serv
4601/tcp   open  unknown
9675/tcp   open  unknown
10000/tcp open   snet-sensor-mgmt
MAC Address: 00:07:E9:82:6B:D8 (Intel)

Nmap done: 1 IP address (1 host up) scanned in 17.80 seconds
```

This scan took a little bit longer, but it showed us an additional three open TCP ports that the default scan did not show.

Example 2

Attempt to perform an "OS fingerprint" on a remote system:

```
# nmap -O 192.168.1.220

Starting Nmap 5.00 ( http://nmap.org ) at 2010-01-14 21:18 CST
Interesting ports on server.domain.com (192.168.1.220):
Not shown: 979 closed ports
PORT       STATE SERVICE
42/tcp     open  nameserver
<...output truncated...>
10000/tcp open  snet-sensor-mgmt
MAC Address: 00:07:E9:82:6B:D8 (Intel)
Device type: general purpose
Running: Microsoft Windows 2003
OS details: Microsoft Windows Server 2003 SP1 or SP2
Network Distance: 1 hop

OS detection performed. Please report any incorrect results \
at http://nmap.org/submit/.
```

Security

nmap performs some interesting manipulations of the standard TCP connection states in an attempt to guess what operating system the scanned host is running. For more information, visit the *nmap* site (*http://insecure.org*).

Example 3

Discover what hosts are "up" on a subnet (or at least which ones are responding to *ping*). This example was run on a different machine, so the version of *nmap* and the IP subnet are different from the previous example:

```
# nmap -sP 10.0.0.0/24

Starting Nmap 4.52 ( http://insecure.org ) at 2010-01-14 21:21 CST
Host 10.0.0.1 appears to be up.
Host 10.0.0.100 appears to be up.
MAC Address: 00:1B:EA:F2:C4:70 (Nintendo Co.)
Host 10.0.0.101 appears to be up.
MAC Address: 00:21:00:9E:45:15 (Unknown)
Host 10.0.0.102 appears to be up.
MAC Address: 00:21:00:72:54:4A (Unknown)
Host 10.0.0.103 appears to be up.
MAC Address: 00:21:85:C2:2D:A5 (Unknown)
Host 10.0.0.104 appears to be up.
MAC Address: 00:19:21:27:8E:83 (Elitegroup Computer System Co.)
Host 10.0.0.106 appears to be up.
MAC Address: 00:14:22:61:E3:D9 (Dell)
Host router (10.0.0.210) appears to be up.
MAC Address: 00:12:17:30:B4:9C (Cisco-Linksys)
Nmap done: 256 IP addresses (8 hosts up) scanned in 4.928 seconds
```

lsof

Syntax

```
lsof [options] [names]
```

Description

lsof lists open files. Since everything in Linux is a file, this tool can tell you a fantastic amount of information about your running system. It is primarily used to tell what processes have what files open, but it can also be used to view TCP and UDP connection information, among other things.

Frequently used options

-c x

Only show files that are open by processes whose executable starts with the character(s) specified by *x*.

-i x

Instead of showing open files, show sockets whose Internet address is *x*. If *x* is not specified, show all IP connections. This is functionally equivalent to *netstat –anp*.

-u username

Show only the files that *username* has open.

-P

Do not convert port numbers to port names (for example, show 25 instead of smtp).

Example 1

The *lsof* command is often used to determine what processes have files open on removable media so they can be terminated, allowing the media to be unmounted:

```
# pwd
/public
# umount /public
umount: /public: device is busy
# lsof | grep "/public"
smbd    17728    adamh  cwd    DIR    8,65    8192    5 /public
bash    21712    root   cwd    DIR    8,65    8192    5 /public
lsof    21841    root   cwd    DIR    8,65    8192    5 /public
grep    21842    root   cwd    DIR    8,65    8192    5 /public
lsof    21843    root   cwd    DIR    8,65    8192    5 /public
```

This shows us that the *smbd* process (controlled by user *adamh*) and a *bash*, *lsof*, and *grep* process all have the file handle for the directory */public* open. Now we'll change directories and run *lsof* again:

```
# cd /
# lsof | grep "/public"
smbd    17728    adamh  cwd    DIR    8,65    8192    5 /public
```

We see now that only *smdb* has a file open on the */public* directory.

Example 2

In this example, we'll see how *lsof* can be used to determine what connections exist between a machine and a remote host. Our machine in this case has an IP address of 10.0.0.1 and is running the Samba daemon (*smbd*). The remote machine at 10.0.0.104 is connected to the Samba daemon:

```
# lsof -P -i@10.0.0.104
COMMAND  PID USER   FD   TYPE DEVICE SIZE NODE NAME
smbd 1329 root 5u IPv4 252713 TCP 10.0.0.1:139->\
                      10.0.0.104:1568 (ESTABLISHED)
```

The machine at 10.0.0.104 is connected to TCP port 139 on 10.0.0.1, and is communicating with the processes named *smbd*, which has a PID of 1329.

On the Exam

The *lsof* command is an important tool for any good system administrator to have in his arsenal. Be prepared to answer questions about its general usage, and be familiar with common options, including viewing socket information and files open by process name and username.

23

Set Up Host Security (Topic 110.2)

This chapter describes the practical steps one needs to take to begin to secure a Linux system. The important thing to remember regarding security is that it is a process, not a destination. Maintaining a secure system is a job that is never complete. This chapter covers the second objective of Topic 110:

Objective 2: Set Up Host Security
   Candidates should know how to set up a basic level of host security. Weight: 3.

Objective 2: Set Up Host Security

As mentioned previously, the key to good host security is knowledge. A good system administrator knows at all times what is happening on systems he manages, and has processes in place to tell him when things stray from the norm.

Previous chapters have covered the topics of shadow passwords, knowledge of the */proc* filesystem, maintaining startup services in */etc/rc.d*, and other areas of host-based security. This chapter will finish this topic by discussing the *inetd* and *xinetd* services, and their role in system security.

The Super-Server

Modern Linux systems are often asked to perform many functions. Because of the broad appeal of Linux, its use is in everything from firewalls to set-top boxes. Because of this, there are many network services that are commonly seen on a Linux system. These services oftentimes do not see constant use, but need to be active and available when the need arises. Some examples of these important but often seldom used services are *ftp*, *finger*, *telnet*, *imap*, and *pop3*.

You may notice that these examples all represent network services that are considered relatively "old" (at least in terms of modern day computing). This is essentially true. Years ago, when hardware was more expensive and harder to come by, the amount of system resources, especially memory, that each process consumed was of great importance. The problem was that administrators wanted to consolidate a lot of their network services on one Linux machine, but were running into memory limitations. The solution was to come up with a listening service, or "super-server," that handled incoming connections and started the correct networking service to handle them. Thus the *inetd* service was born.

The *inetd* service has two important characteristics: It is a single process that can listen on multiple ports for incoming connections, starting the appropriate service when a connection comes in and connecting the inbound connection with the service. Also, *inetd* supports a sophisticated security scheme for allowing and disallowing access to these "simpler" networking services, many of which don't have advanced access controls built into them. So the creation of *inetd* solved two problems: limited memory was conserved, and administrators gained a finer level of control over what systems or networks could access their services.

inetd syntax

The main configuration file for *inetd* is */etc/inetd.conf*. An example looks like this:

```
#echo      stream   tcp   nowait    root    internal
#echo      dgram    udp    wait      root    internal
#discard   stream   tcp    nowait    root    internal
#discard   dgram    udp    wait      root    internal
#daytime   stream   tcp    nowait    root    internal
#daytime   dgram    udp    wait      root    internal
#chargen   stream   tcp    nowait    root    internal
#chargen   dgram    udp    wait      root    internal
#time      stream   tcp   nowait    root    internal
#time      dgram    udp    wait      root    internal
#
# These are standard services.
#
ftp      stream   tcp   nowait    root    /usr/sbin/tcpd    in.ftpd -l -a
telnet    stream    tcp    nowait    root    /usr/sbin/tcpd    in.telnetd
#
# Shell, login, exec, comsat and talk are BSD protocols.
#
#shell    stream   tcp    nowait    root      /usr/sbin/tcpd    in.rshd
#login    stream   tcp    nowait    root      /usr/sbin/tcpd    in.rlogind
#exec     stream   tcp    nowait    root      /usr/sbin/tcpd    in.rexecd
#comsat   dgram    udp    wait      root      /usr/sbin/tcpd    in.comsat
#talk     dgram    udp    wait      root      /usr/sbin/tcpd    in.talkd
#ntalk    dgram    udp    wait      root      /usr/sbin/tcpd    in.ntalkd
#dtalk    stream   tcp    wait      nobody    /usr/sbin/tcpd    in.dtalkd
#
# Pop and imap mail services et al
#
#pop-2    stream   tcp    nowait    root    /usr/sbin/tcpd    ipop2d
#pop-3    stream   tcp    nowait    root    /usr/sbin/tcpd    ipop3d
imap     stream   tcp    nowait    root    /usr/sbin/tcpd    imapd
#
# The Internet UUCP service.
#
#uucp  stream  tcp  nowait  uucp  /usr/sbin/tcpd  /usr/lib/uucp/uucico -l
#
```

```
# Tftp service is provided primarily for booting.  Most sites
# run this only on machines acting as "boot servers." Do not uncomment
# this unless you *need* it.
#
#tftp    dgram    udp    wait    root    /usr/sbin/tcpd    in.tftpd
#bootps  dgram    udp    wait    root    /usr/sbin/tcpd    bootpd
#
# Finger, systat and netstat give out user information which may be
# valuable to potential "system crackers."  Many sites choose to disable
# some or all of these services to improve security.
#
#finger   stream   tcp   nowait   root    /usr/sbin/tcpd    in.fingerd
#cfinger  stream   tcp   nowait   root    /usr/sbin/tcpd    in.cfingerd
#systat   stream   tcp   nowait   guest   /usr/sbin/tcpd    /bin/ps -auwwx
#netstat  stream   tcp   nowait   guest   /usr/sbin/tcpd    /bin/netstat -f inet
#
# Authentication
#
#auth   stream   tcp   nowait   nobody   /usr/sbin/in.identd   in.identd -l -e -o
#
# End of inetd.conf
```

Like most Linux configuration files, a line starting with a # symbol denotes a comment. In this example, only the *ftp*, *telnet*, and *imap* services are active. Each line of the file describes a unique service and is made up of seven sections, described in Table 23-1.

Table 23-1. Fields in /etc/inetd.conf

Field position	Name	Description
1	Service name	The name of the service, which must correspond to a name in the file */etc/services*. This determines what port *inetd* will listen on for requests to this service.
2	Socket type	One of *stream, dgram, raw,* or *seqpacket*. TCP services use *stream*, whereas UDP services use *dgram*.
3	Protocol	One of the following: • *tcp,tcp4* = TCP IPv4 • *udp,udp4* = UDP IPv4 • *tcp6* = TCP IPv6 • *udp6* = UDP IPv6 • *tcp46* = Both TCP IPv4 and v6 • *udp46* = Both UDP IPv4 and v6
4	Connection options	{wait|nowait}[/*max-child*[/*max-connections-per-ip-per-minute*[/*max-child-per-ip*]]] The *wait* or *nowait* option defines how *inted* handles the incoming connection. If *wait* is indicated, *inetd* will hand off multiple incoming requests to a single daemon, whereas *nowait* means that *inetd* should start a new server process for each incoming connection. /*max-child* limits the amount of connections that will be accepted at one time.

Field position	Name	Description
		/max-connections-per-ip-per-minute and /max-child-per-ip are optional limits you can place on this resource, to prevent abuse and denial of service attacks.
5	User	What user account the service should start as.
6	Server	Full path to the service that *inetd* should start.
7	Server options	Command-line arguments (if any) that should be passed to the server.

Using this table as a guide, if we want to enable the *imap* service in our *inetd* configuration but limit *imap* to a maximum of 10 concurrent connections and prevent more than 5 concurrent connections from a single IP address, the line would look like this:

```
imap    stream    tcp    nowait/10/0/5    root    /usr/sbin/tcpd    imapd
```

Notice that we're not actually starting the *imapd* service, but instead the server */usr/sbin/tcpd* with an argument of *imapd*. This is the TCP_WRAPPERS service, which is described later in this chapter.

The real advantage of *inetd* comes into play only when you have many services enabled, thus maximizing the amount of memory you are saving by not running all of these little-used services all the time, listening for connections.

xinetd

The original *inetd* service is seldom seen in more recent Linux distributions. It has been replaced with *xinetd*, the Extended Internet Daemon. *xinetd* improves upon the original goals of *inetd* by increasing the logging and access control ability around the managed services, in addition to adding defense mechanisms to protect against attacks, such as port scanners or denial of service.

The *xinetd* configuration file is */etc/xinetd.conf*, but most services are configured as individual files in the directory */etc/xinetd.d*. This makes adding and removing services much easier for a distribution's package management utility. The */etc/xinetd.conf* file contains global configuration options, as seen in this example:

```
# This is the master xinetd configuration file. Settings in the
# default section will be inherited by all service configurations
# unless explicitly overridden in the service configuration. See
# xinetd.conf in the man pages for a more detailed explanation of
# these attributes.

defaults
{
# The next two items are intended to be a quick access place to
# temporarily enable or disable services.
#
#       enabled      =
#       disabled     =

# Define general logging characteristics.
```

```
        log_type        = SYSLOG daemon info
        log_on_failure  = HOST
        log_on_success  = PID HOST DURATION EXIT

# Define access restriction defaults
#
#       no_access       =
#       only_from       =
#       max_load        = 0
        cps             = 50 10
        instances       = 50
        per_source      = 10

# Address and networking defaults
#
#       bind            =
#       mdns            = yes
        v6only          = no

# setup environmental attributes
#
#       passenv         =
        groups          = yes
        umask           = 002

# Generally, banners are not used. This sets up their global defaults
#
#       banner          =
#       banner_fail     =
#       banner_success  =
}

includedir /etc/xinetd.d
```

As you can see, *xinetd* offers some more advanced configuration options, such as *cps* (connections per second) and the ability to set the *umask* for files created by the managed services. Here is the example *imap* configuration file at */etc/xinetd.d/imap*:

```
service imap
{
        socket_type         = stream
        wait                = no
        user                = root
        server              = /usr/sbin/imapd
        log_on_success  += HOST DURATION
        log_on_failure  += HOST
        disable             = no
}
```

Table 23-2 describes the different popular configuration options available in these service files. For a complete list of options, consult the manpage for *xinetd.conf*.

Table 23-2. Popular fields in /etc/xinetd.d/servicename

Field name	Description
id	Name of the service.
flags	Common flags are:
	• NORETRY = Don't retry in case of a service failure.
	• KEEPALIVE = Set the keepalive flag on the TCP socket.
	• SENSOR = Don't run a service; just listen on this port and log all attempts to access.
	• IPv4 = Use IPv4 only.
	• IPv6 = Use IPv6 only.
disable	Boolean option determining whether this service is on.
socket_type	• stream
	• dgram
	• raw
	• seqpacket
protocol	Must be a valid protocol listed in /etc/protocols.
wait	Normally, TCP services have wait set to 'no', whereas UDP services have wait set to 'yes'.
user	Username the service runs as.
group	Group the service runs as.
instances	The number of services that can run at once. The default is no limit.
nice	Server priority (nice value).
server	Full path to the server program that will run.
server_args	Command-line arguments passed to the server.
only_from	Allows you to restrict access by IP address, network, or hostname.
no_access	Deny access from this IP address, network, or hostname.
access_times	Determines what hours of the day this service is available, in the form *HH:MM* - *HH:MM*.
log_type	Options are SYSLOG or FILE.
log_on_success	What variables will be logged on a successful connection.
log_on_failure	What variables will be logged on a failed connection.
port	What port *xinetd* should listen on for this service.
bind	What IP address *xinetd* should listen on. Useful for multihomed machines.
per_source	Maximum number of connections from a single IP address.
max_load	After the one-minute load average of the machine reaches this amount, stop accepting connections until the load goes below this number.

Once the *disable = no* option is set in our */etc/xinetd.d/imap* file and the *xinetd* service is restarted, we can use the *netstat* command to verify that *xinetd* is ready for incoming *imap* connections:

```
# netstat --tcp -anp | grep ":143"
tcp        0      0       :::143      :::*      LISTEN      15959/xinetd
```

Security with TCP_WRAPPERS

With the original *inetd* service, the servers that were managed rarely had any advanced access control options of their own. These services were often remnants of the early days of the Internet, when systems were a little more trusted than they are today. Examples of these mostly deprecated services are *finger*, *echo*, *daytime*, *telnet*, *shell*, *exec*, and *talk*, to name a few. *xinetd* added some more advanced controls, but both *inetd* and *xinetd* are able to utilize the TCP_WRAPPER service to aid in access control.

In order to utilize TCP_WRAPPERS, *inetd* needs to call the user-space program */usr/bin/tcpd* with an argument of the desired service, in order to "wrap" that service in the access control. This is not necessary with *xinetd*, as the *xinetd* binary has TCP_WRAPPERS support built-in, by nature of its link with the *libwrap* library. You can see this with the */usr/bin/ldd* command:

```
# ldd /usr/sbin/xinetd
        linux-gate.so.1 =>  (0x0012d000)
        libselinux.so.1 => /lib/libselinux.so.1 (0x0012e000)
        libwrap.so.0 => /lib/libwrap.so.0 (0x00149000)
        libnsl.so.1 => /lib/libnsl.so.1 (0x00151000)
        libm.so.6 => /lib/libm.so.6 (0x0016a000)
        libcrypt.so.1 => /lib/libcrypt.so.1 (0x00193000)
        libc.so.6 => /lib/libc.so.6 (0x001c5000)
        libdl.so.2 => /lib/libdl.so.2 (0x0031e000)
        /lib/ld-linux.so.2 (0x00110000)
```

Other services also have native TCP_WRAPPERS support by nature of their links to *libwrap.so*, including */usr/sbin/sshd* and */usr/sbin/sendmail*. You can run a simple shell script to determine what binaries in */usr/sbin/* are linked against *libwrap.so*:

```
# cd /usr/sbin
# for file in *
> {
> if [ -f $file ]; then
> result=`ldd $file | grep -c libwrap`
> if [ "$result" -gt "0" ]; then
> echo "/usr/sbin/$file is linked to libwrap.so"
> fi
> fi
> }
/usr/sbin/exportfs is linked to libwrap.so
/usr/sbin/gdm-binary is linked to libwrap.so
/usr/sbin/mailstats is linked to libwrap.so
/usr/sbin/makemap is linked to libwrap.so
/usr/sbin/praliases is linked to libwrap.so
/usr/sbin/rpcinfo is linked to libwrap.so
/usr/sbin/rpc.mountd is linked to libwrap.so
/usr/sbin/rpc.rquotad is linked to libwrap.so
/usr/sbin/sendmail is linked to libwrap.so
/usr/sbin/sendmail.sendmail is linked to libwrap.so
/usr/sbin/smrsh is linked to libwrap.so
/usr/sbin/snmpd is linked to libwrap.so
/usr/sbin/snmptrapd is linked to libwrap.so
/usr/sbin/sshd is linked to libwrap.so
```

```
/usr/sbin/stunnel is linked to libwrap.so
/usr/sbin/vsftpd is linked to libwrap.so
/usr/sbin/xinetd is linked to libwrap.so
```

Configuration

TCP_WRAPPERS is configured in two files, */etc/hosts.allow* and */etc/hosts.deny*.
These files contain rules that govern either all services or individual services. Like a
firewall, it is usually good practice to adopt either a "block everything, only open
what you need" mentality or an "open everything, block only what you don't need"
mentality when it comes to TCP_WRAPPERS. Here is an example of a sample configuration that blocks everything by default, but opens up access for a few services:

```
# more /etc/hosts.deny
ALL: ALL
```

```
# more /etc/hosts.allow
sshd: ALL EXCEPT 192.168.1.10
vsftpd: 192.168.1.0/24 EXCEPT 192.168.1.10
```

The TCP_WRAPPERS files are read in real time by the servers that support them,
so changes made to these files go into effect immediately. The example configuration
denies all access by default, and then opens it up specifically for the *sshd* and
vsftpd services. Users from everywhere except the system 192.168.1.10 are allowed
to connect to the *sshd* service, and all users on the 192.168.1.0/24 network, except
for 192.168.1.10, are allowed to connect to *vsftpd*.

Let's assume that we have *xinetd* configured and running, with the *imap* configuration as listed earlier. In addition, the */etc/hosts.deny* and */etc/hosts.allow* files are the
same as our example. Our server system has an IP address of 10.0.0.1, and our client
system has an IP address of 10.0.0.112. When an attempt is made to connect to the
imap server on 10.0.0.1 from 10.0.0.112, the connection times out. We can see the
details in */var/log/messages* on the server:

```
# tail /var/log/messages
Jan 26 15:22:42 server xinetd[15959]: xinetd Version 2.3.14 started with \
libwrap loadavg labelednetworking options compiled in.
Jan 26 15:22:42 server xinetd[15959]: Started working: 1 available service
Jan 26 15:23:23 server xinetd[15959]: START: imap pid=15975 \
from=::ffff:10.0.0.112
Jan 26 15:23:28 server xinetd[15959]: EXIT: imap status=1 pid=15975 \
duration=5(sec)
Jan 26 15:26:30 server xinetd[15959]: START: imap pid=16035 \
from=::ffff:10.0.0.112
Jan 26 15:26:30 server xinetd[16035]: libwrap refused connection to \
imap (libwrap=imapd) from ::ffff:10.0.0.112
Jan 26 15:26:30 server xinetd[16035]: FAIL: imap libwrap \
from=::ffff:10.0.0.112
Jan 26 15:26:30 server xinetd[15959]: EXIT: imap status=0 \
pid=16035 duration=0(sec)
```

We can see from the *syslog* messages that our attempt to connect to *imapd* was denied. In order to enable this access, we need to add the following line to */etc/hosts.allow*:

```
imapd: ALL
```

or, if we want to limit it somewhat:

```
imapd: 10.0.0.0/24
```

After this change, we try our *imap* connection from the client again, and we get a connection. Logfiles on the server show our success:

```
# tail /var/log/messages
Jan 26 15:34:37 fileserv xinetd[15959]: START: imap pid=16083 \
from=::ffff:10.0.0.112
Jan 26 15:34:42 fileserv xinetd[15959]: EXIT: imap status=1 \
pid=16083 duration=5(sec)
```

Remember that you need to do more than simply configure */etc/hosts.deny* and */etc/hosts.allow* to secure your system. Many popular applications, such as the Apache web server, do not link against *libwrap.so*, so they do not honor the entries you place in these configuration files.

Also, it is more and more common on network-enabled Linux machines (especially those connected directly to the Internet) to not run *inetd* or *xinetd* at all. If there are services that need to be run, such as *imapd* or *ftpd*, they are often run as standalone daemons, largely because the lack of necessary memory in a server is not as much of a concern as it was years ago, and many of these newer services have built-in access controls that rival the ability of TCP_WRAPPERS. So if you are in doubt about whether or not you need a service that is handled by *xinetd*, you are probably safe to disable it, rather than having to worry about securing a service that might not be necessary.

On the Exam

Although the *inetd* service has largely been replaced by *xinetd*, be familiar with the syntax of the *inetd.conf* file, because there is a good chance you will encounter questions about it on the LPI exams. The syntax of the */etc/hosts.deny* and */etc/hosts.allow* files also will be a focus.

24

Securing Data with Encryption (Topic 110.3)

This Topic focuses on the methods used to secure Linux servers and workstations. Securing servers includes two basics steps: communicating between servers in a secure way, and then encrypting data on the servers themselves. The LPI knows that SSH is the most common method for communicating securely between servers. Therefore, the topic is covered fairly extensively on the exam and in this chapter.

SSH is used for many more purposes than simply communicating across insecure networks; it is used throughout the industry to configure remote systems and tunnel all sorts of traffic, from X Windows to email and FTP.

The second part of securing a server—making sure that stored data is properly encrypted—can be handled in myriad ways. However, the LPI recognizes that GNU Privacy Guard (GPG) has become the standard. Before we take a deep look at how SSH and GPG work, make sure that you understand this LPI Objective's description perfectly:

Objective 3: Securing Data with Encryption
> The candidate should be able to use public key techniques to secure data and communication. The key knowledge areas are:

- Perform basic OpenSSH 2 client configuration and usage.
- Understand the role of OpenSSH 2 server host keys.
- Perform basic GnuPG configuration and usage.
- Understand SSH port tunnels (including X11 tunnels).

Following is the list of the used files, terms, and utilities:

- *ssh*
- *ssh-keygen*
- *ssh-agent*
- *ssh-add*

- *~/.ssh/id_rsa and id_rsa.pub*
- *~/.ssh/id_dsa and id_dsa.pub*
- */etc/ssh/ssh_host_rsa_key and /etc/ssh/ssh_host_rsa_key.pub*
- */etc/ssh/ssh_host_dsa_key and /etc/ssh/ssh_host_dsa_key.pub*
- *~/.ssh/authorized_keys and ~/.ssh/authorized_keys2*
- */etc/ssh_known_hosts*
- *gpg*
- *~/.gnupg/**

Objective 3: Securing Data With Encryption

As you can see from this Objective, you need to know more than how to issue a couple of commands on a remote system. You also have to understand how to configure systems for public key encryption and how to use common SSH and encryption commands, including GPG.

Using Secure Shell (SSH)

SSH, also known as Secure Shell, is a replacement for the obsolete *telnet* command and *rsh/rlogin/rcp* suite. The primary use for SSH is to conduct encrypted shell sessions to remote hosts. However, it can also be used to copy files and to tunnel other protocols.

SSH is a server/client protocol offering *sshd* as the server and the *ssh* and *scp* commands as the client. The client connects to the server, they establish an encrypted session, and then the server demands authentication before finally logging in the client.

The *ssh* command can be used either to execute a single command and return to the local terminal, or to establish a remote session that acts and feels just like logging into the remote system. In this regard, *ssh* acts like the obsolete *rsh* command; used to log in, *ssh* acts like *rlogin* and *telnet*.

The *scp* command copies files and directories to or from a remote system, acting like the obsolete *rcp* command.

In addition to simple login sessions and file copying, SSH can also provide transparent port forwarding, and as an extension of this, X authentication and forwarding. When you have an SSH session, you can start an X client on the remote machine, and the X Window System protocol will travel encrypted over your connection and display on your local machine without the need for settings such as `DISPLAY=foo:0` or the *xhost* or *xauth* commands.

The implementation of SSH generally used on Linux systems is OpenSSH (*http://www.openssh.com*).

Installation and Configuration

OpenSSH may or may not be installed on your system by default. When the SSH server (*sshd*) runs for the first time, it generates a host key for your machine. This key will serve to authenticate your host in subsequent SSH sessions. Then you will typically want to create SSH authentication keys for your own personal account, as well as the root account. After that, as the administrator you should review the configuration of *sshd*, to see that you are comfortable with it.

The standard place for the central configuration of OpenSSH is the */etc/ssh* directory. Here you will find the server configuration in *sshd_config* and default client configuration in *ssh_config*. Here are some highlights from the server configuration as installed on Debian:

```
# What ports, IPs and protocols we listen for
Port 22
Protocol 2
```

Port 22 is the standard port for the SSH protocol. Version 2 of the protocol is the most secure, whereas version 1 has some flaws that were hard to overcome. It is recommended to accept only version 2 now. To support both versions, put 2, 1 on the Protocol line of the configuration file.

On the Exam

SSH uses TCP port 22. Be prepared to know the preferred version of SSH (2) as well. The second version of SSH is preferable, because version 1 has long been known to have a weak encryption algorithm that has been broken.

Example /etc/ssh/sshd_config file

```
# Authentication:
PermitRootLogin yes

PubkeyAuthentication yes

# rhosts authentication should not be used
RhostsAuthentication no
# Don't read the user's ~/.rhosts and ~/.shosts files
IgnoreRhosts yes
# For this to work you will also need host keys in /etc/ssh_known_hosts
# (for protocol version 2)
HostbasedAuthentication no

# To disable tunneled clear text passwords, change to no here!
PasswordAuthentication yes
```

OpenSSH ignores the host operating system setting for permitting root logins on nonconsole terminals. Instead, OpenSSH has its own setting in PermitRootLogin. The PubkeyAuthentication setting allows or denies login authentication based purely on public-key cryptography. You can trust this as far as you can trust the host on which the private parts of those keys are stored (unless they are protected by pass-phrases, in which case you can trust them a bit further).

IgnoreRhosts allows or denies the old-fashioned—and very insecure—rhosts authentication, used by the *rsh/rlogin/rcp* suite. This way of authenticating connections is not only insecure, but also made obsolete by public-key authentication. If you combine rhosts authentication with public-key authentication of the connecting host, on the other hand, it's immediately a lot more secure—but host keys cannot be protected by passphrases. Use of the rhosts authentication is still not recommended, but in some settings it is appropriate, and HostbasedAuthentication enables it.

PasswordAuthentication allows or denies authentication by the old-fashioned passwords read and stored by rhosts authentication. This requires that your users exercise good password maintenance, as with all other password-based authentication schemes.

    X11Forwarding yes

If X11 forwarding is enabled on the server and your client requests it (using the -X option), the client and server will forward traffic from a port on the server side to your DISPLAY. The server sets the remote DISPLAY to the local port that *sshd* uses to transfer X Window System traffic to your local screen, as well as to accept input from your local devices. To secure this forwarding activity, the server will install an *xauth* authentication token that it will enforce for all new connections. This port forwarding and extra authentication, which we'll return to, makes OpenSSH a very versatile remote terminal program.

DSA and RSA Overview

The Digital Signature Algorithm (DSA) is an open standard used for creating digital signatures based on public key encryption. DSA is used in many different applications, including SSH and GPG, because it is an open standard and not subject to traditional copyright. The Rivest, Shamir, Adleman (RSA) algorithm is the first algorithm widely used to create digital signatures, but it is subject to copyright restrictions that some developers find onerous.

You will find that SSH uses RSA by default, whereas GPG uses DSA. As with many algorithms, you can specify various bit lengths; 1024 and 2048 are common lengths, but given the increase in processor speeds that permit ever-faster brute force attacks, 2048 is currently considered the minimal length to provide acceptable security.

Generating and Using Keys

In most cases, you will want to generate SSH keys for your own accounts and perhaps your root account. Use *ssh-keygen* for this. A reference for the needed commands appears at the end of this section (the short of it is: run *ssh-keygen -t dsa* and press the Enter key at all the prompts). This key allows password-less remote logins, as long as PubkeyAuthentication is enabled in the server configuration file.

In *~/.ssh/id_dsa.pub* you can find the public key you've generated through *ssh-key-gen*. You need to transport this key to the remote machine. Because it's a public key, it does not need to be secure. On the remote machine, put the key at the end of *~/.ssh/authorized_keys2*. Once the key is in that file, all users who have the private-key counterpart will be able to log in to that remote account without a password.

Enabling bulk logins on multiple hosts for multiple users

Sometimes it makes sense to let users log into other machines without having to set up authentication themselves. The easiest way to do this is to create and modify all the files on one machine, as described in the following procedure, and then use *tar* and *ssh* in a pipe to transfer them to the other hosts.

1. Enable `HostbasedAuthentication` in */etc/ssh/sshd_config* configuration files on all hosts.

> ## On the Exam
>
> The exam may ask you about the `HostbasedAuthentication` feature and its purpose. Make sure that you know its purpose, as well as the exact location of the */etc/ssh/sshd_config* file.

2. Your client configuration is in */etc/ssh/ssh_config*. All hosts should have `Hostba sedAuthentication yes` set there, and if they have a `PreferredAuthentications` statement, it should list `hostbased` first. The hosts' private keys should be readable only by *root* (otherwise, the key would not be all that secret). Exactly what is needed to get SSH access to the keys depends on the version. If your SSH package includes an executable called *ssh-keysign*, it must be SUID root (it may not be installed that way, so you must check this manually) and must provide the signing service that proves the host's identity in the key exchange. If the package does not contain *ssh-keysign*, make sure the *ssh* executable is SUID root through *chmod u+s /usr/bin/ssh*.

3. On each host, create */etc/ssh/shosts.equiv*. This file defines the hosts with equivalent security levels. In these files, enter the hostnames of all the hosts as they appear in reverse lookups.

4. On each host, create */etc/ssh/ssh_known_hosts*. This file must contain the host keys of all the hosts involved, under the names you used in the previous item. The easiest way to do this is to connect to all the hosts using the right names. After doing that, the user account that made the connections will have all the correct entries in its *~/.ssh/known_hosts* file. Simply transfer the entries to the system file.

After the previous steps are carried out on all the hosts, all ordinary users should be able to use *ssh* back and forth between all the nodes with no other authentication. However, this is not true for the *root* user; she still needs user key or password authentication. Trusting a remote *root* is far more serious than trusting a mundane remote user.

Using the RSA algorithm

The RSA algorithm has become the *de facto* standard used in SSH and is employed by default, although it is possible to use additional algorithms. When it comes time to save the key you generate using RSA, you can use any name you wish. However, most people stick to the defaults:

~/.ssh/id_rsa
> The name of the file that contains the private key. This file should be readable and writable only by the owner and no one else. If anyone else were to obtain a copy of this file, he would be able to decipher all communications encrypted by your copy of SSH.

~/.id_rsa.pub
> The name of the file that contains the public key. You can give this key to anyone you wish. Individuals will import this key into their keychains. Once a user imports this key, they can decipher encrypted text or files that you send to them.

ssh-keygen

Syntax

```
ssh-keygen [-b bits] -t type
ssh-keygen -p [ -t type ]
ssh-keygen -q -t rsa1 -f /etc/ssh/ssh_host_key -C '' -N ''
ssh-keygen -q -t rsa -f /etc/ssh/ssh_host_rsa_key -C '' -N ''
ssh-keygen -q -t dsa -f /etc/ssh/ssh_host_dsa_key -C '' -N ''
```

Description

ssh-keygen generates keys to identify hosts or users in the SSH protocol, versions 1 and 2.

The first form creates a key. For version 1 of the protocol, the type should be **rsa1**. For version 2, it can be either **rsa** or **dsa**. The **-b** option sets the number of bits in the keys: 512 is the minimum, and 1024 bits is the default. In general, you can use as many bits as you like. During key generation, you will be asked to give a passphrase. A passphrase is different from a password in that it is a phrase, not simply a word, and is expected to be long. If a key pair has a passphrase associated with it, you will be expected to provide that passphrase interactively every time you need to access that key pair. If this is undesirable (for example, if you have unattended processes accessing the key pair), you don't want to provide a passphrase.

The second form is used to change your passphrase.

The three last forms are used to generate the three different kinds of host keys. The first is for version 1 of the protocol; the two others are for version 2. The **-f** option sets the output filename; if you omit the option, you will be prompted for the name. The **-C** option sets a comment on the key, and **-N** sets the passphrase.

Example

Generate a private key and then change its passphrase:

```
$ ssh-keygen -t dsa -b 2048
Generating public/private dsa key pair. Enter file in which to save the key
(/home/janl/.ssh/id_dsa): <Press the Enter key>
```

```
Created directory '/home/jan1/.ssh'.Enter passphrase \
        (empty for no passphrase): passphrase
Enter same passphrase again: passphrase
Your identification has been saved in /home/jan1/.ssh/id_dsa.
Your public key has been saved in /home/jan1/.ssh/id_dsa.pub.
The key fingerprint is:
c2:be:20:4a:17:2e:3f:b2:73:46:5c:00:ef:38:ca:03 jan1@debian
$ ssh-keygen -p -t dsa
Enter file in which the key is (/home/jan1/.ssh/id_dsa): <Press the Enter key>
Enter old passphrase: passphrase
Key has comment '/home/jan1/.ssh/id_dsa'
Enter new passphrase (empty for no passphrase): passphrase
Enter same passphrase again: passphrase
Your identification has been saved with the new passphrase.
```

The Server Public and Private Key

When SSH first starts after installation, it will create a key pair, namely */etc/ssh/ ssh_host_rsa_key* and */etc/ssh/ssh_host_rsa_key.pub*, assuming that the server is using the default RSA algorithm. This public key always has a *.pub* ending, and resides in the */etc/ssh/* directory. The SSH server on your system uses this file to authenticate itself to anyone who logs on. The *ssh-keygen* command can be used to view the contents of the public key file:

```
$ ssh-keygen -l -f /etc/ssh/ssh_host_rsa_key.pub
1024 98:2g:h8:k9:de:9f:fg:90:34:v3:35:3j:26:24:26:7k ssh_host_rsa_key.pub
```

If the server is using the DSA algorithm, the key names will be as follows:

- */etc/ssh/ssh_host_dsa_key*
- */etc/ssh/ssh_host_dsa_key.pub*

On the Exam

Make sure that you know the syntax for the -t option of *ssh-keygen*. Make sure that you understand the differences in filenames created between specifying the dsa and the default rsa arguments to the -t option.

---

ssh-agent

ssh-agent makes it practical to use passphrases on your private keys. The principle is to use *ssh-agent* to add your keys to a background agent on the system that will hold them in escrow. You give your passphrase only once, when you add the key. The agent will give the keys out to other processes owned by you that request the keys. You should be aware that the *root* user can also request the keys without your noticing, so you must trust the *root* user.

The process is quite simple; start the agent, and then add the passphrase you used to create the key:

```
$ eval `ssh-agent`
Agent pid 11487
```

Securing Data with Encryption

```
$ ssh-add
Enter passphrase for /home/janl/.ssh/id_dsa: passphrase
Identity added: /home/janl/.ssh/id_dsa (/home/janl/.ssh/id_dsa)
```

By default, all your keys will be added. If several of your keys have the same pass-phrase, they will all be added without further questions. If they have different pass-phrases, *ssh-add* will be prompted for them. If you include a file on the *ssh-add* command line, the key in that file will be added and the command will not prompt for keys.

ssh-agent works by setting two environment variables: SSH_AUTH_SOCK, which names the socket on which to communicate with the agent, and SSH_AGENT_PID, which makes it easy to kill the agent. That is also why the PID (process ID) shows up in the previous listing. The agent emits a shell script that, when evaluated, sets those variables correctly.

Since using passphrases makes remote logins immeasurably more convenient, it may be a good idea to make it simple for your users to use passphrases by starting *ssh-agent* whenever they log in. However, the users' *.bashrc* or *.login* scripts are not a good place for the command, nor is the system */etc/profile*, because you don't need the command to run every time a new terminal is started. A good place to put it is in the system-wide *Xsession* scripts. Exactly which script is used to start an X session depends on which distribution and which desktop people use (KDE, GNOME, classical X, their own custom session). But on Debian-based and Red Hat-based systems, there are standard ways to do it.

On Debian-based systems, if you put use-ssh-agent on a line by itself in */etc/X11/xdm/xdm.options*, anyone who later logs in with the X Window System will cause the script */etc/X11/Xsession.d/90xfree86-common_ssh-agent* to run. It is reproduced here for convenience:

```
STARTSSH=
SSHAGENT=/usr/bin/ssh-agent
SSHAGENTARGS=

if grep -qs ^use-ssh-agent "$OPTIONFILE"; then
 if [ -x "$SSHAGENT" -a -z "$SSH_AUTH_SOCK" -a -z "$SSH2_AUTH_SOCK" ]; then
  STARTSSH=yes
  if [ -f /usr/bin/ssh-add1 ] && cmp -s $SSHAGENT /usr/bin/ssh-agent2; then
   # use ssh-agent2's ssh-agent1 compatibility mode
   SSHAGENTARGS=-1
  fi
 fi
fi

if [ -n "$STARTSSH" ]; then
 REALSTARTUP="$SSHAGENT $SSHAGENTARGS $REALSTARTUP"
fi
```

This script first looks for the system-wide use-ssh-agent setting, then very carefully checks whether any of the *ssh-agent*-related variables are set already, because if they are set, an agent should already be running. Finally, it redefines REALSTARTUP so that the agent will be started later in the Debian scripts. The script could just as well have run `eval 'ssh-agent'` directly.

On Red Hat–based systems, you can accomplish the same effect by adding the preceding script to */etc/X11/xinit/xinitrc.d*, but it should be changed to run the agent directly, as Red Hat–based systems do not set up all the environment variables that Debian-based systems do. In most versions of Linux, the agent is started automatically. This includes, for example, all recent versions of Ubuntu and other Debian-based systems.

But none of these automated systems adds any keys to the agent. That means that users will still be prompted for a passphrase. Users can run *ssh-add* (perhaps in their *.bashrc* files) and enter their passphrases once into a shell terminal each time X starts.

It may be a good idea to doctor the automated X setup further with an *ssh-add* command. If run without a terminal, *ssh-add* pops up a graphical passphrase input box.

On the Exam

You may be asked to provide the proper syntax for making sure *ssh-agent* is running (which is `eval ` ssh-agent``). Also be ready to show how to use *ssh-add* after the user has generated a key.

Other SSH Tricks

OpenSSH respects TCP wrapper configurations, described in Chapter 23.

sshd, like the Linux *login* program, denies logins when the file */etc/nologin* exists. When remotely maintaining hosts in a way that may disrupt user activities, you should create this file with a helpful explanation of what is happening. This will stop all nonroot logins by any method, so you can do your maintenance undisturbed. The file is usually created by the *shutdown* command as well, to keep users from logging in while the machine is shutting down. The file is removed after a complete boot:

```
# cat >/etc/nologin
```

If there is any reason to suspect that your maintenance work can disconnect you or break the login mechanism, you should keep multiple login sessions open while doing the work. Test logging in again before closing them. Otherwise, doing a tiny PAM change that breaks all authentication could force you to reboot the machine into single-user mode to recover.

Consider scheduling an *at* or *cron* job to remove */etc/nologin* at a particular time, in the event you log yourself out. Such a job can be handy when restarting *sshd* from a remote location as well.

Securing Data with Encryption

SSH Port Forwarding

ssh has the ability to forward arbitrary IP-based protocols. The syntax is given next.

ssh -R|L

Syntax

```
ssh -R|L port:host:host_port [user@]hostname [command]
```

Description

When the main option is *-L*, *ssh* redirects traffic from the local port *port* to the remote machine and port given by *host:host_port*. The *host* is resolved by the resolver on the host you connect to. For security reasons, it binds only to the localhost address, not to any ethernet or other interfaces you may have.

When a program connects to the localhost port, the connection is forwarded to the remote side. A very useful application for this is to forward local ports to your company's mail server so you can send email as if you were at the office. All you have to do then is configure your email client to connect to the right port on `localhost`. This is shown by the example in the following section.

When using *-R*, the reverse happens. The *port* port of the remote host's localhost interface is bound to the local machine, and connections to it will be forwarded to the local machine given by *host:host_port*.

Example

Log into *login.example.com*. Then, forward connections that come into localhost port 2525 to port 25 on *mail.example.com*, which would otherwise reject relaying for you. The reason for binding to port 2525 is that you need to be *root* to bind to port 25:

```
$ ssh -L 2525:mail.example.com:25 login.example.com
```

Configuring OpenSSH

This section explains how to acquire, compile, install, and configure OpenSSH for Linux, so that you can use it in place of *telnet*, *rsh*, and *rlogin*.

In the unlikely event that your Linux distribution does not include OpenSSH, it is available at *http://www.openssh.com/portable.html* and at many mirror sites around the world. It is a simple matter to compile and install OpenSSH if you have *gcc*, *make*, and the necessary libraries and header files installed. The OpenSSH build uses *autoconf* (the usual *configure*, *make*, and so on) like most other free software/open source projects.

To enable login from remote systems using OpenSSH, you must start *sshd*, which may be done simply by issuing the following command:

```
# sshd
```

Note that you do not need to put this command in the background, as it handles this detail itself. Once the *sshd* daemon is running, you may connect from another SSH-equipped system:

```
# ssh mysecurehost
```

The default configuration should be adequate for basic use of SSH.

On the Exam

SSH is an involved and highly configurable piece of software, and detailed knowledge of its setup is not required. However, SSH is an important part of the security landscape. Be aware that all communications using SSH are encrypted using public/private key encryption, which means that plain-text passwords are not exposed by SSH and are therefore unlikely to be compromised.

Configuring and Using GNU Privacy Guard (GPG)

This book isn't the place for a full GPG tutorial. However, the LPI 102 exam requires you to understand how to use the standard GPG command to:

- Generate a key pair
- Import (i.e., add) a public key to a GPG keyring
- Sign keys
- List keys
- Export both a public and private key
- Encrypt and decrypt a file

You will also be expected to troubleshoot a standard implementation, which means that you'll need to understand the files in the *~/.gnupg/* directory.

Generating a Key Pair

Following is an example of the sequence necessary for generating a key pair in GPG:

```
$ gpg --gen-key
pg (GnuPG) 1.2.1; Copyright (C) 2008 Free Software Foundation, Inc.
This program comes with ABSOLUTELY NO WARRANTY.
This is free software: you are free to change and redistribute it.

There is NO WARRANTY, to the extent permitted by law.


gpg: keyring '/home/james/.gnupg/secring.gpg' created
gpg: keyring '/home/james/.gnupg/pubring.gpg' created
Please select what kind of key you want:
   (1) DSA and ElGamal (default)
   (2) DSA (sign only)
   (5) RSA (sign only)
Your selection? 5
What keysize do you want? (1024) 2048
Requested keysize is 2048 bits
Please specify how long the key should be valid.
        0 = key does not expire
      <n> = key expires in n days
     <n>w = key expires in n weeks
     <n>m = key expires in n months
```

```
        <n>y = key expires in n years
Key is valid for? (0) 3y
Key expires at Fri Sep 18 00:23:00 2009 CET
Is this correct (y/n)? y

You need a User-ID to identify your key; the software constructs the user id
from Real Name, Comment and Email Address in this form:
    "James Stanger (James Stanger) <stangernet@comcast.net>"
Real name: James Stanger
Email address: stangernet@comcast.net
Comment: <nothing>
You selected this USER-ID:
    "James Stanger <stangernet@comcast.net>"
Change (N)ame, (C)omment, (E)mail or (O)kay/(Q)uit? o
You need a Passphrase to protect your secret key.
Enter passphrase: <passphrase>
Repeat passphrase: <passphrase>

We need to generate a lot of random bytes. It is a good idea to perform
some other action (type on the keyboard, move the mouse, utilize the
disks) during the prime generation; this gives the random number
generator a better chance to gain enough entropy.
..+++++
+++++
public and secret key created and signed.
key marked as ultimately trusted.

pub  2048R/97DAFDB2 2004-01-12 James Stanger <stangernet@comcast.net>
Key fingerprint = 85B2 0933 AC51 430B 3A38  D673 3437 9CAC 97DA FDB2

Note that this key cannot be used for encryption.  You may want to use
the command "--edit-key" to generate a secondary key for this purpose.
```

Notice that you have several options when you first issue the *gpg --gen-key*
command:

DSA and ElGamal
    A DSA key pair is created for making signatures to sign files, and an ElGamal
    key pair is created to encrypt files.

DSA sign only
    A faster method, but only creates a key pair that can sign files.

RSA sign only
    Same as option 2 but uses RSA encryption instead of DSA.

On the Exam

You will only need to know about option 1, DSA and ElGamal. You will not be
expected to know how to use GPG with email applications, such as Mozilla
Thunderbird.

Importing a Public Key to a GPG Keyring

The GPG public key repository is called a "keyring." The keyring contains your private key (or multiple private keys), plus all of the public keys of individuals you wish to communicate with. To add a public key to your keyring, you generally obtain a text file that contains the public key. If, for example, the file were named *andy_oram_oreilly.asc*, you would issue the following command:

```
$ gpg --import andy_oram_oreilly.asc
```

Signing Keys

Before you can safely use an imported key, you need to sign it. To do so, issue the following command from your terminal:

```
$ gpg --edit-key username
```

If, for example, you wished to sign the key within the *andy_oram_oreilly.asc* file, you would need to obtain the username of that key. Let's assume that the username is *Andyo*. You would then issue the following command:

```
$ gpg --edit-key "Andyo"
```

You will then be asked if you wish to really sign the key. As your reply, you need to provide the password for your private key. Once you do this, GPG will sign the key you have just imported.

Listing Keys

Once you have imported keys, you can then list all of them by using the *--list-keys* option:

```
$ gpg --list-keys
```

This command lists both your private key (you usually have only one, but you can have as many as you like) as well as the public keys you have imported. An example of output from the command on a keyring that contains keys for James Stanger and Andy Oram would appear as follows:

```
/home/james/.gnupg/pubring.gpg
---------------------------------------
pub   2048g/CC7877gh 2009-09-11 James (Stanger) <stangernet@comcast.net>
sub   2048g/89G5B4KM 2009-09-11

pub   2048D/4g37NJ27 2009-12-09 Andyo (Oram) <andyo@oreilly.com>
sub   2048D/4g37GK38 2009-12-09
```

The pub defines the DSA master signing key, and the sub defines the ElGamal encryption subkey.

If you wish to list just the private keys, or what GPG calls "secret keys," use the *--list-secret-keys* option. To list just the public keys, use the *--list-public-keys* option.

Export both a Public and Private Key

Exporting your private key is useful because you will want to create a backup should your system somehow become unavailable or experience a problem. To create a backup of all keys to a single file, issue the following command:

```
$ gpg --export -o gpg_backup_file
```

If, for example, your username were James Stanger, the following command would export only your private key to a file named *private.key*:

```
$ gpg --export-secret-key -a "James Stanger" -o private.key
```

To export your public key, you would issue the following command:

```
$ gpg -- export-public-key -a "James Stanger" -o stanger.pub
```

Encrypting a File

Now suppose that you wish to encrypt a file named *chapter24.odt* so that only the user named Andy Oram can use it. You would issue the following command:

```
$ gpg -e -u "James Stanger" -r "Andy Oram" chapter24.odt
```

The resulting file would be called *chapter24.odt.gpg*.

Once Andy receives this file, he would issue the following command:

```
$ gpg -d chapter24.odt.gpg
```

He would then be able to read the file using OpenOffice.

Troubleshooting Files in the ~/.gnupg/ Directory

The LPI exam also expects you to identify the files in the *~/.gnupg* directory, mainly because you may need to troubleshoot an installation or obtain a private key. Following is a listing of the files found in a typical GPG implementation, regardless of Linux distribution:

gpg.conf
　　Allows you to create default settings for GPG, including a preferred key server. A key server contains the public keys of any user who wishes to upload her keys.

pubring.gpg
　　Contains the public keys that you have imported.

random_seed
　　A text file containing settings that enable GPG to create random numbers more quickly and easily.

secring.gpg
　　Contains the private key that determines your identity.

trustdb.gpg
　　The trust database, which contains the information concerning the trust values you have assigned to various public keys. A user may set variable levels of trust

---

to public keys in his key ring. More information on trust can be found in the GPG documentation (*http://www.gnupg.org/gph/en/manual.html*).

On the Exam

Make sure that you understand how to import a public key and export both public and private keys.

25

Exam 102 Review Questions and Exercises

This chapter presents review questions to highlight important concepts and hands-on exercises that you can use to gain experience with the Topics covered on the LPI Exam 102. The exercises can be particularly useful if you're not accustomed to more advanced Linux administration, and they should help you better prepare for the exam. To complete the exercises, you need a working Linux system that is not in production use. You might also find it useful to have a pen and paper handy to write down your responses as you work your way through the review questions and exercises.

Shells, Scripting, and Data Management (Topic 105)

Review Questions

1. Why is it dangerous to have "." (the current working directory) in your $PATH variable?

2. What characteristic of a *bash* variable changes when the variable is exported?

3. What configuration files will *bash* read when a shell is started?

4. Describe the concept of shell aliases.

5. When is a shell function more suitable than a shell alias?

6. Describe the function of */etc/profile*.

7. What must the author of a new script file do to the file's mode in order to make it executable?

8. How does the shell determine what interpreter to execute when starting a script?

9. How can a shell script use return values of the commands it executes?

10. What are some common open source databases available on Linux systems?

11. Describe the common MySQL datatypes and when they are appropriate to use.

12. What is the difference between a join and a left join in a SQL query?

Exercises

1. Using *bash*, enter the *export* command and the *set* command. Which set of variables is a subset of the other? What is the difference between the variables reported by *export* and those reported by *set*? Finally, enter *which export*. Where is the *export* command located?

2. Examine */etc/profile*. How is the default umask set? What customizations are done in the file for system users?

3. Create a simple *bash* script using the #!/bin/bash syntax, set the executable mode bits, and execute the shell. If it runs correctly, add errors to see the diagnostic messages. Have the script report both exported and nonexported variables. Verify that the nonexported variables do not survive the startup of the new shell.

4. Create some bash aliases in your current shell. Start a new shell by running the command *bash* in your current shell. Do your aliases work in this child shell? Why or why not?

5. Create a MySQL table structure that could be used to store the fields in the file */etc/passwd*. Write a shell script to parse this file, one line at a time, and call the *mysql* command-line program to insert the users defined in */etc/passwd* into your table. Once this is complete, write a SQL query to list all usernames that have a shell of */bin/bash*.

The X Window System (Topic 106)

Review questions

1. What is the main X Windows configuration file?

2. What are the troubleshooting steps you need to take when X Windows won't start?

3. How can you switch between desktop environments (for example, running KDE instead of Gnome)?

4. What are some common functions that can be used to assist visually impaired users with using X Windows?

5. What file would you edit to make an application run every time you log into X Windows?

Exercises

1. Boot your system into runlevel 3. Log in as root and type the command */usr/bin/startx*. Exit X Windows and examine the logfile */var/log/Xorg.0.log*. What specific things does this file tell you about your graphical environment? From

this file, can you determine what video card you have and what resolutions it supports?

2. Exit X Windows and use the */sbin/init* command to change your system to run-level 5. Once X Windows starts, hit the key combination Ctrl-Alt-backspace. What happens to X Windows? Why does this happen?

Administrative Tasks (Topic 107)

Review questions

1. What would happen to a user account if the default shell were changed to */bin/false*?

2. When a new account is created with *useradd -m*, what files are used to populate the new home directory?

3. Compare and contrast the execution of */etc/profile* and */etc/bashrc*.

4. Compare and contrast *cron* and *at*.

5. Is there a *cron* command?

6. Describe the format of a *crontab* file, describing each of the six fields.

7. What does an asterisk mean in *crontab* fields 1 through 5?

Exercises

1. Add a user with *useradd*, including a new home directory populated with files from */etc/skel*.

2. Add a group with *groupadd*.

3. Use *usermod* to add your new user to the new group.

4. Set the new user's password using *passwd*.

5. Log into the new account, and use *newgrp* to change to the new group.

6. Delete the new group and user (including home directory) using *groupdel* and *userdel*.

7. Examine the contents of */etc/skel*. How similar are they to your own home directory?

8. Review the contents of */etc/profile* and */etc/bashrc*.

9. Add an entry in your personal *crontab* file to perform a task, such as sending you an email message. Confirm that the action occurs as expected. Experiment with the five time specifiers.

10. Schedule a command in the future with *at*. How is *at* different from *cron*?

Essential System Services (Topic 108)

Review Questions

1. Why is accurate time important on a Linux system? What options exist to keep time in sync?

2. Describe the difference between system time and the hardware clock.

3. How is time stored on a Linux system? How is the time zone used to modify this value?

4. What two things does the *syslogd* server use to categorize log entries? What are the limitations of this format?

5. Give some examples of what kinds of messages you would expect to see in */var/log/messages*.

6. What does *lpd* do to handle incoming print jobs destined for empty print queues?

7. Describe the kinds of information included in */etc/printcap*.

8. What is the function of a print filter?

9. What does the *-P* option specify to the print commands?

10. When is it useful to pipe into the standard input of *lpr* instead of simply using a filename as an argument?

11. How is the Ghostscript program used in printing to a non-PostScript printer?

12. What filter is used on a Linux system to print to remote printers on Windows clients?

13. What are the common Mail Transport Agents (MTAs) used on Linux systems? Give a brief description of each.

14. What command would you use to view the contents of the mail queue on a system running sendmail? What command would you use to force a resend of that queue?

15. What is the easiest way to forward all email coming into an account to another email address?

16. What file is used to maintain email aliases for local users? Describe the maintenance procedure for this file.

Exercises

1. Run the *date* command on your system. Is your system clock accurate? Run the command *ntpd –gnq*. Did you system time change? By how much?

2. Add this line:

   ```
   *.*     /var/log/everything
   ```

   to */etc/syslog.conf* and restart *syslog*. Now run *tail –f /var/log/everything*. What kinds of things do you see? How often are events written to this log?

3. Add the `local5` facility to your configuration. Use *logger* to write to your new logfile, and verify its contents. Compare your log entries with those in */var/log/messages*.

4. Examine */etc/logrotate.conf*. What happens after */var/log/messages* is rotated?

5. On a system with an existing printer, examine */etc/printcap*. Which print filter is used for the printer? Which queue or queues are directed at the printer?

6. Check the printer status with *lpq -P printer* and *lpc status*. Print to the queue using *lpr -P printer file*.

7. Examine */var/spool/lpd* for the spool directory of your print queue. Examine the files you find there.

8. Determine what MTA is installed on your system. Is it listening on TCP port 25? How can you tell?

9. Type the command *telnet localhost 25*. What do you see?

10. Type the command *echo "test" | mail root*. Now type *tail /var/log/maillog*. Was your mail delivered? How can you tell?

Networking Fundamentals (Topic 109)

Review Questions

1. Describe how the subnet mask affects the maximum number of hosts that can be put on a TCP/IP network.

2. Name the three default address classes and the subnet masks associated with them.

3. Identify the IPv4 private address ranges.

4. What are some advantages IPv6 has over IPv4?

5. The UDP protocol is said to be connectionless. Describe this concept and its consequences for applications that use UDP.

6. What is a TCP port? Give some examples of common TCP ports and the applications and protocols that use them.

7. What user command is frequently used to send ICMP messages to remote hosts to verify those hosts' connectivity?

8. Describe the contents and use of */etc/hosts*.

9. In what configuration file are DNS servers listed? What is intended if the local loopback address is included there on a workstation?

10. Name two modes of the *netstat* command and the program's output in each case.

11. Describe why the *route* command is needed for a single interface on a nonrouting workstation.

12. How does *traceroute* determine the identities of intermediate gateways?

13. Describe the advantages and consequences of implementing DHCP.

Exercises

1. Examine your system's TCP/IP configuration using *ifconfig eth0* or a similar command for your network interface. Are you using DHCP? What type of subnet are you running with? Is it a class A, B, or C address? Are you using a private address? Experiment with taking the interface offline using *ifconfig eth0 down* and *ifconfig eth0 up*.

2. Examine the contents of */etc/services*. How many protocols do you recognize?

3. Use the *dig* command to locate information from DNS servers about a domain name.

4. Examine your */etc/hosts* file. How much name resolution is accomplished in this file manually?

5. Examine your */etc/resolv.conf* file. How many DNS servers do you have available?

6. Execute *netstat -r*. How many routes are reported? What are the routes to the local network and interface for?

7. Use *traceroute* to examine the route to a favorite website.

Security (Topic 110)

Review Questions

1. What daemon is associated with the control files */etc/hosts.allow* and */etc/hosts.deny*?

2. In general terms, describe a method to locate SUID programs in the local filesystem. Why might an administrator do this routinely?

3. What is the danger of making */bin/vi* SUID?

4. Why should a user run *ssh* instead of *telnet*?

5. Describe shadow passwords and the file where the passwords are stored. Why don't we store encrypted password strings in */etc/passwd* anymore?

6. How can the tool */usr/sbin/lsof* help you identify potential security issues?

7. What is the difference between a hard limit and a soft limit, with regard to the *ulimit* command?

8. Why is it advisable to use *sudo* rather than *su* in an environment with multiple administrators?

9. What kinds of things can you ascertain about a remote system with the *nmap* command?

10. Describe the process of key-based authentication between systems using *ssh*.

11. What is the difference between a public and a private key? What are they used for?

12. Describe how to encrypt a file with *gpg*.

Exercises

1. Use *find* as described in Chapter 22 to locate SUID files. Is the list larger than you expected? Are the entries on your list justifiably SUID programs?

2. Create an entry in */etc/sudoers* that lets your user account run any command as root. Run some commands through *sudo* and watch the file */var/log/messages*. What entries do you see? How would this be useful in a multiadministrator environment?

3. Look at the file */etc/shadow*. What user accounts do not have passwords? Why don't they?

4. Experiment with the *chage* command to set the password age for your account.

5. Run *ulimit –a*. What default limits are set? What would be some useful limits to place on users?

6. Run *netstat --tcp –anp | grep LISTEN*. What processes on your system are listening on TCP ports? If you were to harden this system, how would you change this configuration?

7. Run *nmap localhost*. Does this output match what you saw from the previous *netstat* command? Why or why not?

8. If you have *xinetd* installed, go to the */etc/xinetd.d* directory and determine what services are enabled.

9. Run *ssh-keygen –t dsa*. What files were created in *~/.ssh*? What are the permissions on those files?

On the Exam

Practice, practice, practice! The best way to get familiar with Linux is by interacting with a working Linux system. Become familiar with the command line and how to read logfiles. Nothing is hidden from you in Linux; if you know where to look, simple tools such as *cat*, *ls*, and *grep* will tell you everything you need to know about your system. Spend as much time as you can working hands-on with a Linux system before you take the LPI 102 exam.

26

Exam 102 Practice Test

This chapter will give you an idea of what kinds of questions you can expect to see on the LPI 102 test. All questions are either multiple-choice single answer, multiple-choice multiple answer, or fill in the blank.

The questions are not designed to trick you; they are designed to test your knowledge of the Linux operating system.

As of April 1, 2009, all exam weights for LPI exams have been standardized to 60 weights.

Regardless of weight totals, each exam score is between 200 and 800. A passing score is 500. However, the number of correct questions required to achieve a score of 500 varies with the overall difficulty of the specific exam that is taken.

The number of questions on the exam is also tied to the total of the weights of the Objectives on the exam. With a total weight count of 60, the exam will have 60 questions. For each weighting, there will be one question. For example, if an Objective has a weight of 4, there will be 4 questions on the exam related to the objective.

The answers for these sample questions are at the end of this chapter.

Questions

1. What environment variable holds the list of all directories that are searched by the shell when you type a command name?

    a. $LIST

    b. $VIEW

    c. $PATH

    d. $ENV

    e. None of the above

2. In the *bash* shell, entering the !! command has the same effect as which one of the following (assuming *bash* is in emacs mode)?

   a. Ctrl-P and Enter

   b. Ctrl-N and Enter

   c. Ctrl-U and Enter

   d. !-2

   e. !2

3. Name the command that displays pages from the online user's manual and command reference.

4. Which of the following commands displays the comments from a *bash* script? Select all that apply.

   a. *find "^#" /etc/rc.d/rc.local*

   b. *sed '/^#/ !d' /etc/init.d/httpd*

   c. *grep ^# /etc/init.d/httpd*

   d. *grep ^# /etc/passwd*

   e. *locate "^#" /etc/skel/.bashrc*

5. Which one of the following answers creates an environment variable VAR1, present in the environment of a *bash* child process?

   a. *VAR1="fail" ; export VAR1*

   b. *VAR1="fail" \ export VAR1*

   c. *VAR1="fail"*

   d. *set VAR1="fail" ; enable VAR1*

   e. *export VAR1 \ VAR1="fail"*

6. What SQL command is used to modify data present in a table?

   a. INSERT

   b. WHERE

   c. UPDATE

   d. OVERWRITE

   e. JOIN

7. What output will the following command generate: *seq -s";" -w 1 10*

   a. 01;02;03;04;05;06;07;08;09;10

   b. 1;2;3;4;5;6;7;8;9;10

   c. 1;10

   d. 01;02;03;04;05;06;07;08;09;010

   e. None of the above

8. Adam wants to protect himself from inadvertently overwriting files when copying them, so he wants to alias *cp* to prevent overwrite. How should he go about this? Select one.

   a. Put `alias cp='cp -i'` in ~/.bashrc

   b. Put `alias cp='cp -i'` in ~/.bash_profile

   c. Put `alias cp='cp -p'` in ~/.bashrc

   d. Put `alias cp='cp -p'` in ~/.bash_profile

   e. Put `alias cp = 'cp -I'` in ~/.bashrc

9. Consider the following script, stored in a file with proper modes for execution:

   ```
   #!/bin/bash
   for $v1 in a1 a2
   do
   echo $v1
   done
   ```

   Which one of the following best represents the output produced on a terminal by this script?

   a. in

      a1

      a2

   b. a1

      a2

   c. $v1

      $v1

      $v1

   d. No output is produced, but the script executes correctly.

   e. No output is produced, because the script has an error.

10. Monica consults the */etc/passwd* file expecting to find encrypted passwords for all of the users on her system. She sees the following:

    ```
    jdoe:x:500:500::/home/jdoe:/bin/bash
    bsmith:x:501:501::/home/bsmith:/bin/tcsh
    ```

    Which of the following is true? Select one.

    a. Accounts *jdoe* and *bsmith* have no passwords.

    b. Accounts *jdoe* and *bsmith* are disabled.

    c. The passwords are in */etc/passwd-*.

    d. The passwords are in */etc/shadow*.

    e. The passwords are in */etc/shadow-*.

11. What is the main configuration file for X Windows?

    a. */etc/xorg.conf*

    b. */etc/x11.conf*

c. */etc/X11/x11.conf*

d. */etc/X11/xorg.conf*

e. None of the above

12. What file in the user's home directory will an X Windows application look to for configuration settings such as color and video mode?

a. *~/.xinitrc*

b. *~/.xconfig*

c. *~/.Xresources*

d. *~/.xorg.conf*

e. *~/.bashrc*

13. What is the protocol XDMCP used for?

a. Remote logging of X Windows events.

b. Remote control of a running X Windows display.

c. Graphical login support for the local host.

d. Graphical login support for remote hosts on the network.

e. None of the above.

14. Which of the following are *not* commonly used display managers for X Windows? Choose two.

a. *xdm*

b. *gdm*

c. *kdm*

d. *xfce*

e. *X11*

15. Emacspeak is:

a. A popular text editor for Linux.

b. A window manager.

c. An assistive technology that handles screen reading for a number of console applications.

d. An assistive technology that provides a user with an on-screen keyboard.

e. None of the above.

16. Which one of the following outcomes results from the following command?

```
# chmod g+s /home/software
```

a. The SUID bit will be set for */home/software*.

b. The SGID bit will be set for */home/software*, preventing access by those not a member of the *software* group.

c. The SGID bit will be set for */home/software*, to keep group membership of the directory consistent for all files created.

d. The sticky bit will be set for */home/software*.

e. The sticky bit will be applied to all files in */home/software*.

17. Which one of these files determines how messages are stored using *syslogd*?

    a. */etc/sysconfig/logger.conf*

    b. */etc/syslog.conf*

    c. */etc/syslogd.conf*

    d. */etc/conf.syslog*

    e. */etc/conf.syslogd*

18. Which MTA was designed specifically with security in mind?

    a. Sendmail

    b. Postfix

    c. Qmail

    d. Exim

    e. None of the above

19. Where are mail logs usually stored in a standard *syslog* setup?

    a. */var/log/messages*

    b. */var/log/secure*

    c. */var/log/dmesg*

    d. */var/log/maillog*

    e. */var/maillog*

20. How many hosts can exist on a subnet with mask 255.255.255.128? Select one.

    a. 512

    b. 256

    c. 128

    d. 127

    e. 126

21. For an Internet workstation with a single network interface, what routes must be added to interface *eth0* after it is initialized? Select one.

    a. None

    b. Interface

    c. Interface and default gateway

    d. Interface, local network, and default gateway

22. On a Linux server, what service is most likely "listening" on port 25? Select one.

    a. Apache

    b. SSHd

    c. Postfix

d. Samba

e. FTP

23. Which one of these protocols is a Layer 4 connection-oriented protocol? Select one.

    a. TCP

    b. IP

    c. UDP

    d. ICMP

24. Which command will display information about Ethernet interface *eth0*? Select one.

    a. *cat /proc/eth/0*

    b. *ifconfig eth0*

    c. *ipconfig eth0*

    d. *ipconfig /dev/eth0*

    e. *cat /etc/eth0.conf*

25. What does the *printcap* entry `sd` indicate? Select one.

    a. The system default printer

    b. A printer's spool directory

    c. A device file for the printer

    d. A location where errors are stored

    e. The printer driver

26. Which of the following is a valid entry in */etc/fstab* for a remote NFS mount from server *fs1*? Select one.

    a. `fs1:/proc /mnt/fs1 nfs defaults 9 9`

    b. `/mnt/fs1 fs1:/proc nfs defaults 0 0`

    c. `fs1:/home /mnt/fs1 nfs defaults 0 0`

    d. `/mnt/fs1 fs1:/home nfs defaults 0 0`

    e. `/home:fs1 /mnt/fs1 nfs defaults 0 0`

27. Which network protocol is used by SSH and FTP? Select one.

    a. ICMP

    b. UDP

    c. TCP

    d. DHCP

    e. PPP

28. Which of the following programs will display DNS information for a host? Choose all that apply.

    a. *host*

    b. *nslookup*

c. *nsstat*

d. *dig*

e. *ping*

29. Which of the following statements regarding the ICMP protocol is *not* true? Select one.

    a. ICMP is connectionless.

    b. ICMP provides network flow control.

    c. ICMP is also known as UDP.

    d. ICMP is used by *ping*.

30. What server daemon resolves domain names to IP addresses for requesting hosts?

31. What function does a print filter serve? Select one.

    a. It collates output from multiple users.

    b. It translates various data formats into a page description language.

    c. It rejects print requests from unauthorized users.

    d. It rejects print requests from unauthorized hosts.

    e. It analyzes print data and directs print requests to the appropriate *lpd*.

32. Consider the following excerpt from the file */etc/resolv.conf* on a Linux workstation:

```
nameserver 127.0.0.1
nameserver 192.168.1.5
nameserver 192.168.250.2
```

What can be said about this configuration? Select one.

    a. Two DNS servers on the public network are being used for resolution.

    b. One DNS server on the local network is being used for resolution.

    c. The configuration contains errors that will prevent the resolver from functioning.

    d. A caching-only nameserver is the first nameserver queried.

    e. The resolver library will consult `nameserver 192.168.250.2` first.

33. Name the file that contains simple mappings between IP addresses and system names.

34. What program can be used to interactively change the behavior of a print queue? Select one.

    a. *lpd*

    b. *lpr*

    c. *lpq*

    d. *lprm*

    e. *lpc*

35. What program will display a list of each hop across the network to a specified destination? Select one.

    a. *tracert*

    b. *rttrace*

    c. *traceroute*

    d. *routetrace*

    e. *init*

36. What is the system-wide *bash* configuration file called? Include the entire path.

37. How can a nonprivileged user configure *sendmail* to forward mail to another account? Select one.

    a. She can add a new entry in */etc/aliases*.

    b. She can create a *.forward* file containing the new address.

    c. She can create an *.alias* file containing the new address.

    d. She can create a *sendmail.cf* file containing the new address.

    e. She cannot forward mail without assistance from the administrator.

38. How does a process indicate to the controlling shell that it has exited with an error condition? Select one.

    a. It prints an error message to *stderr*.

    b. It prints an error message to *stdout*.

    c. It sets an exit code with a zero value.

    d. It sets an exit code with a nonzero value.

    e. It causes a segmentation fault.

39. Consider the following trivial script called *myscript*:

```
#!/bin/bash
echo "Hello"
echo $myvar
```

Also consider this command sequence and result:

```
# set myvar='World'
# ./myscript
Hello
```

The script ran without error but didn't *echo* World. Why not? Select one.

    a. The syntax of the *set* command is incorrect.

    b. The script executes in a new shell, and `myvar` wasn't exported.

    c. The `#!/bin/bash` syntax is incorrect.

    d. The `$myvar` syntax is incorrect.

    e. The script is sourced by the current shell, and `myvar` is available only to new shells.

40. Consider the following line from */etc/passwd*:

```
adamh:x:500:1000:Adam Haeder:/home/adamh:/bin/bash
```

What does the number 1000 mean?

   a. User *adamh* has a UID of 1000.

   b. The primary group that *adamh* belongs to is group 1000.

   c. User *adamh* was the 1000th user created on this system

   d. The password for *adamh* expires in 1000 days.

   e. The secondary group that *adamh* belongs to is group 1000.

Answers

1. **c.** $PATH

2. **a.** The !! command history expansion executes the previous command. Entering the Ctrl-P keystroke uses the Emacs key-binding *bash* to move up one line in the history; pressing Enter executes that command.

3. The *man* command displays manpages.

4. **b** AND **c.** *find* and *locate* do not search the contents of files. */etc/passwd* is not a script.

5. **a.** The variable must be set and exported. The semicolon separates the two commands.

6. **c.** UPDATE

7. **a.** 01;02;03;04;05;06;07;08;09;10. The -*w* option to *seq* instructs it to pad with zeros.

8. **a.** *cp* should be aliased to the interactive mode with the -*i* option in *.bashrc*. *.bash_profile* normally doesn't include aliases.

9. **e.** The script has an error and will not produce the expected output. In a **for** statement, the loop variable does not have the dollar sign. Changing line 2 to **for** *v1* **in** a1 a2 will correct the error and produce the output in answer b.

10. **d.** The shadow password system has been implemented, placing all passwords in */etc/shadow* as denoted by the x following the username.

11. **d.** */etc/X11/xorg.conf*

12. **c.** *~/.Xresources*

13. **d.** Graphical login support for remote hosts on the network

14. **d.** *xfce* and e. *X11*.

15. **c.** An assistive technology that handles screen reading for a number of console applications

16. **c.** The g indicates that we're operating on the group privilege, and the +s indicates that we should add the "set id" bit, which means that the SGID property will be applied.

17. **b.** */etc/syslog.conf*

18. **c.** Qmail

19. **d.** */var/log/maillog*

20. **e.** With the top bit of the last byte set in the subnet mask (.128), there are 7 bits left. 2^7 is 128, less the network address and broadcast address, leaving 126 addresses for hosts.

21. **d.** Routes to the interface and the network are required to exchange information on the local LAN. To access the Internet or other nonlocal networks, a default gateway is also necessary.

22. **c.** As defined in */etc/services*, port 25 is the SMTP port, often monitored by *postfix*.

23. **a.** TCP. UDP is also a Layer 4 protocol, but it is connectionless.

24. **b.** The *ifconfig* command is used to configure and display interface information. *ipconfig* is a Windows utility.

25. **b.** The spool directory directive looks like this:

```
sd=/var/spool/lpd/lp
```

26. **c.** Answer a attempts to mount the */proc* filesystem. Answers b, d, and e have incorrect syntax.

27. **c.** Both Telnet and FTP are connection-oriented and use TCP for reliable connections.

28. **a**, **b**, **d**, AND **e.**

29. **c.** Although both ICMP and UDP are connectionless, they are different protocols.

30. The DNS daemon is *named*. It is included in a package called BIND.

31. **b.** A print server translates formats, such as PostScript to PCL.

32. **d.** The presence of the *localhost* address 127.0.0.1 indicates that *named* is running. Since the system is a workstation, it's safe to assume that it is not serving DNS to a wider community.

33. */etc/hosts*.

34. **e.** *lpc* is the line printer control program.

35. **c.** *traceroute*. *tracert* is a Windows utility with the same function as *traceroute*.

36. The file is */etc/profile*.

37. **b.** The *.forward* file is placed in the home directory containing a single line with the target email address.

38. **d.** Zero exit values usually indicate success.

39. **b.** Instead of using *set*, the command should have been:

```
# export myvar='World'
```

This gives the myvar variable to the new shell.

40. **b.** The primary group that *adamh* belongs to is group 1000.

27

Exam 102 Highlighter's Index

Shells, Scripting, and Data Management

Objective 105.1: Customize and Use the Shell Environment

- A shell presents an interactive Textual User Interface, an operating environment, a facility for launching programs, and a programming language.
- Shells can generally be divided into those derived from the Bourne shell, *sh* (including *bash*), and the C-shells, such as *tcsh*.
- Shells are distinct from the kernel and run as user programs.
- Shells can be customized by manipulating variables.
- Shells use configuration files at startup.
- Shells pass environment variables to child processes, including other shells.

Bash

- *bash* is a descendant of *sh*.
- Shell variables are known only to the local shell and are not passed on to other processes.
- Environment variables are passed on to other processes.
- A shell variable is made an environment variable when it is *exported*.
- This sets a shell variable:

      # PI=3.14

- This turns it into an environment variable:

      # export PI

- This definition does both at the same time:

      # export PI=3.14

- Shell aliases conveniently create new commands or modify existing commands:

    ```
    # alias more='less'
    ```

- Functions are defined for and called in scripts. This line creates a function named *lsps*:

    ```
    # lsps () { ls -l; ps; }
    ```

- *bash* configuration files control the shell's behavior. Table 13-1 contains a list of these files.

Objective 105.2: Customize or Write Simple Scripts

- Scripts are executable text files containing commands.
- Scripts must have appropriate execution bits set in the file mode.
- Scripts may define the command interpreter using the syntax #!/bin/bash on the first line.

Environment

- A script that starts using #!/bin/bash operates in a new invocation of the shell. This shell first executes standard system and user startup scripts. It also inherits exported variables from the parent shell.
- Like binary programs, scripts can offer a return value after execution.
- Scripts use file tests to examine and check for specific information on files.
- Scripts can use *command substitution* to utilize the result of an external command.
- Scripts often send email to notify administrators of errors or status.
- Refer to Chapter 13 for details on *bash* commands.

Objective 105.3: SQL Data Management

- Common MySQL datatypes are integer, float, boolean, date, timestamp, date-time, char, varchar, blob, and text.
- The SQL syntax for creating a table with one varchar column and one auto-increment integer column (which is also the primary key) is:

    ```
    CREATE TABLE test (id INTEGER UNSIGNED NOT NULL AUTO_INCREMENT, \
    column1 varchar(255), PRIMARY KEY (id));
    ```

- INSERT is used to insert data into a table, UPDATE is used to modify a data value in an existing table row, and SELECT is used to display values from a table.
- ALTER TABLE is used to add/remove columns to a table, or modify a datatype.
- A LEFT JOIN is used when we want to display items from two or more tables connected by a relationship, where each item present in the left table will display in the results, even if there is not a match with the other table being joined.

The X Window System

Objective 106.1: Install and Configure X11

- X.Org is the most popular X Windows implementation on Linux, replacing XFree86.
- Window managers handle the functions of creating and managing windows and things such as minimization, maximization, and screen placement.
- Desktop environments are collections of common desktop programs that work together to create a unified desktop experience. These will include applications such as window managers, file managers, launch bars, screensavers, and session managers. The two most common desktop environments are Gnome and KDE.
- The main configuration file for X.Org is */etc/X11/xorg.conf*.
- X Windows can be configured to either read fonts from a local directory or access a font server, such as *xfs*, running either on the local machine or on another machine on the network.

Objective 106.2: Set Up a Display Manager

- Display managers are GUI programs that handle the user login process. They are most often invoked when a Linux system enters runlevel 5. Common display managers are *xdm*, *gdm*, and *kdm*. They can all be configured to support remote graphical logins from other terminals through the XDMCP protocol.

Objective 106.3: Accessibility

- Many applications exist to assist with accessibility in Linux, including Emacspeak, Orca, and BLINUX. In addition to these separate applications, most desktop environments support assistive technologies such as StickyKeys, MouseKeys, and RepeatKeys. On-screen keyboards are also a commonly used assistive technology.

Administrative Tasks

Objective 107.1: Manage User and Group Accounts and Related System Files

passwd and group

- User account information is stored in */etc/passwd*.
- Each line in */etc/passwd* contains a username, password, UID, GID, user's name, home directory, and default shell.
- Group information is stored in */etc/group*.

- Each line in *etc/group* contains a group name, group password, GID, and group member list.
- *passwd* and *group* are world-readable.

Shadow files

- To prevent users from obtaining encrypted passwords from *passwd* and *group*, shadow files are implemented.
- Encrypted passwords are moved to a new file, which is readable only by *root*.
- The shadow file for */etc/passwd* is */etc/shadow*.
- The shadow file for */etc/group* is */etc/gshadow*.

User and group management commands

The following commands are commonly used for manual user and group management:

useradd user
> Create the account *user*.

usermod user
> Modify the *user* account.

userdel user
> Delete the *user* account.

groupadd group
> Add *group*.

groupmod group
> Modify the parameters of *group*.

groupdel group
> Delete *group*.

passwd username
> Interactively set the password for *username*.

chage user
> Modify password aging and expiration settings for *user*.

Objective 107.2: Automate System Administration Tasks by Scheduling Jobs

- Both *cron* and *at* can be used to schedule jobs in the future.
- Scheduled jobs can be any executable program or script.

Using cron

- The *cron* facility consists of *crond*, the *cron* daemon, and *crontab* files containing job-scheduling information.
- *cron* is intended for the execution of commands on a periodic basis.

- *crond* examines all *crontab* files every minute.
- Each system user has access to *cron* through a personal *crontab* file.
- The *crontab* command allows the *crontab* file to be viewed and, with the *–e* option, edited.
- Entries in the *crontab* file are in the form of:

    ```
    minute hour day month dayofweek command
    ```
- Asterisks in any of the time fields match all possible values.
- In addition to personal *crontab* files, the system has its own *crontab* files in */etc/crontab*, as well as files in */etc/cron.d*.

Using at

- The *at* facility, shown here, is for setting up one-time future command execution:

    ```
    at time
    ```
    Enter an interactive session with *at*, where commands may be entered. *time* is of the form *hh:mm*, *midnight*, *noon*, and so on.
- The *atd* daemon must be running in order for *at* commands to be processed.

User access

- Access to *cron* can be controlled using lists of users in *cron.allow* and *cron.deny*.
- Access to *at* can be controlled using lists of users in *at.allow* and *at.deny*.

Objective 107.3: Localization and Internationalization

- The suite of programs that comes with the Network Time Protocol (NTP) allow you to keep your system and hardware clocks in sync with accurate time servers over the Internet.
- *ntpd –q* will update a system clock against an NTP server and then exit.
- Hardware clocks are configured to reflect either local time or Universal Coordinated Time (UTC) plus a time zone offset. The command *hwclock* can be used to manipulate a hardware clock from within Linux.
- The file */etc/localtime* should be a symbolic link to the time zone configuration file appropriate for your locale. For example, in the central United States:

    ```
    # ls -l /etc/localtime
    lrwxrwxrwx 1 root root 30 Sep 12 13:56 /etc/localtime \
            -> /usr/share/zoneinfo/US/Central
    ```
- The command *tzselect* can be used to change your system's time zone.

Essential System Services

Objective 108.1: Maintain System Time

- Refer to the previous section on localization and internationalization.

Objective 108.2: System Logging

Syslog

- The syslog system displays and records messages describing system events.
- The syslog program is made up of two processes: *syslogd*, which logs user-level events, and *klogd*, which logs kernel events.
- Messages can be placed on the console, in logfiles, and on the text screens of users.
- Syslog is configured by */etc/syslog.conf* in the form `facility.level action`:

  `facility`
  > The creator of the message, selected from among `auth`, `authpriv`, `cron`, `daemon`, `kern`, `lpr`, `mail`, `mark`, `news`, `syslog`, `user`, or `local0` through `local7`.

  `level`
  > Specifies a severity threshold beyond which messages are logged and is one of (from lowest to highest severity) `debug`, `info`, `notice`, `warning`, `err`, `crit`, `alert`, or `emerg`. The special level `none` disables a facility.

  `action`
  > The destination for messages that correspond to a given selector. It can be a filename, *@hostname*, a comma-separated list of users, or an asterisk (meaning all logged-in users).

- Together, `facility.levels` comprise the *message selector*.
- Most syslog messages go to */var/log/messages*.

Logfile rotation

- Most system logfiles are rotated to expire old information and prevent disks from filling up.
- *logrotate* accomplishes log rotation and is configured using */etc/logrotate.conf*.

Examining logfiles

- Files in */var/log* (such as *messages*) and elsewhere can be examined using utilities such as *tail*, *less*, and *grep*.
- Information in *syslogd* logfiles includes date, time, origin hostname, message sender, and descriptive text.
- To debug problems using logfile information, first look at the hostname and sender, and then at the message text.

Objective 108.3: Mail Transfer Agent (MTA) Basics

- The most common MTAs on Linux are sendmail, postfix, qmail, and exim.
- sendmail, being the oldest MTA, has influenced current MTAs greatly. The other three popular MTAs all have sendmail "compatibility programs" to enable them to act as drop-in replacements for sendmail.
- The file */etc/aliases* stores aliases for inbound mail addresses; it can redirect mail to one or more users.
- Whenever */etc/aliases* is modified, *newaliases* must be executed.
- Each user can forward his own mail using a *.forward* file, containing the forwarding email address, in his home directory.
- Outbound mail that is trapped due to a network or other problem will remain queued; it can be examined using the *mailq* command.

Objective 108.4: Manage Printers and Printing

CUPS

- The Common Unix Printing System (CUPS) is the current standard for printing on Linux.
- The *cupsd* daemon handles print spooling. Configuration files are stored in */etc/cups/*, and configuration usually happens through a web interface accessed through *http://localhost:631/*.
- CUPS maintains backward compatibility with *lpd*.
- CUPS supports printer configuration in the file */etc/printcap* for backward compatibility.

Legacy printing (lpd)

- Printers are assigned to queues, which are managed by *lpd*, the print daemon. *lpd* listens for inbound print requests, forking a copy of itself for each active print queue.
- *lpr* submits jobs to print queues.
- *lpq* queries and displays queue status.
- *lprm* allows jobs to be removed from print queues.
- *lpc* allows root to administer queues; it has both interactive and command-line forms.
- Filters translate data formats into a printer definition language.
- Spool directories hold spooled job data.

/etc/printcap

- New printer definitions are added to */etc/printcap*:

```
lp|ljet:\
        :sd=/var/spool/lpd/lp:\
```

```
:mx#0:\
:sh:\
:lp=/dev/lp0:\
:if=/var/spool/lpd/lp/filter:
:lf=/var/spool/lpd/lp/log:
```

The lines in this example are defined as follows:

lp|ljet:\
> This parameter defines two alternate names for the printer, *lp* or *ljet*.

sd=*spool_directory*
> This parameter specifies the spool directory, under */var/spool/lpd*.

mx=*max_size*
> The maximum size of a print job in blocks. Setting this to #0 indicates no limit.

sh
> Suppress header pages. Placing this attribute in *printcap* sets it, eliminating the headers.

lp=*printer_device*
> The local printer device, such as a parallel port.

if=*input_filter*
> The input filter to be used. See "CUPS filters" on page 359 for additional information.

lf=*log_file*
> The file where error messages are logged.

Networking Fundamentals

Objective 109.1: Fundamentals of Internet Protocols

Addressing and masks

- An address mask separates the network portion from the host portion of the 32-bit IP address.
- Class A addresses have 8 bits of network address and 24 bits of host address.
- Class B addresses have 16 bits of network address and 16 bits of host address.
- Class C addresses have 24 bits of network address and 8 bits of host address.
- Subnets can be defined using the defined "class" schemes or using a locally defined split of network/host bits.
- The all-zero and all-ones addresses are reserved on all subnets for the network and broadcast addresses, respectively. This implies that the maximum number of hosts on a network with n bits in the host portion of the address is 2^n-2. For example, a class C network has 8 bits in the host portion. Therefore, it can have a maximum of $2^8-2=254$ hosts.

Protocols

TCP/IP is a name representing a larger suite of network protocols. Some network protocols maintain a constant connection, whereas others do not.

IP
> The Internet Protocol is the fundamental building block of the Internet. It is used by other protocols.

ICMP
> This connectionless messaging protocol uses IP. It is used for flow control, detection of unreachable destinations, redirecting routes, and checking remote hosts (the *ping* utility).

UDP
> The User Datagram Protocol is a connectionless transport agent. It is used by applications such as DNS and NFS.

TCP
> The Transmission Control Protocol is a connection-oriented transport agent. It is used by applications such as FTP and Telnet.

PPP
> The Point-to-Point Protocol is used over serial lines, including modems.

TCP/IP services

- Inbound network requests to a host include a *port number*.
- Ports are assigned to specific programs. Definitions are stored in */etc/services*.
- Ports 1–1023 are privileged ports, owned by superuser processes.

TCP/IP utilities

- *ftp* implements the File Transfer Protocol client for the exchange of files to and from remote hosts.
- The *ssh* client program implements a secure shell session to a remote host.
- A web browser, such as Firefox, implements an *http* connection to a remote *http* server.
- *ping* sends ICMP echo requests to a remote host to verify functionality.
- *dig* obtains information from DNS servers.
- *traceroute* attempts to display the route over which packets must travel to a remote host.
- *fwhois* queries a *whois* database to determine the owner of a domain or IP address.

Objective 109.2: Basic Network Configuration

- The *ifconfig* command is used to both view information about an interface in addition to changing the network configuration of an interface.

- The program *dhclient* will query the local network for IP addressing information over *dhcp* and use this information to configure the settings for an interface.
- The command *route* will display the path that packets will take when they leave the system. It is also used to manually add routes.

Objective 109.3: Basic Network Troubleshooting

- Interfaces are configured through a number of configuration files.
- */etc/hostname* contains the assigned hostname for the system.
- */etc/networks* sets up equivalence between addresses and names for entire networks.
- The *host* command returns DNS information.
- The *hostname*, *domainname*, and *dnsdomainname* commands set or display the current host, domain, or node name.
- The *netstat* command displays network connections, routing tables, interface statistics, masquerade connections, and multicast memberships.

Objective 109.4: Configuring Client Side DNS

- */etc/hosts* contains static mappings between IP addresses and names.
- */etc/nsswitch.conf* directs system library functions to specific nameserver methods such as local files, DNS, and NIS.
- */etc/host.conf* controls name resolution for older libraries.
- */etc/host.conf* is rarely used and is replaced by */etc/nsswitch.conf*.
- */etc/resolv.conf* contains information to direct the resolver to DNS servers.

Security

Objective 110.1: Perform Security Administration Tasks

- *find* can perform searches for file attributes such as SUID using the *-perm* option.
- The *chage* command is used to maintain password aging on user accounts.
- The *nmap* program can be used to port scan local or remote systems for open ports.
- The *sudo* command is used to give elevated privileges to a defined set of users for a limited command set. The configuration file is */etc/sudoers*.
- The *ulimit* command is used to view and modify limits placed on users. The superuser maintains user limits in the file */etc/security/limits.conf*.
- Hard limits are limits that users cannot exceed, whereas soft limits are limits that users can exceed temporarily by calling the *ulimit* program.

Objective 110.2: Set Up Host Security

TCP wrappers

- Configuring TCP wrappers (*tcpd*) using */etc/hosts.allow* and */etc/hosts.deny* can enhance security for daemons controlled by *inetd* or *xinetd*.
- *tcpd* is often configured to deny access to all systems for all services (a blanket deny), and then specific systems are specified for legitimate access to services (limited allow).
- *tcpd* logs using syslog, commonly to */var/log/secure*.

Shadow passwords

- Enabling the use of *shadow passwords* can enhance local security by making encrypted passwords harder to steal.
- The use of shadow passwords causes the removal of password information from the publicly readable *passwd* file and places it in *shadow*, readable only by root.
- A similar system is implemented for shadow groups, using the *gshadow* file.

Objective 110.3: Securing Data with Encryption

- The best way to communicate securely between two Linux systems is via SSH. SSH can be run either as a command line, opening up a shell into another system, or as a wrapper around other TCP-based applications.
- SSH supports multiple authentication schemes, including standard username/ password and public/private key authentication.
- The command *ssh-keygen –t dsa* will create a public/private keypair. The keys are stored as *~/.ssh/id_dsa* (private key) and *~/.ssh/id_dsa.pub* (public key).
- Placing a copy of your public key in the file *~/.ssh/authorized_keys2* on a remote machine will allow you to perform passwordless, key-based authentication with that machine.
- The command *gpg --gen-key* will create a public/private key pair to use with the Gnu Privacy Guard (GPG). These keys will be stored in *~/.gnupg/*.
- To encrypt a file with another user's public key, you must:
  - Import the user's public key into your keyring: *gpg --import bobskey.asc*
  - Use that key to encrypt a file: *gpg –e –u "My Name" –r "Bobs Name" /tmp/ filename.txt*

Index

Symbols

! (bang) no match, 128
(hash mark) root shell prompt, xvi, 64
$ (dollar sign) command substitution, 273
$ (dollar sign) user prompt, xvi, 64, 124
$# variable, 262
$? variable, 273
* (asterisk) regex modifier, 125
+ (plus) regex modifier, 125
- single dash character, 68, 71
-- double dash character, 68, 110, 121
. (period) shortcut, 98, 125
/etc directory, 21
< redirection operator, 105
> redirection operator, 104
>> redirection operator, 104
? (question mark) regex modifier, 125
\ (backslash) escape, 124
\<\> match word boundaries, 124
^ caret, 124
| vertical line, 125
~ (tilde) shortcut, 98, 135, 262

A

access control, 176–181, 246, 437–439
access logfile, 366
access mode, 176, 180–185
access time, changing, 100
accessibility, 316–318, 477
action directive, 342
addresses
    IP allocation, 390–393
    masks, 482
    network, 370–372
    in sed, 128, 134
administrative tasks, 319–332, 459, 477
Advanced Package Tool (APT), 50
aggregate functions, 292–293
aliases, 256, 259, 267, 350, 476
alien, 52
anacron, 319
anchors, 130
annex, 199
Apache web server, 26
APT (Advanced Package Tool), 50
apt-get, 50
archives, creating/extracting, 94
arguments, 68, 261
ASCII mode, 378
at facility, 326, 329, 479
authentication rhosts, 444
automate sysadmin tasks by scheduling jobs, 326–330, 478
automatic allocation, 390

We'd like to hear your suggestions for improving our indexes. Send email to *index@oreilly.com*.

B

backends, 359
background, 118, 120
backup schemes, 37
bash (Bourne-Again Shell)
    basic scripts, 272–274
    built-in commands, 274–285
    configuration files, 261, 475
    overview, 257–267
    shared libraries, 44
    shell variables, 65
    standard I/O redirections for, 105
.bashrc file, 262, 264
Basic Input/Output System (BIOS), 7–10
basic network configuration, 383–394
basic network troubleshooting, 395–403
basic regular expression patterns, 133
bg command, 119
/bin directory, 195
/bin versus /sbin, 204
binary, 378
binary files, 199
BIOS (Basic Input/Output System), 7–10
BLINUX, 317
block devices, backing up, 95
/boot directory, 21, 196
boot loader, 39
boot manager, 33, 38–43, 231
boot time
    entering BIOS at, 8
    kernel parameters, 21
    messages, 23
bootable media types, 8, 36
booting
    the system, 21–24, 230
    from USB device, 36
BOOTP protocol, 390
BounceKeys, 318
Bourne, Stephen, 65
Bourne-Again Shell (see bash)
break command, 274
BrLTTY, 317
brute force attacks, 414
BSD and System V interfaces, 356
BSD syntax, 185
bulk logins, 445
Burrows-Wheeler block sorting, 92

bzip2 command, 92, 235

C

C-shells, 475
cancel command, 361
case command, 275
case, changing, 88
cat command, 78
chage, 416–418, 484
character sets, 125
check-updates command, 60
checking remote hosts, 375
chgrp command, 185
child processes, 107, 405
chipset, video, 299
chmod command, 74, 182
chown command, 184
CIDR (classless inter-domain routing), 371
class drivers, 11
classes, user, 177
classless inter-domain routing (CIDR), 371
clear command, 266
client side DNS, 383–394, 484
client/server logging, 343
clock, 8, 334–339
coldplugging, 20
command history and editing, 71–75
command line, 63, 64–77, 92, 232
command separator, 71
command substitution, 72, 273, 476
commands
    recursive, 233
    sequencing, 71
    user and group management, 323–326
comments, 262
common code, 285
compressing files, 92, 97
concatenation, 78
configuration files, 39, 257, 384–386
configuring client side DNS, 383–394, 484
continue command, 275
control characters, 88
control mounting and unmounting of filesystems, 139, 161–167, 244
Coordinated Universal Time (UTC), 340

E

e2fsck command, 157
echo command, 65, 127, 275
editing commands, 128
edquota command, 172
egrep command, 123
EHCI (Enhanced Host Controller
    Interface), 10
Emacspeak, 316
email, 347–354
emulation layer, SCSI, 141
encryption, 454
Enhanced Host Controller Interface
    (EHCI), 10
env command, 67
environment variables, 66, 108, 256, 257,
    331, 475
environment, shell, 256–267, 270, 475,
    476
erase command, 61
error detection/classification, 272
error logfile, 365
essential system services, 333–346, 355–
    367, 460, 480
/etc directory, 26, 162, 167, 195
Exam 101
    format, 2
    highlighter's index, 229–249
    objectives/topics, 1, 5
    physical setting, 2
    practice test, 215–228
    preparation for, 5
    review and exercises, 205–214
Exam 102
    format, 251, 252
    highlighter's index, 475–485
    objectives/topics, 253
    physical setting, 252
    practice test, 465–474
    preparation for, 253
    review and exercises, 457–463
exam preparation, 5
executable files, 269
execute command line instructions, 63,
    64–77, 232
execute permissions, 177
exim, 348, 354

exit command, 276, 379
expand command, 79
export command, 67
exporting keys, 454
extended partitions, 142, 243

F

facility directive, 341
fastforward command, 353
fdisk command, 145
fg command, 119
FHS (Filesystem Hierarchy Standard),
    193–199, 204, 211
file command, 96, 235
file descriptors, 102
file globbing, 97, 100–102, 123, 134, 236
file management, 63, 91–102, 235
file tests, 273
file-naming wildcards, 100–102
files, 91
    appending to, 104
    creating, 104
    deleting, 99
    editing using vi/vim, 64, 241
    locating, 200
Filesystem Hierarchy Standard (FHS),
    193–199, 204, 211
filesystems
    checking and repairing, 157–161
    creating, 148
    defined, 140
    disk quotas, 139, 167–174, 246
    hard links, 187
    inodes, 92, 151
    layouts, 35, 192, 248
    managing the table, 161
    modifying, 154
    mounting/unmounting, 163–167, 244
    objects, 91–100
    review questions/exercises, 211
    symbolic links, 187
    tests of, 96
    types of, 165
filters
    CUPS, 359, 363
    printer, 358, 481
    text stream, 63, 77, 127, 233, 235

mkdir command, 98, 236
mkfs command, 149
mkswap command, 150
/mnt directory, 195
mode, 176, 180–185
mode bits, 178
mode strings, 180
modification time, changing, 100
modifiers, 132
modify process execution priorities, 64,
    120–122, 239
modinfo command, 17
modprobe command, 18–20
modularity, 22
modules, manipulating, 14–20
modules.conf, 22
monitoring disk space, 151
monitors, 299, 305
mount command, 163–167, 180
mount points, 35, 143, 161, 167
mounting, 35, 140, 143, 161
MouseKeys, 317
mput command, 378
msdos filesystem module, 16
multiple-line commands, 70
multitable queries, 293–295
multiuser systems, 319
mv command, 99, 236
MySQL server, 285

N

name resolution, 384
netmask mask, 389
netstat command, 398–400, 422–425,
    484
network addressing, 370–372
network configuration, 383–394, 483
network interfaces, 372, 384–386, 400–
    403, 484
Network Time Protocol (NTP), 334–339
network troubleshooting, 395–403, 484
networking fundamentals, 369–382
   highlighter's index, 482
   review and exercises, 461
   standard Linux configuration, 393
Newham, Cameron, 274
newline characters, removing, 79
nice numbers, 120, 239

nice/renice commands, 120–122
nl command, 81
nmap command, 425–439, 484
nohup command, 118, 120
non-printable characters, 89
nonsharable data, 193
ntpd command, 334–336
ntpdate command, 336
ntpdc command, 338
ntpq command, 337
ntptrace command, 339

O

object types, 91
objectives, exam, xiv
objects
   filesystem, 91–100
   shared, 45
octal notation, 178, 247
od command, 82
OHCI (Open Host Controller Interface),
   10
one-way inheritance, 270
Open Host Controller Interface (OHCI),
   10
OpenSSH, 449, 450
/opt directory, 196
options, 68
Orca, 317
OS fingerprints, 425, 427
output redirection operators, 105
overwrite, forcing, 94
ownership, managing, 176–187, 271, 319

P

packages, Debian, 33, 46–52, 47, 232
page logfile, 366
parent process ID (PPID), 108
parent/child relationship, 108, 110
partitioning, 33, 34, 145, 243
partitions
   defined, 142
   extended, 142, 243
   guidelines, 38
   numbering of, 143
   resizing, 145
pass number, 162

passwd command, 325
password file, 320
password, shadow, 322, 414–418
paste command, 83
patterns, 123
PCMCIA driver information, 22
PDF generators, 359
Pearson VUE, xiv
peer, 335, 338
perform basic file editing operations using vi/vim, 64, 241
perform basic file management, 63, 91–102, 235
perform security administration tasks, 405–429, 484
permissions
    default setting, 181
    list of, 177
    managing file, 176–187, 246, 271
    symbolic and numeric, 187
    workgroup directory, 186
PID (Process ID), 108, 110
ping command, 375, 380, 388, 396, 406, 483
ping sweep, 425
pipeline, 104
pipes, 103
pooling, 338
port numbers, 376
position anchors, 125
positional parameters, 261
POSIX character classes, 124
postfix, 348, 351–353
PostScript printers, 359
PPD files, 359
PPP, 376, 483
pr command, 84
practice tests
    Exam 101, 215–228
    Exam 102, 465–474
prefix, 371
primary IDE interface, 142
primary partitions, 142, 243
printing
    overview, 355–367
    print jobs, 360
    queues, 356, 359, 360
    troubleshooting, 365

priorities, 120–122
private IP addresses, 370
private key, 447, 453–454
privileged ports, 376, 483
/proc filesystem, 8–10
process execution priorities, 64, 120–122, 239
process ID (PID), 108
process lifetime, 107
process monitoring, 108–115
process text streams using filters, 63, 77–91, 233
processes, 107
profiles, 262
prompt, 64, 379
protocols, 374–376, 483
ps command, 69, 109, 117
PS1, 65
pstree command, 110
public key, 445, 447, 453–454
public-key cryptography, 443
put command, 378
pwd, 379

Q

qmail, 348, 353
quantity modifiers, 125
query mode, 55–57
querying system services, 422–429
quit, 379
quotacheck command, 171
quotaoff command, 171
quotaon command, 170
quotas
    enabling, 175
    limits, 168

R

ramfs, 20
rc.local, 27
read command, 278
read permissions, 177
readline, 266
reboot system, 24
recursive copying, 93
recursive execution, 74, 233
recursive remove, 100

U

UDP, 375, 483
UHCI (Universal Host Controller Interface), 10
ulimit command, 418–422, 484
umask command, 181
umount command, 165, 166
uncompressing files, 92, 97
unexpand command, 89
unidirectional inheritance, 270
uninstall mode, 55
uniq command, 89
Universal Host Controller Interface (UHCI), 10
Universal Serial Bus (USB), 10–12, 36, 165
Unix System V, 26
unmounting, 166
unprivileged ports, 376
unreachable destinations, 375
unset command, 67
until command, 281
updatedb command, 202
updates, checking for, 60
upgrade mode, 54
uppercase, 88
uptime command, 114
URLs
    assistive technology, 318
    bash home page, 257
    BrLITTY, 317
    CUP, 358
    FHS specification, 193
    Freedesktop, 299
    GPG, 455
    GRUB, 43
    implementation of X, 297
    Linux Documentation Project, 145
    Linux Professional Institute, xiv
    LPI Objectives detailed, 5, 251
    LPRng, 356
    LVM-HOWTO, 145
    Network Time Protocol (NTP), 333
    nmap site, 428
    NTP documentation, 338
    onscreen graphical keyboard, 318
    OpenSSH, 442
    Pearson VUE, xiv
    pooling, 338
    qmail, 353
    tarball example, 207
    Thomson Prometric, xiv
    Vim documentation, 135
    X.Org mirror websites, 300
USB (Universal Serial Bus), 10–12, 36, 165
use Debian package management, 33, 46–52, 232
use RPM (Red Hat) and YUM package manager, 34, 52–61, 232
use streams, pipes, and redirects, 64, 102–107, 237
user access, 330, 418
user accounts, 319
user ID (UID), 108, 411–414
user quota limits, 168
user.group versus user:group syntax, 185
useradd command, 323
userdel command, 324
usermod command, 324, 413
username, 92, 271, 325, 411
users, classes of, 177
/usr directory, 196
UTC (Coordinated Universal Time), 340
utilities, 377–382

V

/var directory, 24, 196, 198
variable data, 193
variables
    environment, 108, 257
    shell, 65–71, 258
verify mode, 58
vi editor, 121, 135
video chipset, 299
video hardware, 299
virtual consoles, 309
virtual memory, 37

W

warning_message, 30
wc command, 90
websites (see URLs)
well-known ports, 376

whereis command, 203
which command, 200
while command, 282
whitespace characters, 89
whois, 381
wildcards, 100–102, 236, 311
window managers, 298
work on the command line, 63, 64–77, 92, 232
workgroup directory, 186
write permissions, 177

X

X display manager (xdm), 308–311
X fonts, 306
X Server, selecting and configuring, 299–305
X terminals, 298, 311
X Window System, 24
    accessibility, 316–318
    install and configure, 298–308
    overview, 298
    set up a display manager, 308–316
    SSH session, 442
X Window system
    highlighter's index, 477
    review and exercises, 458
X.Org, 299–305
Xaccess file, 308
xargs command, 106
xauth authentication, 442, 444
xdm (X display manager), 308–311
xdm-config file, 309
XFree86, 299, 306
xfs_info command, 157
xfs_metadump command, 160
xinetd command, 434–436, 485
xorg.conf, 300–303
.Xresources, 308
Xresources file, 309
Xservers file, 309
Xsession file, 309
Xsetup_0 file, 309
Xzoom, 317

Y

YUM (Yellowdog Updater Modified), 58–61

Z

zombies, 117

About the Authors

As the Vice President of Information Technology for the AIM Institute, **Adam Haeder**'s responsibilities include management of the IT department and all related technology ventures. He has been the lead instructor in AIM's Cisco Regional Networking Academy and is the Vice President of the Omaha Linux Users Group. Adam has written books about the IT job market and Linux certification. He serves on the technology advisory councils of Omaha Public Schools, Millard Public Schools, the University of Nebraska Lincoln and Omaha campuses, and the Linux Professional Institute. Adam has a Bachelor of Science degree in Computer Science from the University of South Dakota.

Stephen Addison Schneiter is currently the Certification Specialist with Certification Partners, LLC, having been with the company since 2005. Previously, Stephen was a tenured faculty member at the Tennessee Technology Center in Harriman for nine years. Stephen's wide range of expertise includes web-focused customer service, teaching post-secondary students, working with instructors one-on-one, network management and security issues working with Microsoft Windows and Linux, and website development. Stephen is an effective and talented instructor internationally, and his attributes have led to his participation in numerous national conference presentations and the coordination of the 2007 and 2008 Certified Internet Web Professional (CIW) National Conferences. Stephen serves on the advisory boards of several academic institutions and lives with his wife and daughter on their small farm in east Tennessee.

Bruno Gomes Pessanha has been a collaborating translator for the Linux Professional Institute since 2002. He also worked as a consulting analyst for a Brazilian government petroleum enterprise, covering Linux migration and initiatives and administering high-end performance projects, high-availability clusters, and mission-critical services. He currently lives with his family in Amsterdam.

James Stanger has been involved with Linux since 1995, and has worked closely with the Linux Professional Institute (LPI) since its inception in 1999. He is Chair of the LPI Advisory Council, where he helps the LPI coordinate input from corporations and the open source community. James has a unique understanding of LPI's certification exams, as he is an expert in both the certification industry and in Gnu/Linux, networking, and security.

Colophon

The animal on the cover of *LPI Linux Certification in a Nutshell* is a bull, an adult male animal of the species *Bos primigenius*.

Cattle were domesticated early in human history, perhaps more than 8,000 years ago. They are used as work animals, as well as to produce meat, milk, leather, manure, and fuel. Their longstanding economic importance is evident in the etymological relationship of the word "cattle" to "chattel" and "capital." The world cattle population is approximately 1.3 billion.

Cattle are ruminants, meaning that they regurgitate and rechew their food as cud. They spend six hours a day eating and another eight chewing. They may drink 25 to 50 gallons of water a day and produce 15 to 20 gallons of saliva.

The animals are significant in many cultural traditions. The Minotaur, half bull and half man, guards the labyrinth in Greek myth. The constellation Taurus represents a bull, and an ox (the term for cattle used as draft animals) appears in the Chinese zodiac. Cattle are considered sacred in Hinduism, and in Masai myth, all the cattle on earth are believed to be a gift to the Masai people from their god. Bullfighting and the running of the bulls continue to be strongly identified with Spanish culture, as is bull riding in American rodeos.

Though cattle ranching and cowboys are strongly associated with the history of the western United States, domesticated cattle are not native to the Americas. Spanish strains of cattle brought by Columbus and the conquistadores interbred with English strains brought by the pilgrims and other early settlers in the United States, giving rise to some of the iconic American breeds.

The cover image is an original illustration created by Lorrie LeJeune. The cover font is Adobe ITC Garamond. The text font is Linotype Birka; the heading font is Adobe Myriad Condensed; and the code font is LucasFont's TheSansMonoCondensed.

Related Titles from O'Reilly

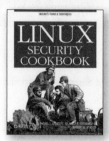

Linux

A Root of all Evil

Building Embedded Linux Systems, *2nd Edition*

The Complete FreeBSD, *4th Edition*

Exploring the JDS Linux Desktop

Extreme Programming Pocket Guide

Fedora Linux

GDB Pocket Reference

Knoppix Hacks, *2nd Edition*

Knoppix Pocket Reference

Learning Red Hat Enterprise Linux & Fedora, *4th Edition*

Linux Annoyances for Geeks

Linux Cookbook

Linux Networking Cookbook

Linux Desktop Hacks

Linux Desktop Pocket Guide

Linux Device Drivers, *3rd Edition*

Linux in a Nutshell, *5th Edition*

Linux in a Windows World

Linux iptables Pocket Reference

Linux Kernel in a Nutshell

Linux Multimedia Hacks

Linux Network Administrator's Guide, *3rd Edition*

Linux Pocket Guide

Linux Security Cookbook

Linux Server Hacks, *Volume 2*

Linux System Administration

Linux System Programming

Linux Unwired

LPI Linux Certification in a Nutshell, *2nd Edition*

Managing RAID on Linux

OpenOffice.org Writer

Producing Open Source Software

Programming with Qt, *2nd Edition*

Running Linux, *5th Edition*

Samba Pocket Reference, *2nd Edition*

SUSE Linux

Test Driving Linux

Ubuntu Hacks

Understanding Linux Network Internals

Understanding the Linux Kernel, *3rd Edition*

Understanding Open Source & Free Software Licensing

Using Samba, *3rd Edition*

Version Control with Subversion, *2nd Edition*

X Power Tools

Our books are available at most retail and online bookstores.
To order direct: 1-800-998-9938 • *order@oreilly.com* • *www.oreilly.com*
Online editions of most O'Reilly titles are available by subscription at *safari.oreilly.com*